Man and Land

Man and Land

The Fundamental Issue in Development

ERICH H. JACOBY

in collaboration with Charlotte F. Jacoby

ANDRE DEUTSCH

First published in 1971 by
André Deutsch Limited
105 Great Russell Street London WC1

Copyright © 1971 by Erich H. Jacoby
All rights reserved

Printed in Great Britain by
Tonbridge Printers Ltd
Tonbridge Kent

ISBN 0 233 96170 4

Contents

List of Tables

Acknowledgments

The genesis of this book dates back many years and consequently I am indebted to all those who during the past twenty years have helped me, directly or indirectly, to grasp the dimensions of the problem of 'Man and Land'. Through this book I sincerely hope to have fulfilled the long chain of obligations and promises accumulated in the course of these years.

My most sincere thanks, however, go to Gunnar Myrdal who gave me the opportunity to write this book at the Institute for International Economic Studies in Stockholm, where I found ideal working conditions in an atmosphere of intellectual independence and congenial contact. His deep understanding of the complexities of development and his imaginative vision have guided me for many years and I am deeply indebted to him for his scholarly advice and never-tiring interest in my work. I am also grateful to Ingvar Svennilson, the present Director of the Institute, and to my colleagues, Östen Johansson and Nils Lundgren for their friendly cooperation.

I remember with gratitude all my colleagues and close collaborators in the Food and Agriculture Organization who in various ways have contributed to my work and studies and I am particularly obliged to my predecessor, the late Sir Bernard Binns and to Mordecai Ezekiel and F. T. Wahlen who supported and encouraged me during the difficult pioneer years at the beginning of the 1950s, when land reform was still an object of disdain in the corridors of FAO.

During many years of study and travel, my wife and I have met scholars and officials in many countries whose knowledge and information increased our understanding of the problems of underdevelopment and helped me to analyse agrarian situations. I am profoundly grateful to the late D. S. Karve and to D. R. Gadgil, Tarlok Singh, Ameer Raza, V. M. Dandekar, M. L. Dantwala and V. S. Vyas in India; to Ungku A. Aziz in Malaysia; to Iso Rekschadipradjo in Indonesia; to the late Vincente Lava in the Philippines; to Seiichi Tobata and Chujiro Ozaki in Japan; to Raanan Weitz in Israel; to Sayed Marei in the UAR; to A. N. Jiménez, Julio le Riverend and Jorge Manfugás in Cuba; to Edmundo Flores and Rudolfo Stavenhagen in Mexico; to Jacques Chonchol in Chile; to H. A. Oluwasanmi in Nigeria; to M. Cepède and René Dumont in France; to S. Herweijer and W. F. Wertheim in the Netherlands; to Thomas Balogh, Ronald Dore, Arthur Gaitskell and J. R. Raeburn in the United Kingdom; to Guiseppe Barbero and Mario Bandini in Italy; and to P. P. Lobanov and G. G. Kotowsky in the USSR. Many of them have become close friends but all of them have given me much time and hospitality and, above all, the possibility of seeing what I wanted to see.

My close friend, Solon Barraclough, Director of the Agrarian Research and Training Institute in Santiago, Chile, has gone through the entire manuscript despite the great demands upon his time and I am immensely indebted to him for his constructive criticism. I also have to thank Gunnar Adler-Karlsson, Frederick Clairmonte, Robert Neild and Tarlok Singh for their valuable comments on parts of the manuscript; Leif Ståhl, a junior research worker at the University of Stockholm, for ably assisting me in the analysis of the agrarian situation in the Philippines which appears as appendix IV to this book; and my devoted secretary, Mrs Caroline Burton, for her patience and attention in preparing the typescript.

Finally I wish to emphasize that the opinions expressed are entirely my own and that I take full responsibility for the content of this book.

The Stockholm University Institute for   ERICH H. JACOBY
International Economic Studies
September, 1970

Preface

When I decided to write this book, it was with the intention of finding out for myself the reasons for the continued suffering of the people in underdeveloped countries and the failure of the advanced world to further their development. Having worked for more than sixteen years with FAO, the United Nations agency that handles most of the multilateral technical assistance to under-developed countries, I am fully aware of the discrepancy that exists between good intentions and small achievements, between lofty ideals and the world of reality. It is my sincere hope that this book may help to explain why so much in the field of development has gone wrong in the past twenty-five years.

There are, of course, always manifold reasons for failure and the establishment of a *causus nexus* depends largely upon the formulation of basic questions. The history of mankind suggests, however, that certain fundamental aspects of life determine the fate of people and nations and that the relationship between man and land is one of these. A conviction that this relationship largely decides the course of economic and political develop-ments has grown on me throughout the years and is what has motivated me to write this book.

Some critics may say that this is a one-sided work because it focuses on a single relationship, fundamental and unique as that may be. I recognize that this may be so, but I believe the im-portance of this relationship justifies such an approach.

The book may also seem to paint a very black picture, partic-ularly to the reader who accepts existing conditions just *because* they do exist. It is my conviction that to determine the reasons for failure is to contribute to general understanding, provided that the analysis brings into clear relief how different actions might have given events a different turn, or, rather, how the adoption of a more auspicious policy could do so in the future. To my regret I have had to base most of my conclusions on qualitative rather than on quantitative evidence. This is partly because the statistical services of underdeveloped countries pay little attention to the impact of institutional factors as the ruling groups want to avoid the reflection of the effects of the power structure in statistical data. Moreover, the available information is lacking in precision due to the vagueness of conceptions and the absence of reliable observations.

I realize, of course, that the relationship between man and land has many facets. In the present study I have chosen to deal mainly with a few: with the socio-economic position of the man working on the land, with his production and productivity, with the returns he derives from his work and with the political power structure that determines his relationship to the land. All these are closely linked to the social stratification of the rural community and to the changing structure of village and city life.

Before the War the distribution of the population implied not only different ways of life but also a dividing line between the relatively pleasant and secure life of the city and the hardship and misery of life in the countryside. But post-war developments have erased this dividing line. The spectacular migrations from the country to the large cities of Asia, Africa and Latin America have carried with them the very essence of rural poverty and insecurity.

At a certain stage in development people begin to perceive social stratification as an expression of the painful difference between wealth and poverty. Social and economic inferiority is felt, not only within the strongly stratified rural community but also between the distressed villages and the better-endowed urban centres and, above all, within the cities themselves where rich and poor live close together and social contrasts appear more obvious and acute. It is awareness of the abyss between social aspirations and reality which makes poverty in modern urban society a more painful experience than was the greater material distress in the homogeneous rural village of the past. To feel poor is largely a psychological phenomenon; it is closely connected to awareness of needs that cannot be satisfied. This is why I underscore the problems of social stratification and why I reject any approach to agricultural and agrarian development which involves the emergence of new privileged groups.

Land reform is no longer as fashionable as in the late 1950s, and structural problems are of less interest. According to the *World Economic Survey 1967* (UN, New York, 1968) it is desirable in the context of a discussion on land problems and policies to limit attention to two aspects, namely, the size of the production unit and 'the question of the capacity of the institutional setup to transmit economic signals to the producer and permit appropriate changes in the organization and methods of production in response to those signals'.

It is sad to see how this Survey reduces the wide implications of land policy to the one point of increasing production and even goes so far as to state that in the past '... political and social motives have indeed often outweighed the purely economic and technical', as if it were possible in the long run to separate economic and socio-political considerations.

The discomfort of thinking about social issues, combined with the simple attractions of new ways of production, have together induced many economists, and still more politicians, to slide into wholehearted support for the new technological approach. At times, it seems as if technological fantasies monopolize current economic thinking. Agricultural development, envisaged only fifteen years ago as a process of socio-economic advance, has been narrowed to the scope of increased agricultural output, while man, in feudal times a tool for the exploitation of the land and thus an essential appendage to the land, seems gradually to be losing his relevance to agriculture; and this, despite the fact that in the underdeveloped countries there is no alternative place for him in urban industries and services. It is not a great exaggeration to say that in several underdeveloped countries the current belief in the panacea of technical innovations may easily lead to the expulsion of the peasants from the land and, as has already happened in some regimes in Latin America, to the new experience of land without man—a dismal paradox for an overpopulated country!

It should be a matter of sound policy, therefore, to harmonize institutional reforms with technical innovations, aiming at a pace and type of technological progress that allows for the necessary adjustments in social conditions. The progress of man and the improvement of his social position are the final objectives of development. Technological advance at the expense of human values is hollow. Unless there is a major change in thinking and in policy, modern technology may reinforce outdated institutions and thereby turn back the feeble forces of social progress. To my mind this will create an unholy alliance which is frightening and will inexorably lead to future conflict.

Problems of this magnitude cannot be solved within the framework of the existing economic and social systems. In order to remedy seriously malignant agrarian structures, radical surgery may be needed; indeed, it is virtually impossible to envisage socio-economic progress without certain revolutionary developments. This may be alarming to those liberal economists who still believe that the underdeveloped world can make progress through peaceful evolution. But most people of this faith used to believe that democracy, too, would prevail in the underdeveloped world. They have silently dropped that belief as the democracies have crumbled. In the years ahead they may also have to drop their faith in evolution.

A special section in this book is devoted to an analysis of multilateral and bilateral Technical Assistance efforts. These have only rarely served the advance of society. The deficiencies of technical aid today reflect most clearly the ambiguous attitude of Western democracies towards the underdeveloped countries—the attitude which is so strongly attacked by the younger generation in the developed countries. Technical Assistance and economic aid have become key issues not only in the struggle between the two worlds, but also in the controversy between the generations in Western countries. A struggle which will be meaningless unless it leads to a levelling up of the standards of living in the underdeveloped and developed countries. Although this can be achieved only at the expense of the industrialized nations, it is, to my mind, a desirable development because it implies the realization of international social justice. The developed countries may still have time to make amends if they discontinue without delay their support of the exponents of the *status quo* in underdeveloped countries and instead extend Technical Assistance to the peasant populations. This, I believe, would alone suffice to start the transformation of the underdeveloped countries and would help to restore the land to the impoverished people to whom it originally belonged.

Agrarian reform, as we see it, is more than an economic programme with certain predictable social effects. It is a process of regeneration after centuries of economic and social underdevelopment which have produced undesirable privileges and led to exploitation and social degradation. What is required is the awakening of the rural people, the acceptance of peasant movements, an increase in contact between isolated rural communities and administrative and urban centres and, finally, general education and efficient and honest administration. These are essential elements in the making of a nation.

Without the emancipation of the peasant populations and the transformation of the economic and social systems, the underdeveloped countries cannot achieve national maturity. Structural reforms and the processes of development and national integration are not separate events: they are one. Failure to recognize this vital fact serves only to strengthen those who, consciously or unconsciously, are perpetuating the undignified position of the underdeveloped countries.

TO RUTH AND HER CONTEMPORARIES

Enseñar la explotación de la tierra, no la del hombre
(Capilla de Chapingo, México, Acta de inauguración 1924)

PART ONE

The Dimensions
of the Problem

CHAPTER ONE

Introduction –
Land and Land Redistribution
in History

The struggle for land and for the right to use land, the vicissitudes of man's relation to land, are ever-recurring features in the history of mankind. The patterns of land distribution and ownership reflect the actual power structure; and the saying 'whoever owns the land wields the power' holds true for entire historical epochs. All that happened before man began to recognize the productivity and value of land belongs to pre-history, and the paintings and carvings in the caves of the Vezère and Dordogne Valleys give evidence only of man's fight against wild beasts and his struggle for survival as a huntsman.

We do not know exactly when and how man discovered land as a source of livelihood, but we may assume that the history of agriculture started with the taming of animals and the seasonal rhythm of nomadic life. Land around the water sources provided ready food for the herds, and man's wandering in search of such pasture reflects his first simple relationship to the land.

But as his numbers increased land and water ceased to be abundant. He began to till the soil and the rotational use of land by distinct migratory groups gave rise to the first forms of organized tribal life. Land became a resource, whose value was determined by the sacrifices in blood made in order to take or protect it. It is this development that changed expanse to *land*, formed society and thus initiated the historical era of mankind.

The fight for land between clans, tribes or nations and, within them, between landowners and landless formed the life of the peoples and determined the pattern of society. Through millenniums history has expressed the gains of the conquerors and the losses of the defeated in terms of land or of rent for the land; the conquerors became landlords and the defeated tenants and serfs.

But during the rise of the Roman Empire, an interplay between conquest of land and commercial transactions introduced a new feature into this traditional pattern. With the conquest of the large fertile areas in Africa and Asia, a succession of Roman emperors and pro-consuls imported vast quantities of wheat and oil and, above all, of slave labour which gradually ruined the economy of the free peasants on the Italian peninsula. Thus the victorious Roman soldiers, mostly country people themselves, soon lost their land to adroit merchants and politicians and were reduced to landless serfs while slave plantations came to dominate the countryside. From then on commerce and land speculation also began to influence the land distribution patterns.

Recorded history, however, also reveals recurrent attempts to adjust land distribution to given social and economic developments: the periodic allocation of land in biblical times, the Gracchian agrarian reform in early Roman history, the repeated settlement of war veterans and the redistribution of Church land and feudal estates during the French Revolution, are all examples of a rehabilitation of the suppressed and of those in need of land and were frequently milestones on the road to socio-economic development and national integration. This may confirm the belief of the optimistic observer that the logic of economic and technical developments is stronger than the brutality of a conqueror or the usurpation of a feudal lord and that in reality only planned changes in the agrarian structure will prevent stagnation and even decline.

Today's urgent demand for agrarian reform is one of the significant features of an age that is marked by the growing contrast between backward agriculture and the subsistence level of peasant life in the underdeveloped countries and the industrialized farming and ever-increasing wealth in Western society. The very fact that land reform is no longer popular with some economists who dedicate themselves to the more fashionable productivity theory, is of little importance; reality and the potential for future socio-economic development is with the peasants of the underdeveloped world and with their claim for agrarian reforms.

Land Redistribution—a Continuing Process

Redistribution of land is thus a recurrent historic event and not merely the invention of idealistic reformers. A permanent land distribution pattern has never existed, and rights in land have been gained and lost by external intervention or internal changes which, at least at the initial stage, led to a deterioration of land use and contributed to peasant poverty and economic and social stagnation. Of all the changes in the land distribution pattern a land reform aiming at the establishment of effective and rational farm units that serve the needs of the entire rural population is the one measure specifically designed to improve the economic and social conditions in agriculture and enhance the dignity of the man on the land.

In substance, land redistribution is the reallocation of agricultural resources. In ancient times, land usually belonged to the community as a whole or was considered the property of the ruling deity whose priests, acting as caretakers—though often abusing their office—were considered trustees for the community. With the gradual disintegration of communal tenure, individual rights in land were established and gave rise to a land distribution pattern that was to release a complex chain of cause and effect. After centuries of *laissez-faire*, and practically unrestricted property rights, a trend towards increased public control of land has emerged which, in some areas, has even reestablished public ownership in land. In retrospect, therefore, it seems as if the historical cycle may be closed in the not too remote future.

By its very nature, the redistribution of land involves changes in ownership and land use patterns which, in turn, affect agricultural productivity in one way or another. During the long periods of history when land was acquired through wars and when changes in ownership were enforced by military conquest, it rarely happened that the new masters immediately improved the land and introduced more efficient cultivation methods in order to secure higher returns from agriculture. To the contrary, almost any such redistribution of land proved detrimental to agriculture. The victorious soldiers usually considered the conquered land their booty and purely an object of exploitation rather than economic opportunity and would either chase the peasant owners from the land or reduce them to serfdom. But even if they did not take over the land themselves, they would generally extort heavy and often unreasonable taxes from the peasant population in order to finance further ventures, and their tax collectors gradually developed into landlords or primary right-holders who further increased the ruthless exploitation of the peasants.

This is not intended to be a world-wide historical summary, but only to give some indication of the misfortunes of the peasantry in a European setting. In other parts of the world the village communities defended their economic and social identity, until conquerors and colonial invaders weakened them beyond the point of recovery by arms, administrative penetration, and the introduction of superior economic forces. Everywhere the peasant communities were the losers, whether because of changes in the land distribution pattern in favour of new privileged groups or because of heavy and unfair taxation.

Land redistribution by way of land reform, however, may serve as a means to interrupt the vicious cycle of poverty, ignorance and stagnation, and start a new chain of cause and effect which will pave the way for agricultural development. Although the mere fact of land redistribution does not necessarily ensure agricultural progress, it is safe to state that rapid agricultural development has often been closely associated with redistribution through land reform.

Yet, we must keep in mind that changes in the size and composition of individual holdings constantly recur as natural adjustments to demographic and technological developments. Normal subdivision by succession within a population equilibrium, minute subdivision and excessive fragmentation in case of population pressure and gradual changes caused by technological progress are submerged aspects of a continued process of land redistribution which is too slow, however, to prevent dangerous tension and friction and possibly social upheavals during critical stages of transition.

The concentration of ownership rights in the most fertile areas, a typical feature in the central plains of Thailand, central Luzon, and in most Latin American countries, has manifold causes. They range from rising land values caused by population increase and subsequent shortage of land to the unrestrained play of economic forces and the practice of rulers and politicians of generously rewarding their loyal supporters with grants in land. This has had, and still has, a decisive influence upon the land use pattern and favours not only the perpetuation of outdated tenure and marketing systems but also an unsound increase of land rents and the brutal exploitation of man.

The establishment of large estates, *haciendas*, and plantations affected the still independent smallholders who through indebtedness to the large landowners gradually lost their land and either had to join the large reserve of landless labour, or were forced to settle on the hilly lands with their rough conditions for agriculture. The concentration of ownership has thus contributed in this most unfortunate way to the gradual destruction of a land distribution pattern that once guaranteed the small peasant owners a relatively secure position.

Objectives of this Study and Attempts at a Definition of Land Reform

The following chapters will deal with the complex problems of the man-land relationship. Although focused on the need for structural reforms and on the dynamic forces which primarily affect the productivity of both man and land, they will necessarily take into account the complex effects of existing land distribution patterns upon the quality of the soil, upon land use, and upon the economic and social position of the peasant within both the rural community and society at large. The substance of the structural reforms will be measured by the efficacy of *institutional improvements*, that is to say, of improvements which direct physical progress to the advantage of man or, more explicitly, *which give first priority in development to the human factor; this is the one and only value premise of this book.*

Redistribution of land is not identical with land reform, but land redistribution through land reform is the specific type of land redistribution that has gained momentum during the past two decades when preference was given to socio-economic engineering in the most sensitive area of society. Yet, land reform initiated by revolutionary action is always identical with land redistribution since it is the prevailing land distribution pattern that is the major, and often even the decisive, cause of revolutionary development. The problems involved in *reforming* the agrarian structure are everywhere substantially the same, despite considerable differences in the implementation and in the attitude towards community structure, credit, education and marketing.

Land reform or *agrarian reform* are the terms most frequently used to denote any integrated programme that aims at reorganizing the institutional framework of agriculture in order to facilitate social and economic progress in accordance with the philosophy, values and creed of the community concerned. The United Nations defines land reform as 'comprising an integrated programme of measures designed to eliminate the obstacles to economic and social development arising out of defects in the agrarian structure.'*

* United Nations, Dept. of Economic and Social Affairs, *Progress in Land Reform, Third Report* (New York, 1962), p. 93. The measures included are:

    (a) provision of opportunities for ownership;

    (b) measures to promote land settlement and security of tenure;

    (c) improvement of tenant conditions; e.g., by the reduction of excessive rent or share payments;

    (d) improvement of conditions of employment and opportunities for agricultural labour;

    (e) protection of cultivators living under tribal, communal and other traditional forms of tenure;

    (f) organization of farms of economic size—land consolidation;

    (g) land title registration;

    (h) extension of agricultural credit and reduction of indebtedness;

    (i) promotion of co-operative organizations used by farmers;

    (j) organization of farm machinery services;

    (k) fiscal and financial policy in relation to land reform, including tax measures to promote improved land utilization and distribution;

    (l) measures concerning land tenure as related to aspects of forestry;

    (m) measures to promote the equitable use of limited water supplies;

    (n) other related measures such as the establishment or expansion of agricultural research and education services.

The *Progress in Land Reform, Fifth Report* (New York, 1970), p. 32 departs from the former line of definitions and states that the term 'agrarian reform' is more comprehensive than land reform as it covers all aspects of institutional development. I do not follow this deviation which will obviously make for considerable difficulties in translation. Land reform in French is *réforme agraire* and in Spanish *reforma agraria*. Difficulties can be avoided by using the term 'structural reform' for the more comprehensive approach to problems of institutional and social development (see p. 30).

To some extent, this inflated definition of the scope of land reform and the rather vague formulation of the measures was the result of a compromise between East and West at the Thirteenth Session of the Economic and Social Council of the United Nations in Geneva, September 1951. The resolution finally adopted by the Session after repeated revision clearly reflects the efforts of the West to prevent *land reform* being considered identical with *land redistribution* as the East claimed to be the case. This compromise, however, is the result of the slipshod approach to land reform which almost paralysed the United Nations agencies in charge of the programmes, until they finally interpreted the resolution to the effect that only measures directly associated with changes in the tenure situation shall be considered part of land reform.

Although a rather useful tool during the first two decades of the United Nations' efforts, even this pragmatic approach has contributed to the present confusion regarding the concept and theory of land reform. In the first place, almost any agricultural programme may be defined as 'land reform', 'agrarian reform' and even as 'agrarian revolution', and consequently these connotations have been used so arbitrarily that they are about to lose their real significance, just as words like 'democracy' and 'liberty' have. And secondly, the terms 'land' or 'agrarian reform' do not contain any reference to the changes in the tenure status of the peasants which, particularly in underdeveloped countries, must be considered the backbone of any real land reform programme.

This lack of clear-cut definitions is due mainly to the uncertain interpretation of the various concepts within the field of agrarian relations. Western economists and sociologists commit the error of applying their familiar concepts without taking into account the cultural and historical differences between developed and underdeveloped countries. It is high time that a more mature interpretation is made in order to clarify the actual economic, social and legal implications of all relevant concepts. It would certainly facilitate the comparative analysis of agrarian structures if concepts like property, possession, leasehold, tenancy, land consolidation, communal tenure, joint farming, cooperative and collective farming and horizontal and vertical integration were defined in their true context. The starting point for such definitions should be the factual situation. Rather than legal terms, the cultural, economic and social implications of existing relations are decisive, and will have to be translated into a new terminology as close to reality as possible; otherwise technical terms will be used arbitrarily and misused in the political debate.

The term *structural reform*, frequently used in this study, covers not only the reform of land tenure systems but the entire range of measures affecting the institutional framework for peasant life and society. Experience has proved that neither land redistribution nor tenancy reform can produce lasting effects without control of the forces which dominate land, credit and village markets. The establishment of a new tenure pattern, therefore, must be an integral part of social and economic reconstruction. Even the most generous land redistribution scheme is doomed to failure unless the peasant is supported by complementary measures in the institutional fields of credit, extension, education, cooperation and marketing, which in their turn must be coordinated with resource development and industrialization. Only such an approach can protect the peasant against the impact of superior market forces and establish new patterns of land and income distribution, of social values, of rural-urban relations which will make possible the transition from subsistence to market economy, and from serfdom to a meaningful life.

It would go far beyond the scope of this book, however, were we to dwell at length upon the inadequate identification of concepts. We will limit ourselves to the socio-economic implications of the man-land relationship and, in this context, deal with a variety of land reform measures, the most important of which are: redistribution of land; tenancy reforms; settlement; land consolidation; cooperative and collective farming; state farming; administration of land reform; taxation; credit and education; and the adjustment of tribal communities to socio-economic progress.

An attempt will also be made to do away with the fictitious division, drawn up during the cold war in the fifties, which has led to the unfortunate notion that collective agriculture is identical with the revolutionary, and individual peasant farming with the evolutionary concept of land reform. We will prove that this dividing line is irrational and in no way relevant to the economic and social aims of a constructive land reform policy in a given environment. In our opinion, the only conceivable line of thought is to consider the agro-economic factors and the cultural and social background of the people as basic elements for planning, since no perfect tenure system exists that infallibly guarantees continued agricultural efficiency. At one time or another all tenure systems have been adequate or inadequate under certain conditions and in certain stages of economic development, and good and bad farming or progressive and regressive agriculture have been encountered under almost every conceivable form of land tenure. The 'tenure chauvinism' of the cold war period has contributed to the present state of confusion and frustration in the rural areas of underdeveloped countries which to an increasing extent are paying for the errors and failures caused by political bias.

CHAPTER TWO

Dynamic Forces in Development

After a long period of stagnation the economic systems and society in underdeveloped countries are being exposed to the interaction of *population expansion* and *technological progress*, the two powerful forces that shape society and are now reaching proportions which present the most formidable challenge to the present generation.* Compared to the dynamism of these two forces, other factors such as industrialization, urbanization and economic growth, significant as they may be, are of secondary importance.

Population Expansion

It was the advances in science and administration that caused the dramatic decline in mortality; and it will be the task of modern science and administration to provide sufficient food and employment for the ever-increasing number of human beings in the world. For decades a race has been under way between multiplying populations and technological progress which will everywhere continue to gain momentum until socio-economic planning has helped to establish a balance between the needs of increasing population and the exploitation of available resources.

The small nations of Europe which had never been affected by colonial domination were able to make the social adjustments reasonably easily and avail themselves fully of modern technology and economic growth.† Their comparative advantages were their

* See particularly the sections in this chapter on: 'Population Expansion and Social Stratification'; 'The Miracle Seeds'; and appendix I.
† S. Kuznets, 'Economic Growth of Small Nations' in E. A. G. Robinson (ed.), *Economic Consequences of the Size of Nations* (London, 1966), pp. 14 ff.

limited populations, their greater homogeneity and stronger internal cohesion. And this may suggest the need for a greater measure of decentralization in the planning and implementation of development projects in order to ensure cooperation at the grassroots level in the necessary adjustment to demographic and technological changes.

POPULATION EXPANSION AND FAMILY PLANNING

The manifold effects of population expansion penetrate all spheres of a nation's economic and social life. They are instrumental in shaping the man-land relationship; they determine the structure of the community, of the labour market, and of urban-rural relations; but above all, they influence the life and work of man by determining the price he receives for his produce and the price he has to pay to keep alive.

To the minds of many scholars, the easiest solution to the problem of population increase in underdeveloped countries is to counter the decline in mortality by controlling fertility. Logical and tempting as such a solution may seem, it is a most unfortunate misunderstanding. The urgent wish for offspring which is deeply rooted in religious beliefs and is justified by prevailing economic and social considerations cannot be diminished substantially by advocating surgical intervention or the taking of a pill. Even if conducted by well-meaning organizations and prominent professionals, this approach is but another sad example of the lack of understanding of the socio-economic reality in underdeveloped countries; no population policy can achieve the desired results before changes in the social structure have created an environment that gives man the possibility of realizing his inherent right to enjoy the fruits of his toil and frees him from the fear of being without support in his old age. Under present conditions, only a large family with at least two or three sons will give him a certain sense of security. In practice this means a 'large' family considering the number of female offspring and the incidence of child mortality.

Birth control, or the so-called 'demographic solution' to the problem of overpopulation, is based on a kind of Malthusian way of thinking and is neither an alternative to nor a substitute for a dynamic socio-economic development policy but, at the very most, an additional remedy only. And this is particularly true as in many underdeveloped countries the propaganda for birth control arouses the suspicion of being yet another device contrived by the developed world to check the feared population explosion without having to introduce any changes that may call for economic sacrifices on its own part.

As a matter of fact, the underutilized labour, covered by the term *excess population*, is to a considerable extent an effect of the economic policy carried out in underdeveloped countries. Cuba, which before the revolution suffered from permanent unemployment of more than 10 per cent of the population (7–800,000 people on the average), has today, ten years later, a painful labour shortage due to expansion and diversification of agriculture, to increased industrialization and more effective and considerate labour utilization. In China, fundamental changes in economic policy with a new approach to problems of labour utilization and organization and particularly the postponement of marriage have reduced the population problem to more manageable proportions, and it can be assumed that a stabilization of the population will be brought about during the next few decades. There is little doubt that in many underdeveloped countries a change in development strategy to make possible a more effective labour utilization and an expansion of agricultural and industrial activities will reduce considerably the drama of the population explosion. The problem of excess population in fact is most explosive wherever man rather than land is subject to exploitation since the ruthless use of manpower reduces the employment potential and prevents improvement in the quality of labour.*

* In March 1969 Carlos Rafael Rodriguez, former president of the Cuban Institute for Agrarian Reform, explained to me the ways in which Cuba had tackled the problem of unemployment: (1) the abolition of child labour through compulsory education; (2) the in-introduction of regular work-days more or less on an 8-hour basis; (3) the expansion of cultivable areas and diversification of agriculture particularly by the introduction of labour-intensive crops such as coffee and citrus fruits; (4) industrialization; and (5) road and dam construction, reforestation, house construction. He further stated that although it is true that the army absorbs part of the available labour force, at the same time it makes labour available for harvesting, reforestation and construction work.

The principle of 'family planning'* is closely related to that of 'saving' and is likely, therefore, to be defeated as an economic objective by the frequently noted 'improvidence' and incapacity of the peasants to reason in terms of economic advantage even if the opportunity were to arise. This well-known psychological fact was superbly analysed more than thirty-five years ago in the following words:

> Saving means present sacrifice and foregoing the satisfaction of a want or need with the expectation, thereby, of satisfying a need in the future. The peasant and his family, who are never quite fully fed, can hardly be expected to lay by for a rainy day when by some good fortune they find themselves in the possession of a few cents.†

The practice of birth control will demand an even greater change of attitude than does 'putting by for a rainy day' and neither attitude can be expected in a society that undervalues man and labour. It is true that education in family planning can do no harm; yet, we would do well to bear in mind that, for reasons deeply imbedded in the social structure, intellectual persuasion will have but little effect outside the already truly urbanized and more or less economically secure upper strata of society.‡

For the mass of the poor rural people in underdeveloped countries the fight against intricate institutional arrangements,

* K. Davis, *Population Policy: Will Current Programs Succeed?* Population Reprint Series, no. 258 (Institute of International Studies, University of California) states that family planning, even if successful, does not achieve the desired population control.

† K. L. Alsberg, *Land Utilization Investigations and their Bearing in International Relations* (New York, 1933), p. 19.

‡ The family-planning schemes carried out in South Korea, Taiwan, India, Pakistan, Turkey, Tunisia, and the UAR by AID and various other agencies should not lead us to believe that the active support of governments and leading intellectuals in these countries is enough to guarantee success; the final outcome will be decided in the remote villages and jungle settlements and not by the educated upper class who for many years have frequently been experienced users of birth control. Not even the absence of religious taboos against birth control, important as this may be, necessarily implies that most of the people are ready to take up the practice. H. Hurrenius and O. Åhs, *The Sweden-Ceylon Family Planning Pilot Project* (Demographic Institute, University of Gothenburg, 1968). Their evaluation did not prove that the family-planning activities had any positive effect during the time of operation.

development impediments and resource limitations is much closer to their daily life than is fear of a growing family. The burdensome exploitation by landowners, moneylenders, traders, and corrupt officials is their most pressing problem—and this cannot be solved by birth control.

Just as extension services frequently have no effect because they fail to reach the bulk of the peasants, the drives for family planning will encounter but little success. Even the most efficient teams cannot be expected to get their ideas across to the impoverished masses whose main worries are land, debt, markets and employment, and who instinctively feel—if anything at all—that less mouths to feed may well be a relief but certainly not the way out of their misery.

However significant some United Nations' schemes and Technical Assistance programmes may have been during the past twenty years, we have to realize that, on the whole, they did not succeed in changing the unfortunate economic and social structure in the underdeveloped world. Food remains the overriding problem for the rapidly increasing populations while poor health and lack of vigour and initiative—the inevitable effects of chronic malnutrition—still mark the bulk of the people. Modern medicine and health services are unable to counteract the inherent socio-economic deficiencies, and the surface appearance of a slow decline in the rate of population increase, largely concentrated in the upper- and middle-class groups in urban areas, can hardly be expected to bring about the necessary fundamental changes. Once again we must emphasize that partial solutions cannot remedy this situation: they are but face-lifting operations that for a short time may improve the countenance without, however, strengthening the socio-economic basis of the underdeveloped society. Like education, agricultural extension, and many other measures, family planning will continue to have no effect unless it is an integral part of a well-designed social and agrarian reconstruction programme.

The Second UNCTAD Conference in New Delhi, 1968, revealed to the more serious observer the complete failure of the 'development decade' of the United Nations which as we shall see in later sections of this book concentrated on partial solutions without recognizing the urgent need for a more comprehensive programme that entails the reorganization of the entire socio-economic system in the underdeveloped countries.

It is unlikely, to say the least, that birth control as an isolated approach can become a successful means of fighting poverty and underdevelopment. Yet, unfortunately, it is likely that the exaggerated emphasis on birth control, well meaning as it may be, will pave the way for yet another 'development decade' of failure and frustration by presenting an alluring formula that may divert our efforts from the key issues and induce taxpayers, governments and professionals to invest considerable amounts of capital and organizational effort which will prove wholly ineffectual in bringing about the intended improvement. Moreover, the recent warnings against oral contraceptives raise strong doubts as to the moral justification of widespread propaganda for 'easy' birth control in underdeveloped areas without adequate health services. Of course, education in family planning should be part of any well-conceived development programme that gives due consideration to the formidable administrative problems involved,* but it should not be considered a miraculous cure for the social and economic ills of underdeveloped countries, since this would be a chimerical and even politically unwise approach.†

POPULATION EXPANSION AND LABOUR PRODUCTIVITY

We know from experience that the true key to agricultural and economic growth in the advanced countries is increasing produc-

* G. Myrdal (*Asian Drama. An Inquiry into the Poverty of Nations*, London and New York, 1968, p. 2151), in dealing with the problems of family-planning policy in India, emphasizes very strongly the administrative problems involved which he rightly considers to be of formidable dimensions. In the view of Myrdal, family-planning programmes will be determined largely by the government's ability to achieve a smooth and effective operation of the huge administrative apparatus. India has chosen to integrate the programme into the regular health administration; this is not only rationally motivated in order to economize efforts but could also be desirable from the point of view of co-ordinating family planning with other related programmes, though, of course, the risk is very considerable for conflicts and delays in action.

† Lester B. Pearson (Chairman), *Partners in Development. Report of the Commission on International Development* (The Pearson Report) (New York, 1969), pp. 194 ff, encourages donor countries and international agencies to 'press' in aid negotiations for adequate analyses of population problems; unfortunately this Report does not recognize that the population explosion and its economic effects are a part of the *structural* problem of underdeveloped societies.

B

tivity per man. This holds true not only for Western Europe but also for Australia, New Zealand and the United States, where growth rates, particularly of farm output and productivity per man, are even higher. Unfortunately, neither population statistics nor agricultural yearbooks contain adequate data for a comparative analysis of this relationship, particularly with regard to the actual number of manhours and the efficiency of labour in agriculture, and little research, therefore, has been directed to these questions. Yet, it is evident that the motivating force in agricultural development is increased labour productivity, which today is 10–20 times higher in the United States and north-western Europe than in South Asia, the Near East, and Latin America. The fact that certain heavily overpopulated rural areas, in the UAR, Malaysia and Ceylon, for instance, exhibit high production figures per area unit is no proof to the contrary since this is but another expression of overpopulation, underutilization, and underpayment of human labour.

True, in some underdeveloped countries specialization in valuable export crops in addition to the plantation industries such as cotton, rubber, tea and coffee, has increased productivity to some extent; but it is equally true that the resulting increase in foreign exchange earnings has never reached the large mass of subsistence and semi-subsistence farmers. On the contrary, their income is declining steadily either because of the increasing population pressure or the deteriorating terms of trade, or both, and they are compelled to concentrate more and more on the cultivation of cereals and starchy root crops in order to produce the bare minimum of calories needed to keep alive. Despite minor improvements here and there, labour productivity in agriculture has remained stagnant for generations in the larger part of the underdeveloped world. And even where it is somewhat higher, as in certain Latin American countries with abundant land resources, inefficient and repressive systems of land tenure and the lack or misuse of capital have impeded development and kept unit yields stationary at very low levels. In fact underdevelopment has become practically identical with the underutilization of labour and with the frequently ineffective work of that part of the labour force which is actually utilized.

We are told time and again that the gap between food needs and supplies in underdeveloped countries is steadily widening, as, due to the explosive population increase, the expansion of the cultivated areas and improved farming methods do not bring about a sufficiently rapid increase in agricultural production although the latter, in some areas, has broken all previous records. An estimated 1.5 billion of the world's population either go hungry or are undernourished and the slightest disturbance upsets the delicate balance between population and food supply. In 1965 and 1966–67, crop failures in India affected the lives of millions of people, and in many of the underdeveloped countries even a small drop in the size of the harvest may mean the step from subsistence to starvation.

It has become fashionable to consider these problems from a purely technical point of view, and public discussion emphasizes *ad infinitum* the need for improved farming methods, more fertilizers, better seeds, increased irrigation, and, recently, for birth control. Yet, only a few voices are heard which advocate an improvement in the institutional framework for agricultural production as a precondition for technical progress. The reasons are obvious: it is far easier to provide the large farmers in backward areas with modern agricultural machinery, fertilizers, and seeds—which serve the interests of international trade and can be obtained without difficulty provided that the necessary capital is available—than to change the economic and social balance in the villages, transform the traditional agrarian structure, and put an end to the destructive practices of money-lenders and middlemen. A development policy directed towards the redistribution of income and opportunities and a more favourable social stratification is not only unpopular, but it is unacceptable to those who, through control of land and labour, wield the economic and political power which they fear to lose if institutional reforms were to be introduced. This does not alter the fact, however, that institutional reforms combined with improved labour utilization are the only possible means of finally establishing the vital balance between growing population numbers and increased productivity per man.

It is true, of course, that greater agricultural productivity could be achieved by, say, highly capitalized commercial estates and plantations operated by hired labour (the slave plantations of the Roman Empire undoubtedly reached a remarkable degree of productivity and profitability). But such an alternative, by necessity associated with great rural misery and often also with expulsions from the land, not only implies a social and political disaster worse than the explosive population increase but also relinquishes the hope of socio-economic progress.

Indeed, a close interdependence exists between agricultural progress and institutional reforms: the peasants living on the brink of starvation cannot be encouraged to accept innovations unless they are given incentives by changes in the institutional framework. This alone can free them from the traditional vicious circle and create an environment that will awaken their interest in the technical requirements of increased food production and planning ahead—including the size of the family.

Agricultural development in north-western Europe bears witness to the thesis that economic and social progress are twin aspects of one and the same process and that technical and institutional improvements must go hand in hand: sustained agricultural development is unattainable without social progress, while social progress cannot be achieved without improved agricultural practices. Only the actual process of labour–intensive agricultural development can reduce the population pressure to manageable proportions and make education in family planning meaningful.

Under the given circumstances rapid population increase may, in fact, be a powerful release mechanism for revolutionary developments. Overloading the physical resources needed for livelihood, and dramatic changes in the age composition arouse the urge to break through the rigid walls of outdated traditions and institutions. But the planners in revolutionary movements realize that, in the underdeveloped world, the combined effect of a rapidly increasing labour force and the inevitable lack of capital urgently calls for a better utilization of human labour, the only asset in abundance.

The divergent opinions on the economic effects of population growth have largely contributed to the current confusion in development planning and policy. Particularly misleading is the theory of *optimum sizes* for populations or resources, which contradicts the very dynamism of development. Of course, it would be so much easier to explain what happens in the world were it possible to define 'objectively' the population problem without being bound by policy assumptions. Yet, considering the rapid changes in technology and in the productivity of labour and land, it is difficult to understand why outstanding economists still accept a theory that is based on the maximization of income or output per head and hence implies the comparison between actual and optimum population numbers. Since, however, the real problem of development planning is how to achieve an *improvement* and not how to reach an *optimum*, we will have to specify the standards by which to judge any improvement and determine a new basis for comparison if we wish to introduce a policy which is satisfactory from the development point of view.* Under conditions of rapid population expansion, economic development implies first of all increased labour productivity through more effective utilization of the labour force and the creation of additional employment opportunities; but this can only be achieved by an adequate reorganization of the institutional framework, by improved nutrition, health and education, and by the training of an efficient managerial and supervisory staff.

POPULATION EXPANSION AND EMPLOYMENT POTENTIAL

One of the most harassing effects of the population increase in underdeveloped countries is the change in the age composition of the population. The fact that a much larger proportion of the rural population than ever is below the age of twenty-five has a most unfortunate effect on both labour market and wage levels, while the large number of children under ten increases the burden of dependents among the peasants. It is obvious that such an age composition will inevitably accelerate the trend towards subdivision and fragmentation of holdings and thus lead to a continued decline in the average farm size and to an alarming increase in the number of landless peasants which will greatly exceed the capacity of both rural and urban industries to absorb them. We do not share the conviction that large-scale birth control programmes, even if successfully implemented, could substantially reduce the burden of the rural people and bring about a fundamental change in the population pattern in the next two decades. The inflated labour force of 1990 is already with us today and in the short time still left even a falling birth rate cannot possibly avert the economic and social consequences of the population increase.

* G. Myrdal, 'Economic Effects of Population Development', *Economic Development Issues and Policies* (Bombay, 1966), pp. 33 ff.

This does not mean, of course, that fewer mouths to feed may not improve to some extent the levels of income and living; but the cumulative effects of circular causation cannot be expected to make themselves felt unless constructive socio-economic changes in the institutional framework are introduced simultaneously with, or preferably prior to, any other measures intended to curb the effect of population increase.

The very fact that economic and social progress in the Western world is closely associated with industrialization has convinced many observers that rapid development of manufacturing industries would be a most effective means of coping with the rampant underutilization of labour in backward areas with an unfavourable man-land ratio. This is partly true, of course, since it is inconceivable that income levels and standards of living in agriculture could be increased or even maintained in the long run unless alternative employment possibilities were to be created. Considering the rapid increase in excess labour, however, it is unlikely that even a considerable expansion of industry could possibly provide employment for the untold masses that will throng the labour market during the next two decades. The immediate effect of increased industrial manufacturing may even be most unfavourable, since it is likely to ruin the economic basis of the cottage industries and force numerous artisans to join the army of landless labour. Particularly in areas of underemployment this serious short-term effect of introducing manufacturing industries may often nullify the intended improvement in the employment situation. Furthermore, a manufacturing industry with some prospect for future development must be built upon a rational basis and not upon the all-too-ready availability of an inflated labour force.

It is inescapable, therefore, that the majority of landless peasants must find a place in agriculture; and it is equally inescapable that the increased utilization of agricultural labour is the only possible means of gradually providing an adequate livelihood for them.

POPULATION EXPANSION AND MIGRATORY MOVEMENTS

The rapidly changing relationship between the size of population, agricultural resources, and the degree of applied technology is undoubtedly the most important variable in socio-economic development. Yet, it has been ignored time and again, and only very few planners seem to understand that this is the principal cause of the formidable migratory movements which, particularly in India and Latin America, have led to what we will call the *semi-urbanization* of rural people:* a suburban slum existence without the slightest possibility for integration into the urban economy and society.

The problems of rapid population increase and migration, however, occur not only in the densely populated underdeveloped areas of Asia and Latin America but also in the still sparsely populated African continent. It has been estimated† that between 1960 and 1980, assuming a moderate increase in life expectancy at birth and a constant fertility rate, the population of Africa will have increased from 271 to 444 million, and that of West Africa alone from 85.6 to 150 million.

A particular aspect of the population problem on the African continent is migration between the erstwhile colonial territories, the artificial boundaries of which have become the borders of the independent countries. Such migratory movements could certainly contribute to the establishment of a better population balance; but in the political turmoil of present-day Africa they only increase tension and friction and often even lead to genocide. Policy-planners in Africa have paid but little attention to this particular problem in the past. They did not understand that the artificial boundaries of the new states, though officially recognized by the United Nations, only rarely correspond to the tribal reality and, consequently, make the mistake of considering these 'international' migrations as a refugee problem to be handled along conventional charitable lines instead of as an important factor in establishing a more adequate man-land ratio.

Several observers are of the opinion that migratory movements may be considered an alternative to birth control; and to some extent this is correct since the migrants are generally young people whose departure not only relieves the pressure on the land but also contributes to a notable decline of the fertility rate in the area of emigration. Still more important, properly directed migratory movements combined with large-scale settlement programmes could well be used as an instrument to even out the discrepancies

* See chapter 4.
† 'The Demographic Situation in West Africa', *Economic Bulletin for Africa*, vol. 6, no. 2 (July 1966).

in population density, since, by their very nature, they call for a reallocation of the natural resources. But here again, success or failure depends upon the objectives and costs of the new settlements and upon the relative increase in labour utilization in the emigration areas obtained by the resultant decrease or, more often, by the reduced rate of increase in the labour force.*

In Kenya, migratory movements have played an important role in the economic development of the country. According to an interesting study,† based on pre-independence census statistics, (1962) on the volume and direction of the migration of the African section of the population, 44 per cent of the total number of migrants had moved to the Rift Valley and 26 per cent to the Nairobi Extra-Provincial District. The clear preference for the Rift Valley Province, the centre of the European estates in the White Highlands, proves the importance of large-scale farming for increased labour utilization. The study reveals furthermore that the majority of migrants came from districts with a high rural population density and extremely fragmented holdings, like the Central Province, Nyanza, and the Southern Province, and this confirms that the pressure on available land resources is a strong motivation for population movements.

The exodus from rural areas in Kenya is also responsible for a rapid expansion of urban centres: in the city of Nairobi it is reckoned that the annual rate of population increase is from three to five times higher than the national rate and, consequently, brings with it serious social and economic problems like acute housing shortages and increasing unemployment with which the urban authorities can hardly be expected to contend in the foreseeable future.

Internal migrations, however, are not confined to the African continent but are a typical feature of many underdeveloped areas, particularly in Latin America and India; wherever they occur they will have a direct bearing upon the agricultural situation and urban employment. The hitherto unprecedented mobility of the rural population due to the development of communications and the gradual disintegration of traditions and prejudices, tend to

---

* G. Myrdal, *Asian Drama*, pp. 2147 ff.

† S. H. Ominde, *The Population Factor in Kenya's Economic Development*, International Institute for Labour Studies, Bulletin no. 3, (November 1967), pp. 14 ff.

deplete agriculture of its more active elements and, at the same time, flood the urban labour market with an increasing number of unskilled workers. The direction of population movements accompanied by adequate changes in the man-land ratio and relationship are, therefore, most pressing problems for economic planning in all underdeveloped areas. In Kenya, the modern commercial agriculture developed by the European settlements in the White Highlands provided a certain outlet for densely populated rural areas and thus diminished somewhat the influx to Nairobi and other urban centres; but such an alternative within one and the same country is the exception in Latin America and Asia.*

POPULATION EXPANSION AND SOCIAL STRATIFICATION

With a little imagination it should not be difficult to understand that growing population pressure and the subsequent increase in the supply of landless labour constitute an imminent menace to the already unfortunate social stratification in underdeveloped countries. In Brazil, according to a well-founded estimate, the number of *minifundistas* and landless agricultural workers is expected to increase from 7.4 million in 1950 to about 12.6 million in 1970. And in India the effects of population increase upon the social stratification is clearly evident from Table 1 which shows the distribution of workers between 1951 and 1961, a notable period in development strategy.

The increase in the number of farm cultivators of close to 30 per cent indubitably indicates a dangerous decline in farm size and, most likely, an equally dangerous increase in the incidence of tenancy. Most striking, however, is the fact that the secondary and tertiary sectors combined were unable to enlarge their share of the labour market and to provide employment possibilities for at least part of the increased rural labour force. In other words, after a decade of strenuous development efforts, the agricultural sector alone still had to 'absorb' the largest part, 72 per cent, of the national population.

In order to counteract the unfortunate trend towards landlessness, attempts have been made in India and other countries to increase the viability of very small holdings by supporting the

* See chapter 4.

TABLE 1

Distribution of Workers, 1951–61

Industrial Category	1951		1961	
	Millions	Percentage	Millions	Percentage
Primary sector	101.4	72	136.2	72
Farm cultivator	69.8		99.5	
Agricultural labourer	27.5		31.5	
In Mining, livestock, forestry	4.1		5.2	
Secondary sector	14.1	11	22.1	12
Tertiary sector	24.0	17	30.2	16

SOURCE: George Rosen, *Democracy and Economic Change In India* (Berkeley, 1967), p. 138.

introduction of modern machinery and farming techniques. But here again, the precondition for any lasting effect would have been coeval changes in the institutional setup and the establishment of rural industries. The gradual lowering of the 'viability minimum' cannot alone prevent the continued subdivision caused by the population pressure which will increase the number of holdings too small for mechanization and thus destroy many small farmers' last hope of gaining their livelihood from agriculture.

It is a fact that all forms of surplus labour merge into the general pool of landless agricultural workers whose numbers increase as the social stratification deteriorates. It has been stated quite rightly that the numbers of rural poor are so great that any increase in these will hardly affect their conditions in those parts of the country where they form a substantial proportion of the population.* Any effort to improve the lot of the landless poor and of indigent peasants on undersized and fragmented holdings by land redistribution alone will fail since the central issue is the organization of production, the intensification of labour utilization and the increase of income.

* Tarlok Singh, *Poverty and Social Change. With a Reappraisal* (New Delhi, 1969), chap. 2, p. 259.

Even in a country like Mexico which underwent an agrarian revolution and agrarian reform fifty years ago, there is a noticeable tendency for the social stratification to deteriorate. And this despite the fact that between 1930 and 1960 the industrial labour force has increased considerably and the farm area, particularly the irrigated area, has been expanded to practically twice its previous size. Nevertheless the much acclaimed industrial growth during these three decades could not absorb the excess agricultural population and prevent the social and economic deterioration of the rural community.

In a brilliant study, R. Stavenhagen* relates the agricultural labour force to the cultivable land and comes to the conclusion that the number of cultivable hectares per person engaged in agriculture did not change significantly between 1930 and 1960; and that the coefficient of 3.9 in 1960 was back where it had been in 1940. Yet, the occupational and social structure of the agricultural population changed considerably during this period largely because of the rapid increase of the agricultural labour force (33 per cent between 1950 and 1960) of which only a tiny fraction could be absorbed by industry. In 1930 almost 2.5 million, or 68 per cent of the agricultural labour force, were landless labourers, but as a result of the agrarian reform their numbers decreased during the following decade to 49 per cent. Between 1950 and 1960, however, when the high rate of population growth had inflated the agricultural labour force by 33 per cent, landlessness increased by not less than 60 per cent, from 2.0 to over 3.3 million, while the number of *ejidatarios* grew by 9 per cent only and that of private farmers decreased by almost 5 per cent due to renewed concentration of landownership in the private sector.

The land distribution pattern in Mexico shows a clear trend towards a sharp concentration of ownership in the private sector. Of the total farm area of 169.1 million hectares in 1960, only 44.5 million (26.3 per cent) had been distributed under the agrarian reform programme to 1.5 million *ejidatarios*. In the remaining non-*ejidal* farm area of 124.6 million hectares, however, there has

---

* R. Stavenhagen ('Social Aspects of Agrarian Structure in Mexico', in *Agrarian Problems and Peasant Movements in Latin America*, New York, 1970), has emphasized the social aspects of the agrarian development in Mexico. In the analysis which follows we have largely drawn upon his findings.

been a continued concentration of ownership and by 1960, a mere 24,000 farm units of over 500 hectares controlled as much as 100 million hectares or 80.2 per cent. On the other hand, nearly 900,000 (66.8 per cent) of the non-*ejidal* farm units are below 5 hectares, and about 668,000 (44.2 per cent) of the plots belonging to the *ejidatarios* are even smaller than 4 hectares. This means that of the 2.7 million farm units in Mexico, almost 1.6 million (about 60 per cent) are in fact undersized and comprise even less than 14 per cent of the total farm area. Given the poor soils and unfavourable climatic conditions in most parts of the country, the majority of these small holdings must be considered sub-family units since they provide neither full employment nor economic security for the peasant family.*

This deterioration in social stratification is further underlined by regional differentiation and racial repression. Stavenhagen talks in this context about 'internal colonialism' and emphasizes that in the more backward regions of the country the differences between social classes at the local and regional levels very often lose their importance as compared with the subordination of the region as a whole to the dominant centres, that is, to the large cities and the areas of rapid economic growth. He also points out that some of these 'internal colonies' are becoming increasingly poorer, losing their best natural and human resources, and that this process is strongest in areas like Guerrero, Oaxaca and Chiapas, where a numerous Indian peasant population is economically and politically subordinated to the *ladino* or *mestizo* ethnic group thus adding a racial element to the exploitation of the peasant population as a social class.

A most distressing feature in Mexico, and in other underdeveloped countries as well, is the process of subdivision and fragmentation of holdings prior to the introduction of technological improvements. Despite a high rate of industrialization, Mexican statistics reveal that in some densely populated rural areas with a serious shortage of cultivable land the possible reduction of the viability minimum through improved cultivation will be offset by the decline in the average farm size due to the continuing subdivision which actually 'pushes' the bulk of the peasant population

* *Censos Agrícola-Ganadero y Ejidal IV, 1960* (Mexico City, 1965). See also C. Tello, 'Agricultural Development and Land Tenure in Mexico', *Weltwirtschaftliches Archiv*, vol. 101, no. 1 (1968), pp. 21 ff.

into the sectors of unviable farm units and landless labour.

Unfortunately the once famous agricultural ladder, leading from landlessness to tenancy and from tenancy to landownership, has ceased to function in the underdeveloped rural regions of the world. It has been recently stated that due to the overwhelming power of the rural capitalists over the rural workers, the situation has been reversed.* The rural workers today 'are going down the up-staircase' under the combined pressures of population increase and commercialization of agriculture; owners will become tenants, and tenants landless workers, while the size of small farms declines. The entire system of outdated social relationships with its inherent trend towards deterioration functions as a gigantic disincentive to increased agricultural productivity.†

The situation is still more complicated in countries where the social stratification can be identified with racial stratification, as is the case in Malaysia, where the suppressed peasants are manipulated in such a way that they see the economic confrontation with the rural capitalists as a racial confrontation. This further increases the danger of violence in the rural areas of the under-developed world and the number of inter-religious and inter-racial social conflicts has never been so high as during the past few years. The recent racial riots in Kuala Lumpur were the protest of the unemployed sons of small or landless Malay peasants, who had migrated to the city, against a social system in which they identified economic suppression with Chinese trade. The exploitation of the Malay peasantry by rural capitalists, who happened to be Chinese, and the government's neglect of the rural areas were clearly at the root of this bitter racial battle.

Another serious menace to social stratification in the rural com-

* Ungku A. Aziz, 'Fundamental Obstacles to Rural Development with Special Reference to Institutional Reforms'. Paper submitted to the South Asia Symposium, Stockholm, September 1969.

† Takashi Tomosugi, 'The Land System in Central Thailand', *The Developing Economies*, vol. 7, no. 3 (Institute of Developing Economies, Tokyo, September 1969). Peasants in the 'floating rice region' round Ayukaya have recently sunk into debt and become tenants. But as rents also tend to increase, many tenants are being reduced to landless labourers. The small peasants are unable to cope with the commercial economy since the credit cooperatives, due to the lack of communal autonomous organization, do not support them adequately.

munity is the elasticity of agricultural wages, pertinent to both relative agrarian prosperity and the increase in labour supply. In our view, wage trends in underdeveloped countries will largely be determined by the extent and type of mechanization, by the degree of unionization of the wage earners, and by the mobility of labour. Although little research has been done on these factors it seems likely that, with the expected increase in labour supply during the next two decades, the social stratification is likely to take a turn for the worse in the rural areas of underdeveloped countries, unless efforts are made to change the institutional framework and intensify labour utilization, control the speed and type of mechanization, organize effective labour unions, and establish rural industries wherever possible.

Rural industrialization would certainly provide a notable increase in non-agricultural employment largely through the external services needed, such as road construction, transportation and other facilities. This is, of course, a strong argument against traditional economic planning which concentrates primarily on the development of industrial and commercial activities in urban centres, profitable as they may be from a capitalistic point of view. Rural industries, however, should not favour the emergence of a new middle class of small industrialists, traders and agents in regional centres, but should be organized on a cooperative basis and conducted by the peasants themselves. Cooperative rural industries will be able to counteract, to some extent at least, the deleterious effect of excess population upon the social structure of the rural communities and reduce the massive flight from the land.* Moreover, the social costs of industrialization in terms of housing and public services will be much lower in the villages and small towns of the rural areas than in the already congested urban centres, where the mere rumour that industrial expansion is intended will attract an overflow of landless labour that far exceeds the needs of any foreseeable industrial programme.

* Government of India, Ministry of Food and Agriculture, Community Development and Cooperation, *Co-operative Sugar Factories in India* (New Delhi, 1966). This publication presents the sugar factories in the states of Maharashtra and Andhra Pradesh as examples of rural enterprises that have visible effects on the socio-economic conditions in rural areas and help to build up an agro-industrial complex.

POPULATION EXPANSION AND THE SUPPLY AND PRICE OF FOOD

Time and again, current discussion emphasizes that the plummeting death rate, particularly in the childbearing period, and the practically unchanged birth rate, may have disastrous effects upon the food situation. The problem of food supply has become of paramount importance and both United Nations' organizations and bilateral agencies are trying to use food shipments not only as a relief measure but also as a vehicle for economic development. Furthermore, it is universally agreed that poverty is the principal reason for deficient food intake and that the degree of a country's well-being or poverty is most clearly expressed in terms of the average daily calorie or protein intake per person,* and the per capita national income. But the latter criterion cannot give a true picture of the degree of poverty in a country because it necessarily ignores the distribution of income. Myrdal† quite rightly points out that income—or output—per head and its rate of change is no more than a rough indication of the degree of development or underdevelopment; this is due to the general weakness of national accounting in most underdeveloped countries and to the fact that a considerable part of the output is not marketed.

Some observers give credence to optimistic forecasts that technical improvements in agriculture will ensure an adequate and sufficient food supply in most of the underdeveloped countries by 1975 or thereabouts. In our view, however, the terms 'adequate' or 'sufficient' food supply are very dangerous indeed because of their ambiguity. The assumption, for example, that India may have achieved a sufficient food supply by 1975, or 1980, simply means that food production will have increased sufficiently to replace the present food aid and other food imports. But this neither implies a change in the current inadequate state of nutrition, nor an improvement in terms of calories and, still more important, in terms of protein. We should also bear in mind that even if these forecasts were to come true, the prevailing unequal distribution of income will automatically preclude the larger part of the population from an adequate diet.

* P. V. Sukhatme, 'The World Hunger and Future Need in Food Supply', *Journal of the Royal Statistical Society*, ser. A, vol. 124 (1963), pp. 463–525.
† *Asian Drama*, chap. 11, p. 474, and vol. 3, app. 13, pp. 2165 ff.

Keynes' well-known observation that the future income level is determined by the present distribution of income is equally valid for the food situation: *the future nutritional level of the masses in underdeveloped countries is determined by the present distribution of income.* It is evident, therefore, that only a fundamental change in the income distribution pattern can call a halt to the permanent state of malnutrition in the underdeveloped world and forestall the disaster of widespread famine. It is true that increased food production is essential; but this alone cannot solve the problem of hunger unless an equitable distribution of income guarantees that it will benefit those who most need it.

With this statement we are in the middle of the current fashionable debate on prices for agricultural products and government price policies as a means of raising agricultural production. If attractive prices to the producers were to serve as an incentive for increased food production in underdeveloped countries, as in the developed markets of the Western world, the problem of institutional changes would be less urgent and an adequate food supply would be available in the foreseeable future for the starving sector of the world's population. Unfortunately, this is not so; and ample evidence contradicts the wishful thinking of some Western economists that rising farm prices will necessarily stimulate agricultural production in underdeveloped countries.*

In India, for example, the subvention of farm prices by government purchases in wholesale markets hardly ever reaches the peasant producers but mostly accrues to the traders and wholesalers. And this because the constantly indebted peasant is virtually bound by contract to sell his produce at prices set by the private moneylender-cum-trader, as no effective marketing cooperatives exist to safeguard his interests.† In many underdeveloped countries, rigid tenancy systems prevent the tenant cultivator from placing even his own share of the crop on the market and force him to

---

* L. G. Sandberg, 'Worldwide Farming Just Around the Corner', *Economic Development and Cultural Change*, vol. 15, no. 1 (October 1966). The author is convinced that the relatively low level of food prices prevents the increasing need for fertilizers, chemicals, and water; and that 'higher prices would bring forth considerable increases in output'. Cf. Asian Development Bank, *Asian Agricultural Survey* (Manila, 1968), pp. 68 ff.

† S. G. Madiman, *Land Reform and Institutional Planning in India* (RU: MISC/68/15, FAO, Rome, April 1968), p. 30.

accept the price set by landlords and moneylenders who hoard the crop until the market offers the best prices.

Price and marketing policies in underdeveloped countries and particularly in Latin America represent a labyrinth of price controls, production limitations, subsidies, state protected monopolies, exchange rate manipulations, and special tax exemptions which clearly reflect the strength of the powerful interests of landowners, traders, processors, manufacturers, and urban consumers in the formation of the market structure. The only group that does not participate in this game are the small agricultural producers who are suppressed by a hostile structure that virtually isolates them from market operation and for whom, therefore, not even higher market prices can possibly provide an incentive for increased production.

A recent attempt in Chile to support small producers by special government loans for marketing did no more to bring about the desired effect. Most of the small producers concerned are either sharecroppers or indebted owner-peasants and in both cases large landholders were able to lay their hands upon the marketing loans, using them as substitutes for the credit customarily extended.*

The very poverty and misery of the rural population, in fact, prevent rising market prices from affecting production, the natural consequence of an imperfect market structure that virtually symbolizes the state of underdevelopment. In times of crop failure, when food is scarce and prices high, the already undernourished peasant producer is forced to reduce his sales in order to feed his family and thus increases the market squeeze which, in turn, pushes prices still higher. On the other hand, in times of bumper crops when food is plentiful and prices exceedingly low, he is forced to sell more than he can really spare in order to meet his burdensome commitments and thus contributes to a further drop in market prices. Agrarian reform will not immediately increase the market supply since the understandable reaction of the farming family to more tolerable living and working conditions is bound to be an increase in home consumption rather than in sales.

Price increases as an incentive to agricultural production can be impracticable in many underdeveloped countries where more

* S. L. Barraclough, *Agricultural Policy and Strategies of Land Reform* (Social Science Institute, Washington University, St. Louis, 1969).

pressing problems must be given first priority. In the first place, there is the permanent shortage of savings for investment and of foreign exchange; in order to increase either, or both, new lines of products and techniques and more realistic profit expectations must be introduced, which necessitate a comprehensive price policy that often may be difficult to reconcile with the concept of price incentives for agricultural producers. And secondly, there is the high statistical weight of food items in the cost of living index which must be reduced considerably as otherwise any increase in agricultural prices automatically leads to a cost-induced inflation of industrial prices. In India, for example, food supplies are considered a major factor when determining the safe limits for monetary expansion.*

The current discussion on food supply is also greatly concerned with the possible effect of food aid upon domestic food production and agricultural prices in underdeveloped countries.† The argument is frequently heard that a relative drop in agricultural prices will not necessarily act as a disincentive to agricultural production since the incidence of the decline will not be with the peasant producer. In our view, however, this is an unrealistic assumption which ignores the still extremely weak bargaining capacity of the peasants in an institutional environment where landowners, traders and middlemen dominate the market. In Malaysia, for example, we find an ingenious Monopoly-Monopsony system for buying and selling agricultural products which completely excludes the peasant producers from any participation in the marketing procedures. This system not only prevents any increase in farm income and, consequently, in production but even swallows up the government subsidies to agriculture and, ultimately, also large parts of the land in government-sponsored settlement schemes.‡

In other words, structural defects are the greatest obstacle to a rational price policy that would ultimately stimulate agricultural

---

* L. K. Tha, 'Price Policy in a Developing Economy', *India and Foreign Review,* vol. 5, nos. 15 and 16 (1968).

† V. M. Dandekar, *The Demand for Food and Conditions Governing Food Aid During Development* (Study No. 1, Gokhale Institute of Political and Economic Research, Poona, 1965).

‡ Ungku A. Aziz, 'Poverty and Rural Development in Malaysia', *Kajian Ekonomi Malaysia,* vol. 1, no. 1 (June 1964), pp. 70 ff.

production. Nothing short of fundamental changes, particularly in the man-land relationship, can improve the imperfect market situation and establish an income distribution pattern that will put an end to the prevailing rationing of food by the purse with its disastrous effects almost everywhere in the underdeveloped world.

Technological Progress

Throughout history, man's faculty for invention has marked the milestones in the various stages of development. But not until the Industrial Revolution did the impact of technological inventions radically upset the economic and social patterns throughout the world.

Like all phenomena that are clearly visible and tangible, and therefore seem easy to appraise, technological progress in agriculture is frequently judged quantitatively only in terms such as yields per unit area, or hectares under irrigation, or degree of farm mechanization, or volume of fertilizers, and is analysed, more scientifically as it were, in terms of returns to scale, capital or labour input and the substitution of capital for labour.*

This approach, important as it may be, is likely to mislead public opinion with regard to the beneficial effect of new technologies, since technological advance always produces effects on the organization of society that are not easily measurable. From the point of view of socio-economic development, therefore, it must also be judged by the extent to which the utilization of the increasing supply of agricultural labour affects the man-land relationship and the social stratification of the rural community. In many underdeveloped countries, in fact, technologically induced growth within the prevailing framework may create an unfortunate situation where, despite increasing numbers of potential consumers, demand on the domestic market will not improve, and the surplus supply will have to enter the export market. This, in turn, will tend to reduce the already low prime commodity prices and accelerate the deterioration of the terms of

---

* M. Brown, *On the Theory and Measurement of Technological Change* (Cambridge, 1966), p. 3.

trade. To use an expression, coined as early as in 1894;* technological progress may cause a 'damnifying growth' that in the end will contribute to the continued destitution of the underdeveloped world.

The transfer of Western technology and research will truly benefit the underdeveloped countries only if adapted to their entirely different circumstances. To be more precise; agricultural technology in underdeveloped countries has to be highly labourintensive, and not capital intensive as in developed countries. Equally important is the fact that underdeveloped countries, by definition, lack the necessary skills to make proper use of advanced technology. Consequently, technical assistance in establishing institutes for localized research in the underdeveloped world would be far more useful than the transfer of research results.

The application of advanced technology may even turn into an impediment to economic and social progress under the prevailing structural and institutional setup. Half-hearted and piecemeal action to change this setup, whether it is rendered ineffectual out of budgetary considerations or by the pressure of vested interests, will merely lead to a further deterioration of the situation. Just as fertilizers without sufficient water result in serious crop failures, and irrigation without drainage leads to salination of the soil, the application of modern technology without a reorganization of the administrative and institutional framework leads to a bottleneck that prevents social and economic progress.

TECHNOLOGICAL PROGRESS AND LABOUR UTILIZATION

The greatest asset of underdeveloped countries is no doubt their abundant supply of labour. But in order to prevent this asset becoming a burdensome liability—and it seems well on the way to being this—the speed and type of mechanization should be determined according to their ultimate effect upon labour utilization. Careful attention should be given to two questions: first, is the new mechanical equipment labour saving only, or does it primarily ensure a better exploitation of the agricultural resources?; and secondly, to what extent does it substitute capital for a more

* F. Y. Edgeworth, 'The Theory of International Values', *Economic Journal*, vol. 4, no. 1 (March 1894), pp. 40–2.

effective utilization of labour, or rather, for a deliberate refraining from purely labour-displacing devices?

It is safe to say that a high man-land ratio does not lead to labour-intensive agriculture; on the contrary, the overpopulated areas of underdeveloped regions are marked by the detrimental effects of an underutilization of labour due largely to outdated cultivation methods. On the other hand, experience has shown time and again that technological progress calls for a higher and more efficient input of labour.* Generally speaking, advanced technology should not reduce but increase the demand for labour since it leads to an expansion of the farm economy and the more abundant crops require additional work in connection with harvesting, replenishing of the soil, weeding, etc.

Western economists, however, are mainly intent upon solving the problem of how to substitute capital for labour and do not seem to realize that the main difficulty in underdeveloped economies is how to utilize most effectively the available labour force and how to substitute labour for capital. At the Overseas Studies Committee Conference in Cambridge in 1968† the discussion reverted repeatedly to the problem of labour utilization and to the reproaches of the African delegates that Technical Assistance ignores this important point and that Western economists do not seem to realize that in China the mobilization and utilization of the labour force is replacing capital to an ever-increasing extent. It proved difficult to gainsay this justified criticism.

Theoretically, of course, it should be possible, as suggested by some experts, to recklessly invest the profits derived from technical progress and, say, within twenty to forty years, depending upon the prevailing social stratification and degree of industrialization, to raise tenfold or more food consumption per head in even the poorest underdeveloped country.‡ But such an iron cure will call for political and social sacrifices no longer possible in our age of socio-political tensions. Equally unfeasible is the theory that even

* G. Myrdal, *Asian Drama*, chap. 26, sect. 11, and sects. 6–19.
† R. Robinson and P. Johnston (eds.), *The Rural Base for National Development. Papers and Impressions of the Sixth Cambridge Conference on Development Problems* (Cambridge University Overseas Studies Committee, 1968).
‡ R. M. Goodwin, 'The Optimal Growth Path for an Underdeveloped Economy', *Economic Journal*, vol. 71, no. 284 (December 1961), pp. 756 ff.

without substantial outside support it should be possible to raise the marginal savings rate to about 75 per cent during part of the take-off period and plough back into capital goods as much as 70–80 per cent of the Gross National Product during the last ten years of the 'big push'.*

Unlike improved biological and chemical techniques, labour-saving mechanization counteracts the objective of intensified labour utilization. In the social environment of an underdeveloped country the large-scale introduction of tractors and heavy machinery may often be considered an unwise investment because of the nature of short-run fixed costs.† Investments of this kind require large management units and uniform agricultural practices in order to hold down unit costs; but this, of course, will lead to an expansion of the capitalist farms and to a decline of individual peasant cultivation and thus in reality to a reduced utilization of labour. Selective mechanization of specific cultivation and post-harvest operations, on the other hand, would be meaningful from the point of view of agricultural progress and labour utilization.

In underdeveloped countries with a surplus population, therefore, modern technology must be appraised in terms of its potential capacity for increasing labour utilization and contributing to the substitution of labour for capital. Though our actual knowledge of experience in the Peoples' Republic of China is still rather incomplete, recent literature‡ indicates that the increased

* L. Currie (*Accelerating Development*, London and New York, 1966) proposes solving Colombia's agrarian problems 'almost overnight by rapid industrialization and out-migration'. See also S. L. Barraclough, 'Employment Problems Affecting Latin American Agricultural Development', *FAO Monthly Bulletin of Agricultural Economics and Statistics*, vol. 18, nos. 7–8 (Rome, July-August, 1969). Barraclough argues rightly that the tripling of the present high migration rate in Colombia, as suggested by Lauchlin Currie, would require political and social changes of dynamic revolutionary dimensions.

† Hiromitsu Kaneda, 'Economic Implications of the "Green Revolution" and the Strategy of Agricultural Development in West Pakistan', *The Pakistan Development Review*, vol. 9, no. 2 (Summer 1969), pp. 111 ff.

‡ W. F. Wertheim, 'Recent Trends in China's Population Policy'. Paper submitted to the UN World Population Conference, Belgrade, August-September 1965; and Isabel and David Crook, *The First Years of Yangyi Commune* (London and New York, 1966), pp. 95 ff.

utilization of agricultural labour has been given a more prominent place in economic planning than has industrialization and increased labour productivity. It seems, moreover that the Chinese have developed a most practical way of achieving quick results in agriculture. On the one hand, they have introduced electric or diesel oil driven pumping machines to replace the primitive type of irrigation by treadle or hand-wheel while, on the other, they use the available manpower rather than tractors for highly labour-intensive types of work like digging canals for irrigation or drainage, and the collection, transport and distribution of manure and fertilizers. At the same time, however, they make full use of all accessible scientific knowledge as well as of the organizational potential of the People's Communes to utilize and direct the manpower to where it is most useful. Even if the part-mechanization of definite elements of the agricultural process actually releases a certain amount of manual labour, it is still acceptable if, at the same time, it helps to increase the number of crops to be harvested from one field and thus creates a new demand for manual labour of a different type in addition to considerably increasing the productivity of the land.*

Contrary to conventional Western concepts, the level of mechanization in China is not determined exclusively by its capital-saving or labour-saving effect but rather by its ultimate influence upon the employment situation. Modern machinery is applied when, in the end, it serves to increase the employment potential and not otherwise. Due to this rational application of modern technology which is not controlled by entrenched interests, a typical picture in the Communes is the planned coexistence of different technological levels in works like irrigation, road construction, sowing and harvesting; whereas in other underdeveloped countries we often see impressive and highly specialized machinery operated by a handful of skilled labourers, while thousands of peasants wander about idle and starving.

Although no statistical data are available on the employment and capital aspects of mechanization in China, the magnitude of the Chinese investment in terms of mobilized labour is clearly evident. If we bear in mind that prior to the Revolution, the labour reserve must have amounted to at least 150 million, about 25 per cent of the population, the full utilization of this reserve,

* W. F. Wertheim, 'Recent Trends in China's Population Policy'.

including the increments created by the population increase, must have called for the unprecedented capital investment of more or less one-quarter of the annual national income.*

Even if Western criticism of certain aspects of the Chinese programme may be partly justified, and even if it were true that the employment of millions of workers has been misdirected, the fact remains that the positive results may well exceed the aggregate achievements in the underdeveloped regions of Asia and Latin America. Recent information seems to indicate that the Chinese way of utilizing agricultural labour has led to a higher level of living, an increased rice production that even allows some rice exports, and a fully employed rural population.† It may be added that this favourable development seems to be facilitated by a reasonable price policy for agricultural products. The criticism of some observers‡ that Chinese agricultural policy concentrates almost exclusively upon labour-intensive farming and is unable to supply the amounts of capital and basic materials required by Western standards, seems unjustified in view of the negative effect upon the employment situation in underdeveloped countries of many bilateral and multi-lateral Technical Assistance programmes.

Although improved agricultural techniques are undoubtedly a prerequisite for higher yields and better-quality products, the introduction of advanced farming methods frequently fails to produce the desired results in underdeveloped countries. This is largely due to the general emphasis in Western research on conditions in the temperate zone, particularly in the fields of soil science and forestry. It is of utmost importance, therefore, to encourage effective localized research and train agricultural scientists *within* the physical and social environment of their respective countries. This would definitely lead to a more appropriate application of modern science in tropical areas which will increase agricultural yields and, ultimately, may even counteract the underutilization of rural labour.

* T. Balogh, 'Agricultural and Economic Development, Linked Public Works', *Oxford Economic Papers*, n.s., vol. 13, no. 1 (February 1961).
† See chapter 6, sub-section on China.
  Le Monde (9.12.1969) states: 'La modernisation de l'agriculture chinoise explique les bonnes récoltes de ces dernières années.'
‡ See A. Eckstein (*Communist China's Economic Growth and Foreign Trade*, New York and London, 1966, p. 69), whose views of the agricultural performance are based on records dating from 1959–61.

Yet, in large parts of the underdeveloped world the very nature of prevailing patterns of land use and land ownership prevents technical progress and increased labour utilization. In Mexico, for example, the employment potential rose sharply in the Laguna Province when the establishment of collective *ejidos* made possible a changeover from labour-extensive wheat farming to labour-intensive cotton cultivation. Such changes in the land use pattern, however, are not always readily accepted by the governments of underdeveloped countries, even if they realize their important effect upon labour utilization. They fear, and sometimes rightly so, that even a partial replacement of food production by increased cultivation of export crops, though the latter is more labour-intensive, may weaken their domestic supply position and at the same time increase their dependence upon world market fluctuations.

The Western concept of landownership upheld in the legal codes of most former colonies, not only helps to preserve the present social stratification but further increases the army of landless and unutilized agricultural labour; it favours enclosure operations and outlaws the traditional practice of squatting on unused land which is deeply rooted in the conviction that the man who has cleared and tilled a piece of land is also its legitimate occupant. At the risk of oversimplifying a highly complex problem, we may state that there are only two ways in which underdeveloped countries can rapidly achieve the needed increase in labour utilization and food production: collective farming and the spontaneous take-over of unused land by squatters.*

PUBLIC WORKS AS AN INSTRUMENT FOR LABOUR UTILIZATION

The importance of public works for the utilization of idle and

* G. Myrdal, *Asian Drama*, p. 1271: '... if squatting were once more made legal, many areas might be quickly opened up for cultivation with little public investment apart from the construction of roads.'

C. Robequain (*Malaya, Indonesia, Borneo and the Philippines*, London, 1954; New York, 1958, p. 290) states that in 1932, 1,000 peasants a month migrated to the Island of Mindanao in the Philippines. Once they had arrived, these peasants 'cleared the lots granted to them by the government along new roads before even the roads were finished.'

underemployed labour is generally recognized not only by economists but, still more important, by politicians. The fact, however,
that public works programmes in the underdeveloped world (excluding the socialist countries) have nowhere been a complete
success needs an explanation. In the feudalistic and class-ridden
societies of the underdeveloped countries the direction of such
programmes is generally determined by the ruling group and
their implementation is often made possible by capital-intensive
foreign assistance which prevents the absorption of idle manpower.
No wonder that the rural people view the organization of public
works with distress and are reluctant to participate in them.* In
Latin America, in Indonesia and the Philippines, the public
works programmes have been decided by those who control
land and labour and have had, at best, little effect upon labour
utilization.

In its Third Five-Year Plan the Government of India declared
that 'the first condition for securing equality of opportunity and
achieving a national minimum is assurance of gainful employment
for everyone who seeks work' and recognizing that for many
years to come, large-scale projects for such things as land improvement and road construction would be the best way of utilizing the abundant manpower resources in rural areas, it proposed
to undertake 'a comprehensive programme of rural works'.†
Dandekar stated quite rightly that 'a complete and total withdrawal of the landless labour population from agriculture might
make some impact on the problem of rural unemployment and
underemployment, since it will reduce the competition for wage
employment and make the latter entirely available to the class of
small landowners'.‡

Yet, despite detailed plans for implementation and the psychologically favourable opportunity provided by the national emergency during the Sino-Indian war, only very modest results were
achieved for two fundamental reasons. First, increasing labour

* G. Huizer, 'Community Development, Land Reform and Political
Participation', *American Journal of Economics and Sociology*, vol. 28,
no. 2 (April 1969), pp. 159 ff.
† Government of India, Planning Commission, *Third Five-Year Plan,
1961–1966* (New Delhi, 1961), chap. I: 'Objectives of Planned
Development'.
‡ V. M. Dandekar, 'Utilization of Rural Manpower', *The Economic
Weekly* (Bombay, February 1962).

utilization through public works is not in agreement with the prevailing socio-economic and structural framework; and secondly, it calls for an attitude that is difficult to reconcile with the prevalent *laissez-faire* approach to agricultural and agrarian problems.

Nor does the success of the community development project of the Academy of Rural Development at Comilla, in central East Pakistan, prove the contrary. It is true that this remarkable project considerably increased manpower utilization and very soon created a total employment of 129 million man-days, or the equivalent of 430,000 man-years. But it is also true that it was directed by efficient and devoted people and received such generous support from the Ford Foundation that there was never any need to impose additional taxes, and the workers received full wages without contributing to future communal benefits as is the case in all other community development schemes. Hence, the Comilla project merely demonstrates the vital importance of employing underutilized manpower in labour-intensive enterprises; but it cannot be considered as a model since it will be well-nigh impossible to obtain foreign assistance on such a scale to promote development in the numerous over-populated areas of the under-developed world. Furthermore, it remains to be seen whether the agrarian structure and the relation between the different social and economic strata in the villages have actually been changed,* and whether any forthcoming data will indicate the extent to which the additional employment has affected the landless workers and underprivileged groups in the community.†

There is no doubt that idle agricultural labour in the under-developed countries could be utilized effectively through public works provided, however, that structural and institutional reforms have fostered a positive attitude at all levels of rural society. Increased labour utilization through public works will then create the means necessary to bridge the gaps caused by the labour force's present immobility and lack of adaptability. It will help to mitigate the effects of population increase and mechanization upon the employment situation and, consequently, upon the in-

* G. Myrdal, *Asian Drama*, p. 1365.
† United Nations Economic Commission for Asia and the Far East, *Economic Survey of Asia and the Far East 1965* (Bangkok, 1966), p. 125.

come distribution in rural areas because the earnings of the labourers in the public works programme will generate new demands and thus release cumulative effects in the villages.

The organization of public works, however, calls for a certain degree of flexibility. In the first place it must avoid possible competition with the large seasonal demand for agricultural labour.* And secondly, it must take into account the fact that if the increase in income is too far above the productive capacity of an area it might have an inflationary effect that will seriously impede overall development. The Chinese seem to have overcome this difficulty by making the villages in the Communes responsible for maintaining the agricultural labour force and in this way tie the increased consumption level to an increase in production. There is no doubt that the conventional *laissez-faire* attitude to socio-economic problems in underdeveloped countries will make it extremely difficult, to say the least, to combat underutilization of agricultural labour by the organization of public works.

THE READINESS TO ACCEPT TECHNOLOGICAL PROGRESS

So far, we have dealt only with the physical and structural obstacles to agricultural progress without touching upon the crucial problem of how to arouse the peasants' interest in innovations and persuade them to give up their traditional practices; of how to mobilize and organize the rural population so that it will take an active part in bringing about agricultural progress.

Development planners in the past did not always realize how extremely difficult it would be to influence the millions of small farmers, an effort involving repetition on an untold number of holdings spread over a vast area. Given the usually insufficient and arduous means of communication in most underdeveloped areas, the individual farm unit, desirable as it seems to many economists, is a serious obstacle to adequate education and effective extension work and entails the risk that, in a time of immense scientific progress, the gap between research results and their useful application is getting increasingly wider.†

Development strategy, therefore, should not be limited to trans-

---

* FAO, 'Interim Report of the FAO Mediterranean Project. Prepared by a team headed by Thomas Balogh' (Rome, 1957, as yet unpublished).
† J. Chonchol, 'From Isolation to Unity', *CERES, FAO Review*, vol. 1, no. 3 (May-June 1968), pp. 41 ff.

ferring modern machinery and technical know-how to underdeveloped countries but should also aim at finding ways and
means of bringing about the urgently needed changes in the attitude
of the people. It has been stated that the progress of change tends
to be uneven, and that this causes development bottlenecks.*
Bottlenecks exist, of course, in fact they are the rule rather than the
exception and they are caused by outdated social systems whose
very nature weakens the overall effect of improved techniques in
all sectors of society.

The psychological aspects of the transfer of innovations have
become a choice topic for social scientists,† who dwell at length
upon the farmer's 'resistance to change' but rarely mention the
pressure to which he is exposed by rigid and outdated tenure
systems. They emphasize time and again the need for improving
the intellectual and moral level of the rural people but hardly
ever touch upon the fundamental problem of how this can be
achieved under the prevailing agrarian conditions. And yet, it is
difficult to conceive an intellectual and moral emancipation of the
peasantry unless adequate tenure reforms have created an environment that will stimulate their interest in agricultural progress and
give them a chance to develop common sense, energy, resourcefulness and prudence; in short, all the qualities needed for active
participation in agricultural development and economic progress.‡
Within the institutional setup in most underdeveloped countries
the insecure and destitute peasant cultivator will hesitate to take
the risk of further indebtedness in order to make the capital
investment required for modern agricultural techniques, as bitter

* I. Svennilson, 'The Strategy of Transfer' in D. L. Spencer and
A. Woroniak (eds.), *The Transfer of Technology to Developing
Countries* (New York, 1967), chap. 7.
† See 'Report on the Seventh Regional FAO Conference for Asia and
the Far East, Manila, 1964' (FAO, Rome, 1965); B. Malinowski, *A
Scientific Theory of Culture* (Chapel Hill, 1944); and F. C. Byrnes,
*Some Missing Variables in Diffusion, Research, and Innovation
Strategy* (The Agricultural Development Council, New York, March
1968).
‡ See E. H. Jacoby, 'Agrarian Structure and Land Settlement', in
*Report of the UN Conference on the Application of Science and
Technology for the Benefit of Less-developed Countries* (UN,
Geneva, October 1962); and United Nations, Dept. of Ec. and Soc.
Affairs, *Progress in Land Reform, Fourth Report* (New York, 1966),
p. 135.

experience has taught him to fear the precariousness of tropical agriculture.

Incentives for additional effort not only increase productivity in general but, more specifically, the application of advanced technology. If they act as a personal material motive they are closely related to the system of private ownership in land and have always provided the strongest argument against the insecurity of tenancy and sharecropping systems. The socialist countries make a clear distinction between self-centred incentives promoting individual enrichment and collective incentives strengthening the group interest. China, Cuba and Tanzania have gone one step further and strive to replace material incentives by ideological principles based on solidarity and faith in a socialist society.

It may be argued that the conception of incentive is over-estimated and that personal effort and initiative are largely determined by the social environment and institutional climate. There is no doubt that the tendency to conformity is of considerable importance in this context, as is clearly evident in such fundamentally different environments as the Communes in China and the suburban communities in the United States.

The literature on the difficulty of promoting technological progress in agriculture deals almost exclusively with the problems of the extension worker-peasant relationship and presents excellent analyses of the shortcomings that will have to be overcome. It has been pointed out that the efforts of extension workers frequently fail because the peasants resist 'on terms of *their* definition of the situation'* and that 'their personalism and status consciousness play an important role'; or that some extension workers are intent upon pleasing their superiors rather than furthering the peasants' interests. In order to remedy the latter shortcoming, it has been proposed that a small number of progressive and intelligent farmers in the extension worker's district should be encouraged to take an active part in agricultural research and experimentation and regularly report their findings to a forum of local peasants.† Given the prevailing socio-economic

* F. C. Byrnes, *Some Missing Variables in Diffusion, Research, and Innovation Strategy*, p. 3.
† V. M. Dandekar, 'Motivating Farmers to Increase Agricultural Production'. Paper submitted to the Seventh Regional FAO Conference for Asia and the Far East, Manila, 1964.

environment, however, it seems unlikely that the 'forum of local peasants' would be able to voice their opinion and make an active choice, or that the 'progressive' and 'intelligent' farmers, who necessarily belong to the village élite, would refrain from using their participation in research and experimentation to strengthen their social position and thus increase the social gap within the village community.

Although some of the various well-meant suggestions for improving the extension worker-peasant relationship may prove useful, they cannot present any solution as long as the material and moral oppression of the peasants remains the major obstacle to the successful introduction of advanced techniques.

THE MIRACLE SEEDS

The present disregard of the need for institutional reforms is nourished by the technocratic euphoria, as Myrdal calls the enthusiasm aroused by the successful experiments with high-yielding varieties of seed.* Economists throughout the world hail the 'green revolution' and the 'miracle' rice but seem to forget that bumper crops alone do not protect peasants in need. This buoyancy, in fact, lends a most dangerous support to the vested interests in underdeveloped countries who are eager to maintain the institutional arrangements that guarantee their economic and social position. It is strange, and indeed almost ironic, that the very scholars who disapproved of land reform under conditions of food shortage because it initially reduces the volume of agricultural production, now maintain that it is no longer necessary, given the new varieties that will multiply harvests and provide ample food for everybody. Their argument, however, is scarcely convincing since even greatly increased production cannot possibly reach the millions of destitute peasants living within an institutional framework that by its very nature restricts their purchasing capacity.

But quite apart from prevailing economic conditions the anticipated massive increase in food production will depend on physical factors such as size of holdings, extent and quality of irrigation, resistance of the new varieties to disease, etc. We must not close

* G. Myrdal, *The Challenge of World Poverty: A World Anti-Poverty Program in Outline* (New York, 1970), chap. 4, pt. 130.

our eyes to the numerous obstacles between scientific discovery and practical application. There is a world of difference between experimental gardens and the vast areas of Asia and Latin America cultivated by millions of poor and ignorant peasant farmers.

A recent study on rice-growing in tropical Asia deals in detail with the physical prerequisites for the successful cultivation of the high-yielding varieties of rice. In the broad deltaic regions of East Pakistan, Burma, Central Thailand and Vietnam, where flood waters make it practically impossible to control the depth of the water in the fields, the long stem of the traditional variety guarantees the survival of the plant. The short-stemmed 'miracle rice', IR-8, however, cannot be grown in such areas, nor can fertilizers, weed-killers or pesticides be used with the measure of precision required to obtain optimal results. Water control, in fact, is so essential in the cultivation of the new varieties that the possibility of increasing yields in the relatively short run is limited by the capacity of the irrigation system. In order to maximize the yields of the 'miracle' rice, it would be necessary to control excess waters in the wet season and provide sufficient water in the dry season; but this, in turn, implies engineering works that inevitably are beyond the technical and financial capacity of the peasant farmer.* The study also points out that a serious defect in the new strain is the quality of the rice produced which has been criticized on grounds of poor milling characteristics and flavour and, therefore, may be less attractive to the people who constitute the market.†

An interesting investigation has recently been made in India on the significance of the new high-yielding varieties for small farms in two areas of the State of Gujarat,‡ where a new programme for the agricultural development of small farms was launched some years ago. The authors come to the conclusion that the younger and more dedicated farmers of the higher castes with the larger

* B. L. C. Johnson, 'Recent Developments in Rice Breeding and Some Implications for Tropical Asia'. Paper submitted to the Conference on South East Asian Society and Environment, 9–11 September 1969, School of Oriental and African Studies, London.
† Ibid., p. 7.
‡ V. S. Vyas, D. S. Tyagi and V. N. Misra, *Significance of the New Strategy of Agricultural Development for Small Farmers – A Cross-Section Study of Two Areas*, (Agro-Economic Research Centre, Sardar Patel University, Vallabh Vidyanagar, 1968).

and better holdings and some money resources at their disposal gained the most from adopting the high-yielding varieties programme. The other, less fortunate farmers with the smaller holdings and no liquid capital could not obtain the same results and gradually ceased to participate. The investigation shows, in fact, that the percentage of drop-outs in both test areas is considerably higher among farmers with holdings of less than 10 hectares than among those with 10–20 hectares at their disposal. Unfortunately, the actual reason for the drop-outs has not been investigated, but it may be assumed that they were largely motivated by unsatisfactory credit arrangements and extension services.

Another interesting observation is that despite the high-yielding varieties, the farm business income of the smaller units was insufficient to meet the customary household consumption requirements and hence a large number of small farms remained non-viable. Although modern techniques, once firmly established, considerably lowered the viability limit, the authors conclude that under the prevailing conditions in the two test areas, a sizeable number of farms, 70 per cent in one district and 39 per cent in the other will remain non-viable and that 'for these farms other alternatives for increasing income and raising the living standards have to be explored'.

The breeding of new high-yielding varieties of rice presents a formidable challenge. From the point of view of economic development, a balance must be established between inputs in agriculture that determine the growth effects and the development of institutions that determine the quality of society. Yet, the hopeful vision of producing yields six, eight, or ten times as great as normal has given rise to a credit policy which concentrates on the highest possible returns and therefore, as in India, tends to promote the introduction of new varieties primarily in the irrigated areas.* This means in effect that the bulk of crop loans go to the larger farms, while the peasant farmer on his dry piece of land will get considerably smaller loans, if any, and thus remains underprivileged despite the miracle seed.

In long-term socio-economic planning, therefore, the input problem is largely a question of how to rescue peasants on the non-viable holdings and at the same time reduce the growing rate of landlessness. The only feasible answer seems to be that the applica-

* A. Hopcraft, *Born to Hunger* (London and Boston, 1968), pp. 96 ff.

C

tion of modern technology must be brought into harmony with the entire system of social relationships in order to establish a society with maximum equality.

We must beware of the illusion that the new high-yielding varieties of cereals will automatically solve the problems of social organization. Indeed, they may further complicate the socio-economic situation.* It is a well-known fact that in many under-developed countries the abundant crops in the irrigated river valleys have caused the emergence of most unfortunate systems of tenure and social organization. A manifold increase in yields through the introduction of new varieties may have a similar effect unless attention is given to the interests of the under-privileged rural people. It is not difficult to foresee that the whole gamut of technological innovation may tempt the governments of underdeveloped countries to adopt an agricultural policy that will favour the most prosperous regions where investments in the economic and social infrastructure have already been made and where the greatest returns can be expected. This will automatically lead to a neglect of the areas of subsistence agriculture and of the

---

* Robert S. McNamara, President of the World Bank Group ('Annual Address by Robert S. McNamara, President of the Bank and its Affiliates' in *1969: Annual Meetings of the Boards of Governors, Summary Proceedings*, Washington D.C., 1969, p. 10), states quite rightly that 'the initial problem of achieving worldwide food suffi-ciency will gradually give way to second generation problems which are even more complex'. '... The new technology is more readily available to richer farmers and thus can paradoxically become punitive to poorer farmers.' See also:

Lester Pearson (Chairman), *Partners in Development*, p. 62.

FAO, *The State of Food and Agriculture 1969* (Rome, 1969), p. 10, while dealing with the agricultural aspects of the 'Green Revolution' makes no mention of the institutional problems involved.

Statement by the Secretary General of the United Nations to the Commission on Social Development (Document E/CN.5/444, December 1969) which concludes that '... the prospect of the Green Revolution has made meaningful land reform more urgent than ever ...'

H. Kaneda, 'Economic Implications of the "Green Revolution" and the Strategy of Agricultural Development in West Pakistan', *The Pakistan Development Review*, loc. cit., pp. 111 ff. Kaneda is partic-ularly concerned with the international as well as domestic marketing prospects of the 'green revolution'. He also points out that, contrary to mechanical engineering technology, bio-chemical technology is not labour displacing.

non-viable farm units which, at best, will receive a handout in order to provide a minimum subsistence for those who otherwise would have none.* These problems are of immense proportions and can only be adequately tackled by a progressive agricultural policy that is not content with protecting subsistence farming, but is ready to support some form of collective landholding system in order to give the small peasants in the subsistence areas a chance to partake in economic development.

Another equally important problem that cannot be solved through 'miracle' seeds is the tendency of rural, economic and political power to become concentrated in the regional towns, where merchants and middlemen skim off the wealth generated by agriculture. This extremely dangerous form of internal colonialism, mentioned earlier in this chapter, may even be strengthened if technological progress is concentrated in privileged areas.

* R. Stavenhagen, 'Social Aspects of Agrarian Structure in Mexico', op. cit., p. 47.

W. Ladejinsky ('The Green Revolution in Punjab: A Field Trip', *Economic and Political Weekly*, vol. 4, no. 26, Bombay, 28 June 1969), deals with the complex aspects of the 'Green revolution' in Punjab which from an agricultural point of view has been a great success. According to Ladejinsky the 'green revolution' is very much in evidence in Punjab. New wheat varieties, sown in May 1969, had a coverage of 90 per cent, and the increase in yields was very considerable. Owner-farmers with irrigated land make a great deal of money: land values are spiralling, rents are going up, and the burden of taxation is light. Despite the fact that the demand and wages for casual labour have increased, it can be expected that, with further mechanization, the Punjab will be confronted by an ever-rising number of underemployed. Ladejinsky had difficulty in establishing the facts and figures of present underemployment, but concludes that 'growth and prosperity cannot hide the fact that the new agricultural policy which has done a yeoman job in generating them is also the indirect cause of the widening of the gap between the rich and the poor. Precisely because the green revolution has found its widest application in Punjab, the probability is that, relatively speaking, the gap is greater there than in any other part of rural India. The assumption that the lot of the landless worker has undergone a change for the better because he earns Rs. 2–3 a day more, or is employed a few weeks more is correct, but it doesn't measure up against the fact that the well-to-do farmers are still better off and that rich farmers are getting very much richer. Nor can one leave out of account the rising insecurity of the remaining tenants, reduced in number though they are, and that the overall conditions of tenants and share-croppers are anything but improving.'

It is far beyond the objectives of this book to analyse the more remote effects of advanced technology. The Philippines' self-sufficiency in rice, for instance, due to the introduction of 'miracle' seeds, will most likely reduce the export market of the rice-cultivating peasants in Thailand and Burma and thus further delay the regional integration which is so needed. Developments of this kind may, in the end, worsen the terms of trade for the underdeveloped countries and prevent any rise in the standard of living of millions of peasants in Asia, the Near East and Latin America. This, of course, does not mean that we should block technological development and prevent the advance of modern technology in the underdeveloped world; either would be impossible and absurd. Any technological progress contains a promise for a better future provided that the man on the land is protected against the single-minded enthusiasm of those who do not, or do not want to, understand the socio-economic implications. But this protection requires a fundamental change in our approach not only to agrarian institutions and agricultural policy but also to the manifold problems of international trade and investments. Such a new approach will act as a safety valve in the powerful machinery of technological progress and reduce the imminent danger that the underdeveloped world be turned into an agricultural slum for countless millions of people. As an instrument for development, therefore, advanced technology is of importance only if and when the agrarian structure and institutions cease to prevent it from reaching those who need it most.

Land reform alone, of course, cannot bring about technical progress. But adequate changes in agrarian structure and institutions can integrate advanced technology into the general pattern of development and create the psychological precondition for the adoption of technical innovations that will make possible a durable development from below.

It would be unfair to blame the technologist for not considering the agrarian structure; he is an expert in his field and his main concern is with problems of agricultural efficiency and growth. But the economist who primarily thinks in terms of technological progress commits the grave error of neglecting the human factor in economic development.

The almost incessant flow of new high-yielding varieties has raised dangerously high hopes that it will be possible to rapidly put an end to underdevelopment and backwardness; and only a few observers openly discuss the intractable social facts that stand as the major obstacle to the fruitful application of the new knowledge.* But many more are carried away by their enthusiasm for this technical achievement which they feel will revolutionize agriculture just as the steam engine revolutionized industry 150 years ago.† And even those who do discuss some of the more important technical and economic problems that may arise such as marketing, storage, extension services, irrigation and even price policies, almost entirely ignore the structural problems.‡

Many writers now consider the green revolution to be an effective tool for a better utilization of agricultural labour. It is true that in the Philippines, for example, the new varieties call for about 50 per cent more labour per crop and yield approximately twice as much rice as does the traditional *intan* variety when cultivated by conventional methods. Yet, this tremendous increase in yield is the crux of the matter, because the actual labour input for each ton of rice thus produced is in reality one-third less than before.§

In other words, due to the application of the new varieties the Philippines will be faced with a decreasing utilization of labour in the rice areas, unless the actual demand for rice is expanding

* B. L. C. Johnson, 'Recent Developments in Rice Breeding', p. 10.

† L. R. Brown, 'A New Era in World Agriculture' (USDA 3773–68). Paper submitted to the First Annual Senator Frank Carlson Symposium on World Population and Food Supply, Kansas State University, December 1968. It is not sufficient to state that the new varieties may be to the agricultural revolution in the underdeveloped world what the steam engine was to the industrial revolution in Europe if we know so little about the direction of the *social* change involved.

‡ C. R. Wharton, Jr. ('The Green Revolution: Cornucopia or Pandora's Box?', *Foreign Affairs*, vol. 47, no. 3, April 1969, pp. 464 ff.), deals brilliantly with some of the most important technical and economic problems of the green revolution such as marketing and storage, credit and extension, the need for more effective irrigation systems and increased susceptibility to disease. He also recognizes the possible effects on markets and price policies and, particularly in the case of Asia, on regional economic integration. But even then he ignores the possible adverse effects on the social structure.

§ R. Barker, S. H. Liao and S. K. De Datta, 'Economic Analysis of Rice Production from Experimental Results to Farmer Fields.' Paper presented at Agronomy Department Seminar, University of the Philippines, 9 August 1960, offset, p. 12.

proportionately with the doubled yields. The much advertised employment effect of the new varieties, therefore, can be realized only if the domestic purchasing power is increasing correspondingly or if, against all expectations, adequate export possibilities should emerge; to produce is certainly easier than to distribute.

Under present conditions, however, the new varieties will further diminish employment in agriculture* since the large commercially managed estates will combine the use of the new varieties with the introduction of modern labour-saving equipment which, in its turn, will inevitably lead to the ejection of tenants and dismissal of workers. There is little hope that in countries such as the Philippines, Thailand and even India this trend can be counteracted by *selective mechanization*, since the large landowning interests who dominate the legislation and administrative machinery are accustomed to react generously to the demands for 'sound' farm management.

It is safe to predict that only countries with a certain degree of structural maturity and a relatively well-balanced land distribution pattern will be able to absorb the shock-effect of the green revolution and profit from the high-yielding varieties. In most underdeveloped countries, therefore, institutional changes, above all through comprehensive land reform programmes, will be necessary in order to avoid the development of rural and urban slums in these countries which are still worse and more widespread than those created in the West by the Industrial Revolution.

Despite 'miracle' seeds, tangible relief in the underdeveloped countries cannot be expected for decades; in the meantime the problem remains of how to pave the way for the transformation needed to cope with the formidable impact of population growth and technological progress. One thing seems certain, however, the time-span allowed for this transformation is getting increasingly shorter: Western Europe needed 150 years for the take-off, while Japan succeeded in half that time, the Soviet Union in less than fifty years, and China seems well on her way to break all records. It is difficult to conceive, therefore, that the combined dynamics of population increase and technological progress can be held back for another generation before tearing asunder the chains of

---

* See Special Release No. 104, Series of 1970, Bureau of Census and Statistics, Manila, according to which agricultural employment has declined considerably between May 1968 and May 1969.

the past. But, unfortunately, precious time for a guided transition is being wasted by the emphasis on technological progress and by the deliberate failure to tackle the fundamental problem of the man-land relationship.

CHAPTER THREE

Fundamental Features of the Man-Land Relationship

An analysis of agrarian conditions in underdeveloped countries which focuses primarily on the factors that determine the man-land relationship may be instrumental in bringing into clear relief the importance of structural reforms for overall economic and social development. But before embarking on such an analysis we must identify the fundamental physical and psychological features which, directly or indirectly, determine man's relation to land and ultimately, therefore, the productivity of agricultural labour. Well aware of the complexity of the world of reality, we have selected the following features which are still extant in most parts of the underdeveloped world, irrespective of race, civilization and stage of development.

1. The agrarian structure;
2. The peasants versus the rural élite;
3. The Agrarian Creed.

The Agrarian Structure

The long historical process by which agriculture was gradually linked to new techniques, new food requirements and living conditions, and to more developed forms of market economy, decisively influenced not only the structure of settlement but also the social stratification in the rural community. From the very beginning of sedentary agriculture, rights in land have determined who has authority, influence and wealth, and formed the different agrarian structures and institutions that decide the productivity of land and labour. In developed and underdeveloped countries alike, productivity of land and labour is fundamentally a function of the incentives and protection offered to the tiller of the soil by the agrarian structure: hence this structure has, or should have, a most important place in economic development planning.

The agrarian structure in Latin America and large parts of Asia is still marked by feudalistic tenure systems in which land owner- ship is concentrated in large estates belonging to a small élite whose social, political and economic power derives from the con- trol of land, labour, market forces and government, while the mass of the rural population lives in poverty and misery.* Under the pressure of commercial and technological forces some of the ex- tensive estates have been transformed into modern plantations and large-scale capitalist farms; yet, the dominant features of feudalistic control are as strong as ever.

Almost everywhere the peasants are used by the owners of the land as a steady source of cash income and, consequently, are considered an appendage to the land rather than an independent production factor. Max Weber traces the origin of this form of exploitation to the medieval feudal lords who never identified land-ownership with farm management, since they were too lazy and too heavily burdened by their many commitments to the Crown.† In addition, though this indirect exploitation of agricul- tural labour is in no way less oppressive than the direct exploita- tion of wage labour, it has probably caused that isolation of the peasants which has delayed and rendered more difficult their struggle for social emancipation.

The degree and form of exploitation is largely determined by changes in the man-land relationship. These are due to demo- graphic or technological factors which, in their turn, affect the interplay of land distribution and productivity of land and labour, and thus the volume of agricultural production and the well-being or misery of the peasant population.

---

* K. M. Parsons, 'Poverty as an Issue in Development Policy: A Com- parison of the United States and Underdeveloped Countries', *Land Economics*, vol. 45, no. 1 (February 1969), pp. 52 ff., states that the underdeveloped countries are typically ruled by oligarchies, in ways which virtually amount to private ownership of government.

† M. Weber, *General Economic History*, trans. by Frank H. Knight (London and New York, 1961).

Despite endless theoretical discussion, labour productivity is rather an elusive term whose importance is the subject of controversy. In advanced countries, where labour is a scarce and expensive commodity, increased productivity is valued in terms of the increase in returns on labour, while in the underdeveloped world, where labour is usually abundant and capital and land are the scarce and costly commodities, it is valued according to the degree to which it replaces capital and is used for reclaiming or cultivating agricultural land. If applied to conditions in underdeveloped countries, the former interpretation may lead to the deterioration of scarce agricultural resources and the increased exploitation of the man on the land, rather than to the full utilization of the abundant labour force, a principal precondition for agricultural development.*

It is universally agreed that overall economic progress in underdeveloped countries is possible only if the agricultural sector provides the food, labour and part of the savings needed for their gradual industrialization. But it is an unfortunate assumption that increased output per area unit, irrespective of the productivity per labour unit, is necessarily identical with development. Such a one-sided criterion can be applied only in the rare instances of static technology and static standards of living and is unsuitable, therefore, as a yardstick for agricultural progress. Yet, the fact that in both theoretical discussion and practical policy increased output is equated, time and again, with agricultural development, has contributed to the dangerous misinterpretation of fundamental development issues which benefits the privileged few without improving the lot of the peasant population.

The relatively large rise in unit yields which can be obtained by increasing the labour input on very small holdings has been used both as a weighty argument against land consolidation or the introduction of collective and joint farming in areas with numerous non-viable holdings too small for mechanized cultivation, and as an excuse for the subdivision and fragmentation of plantation

* United Nations, Dept. of Ec. and Soc. Affairs, *Progress in Land Reform, Third Report* (New York, 1962, p. 39), indicates in this context that a simultaneous increase in output and productivity is not always obtainable because in some cases higher productivity calls for reduction of output which has exceeded the optimum.

land for purely speculative purposes.* It is important, therefore, to briefly discuss the influence of labour productivity on the man-land relationship.

A series of studies on the economics of farm management in selected districts in India† show that gross output per acre tends to increase with the decline in average farm size. Although the most obvious reason for this is that labour costs are lower on small family-operated holdings than on larger farms which must employ hired labour‡ rather vague theories like 'Dis-Economics of Large-Scale Farming'§ have been formulated which emphasize that increased personal participation in operation and management improves the efficiency of small family holdings. But, since the Indian studies also reveal that the gross and net productivity of labour as well as the return on capital invested tend to increase with the size of holding, it is rather difficult to accept the allegedly higher gross output on smaller holdings as an indication of development.

Although farm management data over the entire developed world prove that a positive relationship exists between scale of operation and productivity, some American economists are convinced that this does not apply to agriculture in underdeveloped countries. It has been maintained, among other things, that due to the large hidden agricultural unemployment 'a simple measure of gross value productivity per acre is as relevant to policy decisions in the underdeveloped world as is the net operator income under Western conditions'.‖ This statement is based on the now obsolete assumption that 20–25 per cent of the labour force in underdeveloped countries could well be removed from the land

* Ungku A. Aziz, *Subdivision of Estates in Malaya, 1951–1960* (University of Malaya, Kuala Lumpur, 1962), p. 3.

† K. Bardhan, 'Size of Holdings and Productivity, Further Comment', *Economic Weekly*, vol. 16, no. 34 (Bombay, 22.8.1964), pp. 1401 ff., quotes particularly *The Madras Report*, pp. 63–6, *The Uttar Pradesch Report*, p. 41 and *The West Bengal Report*, p. 65.

‡ E. H. Tuma, 'The Agrarian Based Development Policy in Land Reform', *Land Economics*, vol. 39, no. 3 (August 1963), pp. 265 ff.

§ A. K. Sen, 'An Aspect of Indian Agriculture', *Economic Weekly* (annual no., February 1962), and 'Size of Holdings and Productivity', ibid (annual nos., February and May 1964).

‖ E. J. Long, 'The Economic Basis of Land Reform in Underdeveloped Economies', *Land Economics* (May 1961), p. 115.

without causing any reduction in output, even if a simultaneous improvement of agricultural techniques or an increase in capital investments were to occur.* More recent studies,† in fact, seriously call into question the extent of hidden unemployment and simply state the uncontested fact that the marginal productivity of agricultural labour in underdeveloped countries is exceedingly low and much lower than that of industrial labour.

Myrdal points out quite rightly that the use of the expressions 'unemployment' and 'underemployment' is a symptom of a static approach to the employment situation and that 'waste of labour' would be a more appropriate term from the point of view of dynamic economic planning.‡ Where labour is largely utilized as a substitute for capital, the problem of unemployment and underemployment, with its supposed implication of a near zero marginal labour productivity, does not exist, as in China for instance.

A theory, therefore, which refutes the positive relationship between scale of operation and labour productivity in backward agriculture is not only inconclusive but even dangerous, since it will encourage and justify policy decisions that lead to the exploitation of human labour on undersized holdings. It cannot be emphasized often enough that the waste of labour in underdeveloped countries is a result of the one-sided agricultural policy which neglects the important fact that constructive land use and employment programmes would increase the utilization of agricultural labour and raise its productivity. Under prevailing condi-

---

* See P. N. Rosenstein-Rodan, 'Problems of Industrialization of Eastern and Southeastern Europe', *Economic Journal;* vol. 53, no. 210 (September 1943); and R. Nurkse, *Problems of Capital Formation in Underdeveloped Countries* (Oxford, 1953).

† See J. Viner, 'Stability and Progress in the World Economy' in *The First Congress of the International Economic Association* (London, 1958), p. 50; B. Kenadjian, 'Disguised Unemployment in Underdeveloped Countries', Ph.D. dissertation, Harvard University, 1957; G. v. Haberler, 'An Assessment of the Current Relevance of the Theory of Comparative Advantage to Agricultural Production and Trade', *International Journal of Agrarian Affairs,* vol. 4, no. 3 (May 1964), p. 140 and L. G. Reynolds, *Economic Development with Surplus Labour: Some Complications,* Economic Growth Center Paper, no. 133 (Yale University, New Haven, 1969).

‡ G. Myrdal, *Asian Drama,* chap. 21, pp. 1001 ff. and app. 6, pp. 2041 ff.

tions, where the peasants already carry the burden of the defective agrarian structure, we have to beware of applying a theory which merely calls for an ever-increasing input of peasant labour despite diminishing returns. But the formidable exodus from the land bears eloquent testimony to the fact that under such conditions peasant farming based on family labour will disintegrate long before marginal labour productivity reaches zero. The peasant who works his minute holding for twelve hours a day or more in order to feed his family cannot be expected to think in terms of farm management nor to seek new market outlets for his produce—if any. Neither is he in a position to make wise decisions and invest savings, as Western experts tell him to do, but is chained to the land which, more often than not, he is likely to exhaust and then to leave under threat of starvation.

Accordingly, it is unrealistic to conclude that an inverse relation exists between gross output per acre and size of farm unit and this the more so because none of the data quoted indicates that small farms are actually more efficient in their use of the production factors. On the contrary, one of the surveys even ascertains that the productivity of labour and capital—and in the Punjab also the yield per acre of specific crops—is higher on the larger farms.* Moreover, the advocates of an efficiency-per-acre-criterion utterly neglect the possible effects of its practical application upon the dignity of labour, upon the problem of incentives, and upon soil conservation, although some do admit that agrarian conditions are determined largely by the prevailing institutional framework.

A recent survey of farm productivity in a typical region of the state of Gujarat in India† confirms that small farms are less efficient, on the whole, than the large farms with regard to the use of production factors. Both their input-output ratios and their returns on investment are unfavourable compared to those obtaining on the larger farms; and since even their capacity for surplus

* K. Bardhan, 'Size of Holdings and Productivity', *Economic Weekly,* loc. cit., p. 1402.
† V. S. Vyas, *Economic Efficiency on Small Farms of Central Gujarat. Report of the Seminar on Problems of Small Farmers,* Seminar Series, no. 7 (Indian Society of Agricultural Economics, Bombay, 1968).

production is low, they have practically no prospect of getting out of the poverty trap.*

An economic policy based on the illusive efficiency of small farms will inevitably divert attention from the need for increased labour utilization, for land consolidation and joint farming systems which would raise unit yields over and above the additional labour input, and thus will delay and even prevent modernization and increased capital formation in agriculture. But this is not all. By considering the smallness of holdings an asset, it will discourage the badly needed reexamination of outdated institutions and land distribution patterns in areas where the ever-growing pressure on the land increases the trend towards subdivision and fragmentation, and thus contribute to technological backwardness and the continued servitude of agricultural labour.

Equally dangerous is the now fashionable two-tier theory which unfortunately has caught the fancy of an increasing number of economic planners. In view of the generally limited resources available and the physical impossibility of increasing production in all areas of an underdeveloped country at one and the same time, this theory suggests that intensive investments to boost agricultural production should be made primarily in the already productive areas (the upper tier) from which the greatest returns may be expected. While allocations to the less privileged areas with many small or unviable holdings (the lower tier) should be limited to thinly spread investments that will do little more than maintain income levels.†

This approach, attractive as it may seem to many, entails the great risk that it will further increase the gap between privileged and poor farmers and conveniently hide the less productive tier behind a screen of some limited social and economic improvements. It will ultimately perpetuate the state of backwardness since it deliberately isolates the bulk of the peasant population

* Vyas comes to the conclusion that the extremely limited land base of the small farms is probably the principal reason for the lower productivity of their fixed factors, i.e., family labour and their own draught animals, but their greatest handicap seems to be the lack of ready cash and the limited access to institutional credit.

† M. Yudelman, 'Planning the Rural Sector in the National Economy —From the Donor's Point of View', in R. Robinson and P. Johnston (eds.), *The Rural Base for National Development* (Cambridge University Overseas Studies Committee, 1968). See also p. 119.

from current economic life and thus reduces the level of demand in an expanding economy. Such a development strategy entails hardly more than a rebirth of the old colonial concept of prosperous agricultural oases in deserts of economic stagnation, as happened in colonial Malaya, where investments were concentrated in profitable plantations while the Malay smallholder areas were by-passed by development and the peasants remained backward and destitute despite some protective measures and minor social improvements. The deliberate division of agriculture into favoured and neglected sectors is nothing but an excuse for maintaining defective tenure systems and proves, unintentionally, that structural changes are an essential precondition of the increased productivity of agricultural labour.

In many underdeveloped countries, the low level of agriculture is not necessarily due to demographic and technological factors alone but often to conditions created and maintained explicitly in order to facilitate the exploitation of agricultural labour. In Latin America, the vast area of idle land belonging to the *haciendas* has the specific function of preventing the peasants from using it and thereby ensures their dependence upon the *hacienda* on terms dictated by the *hacendado*.* Although irrational from the point of view of national economy, this 'extensive' land use system is so profitable for the *hacendados* that they forcefully oppose any land redistribution programme which involves the settlement of landless peasants on the idle lands of their estates.

In most underdeveloped countries, in fact, outdated tenure and marketing systems have degraded the peasant from a factor of production to a mere tool for the exploitation of the land. The social and economic subjugation of the tiller is the natural corollary of a social system that does not value human labour but merely uses it to strengthen the position of those who control the land. Landlords, money-lenders and traders, the chief components of any rural hierarchy, did not attain their strong economic position because they increased agricultural production through improved farm management or reasonable investment, but merely because they were able to take advantage of the economic opportunities arising from the weak bargaining power and social helplessness of the peasants. Since money-lending, or rather the

* A. Pearse, 'Trends of Agrarian Changes in Latin America', *Latin American Research Review*, vol. 1, no. 3 (1966).

usurious rates of interest, are the main source of income of all three groups, irrational agricultural production and marketing practices are the principal side-effects of the exploitation of man. The landlord, who calculates the rentability of his estate in terms of interest due from his tenants rather than in terms of agricultural productivity, is no active agriculturist interested in the improvement of his land; the shopkeeper or trader, who extends credit at usurious rates to the peasants while their crop is still standing, is more interested in securing his monopoly in the market than in developing a distribution system that will serve the bulk of the consumers.*

The close collaboration between landlords, money-lenders and traders in using their economic leverage for the exploitation of peasants frustrates even well-meant attempts at organizing self-help or cooperative societies among the peasants. Typical in this context is the fate of the cooperative GRISEK processing plant in Malaya, established shortly before Independence by the government-supported Rural Industrial Development Authority. Although its purpose was to free the rubber smallholders of Johore from their dependence upon landlords and traders by offering them decent prices for their latex, it did not take long before the factory had to close down because the peasants, still heavily indebted to the middlemen, did not dare to sell their produce through other channels.

Even if similar ventures elsewhere did not fail immediately, they were seldom able to fulfil their purpose for very long as they were gradually undermined by powerful vested interests and consequently their services ceased to answer the needs of small owners and tenants but benefited almost exclusively the economically stronger part of the rural population.

The almost unrestricted exploitation of man and land in underdeveloped countries is the true reason for the vicious circle of

---

* In Malaysia, with its specific problems of racial stratification, the exploitation of the peasants, a Monopoly-Monopsony system has gained control of the supply of consumer goods and of the market for rural produce. It has both decapitalizing effects since the traders have bought the peasants' land, their boats and nets, and their buffaloes, and inhibiting effects because it tends to fossilize the rural economy and is a strong obstacle to progress. See Ungku Aziz, 'Poverty and Rural Development in Malaysia', *Kajian Ekonomi Malaysia*, loc. cit., p. 70.

declining returns from agriculture, poverty and indebtedness. Lack of credit at reasonable terms and an infinitesimal opportunity for capital formation keep the peasant in bondage and turn landlord into money-lender. Still, landlord and peasant have one attitude in common, which is that neither is interested in the improvement of the land or is concerned about the possible deterioration of agricultural resources. In large regions of the underdeveloped world it is not difficult to trace the present sad state of agriculture to the degradation and exploitation of the man on the land, though the means applied vary and are not always immediately recognizable.

To some observers the peasants in the paternalistic environment of the Latin American *hacienda*, for example, seem in a less precarious position than those on the large estates in South Asia and the Near East because they form an integral part of a microcosmos and are often linked to the *hacendado* and his family by blood or *compadre* relations. Although this may be a psychological advantage the whole setup is as much a result of the defective institutional framework as in other parts of the underdeveloped world and does not imply either higher incomes or greater security and social mobility. The peasant tilling the soil of the *hacienda* gets no other compensation than a tiny plot of land for private use and a small amount of cash to be spent in the only store available—owned by the *hacienda*. He does not own his plot; nor can he appeal against arbitrary decisions by the *hacendado* or his manager since the *hacienda* is usually an administrative unit with its own police and jurisdiction headed by the *hacendado* himself.

It is a fallacy that the mere allocation of land to the peasants will alleviate rural misery as long as the powerful market forces that dominate economic life in the rural areas of underdeveloped countries are allowed to operate freely. Any redistribution of land or ownership rights which does not simultaneously check the market forces, cannot bring about any lasting improvement, since the latter will soon find ways and means to dictate the terms for the peasants' transactions and jeopardize their newly won position as owners.

The pathetic stagnation of the *ejido* sector in rural Mexico, fifty years after the successful peasant revolution, is due to the impact of uncontrolled market forces on *ejido* economy and society. Even in the relatively recent *ejidal* settlement scheme at Papaloapan, traders and middlemen lay hands upon 40 per cent of the income generated within the scheme while the peasants continue to live at subsistence level.*

About thirty kilometres outside Mexico City, the economy of an *ejido* based almost exclusively on the cultivation of *magüey*, an agave variety used for the production of *pulque*, an alcoholic beverage, is actually paralysed by the continued and heavy indebtedness of the *ejidatarios* to traders and middlemen. When the government started to build a large, modern processing factory in the neighbourhood, to ensure an adequate price for the raw material, the traders began buying the plants themselves from the peasants and thus maintained their control of the production and processing of *magüey* and of the sale of *pulque*. True, the law protects the *ejidatarios* from losing their ownership rights to the land itself, but due to the lack of adequate credit, they have become agricultural labourers on their own land—and for four years the new *pulque* factory has been standing with its gates closed.

In the same area another *ejido* engaged in barley production, is hardly better off for almost the same reason. Here one of its own members, obviously more intelligent and better educated than the rest, has taken over the function of a typical middleman. He uses his own truck to transport the barley crop of the other *ejidatarios* to a brewery in Mexico City, and alone negotiates its sale.

During the past few years increased exports of vegetables to the United States at very profitable prices have also benefited some *ejidos* in the irrigated areas near the border. But since even these privileged *ejidos*, do not have the credit and market contacts needed, they cannot act as producers on their own account but have to lease their land, though obtaining a relatively good price, to private entrepreneurs who produce and sell the export crop. The fathers of the Mexican revolution certainly did not envisage the *ejido* farmer as a kind of absentee landlord, but under present conditions this is his only chance of participating in the new prosperity.

The much acclaimed gesture of the United Fruit Company in

* M. Edel and J. Ballesteros, *The Colonization of Papaloapan*, to be published shortly by the Centro de Investigaciónes Agrarias (Mexico).

Guatemala and other Latin American countries in partly disposing of its plantation land in favour of the peasants will not substantially change agrarian conditions because the company continues to monopolize the market for bananas and other fruit and thus determines both the type of production and the income on agricultural labour. Despite ownership of the land the peasant will remain poor. This is also the case in the provinces of Morelo and Laguna in Mexico where peasant-owners have been induced to abstain from rice farming and take up the less profitable cultivation of sugar since their access to credit is linked to the production of sugar-cane. This proves again that the agrarian problem is part of the whole complex of underdevelopment and, more specifically, that it is a result of the free play of political and economic forces upon the land use pattern and market system.

The relentless disregard of the human factor in agriculture is indeed a significant feature of underdevelopment which leads to painful distortions of human relationships and use of land. This is one reason why economic phenomena in underdeveloped countries should be interpreted primarily in terms of institutional economics since the effects of social relationships do not lend themselves to quantitative measurements and cannot yet be expressed by mathematical models.

The Peasants versus the Rural Élite

For countless generations, the peasantry almost everywhere has built up a kind of psychological defence mechanism and developed a stubborn, almost virtuous, suspicion of new and unexpected developments. At certain times in the course of history, however, the effect of fundamental changes in other sectors of society overcame the inertia of the peasants and induced a desire for a new social equilibrium.* One of the most dramatic outbursts of this kind in the Western world was the revolt of the German peasants in the sixteenth century, which turned into a true 'revolution' with clearly defined objectives. Luther's theses on the rights and freedom of Christian human beings, already accepted by the strong

---

* S. N. Eisenstadt, 'Some New Looks at the Problem of Relations between Traditional Societies and Modernization', *Economic Development and Cultural Change*, vol. 16, no. 3 (August 1968), p. 442.

guilds of the 'free' towns, incited the peasants to fight for a position in society which accorded with the new creed. Unfortunately, their claims were beyond the social reality of the time and since Luther's concept of 'freedom' had but limited social substance, their uprising was drowned in an ocean of blood by the existing political order.*

Such passionate outbursts occurred but seldom and for centuries the life of the European peasant was marked by stagnation, resignation and indifference. Even the gap between generations did not cause any noticeable changes in outlook and action, since the more enterprising of the younger people would migrate to the urban centres, with the result that those who remained on the land came to represent a rather negative selection, at least as regards any eagerness for change. Even the mechanization of Western agriculture proceeded at a relatively slow pace and was only accelerated by the pressure of labour shortage and thus by sheer necessity rather than by foresight.

In other parts of the world, peasant revolutions have played an essential role and contributed to more or less radical changes, particularly in Asia and Latin America where they were frequently combined with a violent protest against racial and national suppression.

Unfortunately, we know little about the social and economic past of the peasantry in those underdeveloped countries whose history has been written by the colonizers with their disregard for peasant life and culture. Modern ethnographers and anthropologists provide interesting and valuable information and psychological interpretations of pre-colonial religious values and behaviour patterns; and social scientists analyse and define the complex aspects of community life. But far too little attention is paid to the factors responsible for the powerful position of the rural élite during the past three generations and to the changes within this rural élite; though its relationship to the peasant population probably constitutes the most important political and socio-economic problems of our day.

In our view the foreign institutions introduced by the colonial powers were at least as influential in the formation of the values and attitudes of the local peasant population as their own time-honoured traditions. A study of the impact of British common

* F. Mehring, *Zur deutschen Geschichte* (Berlin, 1951), pp. 65 ff.

law, of legal codes, of land registration, of tax regulations, and of Western education and moral values upon rural groups would greatly increase our understanding of the complex social relationships in underdeveloped countries, since these very institutions have been, and still are, the tools used by the rural élite in their manipulations.

In dealing with cultural, social and political changes, however, we should distinguish between those adopted voluntarily and those imposed by superior economic or political forces. Either will release a series of cumulative effects; but the compulsion attached to the latter may cause incalculable social reactions that will necessarily influence the direction, speed and content of the change and cause deviations and developments difficult to foresee.

A gradual transmission of new cultural elements will sooner or later end the traditional attitude of 'do-you-pretend-to-be-wiser-than-your-father', and pave the way for a relatively peaceful transitional period which will finally lead to a new cultural integration and a new relative and functional equilibrium.* But if opposed by powerful interests the transmission of new ideas and values will be a painful process that may last for generations.

One of the most revolutionary processes currently taking place in large parts of the underdeveloped world, and particularly in Africa, is the transition from subsistence to market economy which involves the translation from 'status to contract' and introduces new values such as efficiency of work and quality of produce which were hitherto of but minor importance. The two traditional status symbols, cattle and land, can now be bought and sold on the market and their monetary value determines the prestige of their owner. This change in values upsets the principles that safeguard the traditional rights in land and leads to an often uninhibited grabbing of communal land at the expense of the peasants.†

* R. F. Behrendt, *Soziale Strategie für Entwicklungsländer* (Frankfurt am Main, 1965), pp. 115 ff.

† Such a way of acquiring land is not a phenomenon which is confined to the transition from tribal to market economy but was, and still is, common practice where and whenever the institutional setup can no longer secure the rights of the peasants in the land. The Enclosure Act in England at the threshold of the nineteenth century when common land was actually confiscated to benefit the large landowners is a good example of this.

Status symbols now rapidly follow the trends in the Western world and are expressed in terms of glamorous consumption items such as private homes adorned with famous paintings and antique furniture, pleasure trips abroad, cars, yachts, racehorses, and so on. It is only natural that the exponents of this gradual accultura- tion are the rural élites who were once the protégés, and are now the manipulators, of the new institutions.

A new equilibrium is establishing itself and with it a new ruling class whose political power and social ambitions are based on the unrestricted control of land, and on the maximum exploitation of the man on the land in order to increase the production of market- able commodities.

The foreign institutions introduced during the centuries of colonial rule deeply affected not only land tenure and land values, and thus the life of the peasants, but also the general attitude of the leading groups in the colonial environment who later were to form the governments of the new nation states. It is discouraging that social scientists have not dealt more extensively with the impact of foreign institutions and academic training abroad upon the upper-classes of underdeveloped countries. Even a very small privileged group may exercise a decisive influence in an adminis- trative and educational vacuum, an influence which has reper- cussions far beyond their own ranks. The violent claim of the Kikuyu people in Kenya for the same kind of ownership rights to land which had been the privilege of a few thousand successful European settlers in the White Highlands; or the emphasis laid by the British-trained Indian civil service on land registration and administration and its consequent failure to understand any reform aimed at a redistribution of land and wealth; or the feudalistic tenure and land use arrangements of Latin America are but a few examples of this.

In the course of time, however, the foreign influences led to the emergence of strong sentiments in favour of national independence, self-sufficiency, and often of an unrealistic revival of traditional concepts, particularly in areas where the peasants had been com- pelled to give up subsistence farming for the cultivation of cash crops or where, as in Java, subsistence farming ceased to yield a living. In fact, Western concepts and commercial penetration not only upset the social and economic equilibrium of the peasant community and introduced new values that disregarded the conventional authority of the clan and disrupted the protected life of the village but also widened the horizon of the community leaders, who turned into exponents of a fervent nationalism with highly aggressive tendencies. Many of the young intellectuals who had studied abroad now used their acquired knowledge of Western ideology and socio-economic thinking to appraise the domestic problems and fight Western domination. Ironically enough, those leading the attack were at the same time those who had adopted Western culture and modes of life; a fact which frequently alienated them from the peasants who had joined the fight for independence in the hope of regaining their rights in the land. The almost schizophrenic features of current political life in many underdeveloped countries may be traced to this phenomenon, and it partly explains the immense gap between the spearhead of the nationalist movements and the bulk of the people who refuse to participate in the new political game. And, once again, the land problem has moved into the centre of turmoil.

The various concepts and ideologies of the independent governments, almost everywhere dominated by the new national élite, generally work against the real or imaginary fundamental interests of the peasants who despite the political and economic changes have retained their attachment to traditional values. In many of the new African countries the new land policy is inspired by Western concepts and has often a strong anti-tribal bias. The efforts of the national élite to further its own interests, by pressing for the realization of Western-inspired ownership rights, has set the stage for a desperate struggle between the bureaucracy in the capitals and the tribal people who are defending their traditional rights in the land. Only in some countries, like Tanzania, Cameroon, and a few others, do the new governments seem to have succeeded in gradually absorbing and integrating the traditional values into the overall pattern of realistic national land policies.*

* P. J. Idenburg ('Political Structural Development in Tropical Africa', *Orbis,* vol. 11, no. 1, University of Pennsylvania, Spring 1967, pp. 256 ff.), gives an excellent description of this development in the former French and British African colonies. Although political development varies from country to country, a permanent struggle is going on between presidential national centralism and the traditional chiefs who base their power on the control of tribal land.

There is no doubt, however, that the conservatism which safe-guards outdated practices and increases the peasants' resistance to innovation has become ineffectual with the incursion of commercial interests and new technologies into the protected areas and the subsequent distortion of the economic and social equilibrium. The man-land relationship, strained by rigid traditions and abuse in many underdeveloped countries, has to be reshaped in the light of the new economic environment in order to arouse the latent energies of the peasant population and provide the new incentives needed to stimulate their acceptance of innovations and their interest in agricultural development.

The Agrarian Creed

But before we enter into a detailed analysis of the content and import of such structural changes, we must dwell briefly upon one particular psychological aspect of the peasant problem which we have chosen to call—not very originally I fear, but descriptively, I hope—the *Agrarian Creed*: it is the driving force that irrespective of time, place, and civilization has guided and still guides, directly or indirectly, the peasants' way of thought and of those who are concerned with their fate. Though often obscured by local myths and legends, the Agrarian Creed is universal. It is not tied to a particular moment of time or a specific content but is so strongly entrenched in the hearts of the tillers that it has become the recognized expression for the diverse 'ideal' solutions to rural situations and has encouraged the weak to fight their oppressors.

The Agrarian Creed is not a definable doctrine but reflects the hopes and aspirations of countless peasant generations for a time when land will be as free as air and will belong to nobody, and therefore to anybody who is tilling it. That the peasant has to ask for the right to own the land and to be assured of its possession, is not a contradiction of the Agrarian Creed but only a compromise with economic systems and societies based on established property rights.

The fundamental importance of the Agrarian Creed is reflected throughout recorded history. The earliest and probably most complete identification of man and land is expressed in the First Book of the Old Testament (Genesis) where it is more than a semantic coincidence that the Hebrew word for man is *adam* and that for land is *adama*. But the religious interpretation, and what may be regarded as the basic formula of the Agrarian Creed, is to be found in the Third Book of the Old Testament (Leviticus) where the Lord proclaims that every fiftieth year be a 'year of jubilee' when 'ye shall return every man unto his possession' (25:10) and that 'the land shall not be sold for ever: for the land is mine' (25:23). This redemption in the year of jubilee thus guarantees the periodic redistribution of land on the basis of equality and the restoration of a fair economic order. In essence this confirms that the land belongs to everybody and that no one shall be excluded or restricted in the use of land or, to apply a more modern expression, that 'the land shall belong to the tiller of the soil'.

No less powerful is the formulation of the Agrarian Creed by an old Nigerian chief: 'I conceive that land belongs to a vast family of which many are dead, few are living and countless members are still unborn',* or by Proudhon when he exclaims: 'la Propriété c'est le vol!' or 'la terre ne peut être appropriée', and, above all, when he asks: 'comment les biens de la nature, les richesses créées par la Providence peuvent-elles devenir des propriétés privées?'†

The Bhoodan Movement in post-war India, inviting the donation of land by the rich for distribution to the landless poor, was inspired by the ideas of Gandhi and is likewise based on the egalitarian principle that land should be free to all who subsist on it and should be used in the interests of the entire community. The mere fact of this initiative and of the later Gramdan Movement (founded by Acharya Vinoba Bhave) which called upon the village landlords to surrender their individual proprietory rights in favour of the community, prove the strength of the Agrarian Creed in rural India. Although movements of this kind will not contribute much to the solution of the formidable agrarian problems of India, the 4.3 million acres of agricultural land which had

* C. K. Meek, Motto used for *Land Law and Customs in the Colonies* (London, 1949).

† P.-J. Proudhon, *Qu'est-ce que la propriété? Premier Mémoire.* (Paris, 1841), pp. 2, 89, 90.

been collected by 1967 and the almost 38,000 Gramdan villages which had been established, must be considered a concession to the Agrarian Creed and a pioneer move for greater equality in the Indian village.

In the course of history, the Agrarian Creed has found turbulent expression in peasant uprisings and revolts. Although frequently disguised as religious or dynastic feuds these movements were basically concerned with property rights, preservation of common pastures, or socio-agrarian changes. During the Reformation, the German peasants used the concept of Christian freedom as justification for their claim to rights in land, and in 1883, twenty-five years prior to the revolution, the Mexican priest, Maurizio Zavala, in his sermons from the pulpit exhorted the tillers to take possession of the land. Even reform programmes, like improved taxation laws, often refer directly or indirectly to the Agrarian Creed in order to strengthen the moral basis of their objectives.

For more than a century, but particularly during the past thirty years, the claim for land has been an essential element in the struggle of the peasants of South-east Asia and Latin America. And even today, the solution of the land problem outweighs political doctrines and identifies national independence with freedom from oppression, indebtedness and misery.* The Agrarian Creed, used and abused in political propaganda, is so strongly rooted in the minds of the people that it has become their yardstick for the success or failure of the new national government. Though profoundly religious, some are even ready to fight the Church for the sake of land, as has happened time and again in the Philippines and throughout Latin America.

The value and power of the Agrarian Creed is not diminished because it is so far removed from current reality, which is determined by traditionalism and the convenience of political stability. Contrary to the principles of social ethics laid down in the philosophy and law of Western civilization, which have a universal bearing without reference to a particular group or temporary situation,† the Agrarian Creed concerns a specific sector of the

* E. H. Jacoby, *Agrarian Unrest in Southeast Asia* (Bombay, 1961), pp. 37 ff.
† G. Myrdal, *Value in Social Theory. A Selection of Essays on Methodology* (London, 1958), pp. 60, 61.

population and particular socio-economic conditions. And contrary to such Western creeds as 'equality of all men' which are sanctioned by religion and laid down as constitutional principles (*Grundrechte*) in the preambles of Western constitutions, but seldom put into practice in everyday social life, the Agrarian Creed has been taken literally for millenniums by large groups of people and, time and again, peasants and social reformers alike have boldly endeavoured to realize it by direct action or by the organized demand for an effective agrarian policy.

After the French Revolution, the Agrarian Creed of 'land to the tiller of the soil' became reality to an ever-increasing extent in the Western world where, due to the expansion of industry and commerce, it fitted well into the pattern of values of the new ruling class and their representatives in the governments which called for increased productivity and liberalization of trade. In the underdeveloped world, however, where agriculture is still almost identical with the national economy, the prevailing values are antithetical, to say the least, to long overdue changes in the agrarian structure.

The Agrarian Creed has been subject to varying interpretations depending upon the prevailing economic and political theories or socio-economic conditions. Thus, the *Blut und Boden* concept of Nazi Germany must be considered a most unfortunate deviation from the Agrarian Creed. The indivisible farm, the *Erbhof*, which could not be mortgaged and was supposed to ensure the stability of the rural population, became instead an obstacle to technological progress as well as to the horizontal and vertical mobility of the German peasants.

The collective farm, on the other hand, where labour and production are organized on a cooperative basis on common or communal land, represents an approximation to the Agrarian Creed. On the *kolkhozes* in the Soviet Union, on the *ejidos* in Mexico, and on the *kibbutzim* in Israel, the farmer still feels that he is tilling his own soil because he is a member of the community that controls the land.

Time and again, the Agrarian Creed is reflected in political and economic statements, in the programmes of peasant parties and associations, and, above all, in the spirit of cooperative organizations. The individual plots granted to the members of the *kolkhozes* and to the workers of the *sovkhozes* in the Soviet

Union are concessions, as it were, to the strength of the Creed. At the risk of oversimplification, we may even say that the allotments on the outskirts of the large towns in the developed world form a subconscious acknowledgement of the Agrarian Creed by urban people. Even the various efforts to strengthen the economic and social position of the tenant cultivator by reforms providing security of tenure and compensation for improvements are attempts at allying tenancy to ownership and thus at realizing the Agrarian Creed, at least to a certain extent. Despite political realities and the failure of high-sounding programmes, the Agrarian Creed is as alive as ever in the minds and hearts of the people on the land; indeed, it continues to arouse their opposition to the existing order and contributes to the defeat of half-hearted variations.

Considering that the very process of agricultural development entails the reduction of the active agricultural population and, consequently, the decrease in the pressure on land, and long-term prospect for a solution to the land problem in underdeveloped countries is rather encouraging. The immense task remains, however, of finding the shortest and most effective way to release the energies needed for development and it is here that the continued pressure for a realization of the Agrarian Creed may prove a most valuable instrument.

CHAPTER FOUR

Internal Factors Affecting
the Man-Land Relationship

The process of economic development is a dramatic contest between the forces protecting the *status quo* which we will call restraining forces and the progressive forces attacking it. Looked at from this angle underdevelopment emerges as an essentially *political* problem.

For the tradition-bound society, technological progress and innovation represent potential danger to time-honoured values. The *status quo* is maintained in large parts of the underdeveloped world even at the expense of economic stagnation. True, there are partially advanced areas in some underdeveloped countries like India, Thailand, the Philippines and Argentina, where certain economic and technological innovations have been accepted, but this does not affect the internal balance of power or the characteristic features of underdevelopment. The socio-economic structure of the tradition-ridden society is acting as a kind of prophylactic against the emergence of progressive forces sufficiently strong to shake the foundation of the existing order. There are, of course, the side-effects of dissidence between generations reflected often in the more or less erratic migratory movements away from tribal communities; but this alone is not enough to set off a power struggle. The stage of transition from subsistence to market economy must be reached before effective progressive forces in the form of labour and peasant movements can overthrow the *status quo*, or at least try to do so.

In a large number of underdeveloped countries, the current agrarian conflict between the restraining and progressive forces has turned into a contest between profitable individual investments in agriculture and, as I would like to call it, the *social productivity* of agriculture. This contest, in which the restraining forces fight for the maintenance of the political and social, rather than of the economic, *status quo*, is focused on the fundamental problems of agricultural progress: do massive investments exclusively in the upper tier of agriculture produce a commensurate increase in agricultural production, and in employment opportunities in the rural as well as in other sectors of the economy, to the benefit of the bulk of the people? Or do such investments actually benefit the privileged few only and cause a decline in rural employment which will widen the gap between rich and poor?

Forces Protecting the *status quo*

Tradition and religion have established values and principles that guide the life of the common people and strengthen the defences of the existing social order. The conviction that this order has been established by transcendental forces is so deeply rooted in the mind of the peasant that he is by nature inclined to submit to the worldly authorities represented by this order and accept the economic and social structure with its implicit power relations. The fatalism that has marked the rural people in the under-developed world, therefore, is a corollary of this time-honoured belief in the transcendental origin of worldly authority which still rules the life and thinking of untold millions.

In one way or another, traditionalism is encountered in all civilizations, but certain religions and cultural patterns are more effective in paralysing the natural aspirations of man and counter-acting any progressive forces that emerge. There is little doubt that the static character of society in large parts of India, for example, is a direct consequence of the tenets of Hinduism. The powerful concepts that a person's actions in one life determine his fortune and status in the next (*karma*) and that it is his obligation to live in conformity with the rules of his caste and never aspire to any function pertaining to another caste (*dharma*), have created a rigid law of retribution according to which man is born into a particular caste and has a particular function in life.*

Such a set of values makes any opposition to the existing social and economic order difficult and the blind acceptance of predesti-

---

* M. Weber, *The Religion of India*, trans. and ed. by H. H. Gerth and D. Martindale (Glencoe, Ill., 1958: London, 1967), pp. 111 ff.

nation may even soften the bitterness of misery. It has been said quite rightly that the concepts of *karma* and *dharma* lower the sights of human aspiration and place a premium on passive acceptance rather than on the amelioration of the human situation either by hard work or social reform.*

For centuries in the Western world the firm belief in the divine origin of the existing social order and of its representatives on earth turned the fight of the peasants against feudal exploitation into a rebellion against the transcendental forces of Church and State, and thus justified the violent means used to defeat it. Think only of the bloody German Peasant Wars in the sixteenth century, when Martin Luther and Protestantism sided with the established order and thus reaffirmed the transcendency of the social order.

This concept likewise determines and maintains the landlord-peasant relationship in feudalistic societies. The Lord has created the cosmos, including the social order, and, *ipso facto* the landed class has been selected by divine providence and is entitled to riches and power. The combination of high birth, property and a gracious style of living further strengthens their position while the bulk of the people are doomed to accept their humble place in society as part of a divine order. From their powerful heights the masters hand down the rules for crop-sharing; half of the crop to the owner of the land and half of the crop to the tiller of the soil: a benevolent and 'fair' arrangement that professes a neighbourly spirit, and to call in question its righteousness would amount to irreverence and thus contradict the established rules of behaviour. It is interesting to note that the fifty-fifty proportion generally applies when crop-sharing is part of the socio-economic order in agriculture and the assumption follows that this division is considered an expression of 'fairness' and 'moderation' which justifies the position of those who are privileged to own the land.

The belief in a divinely inspired social order was further strengthened during the colonial era when the population was converted more or less by force to a religion whose holy images were representative of the white race and, consequently, of white supremacy. It is beyond all doubt that the close cooperation be-

---

* K. W. Kapp, *Hindu Culture and Economic Planning in India* (London, 1963), p. 16.

tween the colonial and ecclesiastical powers has had most unfavourable psychological effects upon colonial peoples and is largely responsible for the fact that the ruling national élite in so many ex-colonies still draw their greatest strength from their collaboration with the established Church. This is clearly the case in the Philippines and in most Latin American countries.

The very mechanics of economic, social, cultural and often also ethnic interrelations and interactions ensured the dependence of the rural people and guaranteed the perpetuation of the feudalistic political and social order. The vital importance of land and water led automatically to the economic and social dependence of those who needed these resources; the peasants were not given security, but within clearly defined limits they were guaranteed an economic existence, albeit wretched, provided that they were obedient, submissive and loyal to the landlord; and in the end they even accepted the emotional elements of paternalism as their reward for social humiliation. It is this intrinsic power of established feudalistic systems that forms the strength of the restraining forces.

Current agrarian conditions in Brazil, ably depicted and analysed in a comprehensive Comite Interamericano de Desarollo Agrícola (CIDA) report* are a most striking example of the perseverance of such a feudalistic system. In the autocratic rural society of Brazil, the average agricultural labourer works under conditions of nearly complete instability and insecurity and lives in continuous fear of punishment and dismissal—well aware that many others are eager to replace him. The workers do not dare to make demands for improvements in working or living conditions because they know from bitter experience that claims against the landlords mean the end of their meagre existence.

It is no less important, however, that the pattern of latifundisme set by the large landowners has been adopted by all other groups within the community, down to the agricultural labourers themselves. The smallest cultivator, and perhaps even the more imaginative farm worker, is inclined to exploit the degraded position of agricultural labour and hire farm hands at miserable wages and

---

* CIDA, *Brazil: Land Tenure Conditions and Socio-economic Development of the Agricultural Sector* (Pan American Union, Washington DC, 1966).

living conditions in order to make a profit, however modest it may be due to the smallness of their own enterprise. This nationwide acceptance that the way to attain prestige and a better life, is 'not to work, save, invest and produce with one's own effort but to have access to the work of others',* prevents the emergence of effective labour unions which would support the struggle of peasants and workers against the undervaluation and underpayment of human labour by the forces still successfully maintaining the *status quo*.

The elements of the colonial system deriving from the rational and technical superiority of the Western colonizers continue to act as a restraining force, preventing changes in the *status quo* even after the achievement of political independence.† Like their Western predecessors, the new national élites have the prerogative of wealth, higher education and technical knowledge which they use to maintain and even strengthen a sharply differentiated class structure that excludes social mobility. This holds true particularly where ethnic differences, always used and often abused by the former colonial powers, underline the class contrasts, as is still the case in Guatemala, where the *Indians* and *Ladinos* represent respectively the inferior and superior social classes with different sets of values and opportunities. While the social organization of the unstratified Indian community is based primarily on tilling for subsistence, and land, therefore, has never been considered a commodity, the *Ladino* community which was moulded and supported by Spanish colonial rule is based on the Western concept of private ownership and, consequently, upon the accumulation and commercial exploitation of land. With the transition to a money economy the *Ladinos* exploited their land by means of Indian wage labour and established a secondary colonial relationship that has survived the colonial period. It has been stated quite rightly that 'the class and colonial character of ethnic relations are two intimately related aspects of the same phenomenon';‡ and this explains the strength of the restraining forces particularly in the

* Ibid., p. 575.

† R. Firth, *Essays on Social Organization and Values* (London and New York, 1964), pp. 183 ff.

‡ R. Stavenhagen, 'Classes, Colonialism and Acculturation', *Studies in Comparative International Development*, vol. 1, no. 6 (1965), pp. 76 ff.

D

Latin American countries where class and ethnic contrasts are
largely identical.

After the physical withdrawal of the colonial powers class consciousness began to replace the colonial element in social relations
and increased the awareness of inequality and the urge for a
realization of the Agrarian Creed. What we see happening in
large parts of the underdeveloped world is the emergence of
conscious class relations and a new pattern of behaviour that will
encourage the formation of peasant opposition and organization.
The history of development proves that in the final analysis it is
the awakening of class consciousness which paves the way for
progressive forces strong enough to attack rigid social stratification
and introduce new forms of social organization offering alternatives, social mobility and economic opportunities for the bulk of
the people.

Progressive Forces Attacking the *status quo*

1. PEASANT MOVEMENTS*

Given the indisputable fact that agriculture provides the economic
basis of almost all underdeveloped countries and the peasant class
their social foundation, the progressive forces attacking the *status
quo* will always be deeply rooted in the realities of peasant life.
Though they may be analysed and classified otherwise, and
although they are not always progressive in the political sense of
the word, they will be fundamentally peasant movements whose
organization, therefore, is of great importance since it is intimately
connected with the power structure of the rural society.

But before we enter into a more detailed description of peasant
movements and an analysis of their effects and organizational
difficulties, it is important that we clarify the term *peasant* and
discuss briefly the varying forms of rural life and village structure
in the underdeveloped world.

* G. Huizer, 'Report on the Study of the Role of Peasant Organizations in the Process of Agrarian Reform in Latin America—
Preliminary Draft', mimeographed (ILO, Geneva, 1969). We have
drawn on information provided in this outstanding report for this
chapter and elsewhere in the book.

Some writers define the *peasant* as a *rural cultivator who shares in the actual work on the land and whose life is tied to the land*.* Yet, this does not answer the question of whether hired agricultural labour should be considered part of the peasant society. Others have defined *peasants* as *rural people who have substantial responsibility for farm management and whose activity is characterized by a certain stability with respect to both economic position and occupancy of a specific piece of land*. But even this more restrictive definition clearly contradicts reality in rural areas where, following the introduction of a market economy, changes in status from owner-operator to tenant and from tenant to agricultural wage labourer, or vice versa, frequently occur within one and the same generation and even within one and the same household.†

In our view, the term *peasant* should be defined in the broadest manner possible and comprise not only owner-operators, tenants, sharecroppers, landless labourers, serfs and squatters but also the entire group of rural people who have left the land but have not yet been integrated into another sector of the economy. A peasant does not cease to be a peasant because he has moved from misery and stagnation in his village to wretchedness and isolation in the shanty town of a city where he has but an infinitesimal chance of becoming a member of the urban community, and lives in a state of *semi-urbanization*, or *status suspension*, characteristic of the urban conditions in underdeveloped countries. He should rather be defined as a *displaced peasant*, since he will keep in closest possible contact with his village, from where he frequently receives the larger part of his meagre food supply, and thus remains a member of the family relinquishing neither his inheritance rights nor his status in the village community. But most important of all, in the event of structural changes in his area he will return to claim his share of the land and, therefore, is a potential member of any movement pressing for changes in the prevailing man-land relationship.

Although this broad definition of the term *peasant* excludes the possibility of a quantitative analysis, I still consider it a most

* E. R. Wolf, *Peasants* (London and Englewood Cliffs, N.J., 1966), p. 1.
† H. A. Landsberger, *The Role of Peasant Movements and Revolt in Development: An Analytical Framework*, International Institute for Labour Studies, Bulletin no. 4 (Geneva, February 1968).

essential instrument for comprehending agrarian situations, rural-urban relationships and the fundamental socio-economic and political aspects of underdevelopment.

A closer observation of peasant society in underdeveloped regions reveals that the peasant is often labourer, sharecropper and owner-cultivator at the same time and, in addition, may even be semi-urbanized for varying periods. It also reveals the frequent occupational split within the peasant family, where the husband lives in some shanty town or is employed periodically in a mining centre, while his wife and children continue to work on the land as producers or hired labour and have remained active members of the village community. Although these important facts cannot be expressed in statistics, they are of fundamental importance both for the analysis of agrarian situations and in the prognosis of socio-economic development.

The considerable homogeneity of the traditional rural community based on communal ownership of land is disrupted with the introduction of more differentiated economic systems and causes the development of a rural hierarchy in which the different groups are linked to one another by a network of economic and social relationships. Myrdal* has finally done away with the widely held misconception that the typical South Asian village is composed of either a mass of poor tenants, united in opposition to absentee landlords and their local agents, or of self-sufficient cultivating families living together in social harmony. He proves that nearly all villages are composed of a number of groups with highly divergent interests. This also clearly holds true in many rural areas of the Middle East and of Latin America, and accordingly the stratification of the village community may be considered one of the most significant features of underdevelopment and probably the greatest obstacle to the implementation of reform programmes aimed at the development of a more egalitarian society. Colonial administrations were interested in supporting the hierarchical set-up in the villages and further increasing the social differences since this could only strengthen their established policy of 'divide and rule'.

At the top of the hierarchy in the typical South Asian village

* *Asian Drama*, p. 1052.

are the landowners, who should in no way, however, be considered a homogeneous group.* There are the feudalistic landowners, either of pre-colonial standing or created by colonial policy; and there are the non-cultivating owners for whom rents from land may or may not be a primary source of income. Though both groups are generally absentee landlords and as such physically separated from the village community, they still exercise a formidable influence on its life through their managers and agents. Yet, they often prefer to conceal their ownership of land and identify themselves in statistical inquiries as merchants, money-lenders or village officials. It was this type of landowner, exerting political power through the control of land and labour, which was eliminated by the socialist revolutions in order to create a more homogeneous village society. The third and largest group of landowners is composed of those who actually live in the villages and are classified in most statistics as owner-cultivators, whether or not they lease part of their holdings to tenants or own just enough land to maintain themselves and their families without regularly employing hired labour.

Although landownership implies status and prestige, it is frequently impossible to draw a clear line between the owner-cultivator and the still lower groups within the village hierarchy. The former may be forced to rent additional land in order to support a family, and depending upon the relation between the acreage which he owns and that which he rents or sharecrops, he becomes either part-owner or part-tenant, and in both cases he moves down the social ladder. Similarly, many owner-cultivators, tenants and sharecroppers, or members of their families, have to accept wage labour in order to augment the meagre returns from the land, and thus overlap the lowest group within the hierarchy, that of landless agricultural labourers. Nor, given the variety of possible institutional arrangements, can the tenants be considered a homogeneous group. There are cash tenants and 'tenants in kind'; there are privileged tenants who actually manage their farms and market their crops; and there are the tenants 'at will' and the sharecroppers who are entirely at the mercy of their landlords with regard to production, management and marketing.

* In the following we will partly draw upon Myrdal's *Asian Drama*, pp. 1052 ff.

It is unquestionable, however, that the lowest social esteem is attached to manual work performed under the regular supervision and control of another person. Accordingly, the lowest group in the village society is composed of the landless agricultural labourers who are entirely dependent on others for work and frequently remain unemployed for long periods of time. It is this group that eventually supplies the core of the temporarily or permanently semi-urbanized occupants of the hovels in the shanty towns.

Overlapping and duplication of functions are thus characteristic features of village life. They are also a serious obstacle to reliable statistical presentation and analysis, although it may be assumed that the absence of any relevant data regarding the numerical strength of the various social groups is due partly to the concealed vested interests of the upper strata in both rural and urban areas.

In Latin America, the social stratification of the village society is of a different character; but here also overlapping and duplication of functions, and a complex internal organization, affect decisively the life of the rural population. In Brazil,* for example, the *hacendados*, the all-powerful estate owners, form the apex of a low social pyramid in which the group of owner-operators is either very small or non-existent. The broad base of the pyramid is composed of more or less dependent cultivators whose social status is determined by the great variety of contractual arrangements between the *hacendado* and his workers. Thus, they may work as tenants, sharecroppers and herdsmen; or as wage earners who are granted a small plot of land with or without other privileges; or as wage earners who are given a house but no land, with or without other privileges; or as wage earners who receive neither land nor house and do not reside on the farm. Furthermore, small owner-cultivators may be employed under any of the contracts mentioned; and finally, there are the squatters who till the land without any contract. But even this is not all. The *hacendados* may shift the peasants from one type of contract to another for farm management or financial reasons; or the peasants themselves may choose to move from one contract to another particularly if they remain unemployed for any length of time, as is often the case, and the labour market in the community happens

* CIDA, *Brazil: Land Tenure Conditions and Socio-economic Development of the Agricultural Sector*, pp. 178 ff.

to offer them an opportunity to augment their income. The variety of agricultural employment, the frequent changes in contracts and income, and the wide divergence of interests result in insecurity, restlessness and social tension. As in Asia, the underemployed and underpaid landless workers will compete for the scarce job opportunities with the families of the small owner-cultivators whose holdings are too small to provide a living.

Actually, the polyvalent nature of farm labour and the variety of functions fulfilled by the peasants in underdeveloped countries prevent any clear occupational grouping. Instead there is a criss-crossing within the social stratification according to political and economic functions or needs frequently rendered still more complicated by caste or ethnic differences. Hence the difficulties of analysing and defining the values that rule the village community.

Accordingly, it is erroneous to believe that landownership alone secures a higher hierarchical status. The landless agent who supervises the property of the big landowner, or the villager who works for this agent, are held in higher esteem by the community because of their close relation with the representative of worldly power and authority, than the small owner-cultivator who has to perform the despised manual work even if this is on his own land. It is equally erroneous, however, to believe that within the rigid Indian caste system only the higher castes come into possession of land. Studies of Indian village life show, in fact, that despite the high correlation between caste ranking and landownership, low-caste or tribal people may hold a considerable share in land. The over-valuation of landownership and the disdain for manual labour together with the formidable social and economic contrasts within the village community which allow the large landowners to play off one interest against the other are still among the weightiest reasons for the frequent failure of both agrarian reform programmes and the peasants' attempts to establish a common front.

Nevertheless, there have been uprisings in remote villages which have grown into nationwide movements that succeeded in uniting the divergent peasant groups on common objectives and eventually changed the course of history. If we ask how this was possible, the answer is that the widening gap between classes naturally reduces intraclass differences and that consequently these movements were the collective reaction of all strata of peasant society against a common external opponent. It has been stated quite rightly that such a collective reaction was often caused by out-rageous cases of social injustice, such as the eviction of tenants and squatters, intolerable pressure of forced labour and various abuses perpetrated by the authorities.* Frequently, however, it has also arisen out of the invasion of commercial interests or the registration of private rights in communal lands which offended against the creed of the peasants that the land and its produce belong to the community.

The intensity and magnitude of peasant movements depend largely upon the aggressiveness of their opponents, be they the government or the large landowners; the stronger the pressure, the greater the interest of *all* strata of peasant society in overcoming its weaknesses and integrating conflicting interests in collective action for socio-economic progress.

It must not be thought, however, that this collective reaction is identical with the disintegration of the peasant hierarchy or even with diminished respect for higher social status. When it comes to collective action, it is generally the literate and better-off peasants, rather than (as one would expect) the poorest and most miserable villagers, who take initiative and provide most of the active leader-ship. Poverty alone does not suffice to arouse the peasants. They must be intellectually aware of their sad position and its contrast with efficient estates before they are able to take the initiative in the dynamic process of revolutionary change.† But even then, the hierarchic village structure will assert itself and make it extremely difficult for anybody from 'below' to command the respect of those who rank above him socially and economically, unless, of course, he is endowed with outstanding charismatic qualities. It has been asserted that in the German Peasant Wars the 'carriers of the uprising were not the village poor but, on the contrary and practically without exception, the village dignitaries'.‡ Similarly,

* B. Moore, Jr., *Social Origins of Dictatorship and Democracy (Boston,* 1966: London, 1967), pp. 33 ff., 453 ff.
† E. J. Hobsbawm, 'Peasants and Rural Migrants in Politics', in Claudio Veliz (ed.), *The Politics of Conformity in Latin America* (London, 1967), p. 56.
‡ G. Franz, *Der deutsche Bauernkrieg* (Darmstadt, 1956), p. 287. Erich R. Wolf ('On Peasant Rebellions', *International Social Science Journal,* vol. 21, no. 2, UNESCO, Paris, 1969, pp. 286 ff.), indicates that the middle and free peasants are tactically mobile and constitute the pivotal groups of peasant uprisings.

in the Indian state of Kerala, the leader of the Communist Party, who won the election in 1967, and strongly advocates the implementation of radical agrarian reforms, is a Brahmin, a member of the highest caste in Hindu society.

The very complexity of the village structure, on the other hand, makes it possible for both government and landlords to weaken the peasant organizations by playing off the conflicting interests against one another and thus securing the support of those peasant groups which have the highest economic stake in preventing too radical a change in the existing social orde... The history of the European peasant movement shows that, even as late as the second half of the nineteenth century, they were dominated by large landowners. This is still the case today in large parts of Italy where the interests of the small peasants are sadly neglected; or in the Philippines, where the government-sponsored peasant organizations are indirectly controlled by large landowners who, by partially yielding to minor claims which are then given official recognition, use them as a convenient excuse for declaring illegal any serious movement attempting to secure the legitimate rights of the peasants.

In many respects the *Hukbalahap*,* in the Philippines, may serve as a model for the reaction of peasants to the attempts of many governments to use first the carrot, then the whip in dealing with the malignant agrarian situation. It formed the nucleus of Philippine resistance to the Japanese occupation during the Second World War, which was sincerely convinced that political independence would automatically lead to the economic and social emancipation of the peasantry. When, notwithstanding the defeat of the Japanese and the Declaration of Independence issued by the United States government, no move was made to change the agrarian situation and the large landowners regained their dominant position in the government, the *Hukbalahap* turned into a revolutionary guerrilla movement that has now held its ground for twenty-five years. It has alternately been declared annihilated or ready to cooperate whenever any of its leaders have been killed or have surrendered, yet it continues to mobilize the people in the villages against landlord-oriented governments which pass much agrarian legislation, but carefully avoid any reform measures

---

* Abbreviation for the Tagalog '*Hukbo ng Bayan Laban sa Hapon*' (United Front against the Japanese).

which would infringe the prerogatives of the landowning class.

Peasant movements, moreover, may contribute to the process of agrarian reconstruction when a legal and administrative framework has been established within which their interests are openly discussed and duly considered, and when their representatives take part in high-level political decisions, as happened in Mexico under President Cárdenas and during the first years of the Eduardo Frei government in Chile. When discussing peasant movements and peasant organizations, therefore, one must carefully avoid generalizations and classifications since their actions and objectives are substantially, and often even exclusively, determined by the agrarian structure and land policy.

This can readily be seen when comparing different peasant movements. In the advanced countries they have gradually taken on the bureaucratic appearance of labour unions, while in under-developed countries their main features are spontaneity, chance-leadership, un-coordinated group action and a communication system based almost entirely on personal contact and initiative. Under a strong leadership this is not necessarily a disadvantage but if this is incompetent or rendered ineffective by competition and friction between the various peasant groups, the entire movement may easily collapse and disintegrate.

If peasant organizations are thus unable to act as a progressive force, guerrilla movements may emerge and become spearheads in the attack against the *status quo*, as we see happening today in many Latin American countries, in South Vietnam, the Philippines and Thailand. Such peasant guerrillas, often under the leadership of intellectuals such as Fidel Castro and the late Che Guevara in Cuba, have two principal functions. They embarrass the ruling government by undermining its authority and they activate and prepare the peasant population for the revolutionary invasion of the large land holdings and for the final usurpation of political power.

In a feudalistic society the most common tactic of peasant movements was and still is the spontaneous occupation of land, as frequently happens in Latin America where it is even occasionally tolerated particularly if it affects unutilized land. Thus in 1960, groups of Indian peasants in Peru invaded a large estate and hastily established themselves with their families in small huts as a token of actually having taken possession of the land. They were at first expelled brutally by the police of the estate; but when they were given a chance to exhibit documents proving their original communal rights in the land, they were 'permitted' to return and their action was interpreted as recovery of lost property.* This success encouraged other peasant groups to attempt similar action and more than 300,000 peasants participated in subsequent mass invasions of estate land until 1964 when an agrarian reform law was passed and the first redistribution of land was actually carried out.†

The concerted action by the Peruvian Indians was significant for its simplicity. In many cases the occupation amounted to no more than the expulsion of the supervisor and agent of the absentee landowner and was more a demonstration against the illicit claim of the landowner to the crops and lands that the *conquistadores* and their successors had usurped. It should be noted, however, that discord within the ruling class of Peru and political competition for the peasant vote at that time largely contributed to the achievemens of this particular peasant movement. Usually when peasant action is directed against land covered by the registered title of a large landowner, an open conflict will continue until the bitter end: be this the flight of the landlord and the redistribution of 'his' land as was the case in Mexico; or the liquidation of the peasant leaders who will be branded as not only criminals but enemies of the nation.

Other means, frequently employed by peasant organizations to increase their political bargaining power, are open disobedience, passive resistance and mass demonstrations that block thoroughfares or the access to government buildings, as still happens in France today. Or, like the industrial labour unions, they may go on strike and simply stop tilling the land, as happened in Mexico during the thirties, or refuse to deliver the share of the crop or render the services claimed by the landlord. The latter happened in 1963 in Cuzco, a district in Peru, when the landlords, to whom the peasants were obliged to render compulsory services in return

---

* K. L. Karst, *Latin American Land Reform: The Uses of Confiscation,* Land Tenure Center Reprint no. 20 (University of Wisconsin, 1963), p. 333.
† CIDA, *Peru: Land Tenure Conditions and Socio-economic Development of the Agricultural Sector* (Pan American Union, Washington, D.C., 1966).

for the right to cultivate a plot of virgin land, increased their demands as soon as the land was cleared and produced a reasonable yield. An open conflict broke out and organized militant peasant groups successfully fought the police and forced some of the landowners to leave the area. They continued to strike and fight until a special land distribution programme for the area was approved.

In large parts of the underdeveloped world peasant strikes are considered illegal, just as were strikes for legitimate demands in Europe and the United States before they were recognized as an integral part of social relations. It seems doubtful, however, whether a similar development can be expected in the near future in the rural areas of Asia and Latin America where the landlord-controlled governments fear that the social pressures of legal peasant organizations may all too soon change the balance of power. Lin Pao, incidentally, conceives the current political tension in the world as the fight of one large peasant movement (the underdeveloped world) against the urban interests (the developed industrialized nations) in which guerrilla tactics will be the most effective weapon of the peasants.*

We are dealing at some length with peasant movements and organizations because they are an integral part, often deliberately neglected or unintentionally overlooked, of current discussion on the agrarian problem.

From our point of view, the fundamental question is how to increase the participation of the rural people in national development. In most underdeveloped countries, the combination of the prevailing power structure and low levels of education is the greatest obstacle, and peasant representatives succeed only rarely in breaking through the walls of political pressure and entrenched bureaucracy. Modern development strategy has contributed but little to removing this obstacle since it relies mainly upon those social groups accustomed to handling administration and organization. An outstanding example of this neglect is the almost total absence of enthusiasm and active participation on the part of the peasants despite the evident progress achieved in some development blocs, in the otherwise remarkable Indian Community

* Lin Pao, 'Long Live the Victory of the People's War', *The People's Daily*, (Peking, 3.9.1965). He talks about 'the rural areas of the world encircling the cities of the world'.

Development Programme.* Considering the comparatively high level of political democracy in India, it seems unlikely that such programmes will be more successful elsewhere.

One only needs to take as an example the recommendations of the Inter-American Conference of Ministers of Labour, sponsored by the United Nations, which in 1963 urged the Latin American governments to recognize the right of freedom of association of agricultural workers on all levels of development planning.† Although some countries responded to the appeal and introduced peasant participation in agrarian administration this only had a limited effect, if any. Despite new legislation, peasant representatives were either not admitted at all or were out-voted as soon as the occasion arose. It has been emphasized that the absence of peasant participation is particularly evident 'in cases of deliberate resistance to social changes that might threaten the privileged position of large landowners or other members of the rural élite.'‡

It does not call for great psychological insight to understand that dependent and subordinate peasants can hardly be expected to voice strong opinions at committee meetings and that their influence, even if they do dare to speak up, is bound to be very limited because of their extremely weak political and economic bargaining position. Furthermore, their very misery entails the risk that peasant representatives, say on land redistribution committees, may be bribed by the large landowners to sanction fraudulent land transactions, as often happened in Indonesia during the distribution of surplus land. Needless to say, the most essential precondition for successful peasant participation is the elevation

* Government of India, Planning Commission, *Seventh Evaluation Report on Community Development and Some Allied Fields* (New Delhi, 1960) and Government of India, Committee on Plan Projects, *Report of the Team for the Study of Community Projects and National Extension Service, Vols. I-III* (New Delhi, 1957).

† 'Conferencia Interamericana de Ministros de Trabajo sobre la Alianza para el Progreso', *Revista Interamericana de Ciencias Sociales Segunda Epoca*, vol. 2, no. 2 (Pan American Union, Washington, D.C., 1963), p. 172.

‡ United Nations, International Labour Organization (ILO), *Social Development in the Americas. Report of the Director-General on the Eighth Conference of American States Members of the International Labour Organization in Ottawa, 1966* (Report no. 1, Geneva, 1967), pp. 34-5.

of the social, economic and educational levels in rural areas; but this involves the process of emancipation which is still successfully protracted by the opponents of change.

In Japan, it is true, peasant representatives play a decisive role in agrarian policy, but this can hardly be considered a valid example for underdeveloped countries given the high level of education and organization of the Japanese peasantry, and the series of successful agrarian reforms during the past hundred years which have profoundly changed the agrarian situation and improved the use of land.

It is now almost universally agreed that a democratic form of government is not identical with economic democracy and does not necessarily guarantee socio-economic progress and the emancipation of the peasants. In India, where political power has been deliberately dispersed and fully 'democratized', as it were, but where the colonial socio-economic structure has been left essentially intact, we find today 'less educated and more tradition-minded individuals on the local level who are exposed to the pressures of the privileged groups in the state capitals'.*

It is almost self-evident that the political bargaining power of the peasant class determines the extent of their participation in the implementation of land reform programmes. As long as landlord-oriented government representatives play the role of 'neutral' arbiters in local committees, the peasants have lost the struggle. Accordingly, the first task of the agency responsible for the implementation of land reform should be to strengthen the peasants' weak bargaining power by demonstrating a clear bias in favour of their rights in all cases of landlord-tenant conflicts and disputes with local money-lenders and traders. In the current political and social climate of most underdeveloped countries this may be an arduous task. But it is not altogether impossible as has been proved in Nepal where land tenure officers became so strongly inspired by the spirit of the reform programme that they used their authority to support the interests of the peasants in the face of extreme political and administrative opposition. This opposition has so far, however, unfortunately proved the stronger. In the majority of cases, particularly in Latin America, land reform

* M. Weiner, 'India: Two Political Cultures', in L. W. Pye and S. Verba (eds.), *Political Culture and Political Development* (Princetown, N.J., 1965), p. 199.

will remain legislation on paper only until the administration becomes independent enough to openly express its readiness to alter the balance of power in the villages by raising the bargaining capacity of the peasants, as now seems to be the case in Peru.

2. SEMI-URBANIZATION OF RURAL MIGRANTS*

Although it is the peasant and labour movements which at present represent the revolutionary forces in society, the socio-economic reality of peasant life in many underdeveloped countries harbours a potential progressive force that at any time may develop into a formidable attack upon the existing political and social order.

But before entering into a more detailed analysis of this force, we will briefly clarify the terms *semi-urbanization* and *semi-urbanized* or *displaced peasants*, used below to describe the particular socio-economic implications of the migration into the towns. Though these terms are largely self-explanatory, it may be emphasized that *semi-urbanization* indicates the state of rural migrants in the city who, though physically present, have no prospect of being integrated into the urban community in the foreseeable future and, therefore, remain *semi-urbanized* or *displaced peasants* who are still tied to their families and clans in the rural community, still largely dependent upon their support and, above all, still potential applicants for their share of the land in case of land redistribution in their village.†

In an earlier chapter‡ we have already pointed out that mounting population pressure and technological progress in the underdeveloped areas of South Asia, Africa and Latin America

---

* *Semi-urbanization* is the combined effect of migration from rural areas and over-urbanization, and covers the continued economic and social relationship of the excess urban population to their rural base. Thus it is not identical with the problem of *over-urbanization* as dealt with by: Janet L. Abo-Lughod, 'Urbanization in Egypt: Present State and Future Prospects', *Economic Development and Cultural Change*, vol. 13, no. 3 (April 1965); and N. V. Sovani, *Urbanization and Urban India* (Bombay, 1966).

† United Nations, Economic Commission for Latin America (ECLA), *Economic Bulletin for Latin America*, vol. 13, no. 2 (New York, November 1968), states that they demonstrate their non-acceptance of the urban way of life by failing to contribute to the decline in the fertility rate associated with urban life.

‡ Chapter 2.

severely affect the social stratification in the rural communities and that every year hundreds of thousands of peasants migrate to the large cities in the hope of improving their lot.

It has been said that the march of the peasants to the shanty towns of Calcutta, Nairobi, Lima, Caracas and Mexico City is 'a protest with the feet' against an agrarian situation that is as hopeless as ever despite two decades of development efforts. This silent march to urban centres that do not hold out any prospect of immediate industrial employment, is in no way comparable to the exodus from the land which took place in Western Europe and North America during the first half of this century. In effect, this represented a shift in the national economy from agriculture to industry, simultaneously increasing efficiency and labour utilization in the rural areas and providing the labour force needed for industrial expansion. The erratic flight from the land in the under-developed countries, far from being a transfer of labour, is rather an expression of extreme frustration and hopelessness and the urge to escape physically from the bitter reality of landlord oppression or the daily fight for survival on a sub-marginal holding. It is also often subconsciously motivated by the feeling that nearness to the centre of political power offers more of a protection in cases of emergency than does the isolated and remote village.

The expansion of Mexico City, illustrated opposite, where the population increased from 477,000 in 1910 to 3,050,000 in 1950 and to 7,115,000 in 1968 may serve as an example.* Similar or even greater population expansions have occurred in most other large urban centres.

Considering the magnitude of the rural exodus and the still very limited rate of industrialization, the physical presence of the peasants in the large cities of Asia and Latin America is in no way synonymous with their urbanization, since only a tiny fraction of them have any chance of steady employment. But Western demographers are so strongly accustomed to thinking in administrative units that they continue to count any newcomer to an urban area as resident of the urban community and to consider rural-urban migrations in conjunction with industrial developments alone. Accordingly, their analyses of the process of

* E. Flores, *Tratado de Economía Agrícola* (Mexico City, 1968).

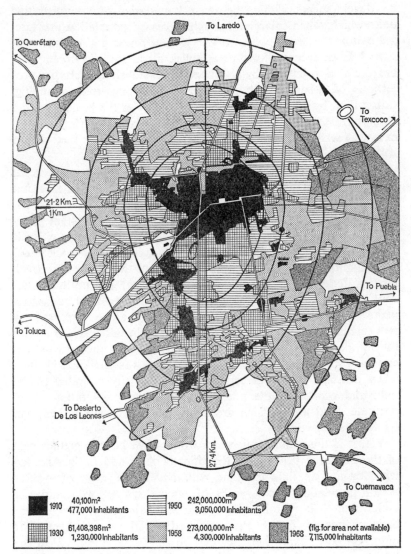

By courtesy of Edmundo Flores

The Expansion of Mexico City

urbanization, and particularly their population forecasts, are based on developments within the fixed boundaries of administrative units which, when enlarged through increased population pressure, are denoted as *metropolitan areas, greater towns* and *conglomerations*.* Even recent efforts to establish more realistic urban units are dictated primarily by the need to establish models for projections of urban growth in order to facilitate urban planning, rather than by the still greater need to consider the position of the *human elements* within the urban unit in order to determine the extent to which they have been urbanized, or whether they should still be considered peasants for all practical purposes.

Economists, sociologists and demographers alike pay scant attention to the social and political implications of the fact that *because the unemployed peasants in the cities remain villagers, the villages have been extended into the cities*. They content themselves with the explanation that the rapid growth of the cities is due largely to rural migrations which, given their social and economic origin, are less predictable than are the other two growth factors, fertility and mortality rates, and that the normally uncontrolled migratory movement in underdeveloped countries makes it almost impossible to estimate, let alone forecast, any movements into or out of the cities. They do not seem to realize the fundamental difference between migratory movements encouraged by growing urban industries, as was the case in Italy when peasants from Calabria, Apulia and Sicily migrated to the industrial centres in the north, and the erratic migrations from destitute rural areas which are motivated by despair rather than by definite objectives.

Yet, it is this aimless migration which furnishes the greater part of the displaced peasants in the cities of Asia and Latin America who for a long time to come will remain the scum of surplus urban population. Long years of unemployment will gradually undermine their moral and physical strength and further reduce their chance of future economic and social advancement. The often voiced opinion that they can be gainfully 'employed' in the tertiary sector where labour is already underutilized, is simply

---

* See K. Davis, 'Conceptual Aspects of Urban Projections in Developing Countries', in *Report of United Nations World Population Conference, 1965*, vol. 3 (UN, New York, 1967); and E. J. Hobsbawm, 'Peasants and Rural Migrants in Politics', op. cit., pp. 57 ff.

fictitious and only helpful to the statisticians, who have to find a convenient heading in their censuses under which to group such people.

It is high time, therefore, that investigations were begun to explore the conditions and economic position of the rapidly increasing unemployed and unqualified population in the shanty towns, and particularly their relations to the other urban, as well as rural, population groups in order to determine the effect of semi-urbanization upon overall social and political developments.

The magnitude of the problem of rural migrations from the highland communities in the Latin American countries of Argentina, Brazil, Chile, Colombia, Ecuador, Guatemala and Peru has been subject to thorough CIDA investigations, aptly analysed by Barraclough.*

In these communities the average per capita income of the peasants amounts to less than $100 per year, whereas that of the large landowners, who constitute only 1–2 per cent of the whole population, is several hundred times that amount. This extremely low income level of the peasants is due to the inadequate land and capital resources of nine out of ten families; to antiquated technology; to lack of services such as transport, education and extension, and of credit facilities which are either non-existent or available only to a few large landowners; and, finally, to the almost total absence of alternative employment possibilities. In this frustrating situation, the migration to urban areas 'seems to be an opportunity'.

Tables 2 and 3 which clearly reflect the migratory trends and the formidable population growth in the urban areas inevitably pose the question of whether the urban employment potential will increase rapidly enough during the next two decades to absorb an influx of this magnitude. The Economic Commission for Latin America† answers this question in the negative and points out that the marginal, unemployed urban population sectors are already very large in every Latin American metropolis while the growth

* S. L. Barraclough, 'Employment Problems Affecting Latin American Agricultural Development', *FAO Monthly Bulletin of Agricultural Economics and Statistics*, vol. 18, nos. 7–8 (Rome, July-August, 1969).
† United Nations, ECLA, *Geographical Distribution of the Population of Latin America and Regional Development Priorities* (E/CN. 12/643, Mar del Plata, May 1963).

of industrial output since 1950 has been declining gradually and during the period 1960–69 amounted to about 5 per cent in urban centres. The situation is particularly unfortunate for the people in the highland communities since migration to the frontier areas or cities can no longer absorb even their annual population increase and the rate of industrial expansion considerably exceeds the increase in employment opportunities due to the wide use of labour-saving equipment.

Thus in Brazil, the number of industrial workers increases only by about 2.8 per cent annually despite very high rates of industrial investment; and in Chile, where the annual growth rate of industrial output in the decade 1950–60 amounted to nearly 6 per cent, the annual employment increase during the same period was only about 2 per cent. In other words, the earlier correlation between rate of industrial expansion and employment has ceased to exist and it can be assumed that the increasing automation will further widen the gap between the two rates.

The socio-economic pressure in the highland villages, however, is still more powerful than the dangers inherent in the disproportion between industrial expansion and employment possibilities; and the peasants will continue to migrate to the cities where they will further accelerate the growth of the semi-urbanized sector. Even if overall economic development were to expand secondary and tertiary employment, it is almost utopian to believe that this will substantially diminish, let alone absorb, the countless numbers who live in the streets or on the roofs of the large cities.

The situation in Peru is particularly dramatic. Between 1940 and 1961, the population in the coastal districts increased from 25 to 40 per cent of the national total, while that of the highlands declined from 62 to 52 per cent; during the same period the average annual rate of population increase was 1.9 per cent in the rural areas but as high as 4.4 per cent in the towns and nearly 5 per cent in the metropolis of Lima-Callao.*

In the light of what we have said so far, it is almost self-evident that semi-urbanization will inevitably affect not only the urban community but the national political climate as well. The fact that an ever-growing sector of the urban population lives under conditions which are incompatible with any hitherto experienced form

* Inter-American Development Bank, *Social Progress Trust Fund. Sixth Annual Report, 1966* (Washington, DC, 1966).

TABLE 2

Urban and Rural Population Trends in CIDA *Study Countries, 1950–70*

Country	No. of people (in thousands)			Percentage	
	Urban	Rural	Total	Urban	Rural
Argentina					
1950	11.199.1	5,893.9	17,093.0	65.5	34.5
1960	15,001.9	5,664.1	20,666.0	72.6	27.4
1970	18,200.8	6,260.2	24,461.0	74.4	25.6
Brazil					
1950	18,783.0	33,161.0	51,944.0	36.2	63.8
1960	31,991.0	38,976.0	70,967.0	45.1	54.9
1970	51,000.0	44,300.0	95,300.0	53.5	46.5
Chile					
1950	3,389.7	2,364.2	5,753.9	58.9	41.1
1960	5,028.0	2,346.0	7,374.0	68.2	31.8
1970	6,925.0	2,467.0	9,392.0	73.7	26.3
Colombia					
1950	3,160.7	8,170.5	11,268.2	28.0	72.0
1960	5,353.0	8,961.0	14,314.0	37.4	62.6
1970	8,394.0	9,897.0	18,291.0	45.9	54.1
Ecuador					
1950	914.0	2,289.0	3,203.0	28.5	71.5
1960	1,422.0	2,787.0	4,209.0	33.8	66.2
1970	2,235.0	3,395.0	5,630.0	39.7	60.3
Guatemala					
1950	701.0	2,101.0	2,802.0	25.0	74.9
1960	963.0	2,579.0	3,542.0	27.2	72.8
1970	1,353.0	3,172.0	4,525.0	29.9	70.1
Peru					
1950	3,058.6	4,773.4	7,832.0	39.0	61.0
1960	4,607.0	5,542.0	10,149.0	45.4	54.6
1970	7,229.0	6,433.0	13,662.0	52.9	47.1

SOURCE: *Land Tenure Conditions and Socio-economic Development of the Agricultural Sector in Seven Latin American Countries.* Edition prepared for the World Land Reform Conference, FAO, Rome, 1966. This CIDA report is based on a series of comprehensive studies hereafter referred to as CIDA Studies.

NOTE: Meta, Chocó, Comisarias and Intendencias are not included in figures for Colombia.

TABLE 3

Estimated Rural to Urban Migration in CIDA *Study Countries, between 1950 and 1960*

Country	Net rural to urban emigration (in thousands)	Net rural to urban emigration, as a percentage of 1950	
		Total population	Rural population
Peru	649	8.3	13.6
Ecuador	390	12.2	17.0
Colombia	1,345	11.9	16.6
Guatemala	75	2.7	3.6
Argentina	1,466	8.6	24.9
Brazil	6,301	12.1	19.0
Chile	685	11.9	29.0

SOURCE: CIDA Studies

of city life presents an insurmountable obstacle to urban development planning and budgeting. Although the rapid post-war development of the urban centres in industrialized countries has given rise to numerous still unsolved problems, it has not altogether paralysed long-term city planning. But in the underdeveloped countries, the influx has been, and still is, so enormous that the cities no longer have a chance to calculate, let alone meet, the needs of the ever-growing groups of people who are separated from the urbanized population and most of whom, in the foreseeable future, will not be in a position to participate in the development of an urban identity.* It seems safe to say that the greater proportion of the turmoil and riots, almost daily occurrences in the cities of Calcutta, Lima and Caracas, must be viewed as a desperate protest by the semi-urbanized peasants for whom there is no room in either village or city.

The phenomenon of semi-urbanization clearly emerges as the formidable social price which the underdeveloped countries of South Asia and Latin America have to pay in order to preserve

* The 1967 *Report on the World Social Situation* (UN, New York, 1969), pp. 131–3 deals with the fact that urbanization in Latin America has proceeded independently of industrialization; but ignores the potential for social dynamics of this development.

the distorted man-land relationship within the existing political and economic order. It seems likely that this price will increase during the coming decade; whereas in China it seems to have been possible to block the flight from the rural areas, and even encourage a return to these, more by persuasion and a greatly increased utilization of the labour force than by force.

It has been argued* that migrations from the country tend to preserve the existing agrarian order because generally the most energetic and enterprising—and, therefore, the most 'dangerous' elements—of the younger generation leave the villages so that those who remain behind are the conservative elements which are less likely to continue pressurizing for changes in the agrarian structure.

This argument, however, is only valid to a certain extent since the massive migration to the large cities and the subsequent semi-urbanization involves potential forces which may profoundly affect overall social and political developments. For the ever-increasing number of displaced peasants, crammed together in the shanty towns of the large cities without any future prospects, the rural community with its problems and political tensions remains a reality. It is true that to some extent they may weaken its economic and social structure because they return from time to time to collect their share of the crop which they did not help to produce. But the very fact that they comprise the most energetic and 'dangerous' elements from the villages means in effect that with them the latent agrarian unrest has actually reached the city gates.

To our mind there is little doubt that, sooner or later, the semi-urbanized peasants in the large cities of South Asia and Latin America will become a gigantic pressure group for agrarian changes within the very precincts of political power. They will counterbalance the influence of the new urban middle class, above all of its corrupt upper strata which, particularly in Latin America, has reinforced the position of large landowners and foreign capital.†

While currently large numbers of peasants and workers are

---

* By E. Feder, in an ECLA Report on 'Land Tenure Problems in Latin America' (as yet unpublished).

† This is also underlined in the outstanding Swedish study by S. Lindqvist, *Slagskuggan—Latinamerika inför 70 talet* (Stockholm, 1969), pp. 41 ff.

being deceived by radical slogans and deceptive reform programmes, the semi-urbanized peasants lost their illusions a long
time ago and are suspicious of the policies and propaganda of the
groups in power. Since they are also difficult to control, it is more
than likely that they will swell the ranks of organized peasant
and worker movements,* and even become the spearhead of the
assault on the *status quo*. The accumulated pressure of a landless
peasant population in both villages and urban centres may
eventually force the ruling class to sacrifice its rural interests in
order to survive politically and economically, as happened in
Mexico at the beginning of this century—though whether, under
present conditions, such a sacrifice will in fact safeguard the
national position of the ruling class is another question.

* The *Tupamaros* in Uruguay and similar groups in Guatemala,
Brazil and Argentina bear evidence of the increased activity of city
based guerrilla movements.

CHAPTER FIVE

External Forces Affecting
The Man-Land Relationship

Colonial Rule and Neo-Colonialism

In the last analysis, it could be said that the particular socio-economic and political conditions which prevail in the majority of underdeveloped countries are the product of powerful, though not always obvious, forces that operate from the outside and by their very nature affect the man-land relationship. But before we proceed to determine and analyse these forces, we must first briefly describe the present position of the peasantry in these countries.

Insecurity of tenure, permanent indebtedness and a generally low level of agricultural technique, epitomize the three principal functions of the peasants in the process of economic growth: they constitute the unskilled labour force for the plantations and mines; they cultivate on their smallholdings the primary products sold on the world market; and they are the principal consumers of imported goods. But due to a total lack of any bargaining power, they are entirely at the mercy of superior economic forces—either foreign, or closely associated with foreign enterprises —which buy their labour and crops at the cheapest price possible and sell them the commodities they need for their frugal existence at prices that often exceed those obtaining in the developed parts of the world.

Post-war developments have not substantially changed the typical economic features of colonialism; with, perhaps, the single exception that the number of trading partners and the subsidiaries of foreign monopolies are steadily increasing. The *free play of economic forces* encourages the disequalizing factors* whose action upon demand and supply is ultimately responsible

* See H. Myint, 'An Interpretation of Economic Backwardness' in A. N. Agarwala and S. P. Singh (eds.), *The Economics of Under-Development* (London, 1958), pp. 109 ff.

for the unequal distribution of income and opportunities, the greatest obstacle to overall development. Galbraith's theory of the emergence of a 'countervailing power'* in the course of economic growth may ultimately prove true, of course, also when applied to underdeveloped countries. But such a self-regulatory mechanism has not appeared anywhere as yet and economic, and even political, dependence reasserts itself in all former colonies although years have passed since the last foreign soldier left and the national banner replaced the flag of the colonial power.

To consider the actions of superior external economic forces merely as wicked manoeuvres on the part of ruthless entrepreneurs and business corporations, when in reality they represent the effective monopolistic exploitation of a socio-economic situation that offers almost unlimited business opportunities, would be an oversimplification of a complex process. With all proper reservations for the differences in political systems and in the ways and means of foreign penetration, the situation in many underdeveloped countries today could well be compared with conditions in China half a century ago. Strictly speaking, China has never been a colony and officially has always retained its political independence. Yet, its central government was usually weak and frequently paralysed by inner strife because it was based on a social order that did not grant the majority of people even the minimum needed for survival, and unmercifully exposed them to the interplay of disequalizing factors. Trading, banking and other economic activities were part of a sophisticated system of contracts and concessions dictated by foreigners who used warlords and provincial officials as their agents, repaying their good offices with the opportunity of immense gains. Sun Yat Sen describes the China of his time in the following words:

> The rest of mankind is the carving knife and the serving dish while we are the fish and the meat ... Our position is extremely perilous; if we do not earnestly promote nationalism and weld together our four hundred millions into a strong nation, we face a tragedy—the loss of our country and the destruction of our race ... From now on, the Chinese people will be feeling the pressure simultaneously of natural, political and economic forces.†

* J. K. Galbraith, *American Capitalism. The Concept of Countervailing Power*, 2nd rev. ed. (Boston, 1965).
† Sun Yat Sen, *San Min Chu I, Three Principles of the People* (Shanghai, 1927), pp. 12, 32.

As happened in China in the past, the present socio-economic foundation in almost all underdeveloped countries is too weak to prevent the combined pressure of outside economic forces and powerful local groups from shaping the national economic and political situation.

What we witness today in the underdeveloped world is a reproduction of the colonial situation, reflected with unmistakable clarity in the socio-economic position of the peasant population. Now, as then, the peasant producer is in the hands of middlemen, traders or large landowners, who exclude him from the market and thus from any share in the profits and incentives of expanding world trade; while the ever-increasing number of landless agricultural workers play no part in the skilled work for the export market but constitute an undifferentiated labour force exclusively serving the interests of the landed groups and a few powerful monopolies.* It may be argued, of course, that the continued economic domination of Western monopolies and local ologopolies is a kind of division of labour which is desirable from the point of view of liberal economics; but then we must add that this is a compulsory division of labour which is based exclusively on the effects of disequalizing factors and the absence of an effective countervailing power.

Despite their political independence, most underdeveloped countries are thus faced with socio-economic conditions which are so closely related to colonialism that we feel justified in defining them as *neo-colonialism*. That is to say, circumstances in which outside forces profit almost unrestrictedly by their economic and, at times, political superiority in the third world whose defective institutional framework cannot counteract the disequalizing factors in the economy of underdevelopment. Considering that agriculture provides the livelihood for the bulk of the people in these countries, it is self-evident that the cumulative effects of neo-colonialism are felt most intensely by the peasant population and, consequently, they are of extreme relevance for our analysis of the man-land relationship.

It has been pointed out rightly that economic development and underdevelopment cannot be viewed as the 'products of supposedly different economic structures or systems, or of supposed

* H. Myint, 'An Interpretation of Economic Backwardness', op. cit., p. 119.

differences in stages of economic growth achieved within the same system', but that 'one and the same historical process of the expansion and development of capitalism throughout the world has simultaneously generated—and continues to generate—both economic development and structural underdevelopment.'* It is difficult to conceive, in fact, how the mere development of natural resources by Western or local private enterprises could possibly overcome the backwardness due to the weak social foundations and economic maladjustment. It must be kept in mind, however, that the implications of backwardness do not fully manifest themselves until the 'development' of the natural resources has reached the stage when the people have become aware of new wants and aspirations, but find themselves without a corresponding increase in their earning capacity and with a minimal share in the economic activities and national income of their countries, although these may be rapidly increasing in the aggregate.†

In South Asia, colonial exploitation was originally almost entirely in the hands of large Western trading companies which, either by force of arms or through collaboration with local dignitaries, collected taxes from the rural population and exploited the natural resources and agricultural raw materials. In Latin America, on the other hand, the commercial interests following in the wake of the *conquistadores* established in conjunction with them a feudalistic system that gradually replaced the indigenous peasant communities. Landownership became the key to political power, a process well-known from the history of the European Middle Ages,‡ and soon the principal agents for external commercial interests became the *de facto* rulers of the colonial territories.

To present an exhaustive description of the ways and means of colonial penetration and exploitation in the various parts of the

* A. G. Frank, *Capitalism and Underdevelopment in Latin America. Historical Studies of Chile and Brazil* (London and New York, 1967), p. 9.
† See H. Myint, 'An Interpretation of Economic Backwardness', op. cit., p. 116.
‡ M. Weber (*General Economic History,* p. 68) distinguishes between colonial and European feudalism, because the basis of the latter was the grants in land conferred on loyal vassals by absolute kings or emperors as recognition for faithful service.

world would go beyond the scope of this study. We will limit ourselves, therefore, to briefly mentioning certain aspects, important for our interpretation of post-colonial developments.

Western colonial penetration, particularly in South Asia and Africa, was carried out mainly by two distinct methods which, according to circumstances, were applied either separately or conjointly. The first was a system of *indirect rule* which, by supporting local chiefs and princes in their conflicts with neighbouring rivals, made them dependent upon Western advice and assistance. The other was the system of *direct rule* which implied the actual conquest of a territory and the intensive exploitation of its natural resources. With the end of mercantilism and the coming of the industrial age in the latter part of the nineteenth century, direct rule proved more appropriate to the demands of the rapidly developing Western industries. Due to the rapid expansion of the colonial empires, however, it became rather costly, and soon a combination of direct and indirect rule evolved as the most efficient form of colonial administration. Indirect rule, in fact, became an expedient of great psychological value for intensive colonial exploitation, since it mitigated the humiliation of dependence and inspired a feeling of voluntary and rewarding cooperation in the ruling class that it had itself created. For the peasant population, however, either system of colonial penetration meant concentration of landownership, sharecropping, unsatisfied credit needs and the vicious circle of usury, indebtedness and permanent bondage which turned many small owners into tenants and tenants into landless agricultural labourers.

This was the essence of the socio-economic setup in almost all colonial territories by the end of the Second World War, when the Western powers started to withdraw from their overseas dependencies. The 'decolonization', however, consisted primarily in the promulgation of *political* independence for the colonies and hardly implied more than the issuing of a 'certificate of maturity' to the most powerful local groups. For generations, the latter had been trained by effective colonial administrators in the application of Western concepts and, accordingly, it is not surprising that they automatically continued the economic and political course of their erstwhile Western masters. The process of decolonization may be interpreted as a return to the *indirect rule* of the early colonial periods since, now as then, Western business interests operate more or less amicable trade relations with the ruling élite in underdeveloped countries.

It would be wrong to assume that the change from colonialism to self-rule has substantially improved the position of the peasant population in the great majority of underdeveloped countries. Although variations in the efficiency of the new governments, in the intensity of class conflicts and in the aggressiveness of outside economic and political forces make a generalization impossible, the vulnerable socio-economic situation of the peasants is evident everywhere and the lack of identification between government and the bulk of the people is as pronounced as it was in the heyday of colonialism. The character of the frequent so-called 'revolutions' and *coups d'état* that flare up and fade away in the underdeveloped countries, indicates that they are merely the result of a competition for power between factions within the national élite, combined at times with some intervention from abroad, and that they hardly ever concern the bulk of the people who have remained economically and politically too weak to press for claims of their own. The state of political independence, in fact, frequently underscores the disparity between the poverty-stricken peasant population, tied to the land without any prospect of economic and social mobility and the ruling élite composed of Westernized lawyers, landlords, traders and soldiers. The latter often seek their own ends more unashamedly than did their foreign predecessors who, with some benevolence and objectivity, tried to ensure at least a small measure of security for all, even if this seldom amounted to more than equality in misery. The policy of the new national governments is particularly relentless in areas of tribal conflicts, as in large parts of Africa today, where it is often guided by their particular tribal prejudices and contributes to increased instability and oppression.

With a few exceptions, the new governments seem less balanced and less efficient than the former colonial administrations though certainly no less eager to seek their own advantage through cooperation with outside economic and political forces. The difference between colonial and national rule seldom amounts to more than the difference between good and bad colonial administration. According to the CIDA Report on Brazil, police force and judiciary are still in the hands of or at least controlled by the *hacendados*, so that any interference, including eventual government action, with the internal affairs of the *hacienda* is met with by strong, often armed resistance. As a result, the present rural society is 'autocratic and a source of serfdom' and 'the average agricultural worker is being shortchanged at every turn of his life: at the moment of hiring, when wages are paid, when the product is shared, or at his dismissal'.*

Conditions are hardly better in many of the new states of Africa south of the Sahara. In Ghana, the colonial administration has fostered a local ruling class, composed of British-educated lawyers, officials and army officers as well as of local chiefs who wish to maintain their controlling position within the tribal community, ready to protect British interests at any price. This influential group residing in the capital is not interested in pursuing an independent economic policy but rather uses its economic leverage to share the large part of the income from cocoa and palm-oil, the principal products of the country, with foreign business corporations.

Decolonization, in the true sense of the word, has not even started, and all that has happened so far is the concession of political independence along with a changing of the guard. No serious effort has been made to tackle the crucial conflict of interests between the bulk of the people and the privileged few who control the exploitation of the natural resources and the appropriation of the surplus production. On the contrary, the persistence of colonial attitudes has prevented the reconciliation of these two interests which, in fact, 'owe their originality to that sort of substantification which results from and is nourished by the situation in the colonies'.†

This holds even more true in many of the recently independent countries of South Asia where the peasants had formed the spearhead of the national movements and parties which moved to the fore during the years of occupation and devastation. Although they had been instrumental in obtaining the political freedom for their countries, their weak socio-economic position almost everywhere prevented them from holding their ground in the new national governments which succeeded the colonial administrations. It did

* CIDA, *Brazil: Land Tenure Conditions and Socio-economic Development of the Agricultural Sector*, p. 572.
† F. Fanon, *The Wretched of the Earth* (London and New York, 1965), p. 30.

not take long before the old national élite, with the effective
support of foreign vested interests, regained its strategic political
and economic position and ever since it has successfully prevented
the agrarian reconstruction and any fundamental changes in the
socio-economic balance.

True, some of the new governments seriously attempt to promote economic growth. But since they usually fail to combine their
efforts with changes in the quality of society, even their most
generous investments fail to improve the overall situation and
rather reproduce the colonial pattern of development with its
sharp gulf between the privileged few and the poor masses.

Accordingly, all that has happened during the past twenty
years is a gradual transition from a colonial to a neo-colonial
economy that has nowhere substantially improved the lot of the
peasants. Instead, almost everywhere, the attainment of political
independence has diverted large sections of the peasantry from
their real objectives and weakened the position of their leaders
while, at the same time, it has strengthened the economic and
political power of the national élite.

The subtle workings of neo-colonialism are probably nowhere
as conspicuous as in the Philippines where, within the span of
but two generations, the economic policy of the United States has
accomplished the complete changeover from colonial to neo-
colonial rule in a manner that may well serve as a model for the
impact of external forces upon the man-land relationship.

Seven years after the conquest of the Philippines in 1898, the
United States set up a legislature that was gradually to increase
Philippine participation in internal affairs. The ceremonious procedures caught the imagination of the people and satisfied the
ambitions of local politicians who very soon became proficient
in the art of parliamentary conduct. During this first stage of
political assimilation which was successfully completed in the
course of about twenty years, the judiciary and the civil service
were gradually Filipinized and a corps of faithful bureaucrats,
drawn from the educated landowning upper class, was established
which soon adopted the customs, values and concepts of its
American protectors.

Simultaneously, a kind of business partnership was established between the United States and the Philippines which was legally laid down in the Philippine Tariff Act of 1909. This legislation introduced reciprocal free trade between the two countries and actually adjusted Philippine agriculture, particularly the cultivation of sugar-cane, to the needs of the American market while it ensured American manufacturing industries an almost uncontested monopoly in the islands. These free trade relations not only prevented the diversification of the Philippine economy but also firmly entrenched the economic and political power of the large landowners who controlled the cultivation of sugarcane.

During the following twenty-five years the economic partnership was so closely welded together that the Japanese occupation of the islands during the Second World War was only a temporary interruption. Less than a year after the end of hostilities, it was resumed in the Philippine Trade Act of 1946 which assured American investors and the Filipino landowning class equal rights in the development of a free trade relationship with the United States. Only a few months prior to the promulgation of political independence on 4 July 1946, this Act stabilized the former colonial economic pattern and thus ensured a perpetuation of the agrarian system in the islands despite the mounting dissatisfaction of the peasant population in the sugar provinces and the opposition of their supporters amongst Filipino intellectuals.

It is only natural that the very groups which carried the Trade Act through the Philippine Congress strongly opposed any fundamental agrarian reform and successfully prevented the implementation of even the most modest changes. At the same time, however, they supported wholeheartedly the resumption of the mutual defence treaty which, prior to the war, had given the United States the right to maintain strong military bases in the islands. Needless to say, this further strengthened the position of these groups and today, almost twenty-five years after independence, the United States exercises more or less openly a power of veto against any unwelcome political decision of the national government of the Philippines.

Another significant effect of neo-colonialism in the Philippines is the gradual integration of many Filipino peasant and labour leaders and their organizations into the political and economic machinery of the ruling élite. This has almost done away with the legal opposition and thus increased the incidence of revolutionary action.*

On the surface, political life in the Philippines seems governed by a democratic two-party system; but in reality, as was proved by the elections in 1969, this is far from being so. Due to their common vested interests, the political differences between the parties have gradually diminished so much that presidential candidates can afford to switch from one party to another immediately before elections without losing prestige. The true reason for this high degree of political homogeneity is the silent unanimity among all factions of the national élite to perpetuate the prevailing agrarian system and trade relations.

The physical presence of the United States is most noticeable of course, in times of political crises. Immediately after the War, it was the American army which decimated the *Hukbalahap*; and it was American guidance and equipment that helped the Philippine government to quench a renewed *Hukbalahap* revolt in Pampanga, one of the principal sugar regions.

The establishment of a neo-colonial relationship, however, is not always based on such lengthy and careful preparation except when necessitated by the political and cultural history of the country concerned, as was the case with the Philippines. In many of the new African states, effective neo-colonial systems have been introduced by much less complicated procedures. In Ghana, the government of Kwame Nkrumah, which strongly opposed both the neo-colonial British interests in Africa and the powerful position of tradition-bound tribal chiefs, was overthrown in a military coup by generals and officers trained in Great Britain or by British cadres in Ghana. The neo-colonial interests in this case were vindicated not by direct intervention but by means of an educational system that had formed the political and ideological outlook of a powerful group of Chanaian society, the Army, according to the norms and values of the former colonial power.† In Chad, on the other hand, France simply had, and still has, to

* See E. H. Jacoby, *Agrarian Unrest in Southeast Asia*, pp. 210 ff.
† Bob Finch and Mary Oppenheimer, 'Ghana: End of an Illusion', *Monthly Review* (July-August 1966).

give direct military support to the national government in order to subdue the frequent tribal insurrections that seriously threaten her neo-colonial interests in the former colony.

In most Latin American countries, on the other hand, the neo-colonial penetration differs from the common pattern in South Asia and Africa inasmuch as it is not connected with the erstwhile colonial powers of Spain and Portugal, but almost exclusively with the United States. Accordingly, whenever any opposition endangers the neo-colonial order in this part of the world, the national governments, almost all of whom depend entirely upon American assistance (either directly or indirectly through the Organization of American States and the Inter-American Bank, or the Alliance for Progress), request and obtain adequate political and, if necessary, military support.

It ought to be mentioned in parenthesis that neo-colonialism does not only affect the political and economic development of underdeveloped countries but also tends to impose a technological pattern that is frequently contradictory to their actual needs. To further their own interests, Western commercial enterprises are inclined to transfer technical innovations for the cultivation and extraction of raw materials, without considering, let alone investigating beforehand, whether they will adversely affect overall production and labour utilization in the country concerned. The introduction of modern Western techniques, if not adjusted to the particular environmental conditions, is in fact a kind of technological neo-colonialism that only further increases the dependence of the underdeveloped countries.*

From what we have said so far, it is clearly evident that the continued pressures of external economic forces jeopardize socioeconomic development and perpetuate an agrarian structure that is harmful to the bulk of the people. As we have said above, the action of these forces is not inspired primarily by the desire to dominate the economy of underdeveloped countries or to actually prevent their independent development; it is rather the natural consequence of an economic relationship within which the disequalizing factors operating in the economically weaker country ensure foreign or foreign-controlled commercial enterprises a wide

* See J. D. Sethi, 'Technological Development and Economic Growth', *Indian and Foreign Review*, vol. 6, no. 3 (New Delhi, November 1968).

range of business opportunities and a privileged, almost extra-territorial, status within the society.*

This holds true particularly in the realm of *banking* which is still largely controlled by the very branches of the Western banking houses that used to handle commerce in colonial times. Now as then, their main responsibility is to serve the interests of their shareholders and keep the larger part of their reserves in the currency of their home countries. Due to the self-liquidating nature of commercial banking, even their sub-branches in the more important agricultural districts avoid the long-term risky agricultural credit transactions and prefer to channel the deposits to the main branches located in the principal commercial centres for financing the more profitable business of exporting raw materials and importing manufactured goods. In the last analysis, therefore, the capital-starved agricultural sector still provides a considerable part of the liquid resources for an economic policy that favours the foreign commercial activities rather than providing the investment and long-term loans needed for the improvement of agriculture and for the urgent diversification of the economy.

It has been pointed out that the export of liquid savings, and the subsequent reliance on foreign long-term capital for development purposes, secures for the commercial banking houses a useful income, and reinforces their control over the economic policy of the underdeveloped countries.†

The scarcity of capital for investment in agriculture created by the neo-colonial relationship is responsible, among other things, for the general shortage of storage facilities for the peasant producers. Most of the modern storehouses in rural areas are built by large, often foreign, commercial enterprises for laying up buffer stocks in times of slack markets, while the small cultivators are forced to sell their produce immediately, whatever the market price, in order to avoid loss by spoilage.

---

* F. Clairmonte (*Economic Liberalism and Underdevelopment. Studies in the Disintegration of an Idea*, Bombay, 1960) gives a brilliant picture of the emergence of intervention in the under-developed world (pp. 225 ff.). Note particularly the case of the Anglo-Iranian Oil Company and the quotation of Dr Mossadeg's statement in the UN Security Council (15.10.1951), p. 276.

† T. Balogh, 'The Mechanism of Neo-Imperialism', *Bulletin of the Oxford Institute of Statistics*, vol. 24, no. 3 (1962).

Thus the strong position of Western banking houses has out-lived colonial rule. The young processing industries in the new independent countries have to cope not only with the competition of imported goods on the domestic markets, but also with a credit policy that retards and often inhibits their growth. This, it need hardly be said, worsens the precarious economic structure and social stratification and further widens the gap between the bulk of the people and the privileged few who are partners in the neo-colonial relationship. In the Philippines the disguised but close association in the sphere of banking gives American banking im-mediate access to local deposits which are then channelled into financing American commercial activities in the islands.* This has the additional psychological advantage of rendering general American business in the Philippines less vulnerable to nationalist attacks against conspicuous 'foreign' commercial activities.

It would take us too long to present the amply available evi-dence of the practices of foreign banking institutions in other underdeveloped countries; suffice it to point out that it is one of the most characteristic features of the neo-colonial relationship. To mention just one glaring example, the construction of the extravagant Hilton Hotel in Havana (now called the *Habana Libre*), completed shortly before the revolution, was largely financed by the retirement fund of the Gastronomic Workers of Cuba which contributed $27 million out of a total of $35 million.

Another equally important aspect of neo-colonialism is the de-terioration of the *terms of trade* for primary commodities. Despite greatly increased consumption in the developed world, the weakened position of agricultural products in the world market literally stultifies the efforts of international agencies to raise the economic potential and promote self-sustaining growth in under-developed countries. This unexpected development is largely a consequence of the neo-colonial trade policy, based on the classical nineteenth-century concept of 'equal treatment', which ignores the structural differences between industrialized and agricultural countries and which was the very substance of colonial exploitation.

* Statement by David Rockefeller, President of the Chase Manhattan Bank, at the annual meeting in New York, 22 March 1966. Quoted in H. J. Abaya, *The Untold Story of the Philippines* (Quezon City, 1967).

It is most unfortunate, therefore, that an important international organization like GATT (General Agreement on Tariffs and Trade) is influenced by this concept and through its rules and regulations still aims primarily at facilitating trade for the sake of trade without paying sufficient attention to the need of the underdeveloped countries for a more constructive trade policy. Accordingly, UNCTAD (United Nations Conference on Trade and Development), as we shall see below, fails time and again to convince the developed countries of the imperative need for a deliberate change in conventional trade and aid practices given their harmful effect upon the poor nations.

It cannot be denied that the increased manufacture of exportable goods in underdeveloped countries has not been supported, let alone encouraged, by any significant reduction of tariffs or of quantitative restrictions on imports in the industrialized countries.* The World Bank has looked into this question and concludes that the tariff reductions negotiated by the Kennedy Round of GATT in 1967 chiefly benefited the commodity trade within the developed world since 'the industrialized countries made larger concessions to other industrialized countries than to the developing ones'.†

During the past twenty-five years, in fact, the rate of growth of the world's industrial production has been considerably larger than that of world trade. And this implies evidently that overall world trade has increased more than world trade in primary commodities. Accordingly, the underdeveloped countries are faced with a growing external imbalance caused partly by an actual contraction of their exports but, above all, by their slow rate of

---

* Although the Soviet Technical Assistance does not aim directly at changing the socio-economic framework in the recipient countries, its programmes seem more realistic from the point of view of trade development than those of Western bilateral aid. By combining aid with an increased import of manufactured goods from the recipient countries it not only helps them to repay their loans but also encourages the gradual diversification of their economy which ultimately will also lead to socio-economic development. Dept. of Ec. and Soc. Affairs, *World Economic Survey 1965*, pt. 1, chap. 4, pp. 110 ff.

† International Bank for Reconstruction and Development (IBRD), *World Bank and International Development Association, Annual Report, 1968*, pp. 33 ff.

growth.* Despite a relatively stable demand for certain primary commodities like coffee and tea, the increasing production of synthetic substitutes severely affects other major export crops like sugar, cotton, jute and rubber the demand for which is currently lagging well behind economic growth in the developed world.

The low elasticity of supply makes the prices for primary commodities extremely sensitive to changes in the demand position and market fluctuations in the developed world. This is the more unfortunate because prices for Western industrial products, and particularly for capital equipment, are largely cost-determined and less sensitive to changing business cycles. Accordingly, in times of favourable markets, both industrial and primary commodity prices tend to rise (the former generally more than the latter), while declining markets affect the prices of primary commodities only. It has been observed correctly that 'the advanced countries take a larger share of the poorer countries output when prices are favourable, but leave them to bear the brunt of years of low prices'.†

The small volume of manufactured goods, produced almost exclusively for the purpose of import substitution, and the financial assistance from international agencies may momentarily relieve the external imbalance. But in the long run the increasing disparity between the terms of trade for primary commodities and industrial goods will further enfeeble the already weak economic position of underdeveloped countries. It is wishful thinking to imagine that even a revocation of the wide range of import restrictions for primary agricultural products would substantially improve conditions that derive from a defective socio-economic structure, the still powerful vestige of the colonial past.

Since the demand for primary commodities in industrialized countries is also relatively inelastic, partly because of the increasing production of synthetic substitutes, the underdeveloped countries can no longer hold out much hope for the scaling down of protective tariffs and import restrictions in the developed countries, and modestly ask only to be given a share in any

---

* See Report by the Secretary-General of the United Nations Conference on Trade and Development (UNCTAD), *Towards a New Trade Policy for Development* (New York, 1964).

† P. Streeten. *Economic Integration. Aspects and Problems* (Leyden, 1961), p. 146 (quoted by Gunnar Myrdal in *Asian Drama*, p. 611).

eventual increase in demand. But even if this were to materialize, the increase cannot be large enough to provide employment for the annual increment of their active agricultural population, particularly since the ever-mounting application of labour-displacing equipment will further reduce employment opportunities and, it need hardly be said, increase the pressure on the real wage level. The neo-colonial trade relationship reinforces this process by its retarding effect upon industrialization; hence wage levels in underdeveloped countries are generally appallingly low even in times of increasing agricultural production, whereas in the Western world, the relative shortage of labour, combined with an effective trade union policy, guarantees a rise in wages commensurate with and often exceeding the growth in productivity.*

* The deterioration of the terms of trade for primary commodities has been the subject of many scientific investigations. In the following we will largely draw upon the theory of Raul Prebisch, former Secretary-General of UNCTAD, as set forth in *The Economic Development of Latin America and its Principal Problems* (ECLA, New York, 1950); and in *Towards a New Trade Policy for Development*.

Reference is also made to Simon Kuznets' study, 'Quantitative Aspects of the Economic Growth of Nations. Level and Structure of Foreign Trade: Long-Term Trends', *Economic Development and Cultural Change*, vol. 15, no. 2, pt. 2 (January 1967), pp. 69 ff. Kuznets deals with the gap in time between increases in international economic growth and international trade; he emphasizes that 'despite the stagnation and decline after 1913, the foreign trade proportions in those older developed countries that showed the rapid rises in the nineteenth and early twentieth centuries were in recent years (say, 1957–63) still much higher than before those countries' industrialization'. While the distribution of world output moved steadily towards a preponderance of manufactured goods, the distribution of world commodity trade between industrial and agricultural products was practically stable during the last decades (60 per cent to 40 per cent). According to Kuznets, the major reasons for this stability were that despite the growth of their industrial output many developed countries continued to export large quantities of agricultural products and that the overseas offshoots of Europe, such as Australia and New Zealand, have a relatively high proportion of agricultural exports. Thus the apparent stability in the distribution of world commodity trade between industrial and agricultural products does not reflect the actual position of the underdeveloped countries.

A. Lindbeck ('Handelspolitik gentemot U-länder' in *U-hjälp i utveckling?* Stockholm, 1969, p. 85) points out that this decline has been balanced as far as the underdeveloped countries are concerned by a gradual improvement in the quality of manufactured goods.

Accordingly, the apparently 'generous' concessions by the developed countries to modify or eventually remove the import restrictions on primary commodities will not substantially improve the export situation of underdeveloped countries; partly because the remaining, often considerable, excise duties tend to discourage the increased consumption of these commodities. The whole fabric of international trade works against the interests of the underdeveloped countries. The principles of equal treatment and mutual advantage are only fair if the economic potential of the contracting parties is more or less the same. But this is certainly not the case with the usual reciprocal trade agreements between developed and underdeveloped countries. Quite to the contrary, in return for the doubtful advantage of a slight increase in the exports of their primary commodites, usually at declining real prices, the latter have to guarantee the manufacturers of the former a preferential position on their domestic market at world market prices.

Since its first conference in 1964, UNCTAD (explicitly established to support the trade position of the poor countries) has strongly opposed the present form of reciprocal trade and recommended that international trade agreements should at least entitle the underdeveloped nations to import manufactured goods from other underdeveloped countries. Although this is unlikely to seriously impair their industrial exports, not all developed countries fully agree to such a change in trade policy. Their evasive attitude towards this and other proposals that would increase the foreign-exchange receipts of underdeveloped countries was one of the principal reasons for the unfortunate atmosphere and final fiasco of the 1968 UNCTAD Conference in New Delhi.*

This 'improvement', however, is viewed too much in the light of Western situations, for the technical development is dictated by Western requirements and does not necessarily meet the true needs of the underdeveloped world.

For an emphatic vindication of the mutual profitability of the international division of labour, see J. Viner, 'Gains from Foreign Trade', in *International Trade and Economic Development* (Oxford, 1957).

* See United Nations, UNCTAD, *Trade Expansion and Economic Cooperation Among Developing Countries*. Report of the Committee of Experts (Geneva, 1966).

G. Myrdal, *The Challenge of World Poverty: A World Anti-Poverty Program in Outline* (New York, 1970), chap 9, deals extensively with the issues of the Second UNCTAD Conference in New Delhi, 1968.

Yet, it is difficult to imagine that even the establishment of regional markets will in fact substantially increase and accelerate the export of manufactured goods from underdeveloped countries, unless it is supported by a structure of tariffs which, on the one hand, facilitates the intra-regional exchange of goods and, on the other, reduces or, still better prevents, the imports of competitive Western manufactured goods. Without the protection of such a strong external tariff there is neither the time nor occasion for regional planning, and regional industrial integration and the regional markets are bound to remain associations of the poor. But it is precisely this change in the tariff structure that meets with strongest opposition in the developed countries. The spokesmen for the large exporters of manufactured goods continue to advocate low common external tariffs and maintain that 'any protectionist attitude towards foreign investment in order to preserve the prerogatives of domestic entrepreneurs would be a mistake'.*

This is clearly evident in Africa where new regional markets have been established both for the former British-controlled territories of Kenya, Uganda and Tanganyika and for former French colonies in Central Africa. But, like the colonial markets of the past, they are based on the free import of foreign manufactured goods, and contribute little to accelerating the rate of industrial growth in the countries concerned, thus ultimately serving instead the economic interests of the former colonial powers. The same is largely true of the economic cooperation between Latin American countries, which is limited by the activities of the Organization of American States whose policy is determined by the economic and political interests of the United States. In fact, most of the existing market agreements between underdeveloped countries (with the exception, perhaps, of the Indian—United Arab Republic—Yugoslavian Trade Agreement) are exposed to neo-colonial pressures that cannot but retard for a long time to come the economic diversification and overall development of the countries concerned. Furthermore, the establishment of such regional markets is rendered more difficult by the fact that some underdeveloped countries have become associated with the regional markets of the developed countries like the European Common

* J. K. Javits, 'Urgencies in Latin America. Last Chance for a Common Market', *Foreign Affairs*, vol. 45, no. 3 (April 1967), pp. 449, 454, 458.

Market as have the overseas members of the French Union. The economic ties with the former colonial powers are still so overwhelmingly strong that it is difficult to conceive how the former colonies, particularly in South Asia and Africa, can possibly avoid yielding to economic pressures from the Western world. By tradition, their entire business and trading is directed towards the West and, given the growing Western participation in their foreign trade, it is no wonder that intra-regional trade relations are suffering. A recent survey in Asia reveals, in fact, that of the total of manufactured exports, intra-regional trade accounted for 40.2 per cent in 1955–56, but only 26.4 per cent in 1964–65; while the proportions for primary commodities declined from 26.9 to 23.1 per cent.*

True, it is now almost universally agreed that increased intra-regional trade would be an effective means of stimulating economic growth. But considering that the very sluggishness of intra-regional trade is due largely to the slow economic growth in underdeveloped countries, economic diversification and gradual industrialization become prerequisites, neither of which can be achieved without a thaw in the frozen agrarian structure and the reorganization of what are still virtually colonial trade patterns. Insofar as the latter is concerned the removal of the differential tariffs still commonly applied by the industrialized countries to imports of tropical products, is of particular importance because these tariffs are raised almost automatically with any increase in processing and accordingly constitute a formidable obstacle to increasing the alternative employment possibilities in the rural areas of the producer countries. Although time and again the negative effect of differential tariffs upon industrial development in backward areas has been recognized by GATT, its recommendations for customs regulations hardly take this problem into account. And this despite the fact that other international organizations are fully aware of the negative effect of differential tariffs on development planning in underdeveloped countries.†

* *Economic Survey of Asia and the Far East 1967* (UN, Bangkok, 1968), pp. 36 ff. and tables.

† See A. Boerma, 'Trade and Aid', *Mediterranea, Révue des Problèmes Agronomiques Mediterraneens*, no. 23–24 (July-August 1968), p. 440; and the Report of the Secretary-General of UNCTAD, *Towards a Global Strategy of Development* (UN, New York, 1968).

What applies to tariff regulations applies with equal force to the high prices of Western consumer goods in underdeveloped countries which are felt most keenly by the peasants. As a rule, the distribution channels for the limited variety of often inferior manufactured goods, imported by monopolistic enterprises, is controlled by powerful trading groups like the Chinese in large areas of South Asia.

The post-war rate of agricultural development and industrialization in underdeveloped countries has been far too slow to counteract the powerful internal and external forces which still continue to control land, markets, credit and labour; nor has it been able to mobilize the peasant populations to break the stagnation and backwardness of the irrational and retrograde system of agriculture. Considering the problems touched upon in this chapter, one might justly ask whether the aid extended to underdeveloped countries is anywhere comparable to the profits made by the donor countries through their favoured position in international trade. If we add to this the deterioration of the terms of trade for primary commodities and the decline in regional trading, it becomes unmistakably clear that the underdeveloped countries are the losers in the game of international trade. The current discussion on 'Trade or Aid' is therefore often misleading. The real problem is not the *amount of aid* required to neutralize the unfortunate effects of the prevailing trade patterns but a *change in trade relations* which will promote development in underdeveloped countries and make possible the agrarian reconstruction which is so urgently needed.

Multilateral and Bilateral Technical Assistance and Aid

More than two decades ago, the United Nations, aware of the necessity of improving conditions in large parts of the world, put into practice the concept of *Technical Assistance*, that is to say, the organized transfer of capital and technical skills from the rich to the poor countries. But this concept, based on the conviction that the transfer of capital and know-how will, without fail, accelerate development, has in practice ignored the fact that the prevailing social structure in the majority of underdeveloped countries is often the real reason for their predicament.

Technical Assistance, whether in the form of multilateral programmes handled by the United Nations organizations in cooperation with the World Bank Group, or of bilateral programmes designed and implemented by individual donor countries, concentrated from the very beginning on promoting economic growth and was usually limited to certain well-defined projects. Outside financial assistance, when limited to development of the natural resources which almost everywhere are owned, or at least controlled, by a few powerful groups, entails the preservation of the existing, defective, agrarian system; failure to recognize this fact has not only defeated the very purpose of Technical Assistance, but has frequently even reduced the share of the bulk of the people in the national income. The overall effect of Technical Assistance, therefore, has been disappointing and it has hardly achieved more than superficial corrections and adjustments to the economic structure in underdeveloped countries. By ignoring the fundamental issue of shifting the control of agricultural resources and thereby changing the quality of the rural society, Technical Assistance has developed into yet another powerful external force affecting the man-land relationship—in this case by neglecting it.

It is high time that an attempt is made to single out for intensive analysis the true reasons why United Nations Technical Assistance and bilateral aid, the efforts of the developed world, have achieved so little, despite sincere devotion and some noteworthy success here and there. It is our hope that such an analysis will also help to formulate the guidelines for a new development policy, so eagerly sought after by the younger generations in developed and underdeveloped countries alike.

Within a few years of its inception Technical Assistance had developed into a huge machine designing and implementing programmes to mitigate the crucial state of affairs in a world divided between affluence and misery by providing the means to hasten development and forestall the economic effects of the population explosion and the threatening social and political disintegration. In order to attain this end, however, Technical Assistance efforts ought to have been centred on preparing the transition to a quality of society that would enable the underdeveloped countries to determine their own relations with other economic systems and thus gradually undo the prevailing economic dependence and backwardness. Most important of all, they ought to have avoided any semblance to the pre-war colonial policy that promoted resource development in the interests of the 'mother country'.

Unfortunately, however, this was not to be the case, and even today the majority of Technical Assistance programmes represent the purely symptomatic approach to development based upon simple input-output relations which necessarily disregard the non-economic factors. Such a narrow approach is useful to a limited extent but it cannot remedy the distorted economic and social balance in backward societies and instil even that minimum of confidence in the people which would enable them to take the risk of making decisions for their own future. Recently Technical Assistance planners seem to attach greater importance to the question of multilateral versus bilateral aid. We will deal more extensively with this problem later on, and at this point only state that contrary to general belief, it has become less important since multilateral programmes have been exposed to increasing economic pressures both with regard to selection and planning.

Before analysing Technical Assistance as a powerful external force, it may be useful to briefly describe the particular structure and policy of the principal United Nations organizations that channel multilateral aid to underdeveloped countries. Given the particular background of these organizations, it is no wonder that their notions on development are frequently marked by fundamental ideological, professional and political divisions which cannot but influence the final formulation and execution of the aid programmes and the coordination of efforts.

The most influential and authoritative of the international bodies is the *International Bank for Reconstruction and Development* (IBRD) also called the *World Bank*. With a working capital, provided by non-socialist governments from all over the world on a shareholder basis, it functions like an immense private banking institution extending long-term loans at more or less conventional rates of interest for such projects as it considers essential for development. About one-third of the total is used for power generation, another third for the expansion of public transport, while only a part of the remaining third goes to improvements in agriculture. Closely connected with the World Bank, together with which they form the *World Bank Group,* are the *International Development Association* (IDA), which provides credit for long-term development projects at much more favourable terms than those of the World Bank; and the *International Finance Corporation* (IFC), which concentrates on investments in the private sector without requesting government guarantees.* Whereas in other UN organizations all member countries are represented by one vote, underdeveloped countries have only 35 per cent of the votes in the World Bank Group and the International Monetary Fund, where voting power is weighed according to the capital contributed. This means, in effect, that their participation in decision-making is very limited precisely in those organizations which are most important to development. During the past decade the World Bank has worked in close cooperation with other UN agencies, and particularly with FAO and UNESCO.

The *Food and Agriculture Organization* (FAO), to whose working budget all countries in the world contribute except China, the USSR and a few others, handles the largest number of all United Nations Technical Assistance programmes. From the very beginning it has concentrated almost exclusively on agricultural resource development and despite repeated assertions in recent years that it considers rural welfare to be a major requirement for agricultural development, programmes focused on institutional improvements like land reform, agricultural credit, cooperatives and education still rate relatively low among FAO activities. This is due partly to the preponderance of technicians on the FAO staff, but above all to the recipient governments themselves, who are not only fascinated by grandiose multi-purpose projects, but are often reluctant to request Technical Assistance in the sensitive fields of land reform and socio-economic improvements, let alone to follow up suggestions in these fields with proper action. Thus it would be unfair to blame FAO too much for choosing the path of

* Julius Nyerere, President of Tanzania, once stated that the International Finance Corporation appears to demand as a condition for their participation in a scheme that private, preferably local, enterprise should be partners and that in many countries this demand effectively prevents their assistance from being of any use. 'We do not wish to create a class of entrepreneurs', he said, 'especially when we do not at present have any'. *McDougal Memorial Lecture* (FAO, Rome, November 1963), p. 14.

least resistance; its very existence, and the popularity of its leadership, depend upon the consent of the majority of member countries and accordingly its hands are tied—at least to a certain extent.

The increasing number of new nation states and the growing awareness of the urgent need for agricultural development as a means of fighting hunger, misery and dissatisfaction in the underdeveloped world, have caused an unparalleled expansion of FAO during the past decade; this expansion, however, seems to have restricted rather than widened its capacity for independent action. For new activities, like the 'Freedom from Hunger Campaign', outside financial support had to be solicited. Close cooperation was established with large industrial and commercial enterprises in the Western world and soon became an integral part of FAO policy. This, however, has not only increased the predominance of capital intensive projects financed by the World Bank Group, but has actually introduced a significant degree of donor bias into FAO programmes. As a matter of fact, the influence of commercial interests is well on its way to reducing that very impartiality of multilateral aid which should safeguard its freedom of action in underdeveloped countries.

It may be argued, of course, that the cooperation of advanced industries will greatly speed up agricultural development by contributing otherwise inaccessible technical equipment and know-how. Yet, considering the matter more closely, it seems as if FAO went beyond its pledged responsibility towards underdeveloped countries when it established the FAO/Industry Cooperative Programme* which, among other things, undertakes:

(a) to implement FAO's pre-investment field work jointly with Industry and Governments by mobilizing managerial ability, scientific and technical competence and capital resources;

(b) to assist Industry and Governments in implementing project proposals initiated by them;

(c) to organize country reviews and missions jointly with Industry in order to clarify and, if possible, improve the climate for cooperation with foreign enterprises in developing countries and to identify priority projects in the FAO sector as proposed by Member Governments;

(d) to exchange technical and economic information on development activities, and to cooperate in research, demonstration and training programmes.

* United Nations, FAO, *Memorandum on FAO/Industry Cooperative Program* (WS/57103, Rome, 15 March 1967).

The final objective of this programme is expressed with un-mistakable clarity in the following paragraph:

> The cooperative effort between FAO and major international firms is aimed at the expansion of industries related to agricultural production and distribution in the developing countries, thus to assist and collaborate in the creation of new industries for which the General Committee of the FAO/Industry Cooperative Programme has a special knowledge, and to persuade the Governments of the developing countries to remove the obstacles to the fulfilment of this objective. Acceleration of capital investment and active industrial participation in the developing world are vital elements for increased productivity and employment opportunities.

In other words, through their representatives on the General Committee of the FAO/Industry Cooperative Programme, a hand-picked group of large industrial enterprises has been given the opportunity not only for participating actively in FAO-sponsored industrial schemes in underdeveloped countries, but also for gaining valuable advance information on forthcoming investment opportunities. This is clearly evident from paragraph nine of the Memorandum:

> About 40% of the pre-investment projects which Governments request within the UN Development Program (UNDP) are being carried out by FAO. The FAO/Industry Cooperative Program is advising General Committee members of the guide-lines of the UNDP for examining and evaluating Government requests, and of ways and means of close cooperation between UNDP/FAO and Industry. As a result of the cooperative agreements of FAO with the International Bank for Reconstruction and Development (IBRD), with regional development banks (such as IDB), and with Industry, efforts are being increasingly made to identify and prepare projects which offer possibilities for capital investment, either during their execution or as follow-up immediately after their termination.

The Fifth Session of the General Committee (now comprising representatives of not less than seventy-five of the developed world's leading industrial and commercial enterprises) in the spring of 1969, underscored the increasing influence of the FAO/Industry Cooperative Programme not only on FAO activity but on the entire UN-Technical Assistance policy. It was pointed out, among other things, that: the United Nations Development Programme (UNDP) has decided that the ideas of industry may play a part in its projects, provided that there is government support and FAO technical approval; and that the experiences gained in 1968 reveal that the emphasis has changed in the Programme's project work to industry-initiated ideas.*

It is certainly the undisputed right of the industrial and commercial enterprise to use their seat on the General Committee as an opportunity to pursue their legitimate business interests, but it cannot be denied that their influence on the entire Technical Assistance programme must discredit the very concept of multilateral assistance and place it on a footing with bilateral aid. The position of large business enterprises in the 'soft' economic systems of underdeveloped countries will be further strengthened by their close cooperation with international organizations, as it will help them to obtain valuable first-hand information on eventual plans for nationalization or changes in foreign exchange and trade regulations.

It is a logical consequence of this policy that six large private

* See United Nations, FAO, *Summary Record of the Fifth Session of the General Committee, FAO/Industry Cooperative Program* (IP:G/69/13, Rome, May 1969). At this session the Director-General of FAO stated that 'the evolution that had taken place in the thinking of the Industry Program during last year, which led to a new policy, developed in cooperation with UNDP, of formulating preinvestment projects likely to be of interest to industry in such a way as to attract investment'. An interesting illustration of this statement is contained in para. 22 of the *Summary Record* which gives the background to a cooperative project idea developed by Alfa-Laval AB. This important Swedish enterprise, which supplies a wide range of plant and equipment for the food-processing industries and provides technical advice on how to erect the plants and set up associated training and marketing, had presented a project concerning the modernization of the Tunisian olive-oil industry. At first, neither FAO nor the Swedish International Development Authority (SIDA) considered that it should be given any kind of priority, but, 'after Alfa-Laval had drawn the attention of the FAO/Industry Cooperative Program to its interest in this kind of project, as they are one of the main producers of modern olive-oil mills, the project was evaluated anew. At a meeting at the beginning of December 1968, between SIDA representatives, the Director of the Program and representatives of Alfa-Laval, SIDA agreed in principle to adopt the project and also to consider substantial extension into the field of cooperative marketing'. In February 1969, a preparatory mission was sent to Tunisia and the forthcoming discussions between SIDA and FAO on this mission's report will probably lead to concrete measures of implementation.

international banks, among them the Chase Manhattan Bank, Barclays Bank Ltd and the Swedish Skandinaviska Banken, formed a cooperative banking group in June 1970 for the purpose of advising FAO as to which of its agricultural projects are economically most promising. Once again, there is little doubt that 'economically promising' in this context can only mean *commercially promising*.

In other United Nations agencies, like the International Labour Organization (ILO) and the United Nations Educational, Scientific, and Cultural Organization (UNESCO), the voice of the underdeveloped countries carries somewhat greater weight. But due to the financial dependence of these agencies on contributions from the developed world, it is still not strong enough to influence the general direction of the policy of these organizations. This holds true particularly for UNCTAD,* an organ of the United Nations General Assembly, whose demands and recommendations for changes in international trade practices in favour of the underdeveloped countries have encountered various kinds of opposition from the majority of the developed world, which prefers the more moderate GATT (General Agreement on Tariffs and Trade) regulations as a basis for international trade cooperation. Although UNCTAD has no Technical Assistance programme of its own, the substantial contribution by its former Secretary-General, Paul Prebisch, to the analysis of the complex relationship between aid, trade and development deserves notice in this context.

In his report to the First Session of UNCTAD in Geneva 1964,† Raul Prebisch gives a lucid description of the impact of international trade on the economy of underdeveloped countries and of the palliative nature of the remedies adopted. The defeat of essential UNCTAD recommendations was due partly to organizational difficulties but principally to indifference on the part of the developed countries. If only they had been willing, they could easily have prevented the transfer of financial resources to the underdeveloped world diminishing in relation to the gross national product of developed countries. In his honest appraisal of the Second UNCTAD Conference in New Delhi 1968, Prebisch states that 'it seems that prosperity, in people as well as in nations, tends

---

* E. M. Chossudovsky, 'UNCTAD and Co-existence: Part One— From Geneva to New Delhi', *Co-Existence*, vol. 6, no. 2 (July 1969).
† *Towards a New Trade Policy for Development.*

to form an attitude of detachment if not indifference to the well-being of others', and that 'developed countries, with a few exceptions, continue to cónsider the development problem as a residual one that can be tackled here and there with a few and insufficient measures instead of bold and resolute action'.*

It cannot be denied that the first Development Decade fell far short of its main objectives and that the land problem is still the most formidable obstacle to development in large parts of the world. In view of the continued and accelerating adversity in the terms of trade which affects the underdeveloped countries, the boycott by the developed world of the series of concrete measures suggested by the Second UNCTAD Conference to accelerate the rate of economic and social growth in these countries is past comprehension.† The failure of UNCTAD, however, is also partly due to the lack of cooperation between the underdeveloped countries themselves and the failure of the responsible international agencies to establish regional and inter-regional institutions that would strengthen their bargaining capacity.

Prebisch indicates the need for such action and emphasizes that measures for a global strategy of development must be taken jointly by developed *and* underdeveloped countries. The developed countries should increase their financial contributions and improve the terms of trade for primary commodities while the underdeveloped countries should endeavour to mobilize their own resources in order to promote their own growth. But this implies that they will have 'to introduce deep reforms in their economic and social structures, modify their attitudes and policies and follow the reasonable discipline of a sound development plan'. And he notes with concern that great resistance to such a global strategy is encountered not only in the developed countries but also within the underdeveloped countries themselves.

* United Nations, UNCTAD, *The Significance of the Second Session of UNCTAD*. Report by the Secretary-General of UNCTAD to the Secretary-General of the United Nations (TD/96, Geneva, 7 May 1968).
† Despite repeated requests, the governments of the European Common Market have not yet joined the International Sugar Conference and continue to export a surplus of about 900,000 tons of sugar beet in hard competition with the sugar-cane exports of the underdeveloped countries.

The failure of the Second UNCTAD Conference and the analysis of the situation contained in the report of this conference strengthens our conviction that development efforts would be far more effective if an attempt was made to understand the basic problem of Technical Assistance: it is as difficult to convince the governments of underdeveloped countries of the need for structural changes and new institutions as it is to persuade the rich nations to carry out an effective and purposeful aid policy orientated towards improvements in the quality of society.

In recent times, it has become fashionable to put the blame for the failures of Technical Assistance on organizational short-comings of the international agencies,* while in fact it is the political and economic pressure exerted upon them which prevents them attacking the very essence of backwardness, and from becoming a strong progressive force that would be able to overcome the obstacles to socio-economic development and finally break the resistance of the *status quo*.

It is typical of the current operational approach to under-development, that attempts are made to establish aid policy as a proper science based on one particular model for economic development. These attempts, however, are bound to fail since the existing variety of 'developed economies' makes it virtually impossible to design *one* model as the blessed path to progress.

The so-called *aid relationship*,† considered the key issue in Technical Assistance by several Western experts, is in reality nothing but the complex interaction of causal factors that decide any other major policy. The model used to define this aid relationship, however, is based on the fallacious assumption that donor and recipient countries deal with one another on equal terms. And this despite a general recognition of the fact that the governments of underdeveloped countries are seldom representative of the populations, or of the national interest in economic and social development, but generally represent only the numerically small groups which wield the economic and political power. In contrast to the truly representative governments of the donor countries, or to the policy boards of the international organizations, which

* See United Nations, Dept. of Ec. and Soc. Affairs, *A Study of the Capacity of the United Nations Development System* (The Jackson Report), vols. 1 and 2 (Geneva, 1969).

† A. Krassowski, *The Aid Relationship* (London, 1968).

evince a large measure of homogeneity with regard to both outlook and action, the weakness of government structure in recipient
countries will allow separate and often conflicting forces to interfere in the aid relationship. This will inevitably discredit the
'neutrality' of aid, and make Technical Assistance appear as a
buttress of the *status quo.**

In the current catalogue of suggestions for international
assistance, project aid and programme aid top the list. While the
former requires a relatively high degree of effective control by the
donor country or organization, the latter implies rather a vote of
confidence in the recipient country and the assumption that it
will make proper use of the support given. Experience has proved,
however, that a realistic aid policy ought to be based on a proper
combination of both types of aid.

It cannot be denied, however, that donor countries generally
prefer aid tied to specific projects since it entails the purchase of
machinery and capital goods. This, of course, may have the unfortunate effect of inducing the recipient country to import goods
that are useful only in supporting the project or, as an Indian
observer states, of encouraging it to set up prestige industries
which may not always satisfy the criteria of priority.† From the
viewpoint of this study, however, the thing that needs to be
stressed is that it is not the type of aid programme that is of
fundamental importance for its ultimate effect but its content and
direction.

Since the true objective of Technical Assistance is to bring about
revolutionary changes by evolutionary means, it must necessarily
be provocative. But given the formidable resistance of the prevailing institutions and entrenched interests generally in control of
government and administration in underdeveloped countries, one
may question whether current Technical Assistance is really the
correct means for bringing about the needed economic and social
changes.

* See G. C. Lodge, 'U.S. Aid to Latin America: Funding Radical
Change', *Foreign Affairs*, vol. 47, no. 4 (July 1969), pp. 734 ff., 738.
† From a statement by Morarji Desai, former Minister of Finance,
quoted in *The Indian and Foreign Review*, vol. 6, no. 1 (15.10.1968),
p. 19.

In large parts of the underdeveloped world the bulk of the population is rather sceptical of socio-economic programmes; they have lived in isolation for such a long time, economically tied to their masters, that familiar traditions and institutions, burdensome as they may be, give them a feeling of security. In their experience, innovations have mostly implied a change for the worse and it would be unjust to blame them for *not* understanding that to safeguard this security perpetuates stagnation and misery. But the situation may appear in quite a different light when agrarian restlessness and political insecurity shake the stability of the existing order. Provided that they do not receive moral and material support from abroad, even powerful groups may be willing to make concessions for fear of jeopardizing their political and economic position, as was the case in Peru in the summer of 1969. Given the open, or at least latent, restlessness in the underdeveloped world and the potential readiness of its ruling groups to compromise under difficult circumstances, a Technical Assistance orientated towards true development and not only growth could become a most valuable instrument for breaking down the walls of prejudice and outdated values which landlords and tribal chiefs ingeniously use to strengthen the peasants' fear of social change.

But instead of using their strategic position to this end, Technical Assistance programmes continue to attach the greater importance to purely physical development and thus reinforce rather than reduce the forces defending the *status quo*.

Assistance for multi-purpose projects, fertilizer and pesticide factories, and expensive mechanization schemes are still the preferred activities of both the World Bank and individual donor countries. This one-sided emphasis on capital-intensive, long-term investment projects, however, is often at variance with the true needs of underdeveloped countries because of the extremely limited overall effect in areas with low levels of education and outdated agrarian structures. The impressive Ganges-Kobadek irrigation scheme in Pakistan clearly illustrates the shortcomings of a costly resource development project that omits to take institutional factors into consideration. Although the new dam provided an abundant supply of water, the large landowners did not expand crop cultivation as much as was anticipated, for fear of eventual land reform; while the tenants who under the present institutional arrangements do not benefit by growing a second crop, often refused to pay the additional water rates. The latter, in fact, were disproportionately high because excessive fragmentation of holdings had added considerably to the costs of constructing the feeder canals. If a land consolidation scheme had been carried out prior to or even concurrently with the construction of the irrigation system, the water rates would have become cheaper and this alone would have given the whole project a better start.

Another interesting example is the Technical Assistance extended to the UAR some years ago for the widespread use of pesticides in the cotton fields. Despite heavy capital investment in equipment, the programme not only failed to increase the cotton yields but may even have been largely responsible for the catastrophic crop failures in 1965 and 1966: firstly, because officials diluted pesticides intended for distribution among the peasants and sold the surplus on the black market; and secondly, because the programme did not include an efficient extension service to teach the inexperienced and illiterate peasants how to apply the chemical. The inefficacy of this costly programme actually calls into question the feasibility of introducing advanced techniques in an environment that lacks both administrative maturity and practical experience. It is of interest to note in this context that in 1967 the Minister of Agriculture and Land Reform successfully fought the cotton pest by a kind of public works programme which organized effective teams of surplus manpower which followed the proven method of picking the infected buds off the plants by hand.

What applies to the selection of projects, applies with equal if not greater force to the selection of field staff and experts. Most donor countries are inclined to select the experts for their bilateral Technical Assistance programmes from amongst their own nationals. The average Western economist or technician, however, seldom has the training and experience needed for work in underdeveloped countries and is accustomed to think in terms of input-output relations and applied technology rather than in terms of socio-economic development. In theory, United Nations organizations are not bound by national considerations in selecting experts, but in practice they are often faced with the problem of resentment against certain nationalities in recipient countries. But that is not all. Frequently professionally the best qualified candidate for a field post is a former colonial administrator whose wealth of experience, however valuable, often proves to be an obstacle rather than an advantage, unless he realizes that the United Nations expert has quite different responsibilities. Whereas the colonial administrator had the authority to command obedience and was trained to administer his territory with the minimum of active participation on the part of the local population, the Technical Assistance expert must make a serious effort to ensure the cooperation of the people and show them the way to self-determination and decision-making. In addition, a former colonial administrator will be faced with the almost superhuman task of proving to the people that he has not returned as the old master but is determined to remedy the defects of a society which he himself has helped to create.

Some ten years ago, the United Nations established a particular kind of Technical Assistance service (OPEX) in underdeveloped countries. The foreign experts employed by this service not only advise the governments but personally take an active part in the day to day administrative work, in order to increase the efficiency of the staff. Yet, the OPEX experiment is not as successful as might have been expected; for one thing because the more highly qualified and better paid foreign expert seldom succeeds in really becoming part of the administrative machinery, and for another, because the very administration to which he is assigned is frequently on the defensive against any socio-economic changes that he may suggest.

In order to prove that Technical Assistance is not the 'White Man's monopoly', UN agencies are recruiting numbers of experts from underdeveloped countries, preferably civil servants from India, Pakistan, Ceylon and the Sudan, but also young professionals trained in British and American universities. It may be open to doubt whether this recruitment policy will actually change the 'Western' outlook of Technical Assistance, but one thing is certain: the added 'brain drain' can only seriously damage the development efforts in these experts' own countries. The general shortage of qualified people, combined with the fact that it is the most efficient, and also often the most progressive, who are offered UN posts, will inevitably help to weaken the emergence of proficient administration in underdeveloped countries.

In contrast to the colonial civil service which was based on homogeneous staffs and relatively permanent appointments in a particular area, service in Technical Assistance is marked by a lack of continuity and consistency. Teams of experts are sent out for relatively short periods of service and given their international composition, it is only natural that the members differ in their approach to the task in hand according to their cultural background and values, experience and training.

Another serious problem engendered by the very concept of Technical Assistance is the relationship between donor and recipient countries. In the case of bilateral programmes, the position of the donor country is generally so strong that no strings need be attached to the aid extended. The very conception of bilateral assistance has a built-in bias in favour of the donor country and, in the case of long-term programmes, inevitably causes the dependence of the recipient country.* Multilateral programmes, on the other hand, *originally* entailed the exact opposite. As long as the UN agencies provided technical advice only, and were not engaged in the actual transfer of capital or commodities, the recipient countries were still in a position to voice their opinion and be exacting in their demands in UN councils and committees. The increasing influence of private industry and commerce in the sphere of Technical Assistance, however, is well on the way to destroying the fundamental difference between bilateral and multilateral aid.

The Technical Assistance relationship takes on a particular nature when a recipient country has at its disposal large capital resources derived from the exploitation of oil or mineral deposits. In order to obtain technical advice, say for agricultural development, they place considerable cash deposits in trust with international organizations like FAO for the implementation of Technical

---

* F. H. Golay (*The Philippines: Public Policy and National Economic Development*, Ithaca, N.Y., 1968, p. 125) states that the specific placement of financial assistance is rarely related to purely economic considerations and that the distribution of aid appropriation (in this case, from the USA) seems to reflect strategic and political rather than economic considerations.

Assistance programmes. Experience has proved, however, that it is difficult to implement an effective Technical Assistance programme when donor and the recipient country is one and the same. The financial strength of the recipient country reduces the authority and freedom of action of the agency concerned since its political and commercial interests are likely to interfere in the selection of experts as well as in actual planning and implementation.

The nature of economic life, which also governs the operation of Technical Assistance, has led to a close cooperation between the developed countries and the politically powerful and economically strong groups in the underdeveloped countries. We need only take as an example the large coffee planters in Brazil and Guatemala who have undoubtedly strengthened their own economic and political position through Technical Assistance efforts. The similiarity to the indirect rule of the former colonial powers is obvious. To an increasing extent Technical Assistance, and particularly bilateral aid, has become an instrument through which the industrialized nations exercise economic and, consequently, political influence in backward countries. Not necessarily solely through princes and tribal chiefs but through the powerful landlords and plantation owners who benefit most, and thus have become suitable partners with considerable influence upon the programmes. This also partly explains the negative attitude of both donor and recipient countries to structural reforms, since any change in the prevailing socio-economic setup in underdeveloped countries would endanger the continuation of this profitable relationship.

A most serious side-effect of bilateral as well as multilateral credit programmes is the problem of the increasing accumulation of debt and service cost on public and publicly guaranteed external loans to underdeveloped countries. Recent statistics on World Bank activities in seventy-nine underdeveloped countries* clearly reflect the dimensions of this problem; from the end of 1961 to the end of 1967, the outstanding external public debt increased by 114 per cent from $21.6 billion to $46.2 billion and rose by another $1.3 billion during the first half of 1968 to a total of

* IBRD, *World Bank and International Development Association, Annual Report, 1969*, tables 4 ff. and former Annual Reports.

$47.5 billion. During the same period estimated interest and amortization payments increased by about 74 per cent to slightly more than $4 billion in 1968. Considering that most under-developed countries have contracted numerous other medium and short-term obligations, either in the form of suppliers' credits or of purely commercial, often speculative loans, the global figure for outstanding debt-service payments must be much higher. During the past few years the most rapid increase in public debt-service payments was reported for Africa and South Asia, while a certain let up was noticed in Latin America, largely due to a re-scheduling of the terms for Argentina, Brazil and Chile.

Whereas in the mid-1950s the average service payments on the external government debts of underdeveloped countries accounted for less than 4 per cent of their exports of goods, the ratio in 1968 was 21.6 per cent for India (as against 12.6 per cent in 1961) and as high as 26.4 per cent for Argentina despite a slight decrease of 0.2 per cent on the preceding year. For Brazil it was 20.3 per cent (30.4 per cent in 1967), for Mexico 21.2 per cent and for Uruguay 30.4 per cent (as against 13.8 per cent in 1966). The World Bank calculates that, by 1970, the debt-service ratio for Pakistan will amount to about 20 per cent (1968: 18.8 per cent) in spite of that country's relatively fast rate of economic growth. Since this data includes neither unguaranteed export credits nor debts repayable at the option of the borrower in local currencies or commercial arrears, the total of debt-service payments in 1969 may well exceed the five-billion-dollar mark. It is obvious that debt-service liabilities of such magnitude will have detrimental effects not only for countries which have acquired excessive sup-pliers' credits or other loans at high interest rates, but indeed also for those which have followed a 'fairly cautious policy with regard to external debts'.* The interest costs of accumulated debt, have reached such critical proportions in a number of countries during the past decade that increasing rescheduling has taken place particularly since 1966. Where loans for development programmes are of old standing, debt-service ratios have risen to 15–20 per cent or more.

In its preparatory papers for the Delhi Conference in 1968, the

* From a statement by Irving S. Friedman, Economic Adviser to the President of the World Bank to the United Nations Economic and Social Council, Geneva, 13 July 1967.

UNCTAD Secretariat strongly emphasized the dangers of the dramatic increase in debt-service ratios.* In the years 1965 and 1966 public debt-service payments in 34 countries accounted for more than one-half of the external loans received by the public sector or guaranteed by a public authority. In 12 of the 34 countries, they even exceed total public loan disbursements. The time indeed seems far off, when economic growth in under-developed countries will be fast enough to close the gap between domestic savings and investments.† In the meantime, they may even have to ask for aid in order to repay aid.‡

Although the projection of debt-service payments due may be offset to some extent by rescheduling and/or an increase in grants, present trends indicate that they will rise in the aggregate from $4.0 billion in 1968 to close on $10 billion by 1975§ with a threefold increase for the countries of Africa and at least double the amount for South Europe, South Asia and the Middle East. For the Latin American countries whose service payments for 1966 were already higher than anywhere else, the projected increase for 1975 is as high as $1 billion. UNCTAD estimates, assuming an average annual rise in exports of 4 per cent during the projection period and unmodified average annual terms, that an overall average of 18 per cent of export earnings will be pre-empted by debt-service payments in 1975. This figure, how-

* *The Terms of Financial Flows and Problems of Debt-Servicing* (TD/7/supp. 3, 18.10.1967); and *The Outlook for Debt-Service* (TD/7/supp. 5, 31.10.1967).

† Thorkil Kristensen, the former Secretary-General of OECD, also touches upon this problem in 'The Food Problem of Developing Countries', *CERES, FAO Review*, vol. 1, no. 4 (1968), p. 13. His preference for private investment (conditions not mentioned!) rather than official loans, however, is inexplicable considering the political and economic weaknesses of many of the African, Asian and Latin American countries.

‡ See D. R. Gadgil, 'The Fourth Plan: Evolution of New Policy and Planning Strategy—II', *Indian and Foreign Review*, vol. 6, no. 5 (15.12.1968), p. 9.

§ In view of this trend, one may call into question the statement by Mr McNamara, the President of the World Bank, that most under-developed countries can afford the present high interest rate of 6½ per cent on the conventional hard loans issued by the Bank 'because of the high yield of most development projects, if selected carefully'. *New York Herald Tribune* (Paris edition, 27.9.1968).

ever, seems rather optimistic. Excluding the oil-exporting countries, the overall average would amount to as much as 23 per cent.*

In its Annual Report 1964–65 the World Bank stated correctly that part of the indebtedness problem is due to unwise borrowing and unwise lending. 'The trouble arises from high pressure salesmanship on the one side, often facilitated by abuse of export credit insurance, and the desire, on the other side, to avoid all the hard work of preparing and negotiating helpful projects. In these cases, large amounts of short- and medium-term indebtedness are taken on, although foreign exchange earnings are not likely to increase fast enough to meet quickly maturing repayments.' In a subsequent report† it quotes an interesting study prepared by members of its own staff, using these even stronger words in reviewing the problems arising from suppliers' credits. 'In some countries', it says, 'their excessive use has led to unduly high debt-service payments because of maturities considerably shorter than warranted by the country's position'. It then goes on to recommend 'that governments in debtor and creditor countries should assure that only economically sound projects were financed, that the terms were related to the life and productivity of the projects, and that the borrowing country's total capacity to service debt incurred for development should not be impaired'. The Report also advises the creditor countries to more carefully align their widely varying commercial and financial policies with respect to suppliers' credit—an unrealistic request, indeed, considering the relentless competition between export industries.

The close attention given by the World Bank to the banking aspects of the serious increase in the debt and service accumulation of underdeveloped countries is certainly worthy of praise and more careful banking practices and the rescheduling of debt payments may undoubtedly improve the situation. Yet, this does not touch upon the crux of the matter. Increasing external indebtedness in relation to foreign exchange earnings is not due primarily to defects in the debt structure. It is due rather to the fact that

* United Nations, UNCTAD, *Problems and Policies of Financing.* UNCTAD, Second Session, vol. 4 (TD/7, Geneva, 1968).
† IBRD, *World Bank and International Development Association. Annual Report 1966–67*, p. 32.

underdeveloped countries can never increase their productive capacity and foreign exchange earnings so long as the terms of trade are against them and, above all, so long as socio-economic development in general and the unwholesome man-land relationship in particular remain unsolved problems. Neither has received much more than a hand-out in the past be it through multilateral or bilateral programmes and despite some slight improvement in recent times, both are still neglected; as is evident from the following figures:* although in 1968–69 aggregate Bank loans and IDA credits amounted to a total of $1,784.25 million, only $367.30 million were extended to agriculture and $81.80 million to education. Not very impressive amounts, given the overwhelming need for assistance in precisely these two fields.† The World Bank Group remains reluctant to support programmes that may lead to changes in the institutional setup and, accordingly, there is reason to doubt whether any of the new agricultural credit projects totalling $69 million in Colombia, Pakistan, the Philippines and Senegal, will improve the agrarian situation in those countries to any noticeable extent.

It can no longer be denied that multilateral aid has lost its bearings and is reaching the point when larger programmes can only lead to larger failures. Yet, any reorganization of Technical Assistance will be worthwhile only if it leads to a greater understanding of the true reasons for past failures and draws realistic conclusions, inconvenient as they may seem. A reorientation is certainly needed in order to make Technical Assistance the effective tool for development it was originally intended to be and prevent it from assuming features that bring to mind the outdated colonial relationship.

Twenty years of partly frustrated development efforts should suffice to convince anybody concerned with Technical Assistance of the vital importance of the *non-economic factors* in the cumulative process of economic development and of the importance of

* IRBD, *World Bank and International Development Association, Annual Report, 1969*, pp. 10–11.

† Robert S. McNamara, President of the World Bank Group, 'Annual Address to the Board of Governors', *Summary Proceedings* (Washington, DC, 30 September-4 October, 1968, pp. 9 ff.) mentions that the Bank in future will shift a greater part of its resources to agriculture and education; yet, problems of agrarian structure were not mentioned in this context.

extending aid for resource development only if it is combined with socio-economic and structural reform programmes. Nothing less than the combination of institutional reforms and resource development can guarantee the success of Technical Assistance and refute the now famous statement that Technical Assistance is the aid which the poor people in rich countries extend to the rich people in poor countries!

The current re-examination of the entire Technical Assistance machinery, with its large multilateral and bilateral bureaucracies constantly competing with one another, could be a step in the right direction if it keeps in mind that Western history is to a large extent the history of economic and political revolutions. It would be a betrayal of the very foundations of Western prosperity if, motivated by convenience and vested interests, our highly developed societies were to endorse the fallacy that generous support to outdated economic and political systems can solve the problem of underdevelopment. From the viewpoint of historical and socio-economic experience Western development strategy is dilettante, and even irresponsible. Take only the construction of grain silos in Brazil with US aid, which should have improved the marketing opportunities of the peasants but instead reinforced the commanding position of the largest producers.*

The first and chief criterion for aid allocation should be the recipient country's readiness to improve the quality of society rather than maximize the returns per dollar of aid. Mere input-benefit calculations have an unfortunate tendency to confuse localized economic growth with overall development. The argument that any pressure in favour of socio-economic changes, whether brought to bear by the United Nations or by a donor country, is against the accepted rule of non-interference in a sovereign country's internal affairs seems equivocal, to say the least. International agencies and donor countries alike, refuse, almost as a matter of routine, to extend requested assistance or aid whenever the cost-benefit calculations seem too un-

* S. L. Barraclough, *Agricultural Policy and Strategies of Land Reform* (Social Science Institute, Washington University, St. Louis, Mo., 1969).

favourable to justify the investment. Even the statement* by Mr McNamara that the World Bank Group is inclined to consider the population problem in underdeveloped countries as worthy of assistance seems hardly less of an interference in internal affairs than would an emphasis upon structural reforms. The only difference is that the former in no way touches the established property rights of the ruling class. Accordingly, it could scarcely be accounted interference if United Nations Technical Assistance as well as individual donor countries were to include the recipient country's attitude to agrarian reforms since outdated tenure systems are a limiting factor for development. Technical Assistance agencies cannot force the issue, but they could certainly make up their minds to use the limited resources available primarily in those countries which declare themselves ready to make a serious attempt at improving the socio-economic conditions in agriculture.†

Such a new aid policy, however, will call for an entirely different approach to Technical Assistance operations. The large bureaucracies, now standardizing and adjusting multilateral and bilateral programmes to prevailing economic policies in donor and recipient countries, should be reorganized, or maybe even reduced. At the Overseas Study Conference in Cambridge, 1968, on 'The Rural Base for National Development' it was observed correctly that what is needed is a kind of 'guerrilla strategy' in preparing Technical Assistance programmes which will support the peasants and their organizations and make use of shortcuts whenever they promise faster results. Accordingly, priority should be given to programmes that will ultimately benefit the agricultural population in the recipient countries, even if this may entail a transition period of reduced activity. True, such an approach may also contain certain risks and sometimes even lead to failure; but the risks are calculated ones that must be taken in the interests of fast action. As to possible failures, one should not forget that

---

* Robert S. McNamara, 'Annual Address to the Board of Governors', op. cit., pp. 11 ff.
† In the summer of 1970, the Swedish Authority for International Development (SIDA) took a first step in this direction by informing the government of Ethiopia that it will terminate the large CADU development project unless the already drafted land reform legislation is passed by Parliament in the very near future.

F

present projects have certainly not got much to boast of in terms of successful overall development.*

It is inevitable that a Technical Assistance concept of this kind will meet with the disapproval of those groups in both donor and recipient countries who up till now have benefited the most. Yet a fair amount of honest information should suffice to demonstrate to the public in advanced countries that putting an end to misery and stagnation in backward areas can only benefit mankind throughout the world. Once this has been achieved even the ruling national élites in the recipient countries will understand that the sooner they stop opposing social progress the greater will be their chance of finding an acceptable place in a society which is inevitably changing.

A new Technical Assistance strategy, however, calls for a thorough revision of the present recruitment policy. Experts should no longer be chosen exclusively for their professional ability but also for their understanding of the problems of socio-economic development; without the latter, even the most excellent training is of little use. The combination of professional knowledge and social awareness on the part of the Technical Assistance experts will ensure a more homogeneous approach to the programmes and increased coordination at the various stages of implementation. Likewise, replacements for both field officers and expert teams should be chosen with a view to avoiding the present, often harmful succession of conflicting viewpoints within a single programme.

What applies to field experts applies equally to staff at headquarters. At present, far too many of the people responsible for recruiting and supervising field experts show greater concern for the administrative aspects of Technical Assistance than for the actual content and ultimate effect of the programmes upon the process of development. Accordingly, a number of officers,

---

* G. C. Lodge (in 'U.S. Aid to Latin America: Funding Radical Change', *Foreign Affairs*, loc. cit.), is naïve enough to suggest that United States bilateral assistance programmes for Latin American countries should be divided into two general categories: one should support the *status quo* like the old Alliance for Progress receiving 75 per cent of US aid, while the other, to be called the American Foundation, receiving the remaining 25 per cent, should work for *revolutionary changes* which are not likely to be welcomed by existing governments.

appointed to permanent key positions on the ground of social prestige or noteworthy administrative experience are actually against or, at best, indifferent to the very idea of socio-economic reforms. This lack of active sympathy necessarily affects the attitude of their colleagues, frustrates individual efforts and is often detrimental to the very objectives of the programmes.*

It may be objected that the changes suggested will reduce the volume of Technical Assistance for some time to come. But this need not necessarily be a disadvantage since, and this cannot be repeated often enough, it is the *quality*, and *not* the quantity, of the programmes which determines the role of Technical Assistance and aid. Accordingly, any constructive reorganization of Technical Assistance activities should be aimed at reducing the inflated number of programmes through an examination of their quality in the light of their ultimate effect upon *overall* development in underdeveloped countries.

Nonetheless, the recent harsh criticism† of Technical Assistance deliberately, as it seems, diverts public attention from the basic problem of Technical Assistance. It concentrates the attack upon the organizational and administrative shortcomings of intergovernmental agencies without weighing the only question that really matters, namely, whether the selection, planning and effect of current programmes are in accordance with the true needs of the underdeveloped world. Although the failure of the First Development Decade provides ample scope for criticizing the UN organizations, it cannot be denied that their overall performance has been considerably better than that of bilateral assistance programmes in general.

The suggested centralization of all Technical Assistance activity into one enormous bureaucracy can only multiply the mistakes of the past. By isolating multilateral Technical Assistance from the regular professional work of the specialized agencies, the projects will have to be farmed out to contracting agencies and firms whose legitimate business interests and connections frequently run

---

* At a most critical stage of land reform in Chile, a large landowner from Paraguay became the UN representative in Santiago. In many other countries, retired colonial and military officials still hold key positions in Technical Assistance programmes.

† In *A Study of the Capacity of the United Nations Development System* (The Jackson Report).

contrary to the needs of the bulk of the people in underdeveloped countries. From the point of view of overall development there is everything to be said for a fundamental reorientation of current efforts; but certainly not in the direction of the Jackson Report whose recommendations, in the final analysis, must lead to the further *commercialization of multilateral Technical Assistance*. All that can be said at the moment is that the suggested reorganization bodes ill not only for the effect of future aid policy but also for the entire relationship between the advanced industrialized nations and the underdeveloped agricultural countries.

We will now briefly outline some principles of a new concept of Technical Assistance which, considering the unique importance of the man-land relationship to the entire question of underdevelopment and backwardness, may be in greater harmony with the true needs of the Third World. It must first be stressed, however, that all of these principles are based on a fundamental prerequisite: Technical Assistance must be completely independent, and free from any organizational ties with private industrial and commercial interests. This is not to deny industry and business their legitimate place and profit in Technical Assistance programmes but rather to prevent Technical Assistance from giving industry and business an opportunity to expand their activities at the expense of the people in the underdeveloped countries.

1. Technical Assistance should be the chief weapon in a concerted effort by the developed world to put an end to the increasing economic and social misery of the peasants in underdeveloped countries, and should single out whatever means seem most likely to achieve this end.

2. Accordingly, Technical Assistance should aim at improving the socio-economic environment in general and the income-distribution pattern in particular. Given the prominent place of agriculture, it should give first priority to agrarian reform programmes, while resource development projects should serve mainly to enhance the effect of socio-economic changes.

3. The appraisal of proposed resource development projects should be focused on their possible effect on both social stratification and income distribution; and such a programme should not even be contemplated unless coordinated with institutional measures that

will guarantee the improved welfare of the largest possible number of people.

4. In order to ensure the cooperation of all parties concerned, and particularly in order to convince public opinion in both developed and underdeveloped countries of the over-riding importance of institutional and structural changes in backward agricultural areas, well-prepared and honest information should be disseminated on the content and objectives of Technical Assistance activities.

5. Obligatory training courses in the theory of socio-economic development and its practical application in underdeveloped countries should be organized for all Technical Assistance experts and supervisory staff.

6. With certain exceptions such as health control, distribution of food and medical supplies, veterinary assistance and localized research, no Technical Assistance and aid should be granted to underdeveloped countries unless their governments agree to implement the institutional reforms necessary to guarantee the greatest possible overall effect.

7. Finally, Technical Assistance should endeavour, as far as possible, to provide alternative investment and employment opportunities for those groups which will lose their present position and function in society through the socio-economic changes brought about by institutional and structural reforms.

Such a change of emphasis in Technical Assistance will have the effect of breaking the present sad relationship between the failure of Technical Assistance programmes and the defective agrarian structure in underdeveloped countries, and will turn Technical Assistance into a useful instrument for promoting development where it is needed most. Given the multifarious economic and political problems involved, only multilateral Technical Assistance will be in a position to assume the leadership in this crucial part of development strategy.

PART TWO

Programmes of Agrarian Reform

CHAPTER SIX

Land Redistribution -
The Determining Factor in the
Organization of Agriculture

An agrarian policy focused on the human factor does not necessarily have to follow a given pattern and its content and formulation should be determined by the specific conditions in the countries concerned. Accordingly, land reform and institutional changes should be planned in the light of the prevailing pressure on land, of alternatives open to crop patterns under the given soil and market conditions, of livestock production, and of the technical and social level of the rural population.

A thorough investigation of the socio-economic conditions surrounding the human factor in a definite area is just as necessary for institutional planning as is a resource survey for the planning of land and water development. Such an advance appraisal would establish, among other things, the extent to which the existing institutions and infrastructures support or prevent the access to, and effective use of, the available physical resources, and thus would not only clarify the actual position of the human factor but also reveal the reasons for the income distribution pattern in the area concerned. In short, it would provide the factual basis for a thorough understanding of agrarian situations that sooner or later stand in need of reform or development programmes. Recent history abounds in hastily and inadequately prepared agrarian reforms which, due to *lack of information*, not only failed to improve conditions but actually squandered human and material values and caused frustration, disillusion and often detrimental political reactions. It has been emphasized, rightly, that an advance appraisal should present the most radical solution that can be based on its findings.*

* By D. R. Gadgil at the Second Panel of Experts on Land Tenure and Settlement convened at FAO Headquarters, Rome, May 1969.

If a comparison is made between the various measures designed over the years to improve agrarian conditions, it will be seen that the *redistribution of land* is the most spectacular and effective of these, provided that it is accompanied by whatever reforms are necessary under the given circumstances. Time and again experience has proved the often tragic consequences of redistribution programmes that are confined to the mere distribution of public domain land and which completely ignore the vital problems of agricultural credit, infrastructures, soil improvement and access to markets. This is still the case, for example, in many countries of Latin America where the peasant families are left to fend for themselves and either slowly perish or move away, while the land reverts to jungle. It has been pointed out that it is inadvisable to redistribute public domain lands before industrial development gets under way since they have frequently been left in a virgin state because of their questionable fertility, their distance from markets, and the prevalence of bad weather and unhealthy living conditions. The large capital outlay required for settlement in such areas could be put to better use elsewhere in the economy.*

It is equally doubtful, however, whether the often recommended dissolution of large estates through a severe taxation policy is a desirable approach to land redistribution. For one thing, it would be difficult to enforce such a policy in areas where landlordism is powerful; and for another, even if such a taxation policy were feasible, the mere dissolution of large estates in an area does not guarantee the establishment of a land distribution pattern that will satisfy the needs of the people. The same holds true for the voluntary distribution of land in times when political instability holds the risk of imminent expropriation, as happened in Italy immediately after the war. In either case the redistribution is motivated by pressure on the land and may lead to an excessive fragmentation which, due to the still prevailing defective market conditions, will prevent the peasants from gaining more than a meagre subsistence despite their ownership of the land.

Accordingly, any purposeful redistribution of land must entail the redistribution of wealth, income, status, capacity for saving, and political influence which not only will provide incentives for

---

* See E. Flores, *Land Reform and the Alliance for Progress* (Center of International Studies, Princeton University, Policy Memorandum no. 27, 1963), pp. 8–9.

increased agricultural production and labour productivity but will strengthen the socio-economic position of the peasant population. In feudalistic environments where, in order to safeguard their political and economic control, the large landowners prevent or delay the development of institutions that may increase the bargaining power of the peasants, land reform programmes should give first priority to land redistribution through expropriation.

This is easier said than done, of course, and how to carry out the redistribution of land and subsequent reform programmes without actual revolution in those countries where landlordism is still so strong that it does not even have to make concessions to the emerging progressive forces is still an open question.

To make a sharp distinction between 'evolutionary' and 'revolutionary' land reforms in underdeveloped countries is a mistake which has led to the confused Western approach to land reform. Any changes in the agrarian structure are part of a socio-economic process that contains revolutionary elements which under certain circumstances move to the fore, while the lasting success of any agrarian revolution depends upon subsequent evolutionary developments. The events in Mexico in 1935–36, when President Cárdenas himself provided the peasants with 60,000 rifles and a number of military advisers to enforce a land redistribution law that had been constitutionally passed by Parliament, are an example of the former. In the Soviet Union, on the other hand, the revolutionary land redistribution was and still is followed up by legislative changes that do not differ essentially from an evolutionary land reform policy.

The entire problem would appear in a different light if one were to consider the 'relative speed' of reform programmes, and then decide whether they are part of the 'normal' range of 'evolutionary' changes or should rather be viewed as 'revolutionary'.* This would bring into clear relief the futility of using 'evolutionary' land reforms in some Latin American countries, for example, as an instrument for agrarian development. (See Table 4.)

Unfortunately, the UN organizations have always adhered to this distinction and based their entire approach to problems of land

* W. F. Wertheim, *Evolution and Revolution: Sociology of a World on the Move* (University of Amsterdam, 1967), p. 30.

TABLE 4

Comparison Between Land Reform Programmes Extrapolated over 20 Years and Land Reform Programmes Based on Rate of Settlement Observed During the 1960s in Brazil, Colombia, Dominican Republic, and Honduras

Country	20-year programme				Number of years required to settle 75 per cent of underprivileged families existing in 1960, at rate of settlement by reform institutes during the 1960s	
	Number of underprivileged families	5 percent of families	Annual increase	Total number of farm families per annum	Approximate rate of settlement by land reform institutes observed in the 1960s	Number of years required to settle families
Brazil	4,535,000[a]	226,000	106,000	332,000	100	34,013
Colombia	961,000	48,000	14,000	62,000	560	1,287
Dominican Republic	350,000	17,500	15,000	32,500	1,150	228
Honduras	183,000	9,150	5,000	14,150	885	155

SOURCE: Compiled by Ernest Feder, Mexico City, 1969 (unpublished).

NOTE: The rate of settlement used in this table corresponds to the annual settlement of farm families in land reform projects undertaken by the respective land reform institutes and does not include colonization projects. The rates are approximations, based on information furnished by the institutes. The number of years required to settle poor farm families (less 25 per cent) does not include the annual increase in farm families, as otherwise the land reform programmes would never catch up with the rural poor.

[a] CIDA data adjusted to 1960.

reform on the belief in 'peaceful evolutionary reforms' from above, which has often led to a fatal misunderstanding of the dynamics of socio-economic changes.

In the present chapter, which deals with the fundamental problems involved in the redistribution of land, with the reasons for the failure or success of this, and with suggestions for future action in this field, we will adhere for the sake of convenience to this conventional classification of land redistribution programmes. We will then distinguish between those programmes introduced by constitutional action, and those initiated by revolutionary action, but it should be understood that the former may be implemented or expanded by revolutionary action and the latter is generally followed up by evolutionary measures. The very dynamics of such a fundamental socio-economic change as the redistribution of agricultural resources will inevitably create new behaviour patterns and institutions equivalent to the changes in status and income, and accordingly the way in which this dynamic process has been started is of little more than incidental importance.

The content and direction of a land redistribution programme should be determined primarily by an appraisal of the prevailing agrarian conditions. Tenancy problems in Japan, for example, posed totally different problems for the redistribution of land, than the combination of large estates and minute peasant holdings in Latin America, which calls for some kind of resettlement in addition to redistribution. In old settled areas, therefore, the first step must be to verify data on existing rights in the land, the size of farms, the land utilization pattern, population densities and the social and economic status of the cultivators. Even if the data needed are non-existent or too spurious, however, redistribution should not be postponed until reliable records have been established but initiated without further delay, since under certain conditions errors in reallocating the land may be less dangerous than the maintenance of the *status quo* for a further period. It has proved possible, in fact, to obtain certain data on the spot, as in Kenya, where village committees were established to handle part of the work and, with the support of mobile survey units, were able to define with reasonable accuracy the existing rights in land. On the basis of these data the local administration drew up plans and invited the villagers to lodge any objections within a given period of time. The same procedure could be applied to the distribution of surplus land, since the villagers generally have a fairly clear idea of the different kinds of farm and size of holdings which prevail.

The way in which the land is then redistributed will depend on whether the reform aims simply at turning tenants into owners without otherwise changing the pattern of land utilization and farm structure, as was the case in Japan and largely also in India, or whether its purpose is to dissolve the large estates and encourage the emergence of new types of operational units, be they individual units, cooperative or collective farms, or state farm enterprises.

It is true that the redistribution of land does not always automatically lead to an increase in production, and may even reduce market supplies. But it is equally true that, in the long run, it will increase the productivity of both land and labour and, above all, decisively improve the well-being and dignity of the man on the land. Accordingly, throughout the entire process of land redistribution, the primary objective should be to establish immediately reasonably viable units. But if this proves impossible, efforts should be made to improve cultivation methods and marketing possibilities, since it would be pointless to simply reproduce conditions which hold no greater promise for a better future than those obtaining previously.

It is against this background that it is necessary to establish specific criteria for the actual expropriation of land. The first, and most important, is the *size of the landed properties to be earmarked for redistribution*. This must be determined not only on the basis of prevailing physical conditions such as soil, contours, and extent of present or potential irrigation, but also on population density, access to markets and the degree of absentee landlordism or intermediary rights. Secondly, there is the current *degree of productivity* which needs to be given particular attention because it can only be applied in conjunction with the overall social and economic situation. Thus, it may be a mistake to use a given degree of mechanization as a criterion for productivity in areas with abundant idle manpower. In certain parts of Iran, for example, the use of agricultural machinery may well create the impression of high productivity, whereas in reality it may mean little else than the squandering of foreign exchange. In the absence of reliable statistical data, fact-finding missions with clearly defined terms of reference should investigate the distribution and use of agricultural resources.

A third criterion is the *scale of the land redistribution programme*, that is to say, whether it should be countrywide and comprehensive or limited to certain areas or particular conditions. The immediate reaction is that a countrywide programme would be more effective and, therefore, desirable. But this is only true if the problems of administration can be handled efficiently,* and if it is based on clearly formulated legislation that leaves no room for arbitrary decisions and evasions. Limited programmes, on the other hand, are always risky since they are necessarily designed in a haphazard manner and based on vague legal formulations that may encourage open corruption, particularly if the expropriation of large estates is left to the arbitrary decisions of local officials. In the Philippines, the provision that entitles the tenants to put in a request for the expropriation of the land which they cultivate has been misused by the landlords, who actually invited their tenants to put in a claim for the expropriation of their estates and with the help of understanding local officials, obtained unduly high compensation payments. The moral climate of the administration thus determines how redistribution is carried out.

What applies to the expropriation procedures applies with equal or even greater force to the organization of the new farms. Once again criteria have to be established for types of tenure, size, and capital investment which together decide the future productivity of both land and labour. The question of farm size has become an extremely controversial issue on which a wealth of literature has been written which, however, seldom touches upon the fundamental structural problem. This is that large landownership in underdeveloped countries becomes synonymous with control of labour, political power and social prestige.

That being the case, the new farm units should be organized according to the desired changes in the balance of economic and political power through the redistribution of agricultural resources and reorganization of agricultural production, and not on the

* See chapter 14.

basis of the many elaborate models for standard or optimum farm sizes. To establish such a model it would be necessary to embark on a complicated analysis in order to isolate the variety of institutional factors, of input-output relationships and of specific farming practices, and to determine the most favourable combination of institutional improvements with agricultural activities. It seems rather doubtful, however, that this would prove a worthwhile exercise, as an optimum farm size calculated in this way may turn out to be unworkable, given the impact of overall development and market trends. The World Land Reform Conference strongly criticized the widespread use of standard farm sizes and emphasized that much greater attention ought to be paid to such aspects as growth of production, increase in income, and enlargement of holdings.* Neither would the much-acclaimed inter-farm comparisons be of any use, since inter-farm differences have the unfortunate tendency of becoming irrelevant or even disappearing altogether when the areas compared are relatively homogeneous with respect to types of farming, degree of fragmentation, and conditions of tenure. There can be no doubt that institutions, efficiency of land use, and even infrastructures are far more relevant factors than the confusing issue of 'optimum size'.

On considering these factors, it can readily be seen that, given the rapid demographic and technological changes in underdeveloped countries, it would be irrational to establish an optimum farm size. The most important thing is that the size of the new farms should meet the requirements of the desired farm type and, to whatever extent possible, fit into the present and even foreseeable demographic pattern.

* United Nations, FAO, *Report of the World Land Reform Conference, Rome 1966*, p. 107.

See also United Nations, Dept. of Ec. and Soc. Affairs, *Progress in Land Reform, Fourth Report*, pp. 59, 60, para. 280. Although theoretically the Report considers it perfectly possible to make economic calculations, it states that 'the chances are that any one of these optimum solutions involves either settling the new farmers on holdings much larger than those enjoyed by the average established farmer, or in endowing them with a much higher level of capital investment, or both. To give such privileges to a tiny fraction of the population may be politically impossible. Economic viability and fairness do not necessarily go hand in hand.'

In the following two sections we will illustrate, through examples, the various procedures, problems and effects of land redistribution in selected underdeveloped countries in Latin America and Asia, as well as in some socialist countries.

Land Redistribution Introduced by Constitutional Action

Whatever the manifestations and impact of existing power relations in underdeveloped countries, any land redistribution programme introduced by constitutional action has to contend with the sustained resistance of powerful vested interests and the problems of evasion and corruption.

Wherever the protection of property rights is written into the constitution, expropriation of land for redistribution entails the payment of compensation to the legal owners. The problems engendered by this obligation are of vital importance because the considerable volume of capital involved may upset the entire national economy by increasing the inflationary trend which is almost always present. But the most complex and vexed problem is how to calculate the actual amount of compensation.* The idea of using the prevailing high market value of agricultural land as a yardstick is most unrealistic since it is determined mainly by the prestige attached to large landownership and the prerogative of virtual tax exemption due to low assessments, and consequently greatly exceeds the actual and even potential production value. The repayment of such a generous compensation will almost everywhere lead to instalment rates which are far beyond the economic capacity of the new peasant owners. The correlation between compensation payments and instalment rates largely determines the ultimate success or failure of the land redistribution programme.

There are three reasons why we have chosen to start with the

* See Appendix 1: 'Technical Assistance for the Financing of Land Reform Programmes'.

Latin American countries;* first, because they provide a wealth
of relatively homogeneous material suitable for a comparative
analysis; secondly, because agrarian tension throughout Latin
America has moved into the forefront of critical attention; and
thirdly, because the effects of ambiguous economic policies and
technical and financial aid are more keenly felt than in other
underdeveloped regions of the world.

With a few exceptions, agrarian conditions throughout Latin
America demonstrate that outdated land distribution patterns
cause social injustice, maintain the wasteful use of agricultural
resources through irrational, labour-extensive farming practices and
thus block the way to economic, social and political development.

Table 5, contained in a report by CIDA†, reveals some impressive facts: in *Chile* and *Peru*, more than 80 per cent of the
farmland is contained in the size group (multi-family large) which
requires a permanent labour force of more than 12 workers, while
in *Ecuador, Guatemala* and *Peru*, 80–90 per cent of the farm units
(sub-family) are not even large enough to provide employment
for two people. A high proportion of these undersized units
(*minifundia*) are operated by tenants or simply squatters who,
even when their lands are not physically included within the
large estates, depend on them for part-time employment, markets
or credit. The distribution of technical means is extremely poor;
in 9 Brazilian municipalities with a total of 26,000 farm units,
there were only 462 tractors and 3,000 vehicles in operation, while
fertilizers were used by only about 4 per cent of all farms. Some
large estates, on the other hand, introduced agricultural machinery
in order to economize on labour expenses rather than to intensify
cultivation, with the net effect that unemployment and insecurity
often increased amongst the peasants. Thus, a 15,000-hectare
hacienda in Ecuador owned by Swedish interests sent half of its
resident workers away when it was transformed into one of the
most 'efficient' farm enterprises in the country.

It is clearly evident from the report that the production and

---

* When we refer to *Latin America* or *Latin American countries* in
the following account, Mexico and Cuba are exempted.

† *Land Tenure Conditions and Socio-economic Development of
the Agricultural Sector in Seven Latin American Countries*
(CIDA Studies).

TABLE 5

Relative Number and Area of Farm Units by Size Groups in CIDA *Study Countries*

(Percentage of country total in each size class)

Country	Sub-family	Family	Multi-family medium	Multi-family large	Total
Argentina					
Number of farm units	43.2	48.7	7.3	0.8	100
Area in farms	3.4	44.7	15.0	36.9	100
Brazil					
Number of farm units	22.5	39.1	33.7	4.7	100
Area in farms	0.5	6.0	34.0	59.5	100
Chile					
Number of farm units	36.9	40.0	16.2	6.9	100
Area in farms	0.2	7.1	11.4	81.3	100
Colombia					
Number of farm units	64.0	30.2	4.5	1.3	100
Area in farms	4.9	22.3	23.3	49.5	100
Ecuador					
Number of farm units	89.9	8.0	1.7	0.4	100
Area in farms	16.6	19.0	19.3	45.1	100
Guatemala					
Number of farm units	88.4	9.5	2.0	0.1	100
Area in farms	14.3	13.4	31.5	40.8	100
Peru (before 1969)					
Number of farm units	88.0	8.5	2.4	1.1	100
Area in farms	7.4	4.5	5.7	82.4	100

SOURCE: CIDA Studies.

NOTES:

Sub-family: Farms large enough to provide employment for less than 2 people with the typical incomes, markets and levels of technology now prevailing in each region.

Family: Farms large enough to provide employment for 2 to 3.9 people, on the assumption that most of the farm work is being carried out by the members of the farm family.

Multi-family medium: Farms large enough to provide employment for 4 to 12 people.

Multi-family large: Farms large enough to provide employment for over 12 people.

employment pattern in all seven countries is motivated by the desire of the large landowners to secure the level of income necessary for a sumptuous way of life and to retain their economic, social, and political position with a minimum of investment and personal effort. No wonder that inefficient farm management is a distinctive feature of so many large landholdings. It has been estimated that the large-scale production of cocoa and coffee in Brazil could be easily doubled by even minimal improvements in management and investment.

On the whole the estate owners make but little effort to meet the growing labour supply with intensified land use that would increase the productive employment on their estates.* They seem to be more interested in maintaining the state of underemployment which will keep wages down and secure their control of land and labour. As a matter of fact, the prevailing tenure arrangements prohibit the use of large areas otherwise suitable for cultivation and thus maintain the vicious circle of low agricultural productivity, inadequate diet and poverty amongst the rural masses.

In the final analysis, conditions of tenure and the attitude of the landowning class are the very reasons why such a small part of the estate land is cultivated intensively and why the relative contribution of the large farms to the national food supply is so grossly disproportionate to their potential (see Table 6). Only a small group of efficiently managed, highly mechanized large estates actually contribute to economic growth in their countries.† The concentration of land ownership is even greater than indicated by the figures in Table 5, since business corporations and even one and the same family own or control several large estates. Table 7,

* The 1967 *Report on the World Social Situation* (UN, New York, 1969, p. 135) emphasizes quite rightly that the wealthiest land-owning families are becoming more dependent on their non-agricultural income sources and more urban in their interests.

† T. W. Schultz, *Transforming Traditional Agriculture* (New Haven, Conn., 1964). The CIDA Studies rightly attack Schultz for trying to reduce the problem of agricultural development in traditional smallholder communities to purely economic terms without resorting to institutional and cultural explanations. His belief in 'unconventional inputs' as education, for example, is rather unrealistic, and it is significant that he is unable to explain why the latifundias 'have not been quicker to introduce new productive factors'.

TABLE 6

Relationships Between the Value of Agricultural Production, Agricultural Land, Cultivated Land and the Agricultural Work Force by Farm Size Class in Selected CIDA Study Countries[a]

Country and size groups	Percentage of total in each country			Relative value of production as percentage of that of sub-family farms		
	Agricultural land	Agricultural work force	Value of production	Per ha. of agricultural land	Per ha. of cultivated land	Per agricultural worker
Argentina (1960)						
Sub-family	3	30	12	100	100	100
Family	46	49	47	30	51	251
Multi-family medium	15	15	26	51	62	471
Multi-family large	36	6	15	12	49	622
Total	100	100	100	30	57	261
Brazil (1950)						
Sub-family	0	11	3	100	100	100
Family	6	26	18	59	80	291
Multi-family medium	34	42	43	24	53	422
Multi-family large	60	21	36	11	42	688
Total	100	100	100	19	52	408

continued overleaf

TABLE 6 continued

Country and size groups	Percentage of total in each country			Relative value of production as percentage of that of sub-family farms		
	Agricultural land	Agricultural work force	Value of production	Per ha. of agricultural land	Per ha. of cultivated land	Per agricultural worker
Colombia (1960)						
Sub-family	5	58	21	100	100	100
Family	25	31	45	47	90	418
Multi-family medium	25	7	19	19	84	753
Multi-family large	45	4	15	7	80	995
Total	100	100	100	23	90	281
Chile (1955)						
Sub-family	0	13	4	100	100	100
Family	8	28	16	14	47	165
Multi-family medium	13	21	23	12	39	309
Multi-family large	79	38	57	5	30	437
Total	100	100	100	7	35	292

TABLE 6 *continued*

Country and size groups	Percentage of total in each country			Relative value of production as percentage of that of sub-family farms		
	Agricultural land	Agricultural work force	Value of production	Per ha. of agricultural land	Per ha. of cultivated land	Per agricultural worker
Ecuador (1954)						
Sub-family	20	b	26	100	100	b
Family	19	b	33	130	179	b
Multi-family medium	19	b	22	87	153	b
Multi-family large	42	b	19	35	126	b
Total	100	b	100	77	135	b
Guatemala (1950)						
Sub-family	15	68	30	100	100	100
Family	13	13	13	56	80	220
Multi-family medium	32	12	36	54	122	670
Multi-family large	40	7	21	25	83	706
Total	100	100	100	48	99	224

SOURCE: CIDA Studies.

a Gross value of agricultural production in all countries except Argentina where the estimates are of added value. Comparable data is not available for Peru.

b No information available.

which among other things relates farm size to the agricultural
work force, throws further light on the present situation.

A study on agrarian conditions in Nicaragua 1966–67, gives a
vivid account of the legal and economic insecurity of the peasants
which may be considered typical in large parts of Latin America.*
Many of the small farm units are either operated by tenants
whose contracts seldom extend over more than a year or simply
used or 'borrowed' by squatters, who are often poor relatives
of the landlords. This insecurity of tenure causes innumerable
conflicts particularly where improved communications are increasing the market value of farm land. As the legal owners,
usually living in distant urban centres, are not interested in developing the land themselves, they do not prevent the local landless peasants from squatting and performing the initial hard work
of clearing the land and preparing it for cultivation. But as soon
as the land begins to yield, the legal owner becomes interested in
the returns and will either eject the squatters or impose harsh
terms of tenancy. In many cases the squatters even claim to have
started working the land before the title was ever issued to the
landlord. Evidently such an agrarian situation contains the risk of
serious conflicts, and to an increasing extent, the ejected or suppressed peasants are inclined to join guerrilla forces, as soon as
the occasion arises.

The typical land distribution pattern in Latin America, however,
is equally detrimental from the point of view of land use. Almost
everywhere the separation of ownership from management of land,
common in many other parts of the world, is aggravated by the
further separation of management from labour. The fact that cultivation practices, such as use of fertilizers, weed-killers, pesticides
etc. which determine the quality of investment, are not decided
by the owner or manager of the land but left entirely to the
agricultural labourer whose miserable wage does not increase with
higher yields, is an additional reason for the very low productivity
of agricultural land.

Accordingly, one of the most important objectives of land redistribution in Latin America should be the abrogation of this

* J. Taylor, 'Some Findings and Implications of Land Tenure
Center Research in Nicaragua', *Land Tenure Center Newsletter*,
no. 26 (April 1967-February 1968).

TABLE 7

Relative Number, Area, Agricultural Work Force and Value of Agricultural Production by Farm Size Class in Selected CIDA *Study Countries*

Country and Size Groups	No. of farm units	Agricultural land	Agricultural work force	Value of production (a)	Owners of family sized farms	Sub-family sized operations	Landless farm workers
Argentina (1960)							
Sub-family	43	3	30	12	..	..	..
Family	49	46	49	47	..	..	..
Multi-family medium	7	15	15	26	..	..	..
Multi-family large	1	36	6	15	..	..	..
Total	100	100	100	100	16	26	35
Brazil (1950)							
Sub-family	22	c	11	3	..	..	..
Family	39	6	26	18	..	..	..
Multi-family medium	34	34	42	43	..	..	..
Multi-family large	5	60	21	36	..	..	..
Total	100	100	100	100	12	9	60
Colombia (1960)							
Sub-family	64	5	58	21	..	..	..
Family	30	25	31	45	..	..	..
Multi-family medium	5	25	7	19	..	..	..
Multi-family large	1	45	4	15	..	..	..
Total	100	100	100	100	18	47	23
Chile (1955)							
Sub-family	37	c	13	4	..	..	..
Family	40	8	28	16	..	..	..
Multi-family medium	16	13	21	23	..	..	..
Multi-family large	7	79	38	57	..	..	..
Total	100	100	100	100	15	23d	48
Ecuador (1954)							
Sub-family	89	20	b	26	..	..	..
Family	8	19	b	33	..	..	..
Multi-family medium	2	19	b	22	..	..	..
Multi-family large	1	42	b	19	..	..	..
Total	100	100	b	100	8	52	35
Guatemala (1950)							
Sub-family	88	15	68	30	..	..	..
Family	10	13	13	13	..	..	..
Multi-family medium	2	32	12	36	..	..	..
Multi-family large	c	40	7	21	..	..	..
Total	100	100	100	100	7	64	25
Peru							
Sub-family	88	7	b	b	b	b	b
Family	9	5	b	b	..	..	..
Multi-family medium	2	6	b	b	..	..	..
Multi-family large	1	82	b	b	..	..	..
Total	100	100	b	b	b	b	b

SOURCE: S. L. Barraclough and A. L. Domike 'Agrarian Structure in Seven Latin American Countries', *Land Economics* (University of Wisconsin, November 1966), pp. 395, 397, 402. This article is based on the CIDA Studies.

NOTES:
Sub-Family: Farms large enough to provide employment for less than 2 people with the typical incomes, markets and levels of technology and capital now prevailing in each region.
Family: Farms large enough to provide employment for 2 to 3.9 people, on the assumption that most of the farm work is being carried out by the members of the farm family.
Multi-family medium: Farms large enough to provide employment for 4 to 12 people.
Multi-family large: Farms large enough to provide employment for over 12 people.
a Gross value of agricultural production in all countries except Argentina where the estimates are of added value. Comparable data are not available for Peru.
b No information available.
c Less than one per cent.
d Including communal owners (16.6 per cent).

outdated type of farm organization, as happened in Mexico. Although the Mexican land reform fell short in many respects, the initial redistribution of land succeeded in breaking up the large estates and essentially improving the farm organization.

Despite general agreement on the fact that the low level of land use in Latin America is caused by concentration of ownership and defective tenure systems, land redistribution programmes have achieved but negligible results either because they were rescinded wholly or in part or, as was mostly the case, because they were rendered useless by gross evasion or corruption. It is a fallacy to believe that better extension services and the increased use of fertilizers and even 'miracle' seeds are adequate substitutes for land redistribution. Were this really so, the generous assistance lavished on Latin American agriculture by United States bilateral aid and by the Alliance for Progress would have changed the agrarian and agricultural situation in Latin America a long time ago. True, it may have increased efficiency to some extent, but this is not enough to alter the income distribution and has in fact widened the income gap between the few who actually own the land and the masses who do the tilling. This type of assistance, therefore, should be given *after* the redistribution of land and not instead of it.*

The land redistribution programme in *Colombia* clearly illustrates how vague and permissive legislation impedes any effective implementation. After a period of renewed agrarian unrest in 1960, stimulated by the successful revolution in Cuba, and after the official acknowledgement of the need for agrarian reform expressed in the Charter of Punta del Este in 1961, the government felt that some kind of legislation was needed in order to appease the dissatisfied peasantry by a programme of land redistribution. In December 1961, it passed the Social Land Agrarian Reform Law (no. 135) which promised the final enforcement of a law dating back to 1936 which had authorized the expropriation of all land left uncultivated for ten years or more. An example of the vagueness of this Law is the fact that it does not set any definite ceilings on land ownership but only provides that 'the natural right to property' should be extended to 'ever

* E. Flores, *Land Reform and the Alliance for Progress*, p. 8.

broader sectors of the rural population' and that, if necessary, private land should also be expropriated, for this purpose.

A Land Reform Institute was set up to handle the difficult task of settling peasant families on individual farms. The land to be made available for settlement is listed by the Law in the following order of priority: suitable public lands; suitable, but un-utilized or inadequately cultivated, private lands; adequately cultivated tenant-operated lands, and, finally, adequately culti-vated, owner-operated lands which preferably shall be acquired by sales agreements and not by expropriation. Even with regard to compensation payments, the Law shows great consideration for the landlords by the ambiguous provision that the compensation is in no case to exceed 130 per cent of the cadastral value. But since this notoriously undervalues land, because of the very low assessments, a decree issued two years later allows the large land-owners an immediate cadastral revaluation which ensures them a very generous compensation in the event of expropriation.

Yet, the budget set aside for compensation payments is most unsatisfactory. Even if the former extremely low assessment rates are used, it would suffice at the most to provide land for only about 100,000 of the estimated one million families in need of land.

Since, furthermore, the Law clearly chooses the piecemeal approach to be applied in particular areas by separate decree, and only contains but one clearly formulated provision that properties of over 2,000 hectares must be declared, it is no wonder that it has not been effectively implemented and has been a serious disappointment to the rural masses.*

In order to have achieved any kind of success, the Land Reform Institute should have been in a position to settle at least 20–30,000 families a year in viable holdings, consolidate the frag-mented smallholdings of at least another 5,000 families and, in addition, improve the working and living conditions of thousands of farm workers through unionization, enforcement of work con-tracts, housing programmes, and social security measures. But, even at that rate it would take decades to change the prevailing

* E. Feder, in 'The Rational Implementation of Land Reform in Colombia and its Significance for the Alliance for Progress', *America Latina*, vol. 6, no. 1 (1963), p. 99, gives a picture of the organizational pattern established by the Law.

system of large estates into a somewhat more equitable tenure pattern. In the course of six years (1962–67), however, the Land Reform Institute obtained new land expropriated from private owners for the settlement of only about 3,800 families who were given an average of some 16 hectares each, and registered titles for some 60,000 peasants, mostly squatters, on remote public domain lands which they had already cleared. Although this has at least improved the tenure status of a large number of poor settlers, it makes little contribution to the badly needed transformation of the agrarian structure in the principal agricultural areas. This is particularly so now that the Institute is under increasing pressure to abandon the idea of solving the land distribution problem and concentrate instead on technical development, particularly irrigation.* In this connection, the following quotation from a statement by the President of the Republic published in *El Tiempo* as early as October 1964, is of more than transitional interest: 'We are carrying through a land reform', he said, 'whose primary objective is not so much to change the number of landowners as to increase the national production in order to bring down the cost and prices of food through a more intensive, more scientific, and more diversified exploitation of land.'†

Considering the failure of land reform in Colombia, it is difficult to understand why the United States, in 1968, granted the livestock industry in Colombia a loan of $12 million, 'to allay fears, which had been engendered among ranchers by the agrarian reform law'; while at the same time, a loan of only $18.5 million was considered sufficient to provide supervised credit for Colombia's hundreds of thousands of small farmers.‡ Yet, the increasing incidence of violence in the countryside and particularly the land invasions in the South Atlantic Department, prove that this is not the last word on the agrarian issue in Colombia.

Despite increased legislation and the growth of active pressure from the peasants themselves, land redistribution has met with little more success in other Latin American countries. Almost everywhere, the acquisition of private land for redistribution is in

* *Progress in Land Reform, Fourth Report.*
† Ibid., p. 21.
‡ US Aid Committee on Foreign Relations, US Senate, 91st Congress, 1st Session, 1 February 1969 (Washington, D.C., 1969), pp. 82 ff.

the hands of national institutes or agencies that all operate on the piecemeal-by-decree principle and usually limit expropriation to public lands or to 'land that does not fulfil its social function', to 'idle land' and to 'land not cultivated or ineffectively exploited'. Legislation in the Dominican Republic provides that the local institute shall acquire land 'by amicable sale' and only resort to expropriation by government action 'if necessary'.

It seems, however, that the new military government in *Peru* which is supported by a nationalistic middle class with strong anti-American feelings is trying to find an alternative to a Cuban solution of the country's permanent crisis. It makes an honest attempt to carry out the *'New* Agrarian Reform', decreed in June 1969, superseding the Agrarian Reform Law of 1964 which had scarcely been implemented. The new Law provides for the subdivision of large private holdings, the regrouping of very small farm units and the formation of farming cooperatives. Ceilings on farm sizes shall be adjusted to the conditions in different regions and compensation payments shall be determined according to the size and condition of the holding and calculated on the basis of the tax return statements for 1968. An essential provision in the reform programme is that of 'intervention', which authorizes the land reform agency to assign high-ranking officials to supervise the administration of large estates, in order to prevent evasive transactions or changes in the course of normal operations. By the end of 1969 the large estates had actually been expropriated and 'interventions' had been arranged.

It is still too early to judge whether or to what extent the military government will succeed in transforming the agrarian structure of Peru, particularly since they seem to hesitate in allowing the peasant organizations to take an active part in implementing such changes and operate in a political and social vacuum. The establishment of farming cooperatives which the law sets up as the ultimate goal, still seems very far away as the peasants are still suspicious. But in the next year or two the reform should have been under way long enough to assess its impact on agricultural development.

In *Venezuela* the implementation of an extensive land redistribution programme between 1959 and 1967 seems to have been rather successful and 143,000 families were settled on land expropriated against compensation from private estates. This success is largely due to the well-organized and coordinated peasant invasions in the early sixties of the estates in densely populated areas like Carabobo and Aragon. In some cases these invasions had even been encouraged by the landlords themselves because the subsequent acquisition of the land by the Instituto Agrario Nazional was good business especially in areas close to the cities.* On the whole, the Venezuelan landlords are not as opposed to selling their land at favourable prices and investing the profit in other sectors of the economy as are their colleagues in other Latin American countries. Modern economic ideas seem to be more widespread in the Venezuelan upper class and this explains the less violent opposition of the large landowners to an agrarian legislation which has facilitated the actual implementation of a moderate reform programme. Although the Venezuelan attitude is rather exceptional compared to that in other Latin American countries, the land redistribution has not solved the land problem, and in the larger part of the country *latifundia*, indebtedness and landlessness still dominate the rural scene.

In *Bolivia*, also, peasants invaded many large estates before they were assigned legal titles to the land, and peasant organizations had already assumed local government functions by the early fifties. But neither the agrarian revolt of 1952 nor the Land Reform Law of 1953† has finally solved the agrarian problem. Despite many changes for the better—an estimated 400,000 peasant families became owner-operators, schools were built in rural areas, and peasant unions formed—new situations have given rise to new conflicts because the Land Reform of 1953 was not followed up by complementary measures.‡

* Gerrit Huizer, 'Report on the Study of the Role of Peasant Organizations in the Process of Agrarian Reform in Latin America' (ILO, Geneva 1969, mimeographed), pp. 298 ff.
† Land Reform Law and Decree no. 03465, 1953, particularly Article 78.
‡ See J. R. Thome, 'The Bolivian Reform: The Need for a Faster Title Distribution Process', *Land Tenure Newsletter*, no. 24 (University of Wisconsin, 1.8.1966); and R. J. Clark, *Problems and Conflicts over Land Ownership in Bolivia*, Land Tenure Center Reprint, no. 54 (University of Wisconsin, 1969).

The last decade has been marked by continuous conflicts between former landlords and new peasant-owners, and intimidation of peasants by landlords who wish to retain title to or obtain payment for their farms are recurring features of the situation. It may even be said that there is a certain trend on the part of the landlords to reassert traditional labour arrangements on all or part of their former holdings.

The revolutionary action of 1952 was followed by a certain amount of ratification and distribution of titles. Between 1953 and 1969, 185,000 peasant families received 263,000 individual and collective titles (titles to land now held in common by the community) amounting to approximately 3.8 million hectares of cultivable land, in addition to pasture lands and lands for school areas. Compared to land redistribution in other Latin American countries this is an outstanding achievement but the process has been erratic and has gradually slowed down; to date only 45 per cent of the peasant families have received their titles to land. Eight thousand large estates comprising more than 5.3 million hectares have not yet been distributed to the approximately 165,000 peasant families who are entitled to this land, and between 1965 and 1967 only about 18,400 cases were settled.

There is no doubt that despite some improvements, the confusion and inefficiency of the expropriation procedures have given rise to numerous problems and conflicts. As in India, the provisions of the law that allow landlords to retain portions of their former holdings have led to considerable difficulties in implementing the expropriation policy, and have created an unhappy atmosphere in the rural areas. The delay in expropriation and the distribution of titles has increased the insecurity of the peasants *vis-à-vis* the landlords who often threaten to repossess their land. In a few cases the landlords have even exploited this uncertainty, and have sent peasants and city dwellers disguised as soldiers or police to demand payment for land to which they no longer have legal rights.*

Frustrated by the ineptitude of the authorities, the peasant is willing to agree to almost anything. In areas where peasant organizations are weak, the landlords have actually reassumed control of all or a part of their lands, and in others they have

* R. J. Clark, op. cit., p. 7.

succeeded in persuading those peasants still waiting for their title, to work their land on a sharecropping basis with the former land-lord.

The delay in the distribution of titles has also caused splits among the peasants and the most frequent source of conflict is the subdivision of the land previously cultivated by the landlords. In many cases the more powerful peasant families, usually those who already had the most land under the landlord, requested larger parcels than allowed under the Land Reform Law, which states that these lands should be used to equalize holdings of all peasant families.* It cannot be denied that bureaucratic pro-cedures, indifference to the interests of the peasant and disloyalty to the spirit of the Agrarian Reform Law of 1953 have created an atmosphere which favours manipulation by the landlords and, unless this can be prevented by the growing strength of peasant unions, may finally jeopardize the implementation of the Law for many of the Bolivian peasants.

After a long series of abortive attempts, *Chile* has tried to tackle the problems of a constitutional land redistribution in a more systematic and realistic manner under difficult circumstances and against powerful opposition. It thus belongs to the small group of Latin American countries (Bolivia, Cuba, Mexico and Venezuela) which in their own way have embarked on reforms that directly affect the rural masses. Up until now, however, only about 5 per cent of the country's agricultural lands has been assigned to approximately 4 per cent of the 250,000 peasant families who, according to the CIDA Studies, are potential land reform beneficiaries.† But even this very modest result could only be achieved in an uphill fight against entrenched vested interests.

Eduardo Frei, who won the presidential election for the Christian Democratic Party in 1964, decided to attack the in-equitable agrarian structure. He submitted the Agrarian Reform Bill, enacted as Law in 1967, whose main objectives were:

1. To give able agricultural workers ownership right to the land which they have cultivated for years.
2. To increase agricultural and live-stock production.

* Ibid., p. 13.
† S. L. Barraclough, 'Employment Problems Affecting Latin American Agricultural Development', loc. cit.

3. To attain upward social mobility for agricultural workers and secure their active participation in the land reform procedure.

The term 'agricultural workers' covers not only labourers and employees whose continued and habitual occupation is carried out on the land, but also occupants, sharecroppers, leaseholders, tenureholders, and even landowners, as long as the size of their holdings does not exceed that of one agricultural family unit. University-trained professional agriculturists do not fall within the category of agricultural workers.

But before the Bill was enacted, the government, on the strength of an earlier Law of 1962, set apart 300,000 hectares of the public domain and expropriated 560,000 hectares of privately owned lands. A total of 860,000 hectares was thus made available for the reform programme and during the first eighteen months, land was actually distributed to some 7,000 families. But most significant in this connection is that, for the first time in the history of Chile, land had been expropriated without the consent of the landowners affected.

The final Agrarian Reform Law was passed in 1967. It entitles the land reform agency, Corporación de la Reforma Agraria de Chile (CORA), to claim expropriation of any property which is abandoned or badly utilized or which is owned by public or private corporations, or by individuals if its area exceeds 80 hectares of first-class irrigated land.* Compensation payments shall equal the assessment value of the property for rates and taxes in force at the time of expropriation, and any additional compensation for improvements shall be valuated by CORA according to their current value. The expropriated land shall be allocated primarily in private ownership to individual agricultural workers; in special cases and for specific technical reasons it may be assigned to them in joint ownership. CORA applies a particular arrangement, *asentamiento*, whereby contracts are made with eligible 'companies' of peasants, *asentados*, to 'settle' on the expropriated land for a transitional period of three years. During this time, CORA retains ownership to the land, all or most of which is operated on a cooperative basis according to a national development plan. The *asentados* have the right to elect the admini-

---

* The 'basic' irrigated hectare is the standard unit of area applicable to determine the maximum size of properties throughout the country.

G

strative committee which shall conduct the management of the
asentamiento. CORA supervises and guides the committee until
the *asentados* can handle matters themselves, but continues to
provide all complementary services such as credits, seeds,
machinery, etc. At the end of each year, returns, minus the repayments due to CORA, are distributed among the *asentados*. This
arrangement which provides proper training in farm management
and cooperative organizations, at the same time tests the ability
of each individual *asentado*. After the three-year period, only the
most able of them will receive titles to the land either as members
of a cooperative, or as individual owners, or as partners in a
mixed system whereby the cooperative holds part of the land
while the remainder is parcelled out to individual owners. The
latter seems to be the most common procedure to date,* but this
is contested by other observers.

The system seems to be highly effective and the aids and services provided have been called 'magnificent', particularly since
the 'seed to sale' service is granted without undue patronizing or
bureaucratic supervision.† There has been pressure from the
asentados to increase the amount of individual ownership, but
the advisability of private exploitation at the post-*asentamiento*
stage is questioned by some experts.‡

A remarkable aspect of the Chilean legislation is the provision
that all water sources are considered part of the public national
domain and, consequently, are subject to expropriation. Private
owners may continue to use the water only with the permission
of the competent authority.

The actual implementation of the Agrarian Reform Law however, was, and still is, an uphill struggle against a powerful political
and economic opposition that is determined to impede any move
which may endanger its control of the land. In this it has been

* J. R. Thome, 'A Brief Survey of the Chilean Agrarian Reform
Program', *Land Tenure Center Newsletter*, no. 28 (University of
Wisconsin, September 1968-February 1969).

† A. Jolly, 'The Economic Evaluation of the Asentamientos of the
Agrarian Reform 1966 and 1967' (ICIRA, Santiago, Chile, April 1968,
mimeographed), p. 17.

‡ Ibid., pp. 19 ff. Jolly argues that the use of the land could be
better planned on a communal basis and that individual activity
occupies and diverts *asentado* labour and interest to an uncontrol-
lable extent.

rather successful. Although the target of the Frei administration was the redistribution of land to 100,000 landless families by 1970, only about 20,000 had received land at the end of 1969 and, even under optimum circumstances, no more than another 10,000 can be expected to benefit in the next year. By the middle of 1968, 10,000 Chilean *campesino* families had been incorporated in *asentamientos*, on land purchased or appropriated in the Land Reform Legislation, which finance themselves in terms of internal credits at a level of 25 per cent of total credit needs.* Yet, for the transformation of the man-land relationship and future changes in the ownership pattern of Chilean agriculture, the increasing extra-legal unionization of rural workers who demand higher wages and social rights, strict enforcement of minimum wages and effective credit and cooperative programmes for 70,000 of the country's smallholders, may become of far greater importance than land distribution at its present limited extent.†

Despite a few remarkable results, the prospects for land redistribution initiated by constitutional action in Latin America are far from encouraging. The 'Declaration of the American Presidents' in 1967 which gives top priority to regional integration, that is, to the establishment of a common Latin American market, openly repudiates the original objectives of the Alliance for Progress which, animated by the Punte del Este Charter, were based on the sound premise that regional integration should *follow* and not *precede* fundamental structural reforms. At the present stage of economic and institutional development in the countries of Latin America, however, the emphasis on regional integration is bound to stabilize the defective agrarian structure and give rise to new vested interests only too anxious to defend and perpetuate it. The 'Declaration of the American Presidents' was far more than a diplomatic postponement of agrarian reforms; it was an

---

* Statement by Rafael Moreno, Vice-President of CORA, and Jacques Chonchol, then Vice-President of INDAP, quoted in *Land Tenure Center Newsletter* no. 27 (University of Wisconsin, March-August 1968). In 1969, the Christian Democratic Party split on the land reform issue with Chonchol leading the left wing.

† In September 1970, Salvador Allende, the leader of the socialist front, won the presidential election. His programme includes a radical agrarian reform focused on peasant cooperation and probably on large-scale collective farming.

important political decision which has shifted the problem of structural changes in Latin America from the evolutionary to the revolutionary level.*

On the continent of *Asia*, a number of countries have implemented comprehensive land redistribution programmes by constitutional action and so we have chosen as examples Japan, India and the Philippines because their content and achievements all differ. Although modern *Japan* is a highly industrialized country, and can no longer be considered underdeveloped, it may be instructive to recall the history of its agrarian reform programme, which was carried out in two distinct phases over a span of almost three generations. The first phase paved the way to industrialization, while the second furthered Japan's successful economic reconstruction after her defeat and devastation in 1945.

Land redistribution and agrarian reforms in Japan have a long history and were not started, as is commonly believed, by the United States Occupation Forces. During the first phase which dates back to the Meiji Restoration (1868–1912) feudal fiefs and stipends were abolished and a revision of the land tax was carried out in order to break the power of the *daimyō*, the feudal lord, and create the financial basis for a modern state. With the introduction of private ownership, a new class of village landlords† gradually emerged, mostly composed of erstwhile farmers, who, however, did not exercise the feudal prerogative of combined

* See W. Thiesenhusen and Marion Brown, 'Paper Prepared for an Overall Survey Conducted by the Subcommittee on American Republic Affairs', *Land Tenure Center Newsletter*, no. 26 (University of Wisconsin, April 1967-February 1968). The Paper sounds a note of warning against the concentration on agricultural production in Latin America at the expense of agrarian reform and states that such a narrow concern for production diverts attention from the revolutionary changes that are taking place in rural Latin America. The authors are of the opinion that it is necessary to incorporate rural income and employment into the concept of modern agriculture and that the lack of enthusiasm for land reform on the part of many Americans working in Latin America is mainly due to the fact that they consider it a danger to orderly procedures and the rights of private property.

† See R. P. Dore, 'Land Reform and Japanese Economic Development,' in Seiichi Tobata (ed.), *The Modernization of Japan I* (Tokyo, 1966).

control over land and labour. With the expansion of the money economy and increased land transactions, absentee landlordism became more and more frequent and tenancy grew rapidly. Due to the comparatively high level of education among Japanese peasants and their time-honoured tradition of organization and cooperation, the tenant-cultivators were responsible for the great increase in agricultural productivity which followed the abolition of feudalism, while the landowners gradually declined to the level of a rent-receiving class.

In the course of time this new agrarian pattern led to mounting unrest; the agrarian disputes of 1918–21, in particular, which coincided with a sharp fall in rice prices, posed serious political problems for the government.

But the continued rise in farm productivity created a crisis for the landlords who, at a certain point, were unable to raise the rate of farm rent to accord with the increased crop yields per unit area.* The effect of this development became evident during the Sino-Japanese war when the landowners were unable to satisfy the demand for increased food production. Aware of the importance of the tenants for agricultural production and of their organizational strength, the government tried to invite their co-operation by partly meeting their social and economic demands. In 1937, a law was adopted which aimed to transfer one-seventh of the tenanted land (460,000 hectares) into the possession of owner-cultivators within twenty-five years. Control of farm rents and prices quickly followed which favoured the tenant-cultivators and provided incentives for increased production. In 1940, when the shortage of food had reached serious proportions, the government officially recognized the tenant-cultivators as the one factor responsible for agricultural production. The Price Autonomous Control Law was passed whereby both the rice produced and sold by the tenant-cultivator and his deliveries to the landlord as rent in kind, were placed directly under government control. Except for the amount needed for his own consumption, the tenant now sold his entire rice crop directly to the government, a change in marketing which gradually led to the substitution of fixed cash amounts for the rent in kind due to the landlord. As a result, government grants and subsidies extended to small owners and

* Takekazu Ogura (ed.), *Agricultural Development in Modern Japan* (Japan-FAO Association, Tokyo, 1963), pp. 125 ff.

tenant-cultivators during the war did not increase the income of
the landlords, but rather became real incentives for additional
effort on the part of the cultivators. It can safely be said that
this step, which had the effect of economically depriving the landlord of his land before he lost it legally, initiated the second
phase of Japanese land reform. All that remained was to establish
the legal framework for the final transfer of ownership rights.

After the defeat of Japan, the administration of the United
States Occupation Forces drew the correct conclusion from the
situation as it actually existed, and, with the cooperation of the
Japanese government, took steps to make it legally effective. On
9 December 1945, it issued a directive for the emancipation of
farmers which was followed, the same year, by an amendment to
the existing Farm Land Adjustments Law. This amendment,
which has erroneously been considered the first land reform legislation in Japan, stipulated that farm land of more than five hectares
let by a resident landlord, and any farm land let by an absentee
landlord should be surrendered to the tenants upon request within
a period of five years. The occupation authorities soon realized,
however, that the figure of five hectares was far too high, since
by tradition the Japanese consider anybody a large landowner
who possesses more than three hectares of farm land. They induced the Diet to re-examine the situation and the result was
a law on 'Special Measures for the Establishment of Owner-
Farmers'.

This legislation authorized the government to acquire for sale
to tenant-farmers all farm units of more than one hectare (in
Hokkeido of more than four hectares) owned by resident landlords and all the farm land belonging to absentee landlords. It
is estimated that within two years following its enactment, 80
per cent of the almost two million hectares of tenanted land
were distributed to tenant-cultivators, as were 450,000 hectares
of pastures and 1,320,000 hectares of uncultivated land. Compensation payments to the landlords had been based on a fair
calculation but were largely absorbed by the post-war inflation.

The entire operation was completed by the autumn of 1949 in
spite of strong opposition and evasive practices on the part of
the landlords, who arbitrarily evicted the tenants, secretly sold
the excess farm land before the government officials arrived or

nominally divided the land among their family and friends. But the strong Japanese peasant organizations were able to cope with the landlords' resistance and ensure the effective implementation of the new law.

Yet, even the Japanese land redistribution had serious defects. Tenants of large landlords were unavoidably favoured compared to those of the small resident landowners who frequently claimed their right to one hectare. No efforts were made in fact to counteract the effects of uneven distribution caused by the application of the simple principle of selling the purchased land to the tenants cultivating it at the time.* The subsequent inequality is still clearly evident in the Japanese villages where at least half of the farmers own minute plots of 0.1 to 0.2 hectares. Although this has created structural problems of considerable dimensions, the spectacular expansion of industry attracts an increasing number of the rural population to the towns so that the Japanese government is now in a position to carry out land consolidation and farm enlargement operations.

Despite certain defects, the Japanese land reform must be considered highly successful. It has released unexpected resources of human energy which promoted agricultural production and, above all, accelerated the emancipation of the Japanese countrywomen. After the reform 'things were better not only economically but spiritually as well'.†

A recent investigation on post-war developments in Japan,‡ shows that today the income from agriculture is retained almost entirely within the farm, whereas prior to land reform, the landlords had withdrawn nearly 25 per cent for capital investments in industry. At Japan's present rate of economic growth this is a favourable development which makes the needed investments in agriculture possible. The formidable growth of agricultural production between 1946 and 1960 is evident from the following figures which also indicate the immediate effect of the post-war land reforms.

* R. P. Dore, *Land Reform in Japan* (London and New York, 1959), p. 179.
† Ibid, p. 370.
‡ Keinosake Baba, 'Structure of Agricultural Income Distribution', *Journal of Agricultural Economy*, vol. 9, no. 3 (Ministry of Agriculture and Forestry, Tokyo).

Agricultural Production Index
1895–1899: 100
1945–1949: 135.0
1950–1954: 176.7
1955–1959: 222.8
1960–1964: 257.6

SOURCE: Ministry of Agriculture and Forestry Survey.

Despite this remarkable development, however, the share of agriculture in overall national income has declined steadily from 31.1 per cent in 1946 to 16.7 in 1954 and 10.8 per cent in 1960.* The unique development of Japanese industry, particularly since the Korean War, has also caused a growing disparity between rural and urban incomes. But this does not reduce the important role which land reform has played in agricultural development. The present gap between agricultural and industrial income is due more to the tremendous industrial expansion than to short-comings within the agricultural sector.

To sum up, the first phase of land reform freed the Japanese peasants from the yoke of feudalism and removed the obstacles to agricultural and industrial progress. The second phase then consolidated their social and economic position by reducing the economic influence of the new landlord class and was accom-panied by a period of industrial development that attracted, and largely absorbed, mass migration to the industrial centres, with the result that pressure on rural land was eased. Although the entire reform was carried out by constitutional action, there is little doubt that the second phase contained certain revolutionary elements which demonstrate the important part played by strong peasant organizations and a fair degree of literacy in rural areas in realizing changes in the *status quo*.

While we are well aware that the underdeveloped countries of today have neither the time nor the patience to extend urgently-needed agrarian reconstruction over a period of almost one hun-dred years, the sequence of developments in Japanese agriculture

---

* Economic Planning Agency, *Kokumin shotoku tokei* (National Income Statistics), 1961. The pre-war level (1934–36) had already been reached in 1954.

translated into terms of modern policies, may still be of some use in evaluating their own situations.

Despite the incontestable fact that the land redistribution programme in *India* was one of the largest of its kind, it has had a limited effect on overall agricultural productivity and on the socio-economic position of the peasant, and on the whole, has failed to counteract the state of stagnation in Indian agriculture.

The guidelines for the wide range of measures designed and put into effect during the first years after independence are contained in the first two Five-Year Plans of the Planning Commission of the Government of India. Though probably unavoidable, it was most unfortunate that legislation and implementation was left to the discretion of the various states. For their administrators, trained in the spirit of the British-Indian Civil Service, although well versed in the principles of tax collection, land administration and land improvement were utterly unfamiliar with, and frequently even hostile to, any policy concerned with the redistribution of wealth. Accordingly, there was a wide gap in understanding between the dynamic and progressive Planning Commission in New Delhi and the administrations in the state capitals where landed interests and caste and class divisions were firmly entrenched. After the economic and industrial development following the first two Five-Year Plans, however, capitalistic and landed interests also gradually gained ground in New Delhi and largely succeeded in diverting attention from the bitter realities in the countryside.

Considering, however, the immense political and administrative difficulties, the Indian land redistribution programme achieved some remarkable results. It abolished the *Zamindari* System, by-product of British rule, and other intermediary rights in land and enabled tenants to acquire ownership to their holdings although the instalment rates for the land payments were quite high. In addition, it attempted to implement ceilings for the size of landed property in the rural areas of the various states.

This is not the place to give a detailed historical account of the unique role of the *Zamindars* in India which originated from their right to collect taxes for the British colonial administration; suffice it to point out that they used this right to build up a system of landholding which guaranteed them a large share of the income produced from agriculture without making any contribution to production, and control over almost a half of rural India. The abolition of *Zamindari* tenure was generally carried out in two stages. First, the state government took over the collection of revenues and rents from the tenants against generous compensation to the *Zamindars*, and secondly the *Zamindar's* tenants were granted rights of occupancy on all his land except that part which was to be considered his 'home-farm' and to which he himself was generally allowed the right of occupancy. This procedure, however, was not altogether effective, and many of the large *Zamindars* resorted to large-scale ejection of tenants and incorporated the holdings into their 'home-farms' before it came to the transfer of rights. Furthermore, they often delayed their decision regarding the area which they could claim for 'self-cultivation' (for which, incidentally, there was no upper limit), and thus increased the tenants' feeling of insecurity. On the whole, however, the abolition of intermediary rights was carried out thoroughly in most of the states, at least to the letter if not always in the spirit of the law. Although this was mainly due to the *Zamindars'* general unpopularity as a class and to the more or less equal social status of the majority of the hereditary tenants in many states, the wholehearted support of the political and administrative machinery was also a contributory factor.*

Yet, from the viewpoint of overall agrarian conditions in India, the effect of this part of the land redistribution programme was almost negligible. It did not affect the large holdings held under *raiyatwari* tenure, the other system of settlement and land administration under which cultivators paid land-revenue directly, and this despite the fact that it is responsible for inequitable land distribution in 57 per cent of the total area under cultivation in the country.† But even where the *Zamindari* system as such had been abolished, large areas of land were exempted from expropriation since the *Zamindars* could claim and generally retain part of their land *sir* to which the tenants were not given the right of occupancy. In some states, like Uttar Pradesh, such an exemption under the legislation led to the establishment of *sir*

* V. S. Vyas, 'Land Reform Legislation', *Seminar*, no. 8 (New Delhi, May 1966), p. 26.
† Government of India, Ministry of Information and Broadcasting, *India: A Reference Annual 1958*, p. 277.

lands by large-scale evictions* which were claimed for 'self-cultivation'.

Compensation payments to the *Zamindars* were very high, amounting to a total of roughly 6,500 million rupees,† which exceeded the original estimate by 2,000 millions. It has been indicated that claims for higher compensation were often directly encouraged by the highest level of the Congress Party which had a pro-landlord bias.‡

Despite some social gains in former *Zamindari* areas, the abolition of intermediary rights changed neither the general production pattern nor the insecurity of tenancy. In fact, sharecropping has remained a significant feature of Indian agriculture and is actually expanding, particularly in the state of Uttar Pradesh, where sample surveys in a number of villages have shown an increasing incidence of sharecropping which does not appear in census statistics and is not regulated by law. According to the *8th Round of the National Sample Survey*, only 20.8 per cent of the total tenanted area in India is under formal contracts with fixed rents, while 'it is not at all certain whether the rest is free from sharecropping'.§

Even the Ministry of Community Development and Cooperation admits in its comments‖ to Wolf Ladejinsky's Report, *Tenurial Conditions and the Package Program* (1965), that the Indian land tenure legislation has not been fairly and promptly implemented, that it has not substantially helped the non-landowning cultivators and that this necessitates new legislation which should be implemented without further delay. The crux of the matter is, however, *how* to enact a law that is truly in favour of the non-landowning cultivators. The abrogation of their

* G. Kotovsky, *Agrarian Reforms in India* (New Delhi, 1964), p. 48.
† Government of India, *Review of the First Five-Year Plan* (New Delhi, 1957), p. 315.
‡ G. Kotovsky, op. cit., p. 50.
§ A. K. Sen and T. C. Varghese, 'Tenancy and Resource Allocation', *Seminar*, no. 8 (New Delhi, May 1966), p. 30.
‖ Government of India, Planning Commission, 1964: 'In some States, the land-owning classes wield a great deal of power and influence and are in authority in government. In many States a considerable number of members of the legislature also come from the land-owning classes and it is too much to expect them to support land reforms at their own cost.'

prerogatives has by no means eliminated the powerful social and political position of the ex-*Zamindars*. They have always held a high rank within the caste hierarchy and since the caste divisions are as strong as ever in rural India, they have automatically become part of the secular élite in the countryside. Since, in addition, they are still in a position to reward loyal ex-tenants with jobs in business or government, they are often the preferred candidates in elections for local, state or central government offices.

It is true that many ex-*Zamindars* have become active farmers and have introduced modern cultivation methods on the land that they claimed for self-cultivation, but, from a general socio-economic point of view they have remained a negative factor that strengthens the caste system in the villages and thus delays the emancipation of the Indian peasants. An investigation of the *Oudh taluqdars*, a particularly powerful group of ex-*Zamindars*, concentrated in the twelve central districts of Uttar Pradesh surrounding the capital city of Lucknow, confirms that the increasing opposition within the Congress Party to further agrarian reforms is due largely to the considerable influence of ex-*Zamindars* on Indian political life.*

This is not to deny that the abolition of intermediary rights has also had some favourable effects. Among other things, it simplified to a considerable extent the landholding systems throughout the country and reduced the countless categories of tenure to two or three principal types. Yet, it did not substantially improve the overall land distribution pattern and local inquiries reveal that, while the incidence of tenancy has declined in some parts of the country, unfortunate new tenancy relations have emerged in others.

Even with regard to land use and agricultural production, the land redistribution programme is far from having fulfilled what it set out to do.† Now, as before, small and uneconomic holdings dominate the land utilization pattern and almost everywhere the

---

* T. R. Metcalf, *Landlords without Land: The U.P.* Zamindars *Today*, South Asia Reprint Series, no. 274 (Institute of International Studies, University of California, 1967).

† Sachin Chaudhuri provides the reasons for this defeat in 'Going Back on Land Reform' in *Economic Planning and Social Organization* (Published by the *Economic and Political Weekly*, Bombay, 1969).

continued fragmentation of holdings far exceeds the modest attempts at land consolidation. In addition, the growing pressure of population further reduces the average size of operational holdings despite the fact that a number of relatively large and efficient holdings have come into being, operated either by former absentee landlords who have resumed land for self-cultivation, or by a new class of financially strong farmers composed of retired army officers, superannuated civil servants, merchants with a pressing need to diversify their wealth, ex-moneylenders and lawyers.* A comparison between national sample surveys for the *Provisional Indicative World Plan for Agricultural Development*† calls attention to the fact that while in 1954–55 farms of 5 acres or less comprised 15.4 per cent of the total farm land in operational agricultural holdings, they comprised 19.2 per cent in 1961–62; and that during the same period land in farms of 20 acres or less increased from 56.5 to 63.7 per cent. It adds that decline in farm sizes also marks countries like Pakistan and Ceylon as well as the Philippines, Indonesia, Thailand and Malaysia.

In the final analysis, reform legislation has primarily favoured the large landowners who have become capitalist farmers who due to their wealth and influence avail themselves of all the facilities which the state gives the agricultural sector, and the better-off part-owners who were given the possibility of enlarging their holdings by acquiring ownership to the rented land. But it gave no relief whatsoever to the small part-owners or landless tenants 'who had to bear the major brunt of evictions and are now mostly tenants-at-will'.‡ And it certainly failed to help the millions of peasants living off tiny plots of exhausted soil whose life continues to be a struggle for bare subsistence whether or not they have the secure occupancy of land. They still work with outdated methods of cultivation at the mercy of landlords and moneylenders and are not even aware of other opportunities be-

* D. Thorner, 'Indian New Farms: New Class Rises in Rural India', *The Statesman* (New Delhi and Calcutta, 1.11.1967); and 'Capitalist Farming in India', *Economic and Political Weekly*, vol. 4, no. 52 (December 1969).

† FAO, Rome, August 1969, p. 409, para. 48.

‡ V. S. Vyas, 'Land Reform Legislation', *Seminar*, no. 8 (New Delhi, May 1966), p. 27.

cause the limited agricultural credit and rural development programmes are monopolized by medium and big farmers.* They will
even sell bags of fertilizers on the black market for a tiny profit
because they have neither the money nor the motivation to use
it themselves.

Agricultural stagnation and widespread rural misery induced
the Congress Party to look for alternative solutions. One result
was the Nagpur Resolution (1959) on cooperative farming after
which the Second and Third Five-Year Plans of the Planning
Commission called for the organization of pilot projects for 'cooperative joint farming'. On the whole, the response of the state
governments was positive and by the end of 1965, about 2,400
cooperative societies had been organized in pilot areas covering
some 265,000 acres. But, unfortunately, they were prepared with
too little foresight and their consequent unsatisfactory achievements have contributed to the disrepute of cooperative farming in
India.

First of all, many of the cooperative farms were established
on inferior land with inexperienced landless people who, depressed
by years of unemployment, were neither able nor ready to overcome the initial difficulties. And secondly, a number of large
landowners used the new emphasis on cooperation to evade
ceilings on size and pooled their land to form fake cooperative
societies through which they could take advantage of the benefits
and privileges assigned by the government to cooperative farming. The Committee of Direction on Cooperative Farming under
the chairmanship of D. R. Gadgil points out in an assessment†
of the results of cooperative farming that in some of the societies,
the landowning members were either non-working or absentees
and had hired a large number of labourers for farm operations.
In two of the societies, the members even belonged to a single
family and cultivated land that twenty years ago had been one
cultivating unit. Although such arrangements may have been use-

* See V. P. Pande, *Village Community Projects in India* (Bombay,
1967), pp. 982 ff.
† Government of India, Ministry of Community Development and
Cooperation, *Report of the Committee of Direction on Cooperative
Farming* (New Delhi, 1965).

ful for the people concerned they have nothing in common either with the spirit or the reality of cooperative farming. A recent investigation in Punjab and Western Uttar Pradesh comes to the conclusion that most of the societies are not true farming cooperatives because they are either family enterprises or associations of people who are largely engaged in occupations other than agriculture.*

Despite considerable efforts, land redistribution in India did not lead to a fundamental change in the old relationship between the large landowners and the hopelessly neglected small owners, tenants, sharecroppers and landless labourers who till more than one-third of the cultivated area. The question is whether it is possible to solve this problem at all within the existing land distribution pattern or whether another redistribution will become imperative in order to mobilize the vast mass of unutilized rural labour that is India's only abundant capital asset.

It might be argued that many of the new modern farms are discharging their functions effectively, but if we consider general rural conditions after two decades of development efforts, it is clearly evident that it is not enough to strengthen the capitalist sector of Indian agriculture, attractive as this may be. The most pressing problem is still how to activate the millions of small cultivators on the unviable holdings in the neglected countryside. Table 8, which reflects the land distribution pattern in 1960–61, reveals the magnitude of this problem which due to the continued trend towards subdivision is probably even greater today.

Nonetheless, present public discussion in India, discouraged by failures in the past, seems to have lost interest in improving village agriculture, and despite some statements in favour of land reform by both camps of the Congress Party, it centres on the importance of enterprise farming, birth control and high-yielding crops for agricultural development and thus for the solution of the agrarian problem. Only a few economists and social scientists seem to realize that 'the social premises of capitalist farming and

---

* H. Laxminarayan and K. Kanungo, *Glimpses of Cooperative Farming in India* (London, 1967), p. 126.

TABLE 8

Agricultural Holdings in India

Class of farmer	Proportion of operational holdings (%)	Proportion of area (%)
Poor farmers	81.81	38.83
Middle farmers	14.80	36.00
Well-off farmers	3.39	25.17

SOURCE: *National Sample Survey*, 16th Round, no. 113 (July 1960–June 1961). Tables with notes on 'Agricultural Holdings in India'.

the economic conditions appropriate to them run counter to the facts inherent in the situation in India ...'*

The idea of a radical land reform is still a popular theme in political statements, but unfortunately, the more important the position of the politician the more he is likely to ultimately tone down any progressive suggestions which he may have made at the beginning.†

But things are now rapidly changing in India and it seems as if the lethargy with respect to the agrarian situation is about to disappear.

Strong social forces are now on the move to break down the taboos and attitudes established by religion and caste division. A new social consciousness is rallying the landless workers and

* Tarlok Singh, *Poverty and Social Change*, pt. 2, p. 285.

See also Government of India, Planning Commission, *Report on the Evaluation of the Rural Electrification Programme* (New Delhi, 1965), pp. 124 ff. In 11 states with advanced electrification the average size of holdings of non-users of electricity was 10 acres, that of prospective users was about 19 acres and that of all users of electric pump sets and tube wells was approximately 28 acres.

† V. V. Giri, President of India, 'Jobs for Our Millions', quoted in the *Indian and Foreign Review*, vol. 7, no. 12 (1 April 1970), pp. 11 ff. In this statement, the President recognizes the need for a constructive policy to combat rural unemployment and actually suggests cooperative land colonization as a possible solution. But in the very next sentence he feels obliged to add that he does not envisage, of course, any changes in the prevailing private ownership rights to land.

sharecroppers into mass movements whose strength should not be underestimated, although they may still be repressed by military force for some time to come.

The peasant riots which started in Naxalbari, West Bengal, in 1967, released a wave of uprisings in the rural areas not only in other parts of Bengal but also in neighbouring Assam and even in Bihar, Rajasthan and Uttar Pradesh. It seems as if the agrarian situation in India has reached a point where the sophisticated formulations suggested by Congress Party politicians and technologists no longer hold out any hope for the impoverished rural masses. Time and again, landless agricultural workers and sharecroppers led by radical peasant organizations or city-based Communist intellectuals invade large estates and forcibly harvest the food crops. Violent clashes with landlords and land-owning peasants have been reported particularly in those areas where the promised implementation of land reform has been delayed and the peasants simply took matters in their own hands and occupied the surplus land.

In large parts of West Bengal, Bihar and Rajasthan landlords are no longer safe and some of them have even been executed by verdict of a peoples' court. As in Latin America, the revolutionary movement has spread to the homeless masses in the cities, who have begun to occupy houses and apartments. It is no coincidence, however, that the radical movements commonly categorised as Naxalite have gained ground at a time when the Congress Party is in the midst of a serious political crisis. Both developments are strongly connected with the growing influence of the new Marxist-Leninist parties in Assam and Bihar who direct their propaganda against the Indian and foreign educational institutions and do not even hesitate to attack the national hero, Mahatma Gandhi.

The Naxalites and the various other Communist movements, are far more than a reaction to the outdated agrarian structure and the social ill-effects of the green revolution. They are a desperate attempt to do away with rural poverty and urban misery by attacking a political system which far too long has served the interests of the privileged classes and has hardly provided more than a hand-out to the impoverished rural and urban people.

It is difficult to predict developments for the coming decade but *one* thing is sure: superficial and half-hearted reform measures will no longer answer the claims of the millions of landless peasants and homeless and unemployed city dwellers for a new egalitarian society, free from caste division and socio-economic privileges. It remains to be seen whether Indian intellectuals will be able to channel the formidable social energies on the move and use them for the establishment of a society which primarily cares for the people in the villages and city slums.

In the *Philippines*, despite almost a century of serious agrarian unrest, the peasants' claims for the redistribution of estate lands and for security of tenure have never been realized. After independence there was a succession of governments each of which came up with some kind of land reform legislation, but since they were usually based on a gross misunderstanding of the agrarian situation they had no practical effect. Equally unsuccessful, however, were, and still are, the continued efforts to quench peasant opposition by force and stabilize the feudalistic land distribution pattern by superficial corrections.

At regular intervals reports are published in the world press that this or that government has finally liquidated the strongholds of the *Hukbalahap* and other peasant movements.* But at equally regular intervals one reads about new riots and fights in the sugar provinces, since the oppression inherent in the Philippine tenure systems calls forth an active opposition in every new peasant generation which remains a potential menace to the existing political and economic order in the islands. It would be a waste of time to discuss any of the many abortive attempts at land reform; let it suffice to state that none of them provided the means for a redistribution of land and that consequently the agrarian structure has hardly changed since the Declaration of Independence. In 1960, approximately 40 per cent of all cultivators were tenants, twice as many as in 1920, while another 10 per cent rented part of the land. †

After a renewed outburst of rural unrest in 1962, the Philippine government, still faced with a strong opposition in Congress against large-scale expropriations, decided to try a different approach. It presented a bill for a Land Reform Code which set down land redistribution as the very last item in a long and in-

* See chapter 5, pp. 128–30.
† *Progress in Land Reform, Fourth Report*, p. 25.

volved programme of transition from tenancy to ownership. Since it clearly deferred the much feared expropriation to the unforeseeable future, it met no further opposition and was enacted in 1963. According to this law, the change in the agrarian structure will be brought about in three stages. During the first stage, sharecropper tenancy will be converted into leasehold against a fixed rent amounting to 25 per cent of average net production during the last three years. During the second stage, the leasehold will be converted into ownership through amortization, while the third and final stage, definite registration of the title, cannot be reached before the tenant has repaid all the costs of land acquisition. Such an approach to land redistribution makes a virtue of a most unfortunate political situation and has been defined correctly as a land productivity policy whose main objective is to remove some of the most oppressive features of an obsolete and defective tenure system* while delaying the actual redistribution of land. Despite the high-minded objective of providing 'a dignified existence for small farmers as owner-cultivators on economic family-size farms conducive to greater productivity and high farm income as the basis of Philippine agriculture', and despite the possible administrative advantage of proceeding by stages, implementation had been started in only 62 of the 1,398 municipalities in the islands by the end of 1968. Even an otherwise cautious FAO appraisal of the Land Reform Code points to the slow implementation, to evasions, to an obvious lack of confidence in the government's desire to implement the law and to a feeling of uncertainty in the rural areas which is likely to adversely affect production. During the 1969 election campaign, President Marcos promised the speedy implementation of the law throughout Central Luzon. But even if this was carried out, the law only holds out a vague hope for the sharecropper as long as the actual conversion of share tenancy to leasehold proceeds as slowly as hitherto. To date, less than 50 per cent of the leasehold grants have actually been formalized and not even 25 per cent have been confirmed in writing. But, in the meantime, illegal share-tenancy increases at a frightening pace.

It cannot be denied, of course, that this very modest programme has provided improved living and working conditions for some

---

* United Nations, FAO, 'FAO Mission to the Philippines, March-May 1967' (Rome, May 1967, mimeographed), p. 29.

new leaseholders and to a certain extent may mitigate some of the worst deficiencies of Philippine farming in limited areas. But, neatly arranged and attractive from a bureaucratic viewpoint as it may be, it is certainly an inadequate response to the passionate claim of the Philippine peasantry for agrarian reform. The extremely slow pace of improvement and land acquisition envisaged by the government is further reduced by the limited provisions in the Code for supporting the tenant after his emancipation. It is difficult to conceive how this piecemeal approach could satisfy the needs of a rather explosive situation;* and how a reform programme, which places land acquisition at the very end of a painfully long process, can possibly avoid being swallowed up by bureaucratic entanglements and political intrigues long before it ever reaches the stage when the actual distribution of estate lands may become a reality.†

CONCLUSIONS

The transformation of obsolete agrarian structures through land redistributions initiated by constitutional action is a protracted and complex process, to say the least. At most it has contributed to the stimulation of agricultural and industrial development, as is the case in Japan and Italy.‡

* Ibid., p. 30: 'The acquisition of land is to be made first from those with the largest holdings over 1,024 hectares and then moved progressively down the scale as needed. The *minimum* residual holding is 75 hectares.'

See also Asian Development Bank, *Asian Agricultural Survey* (Manila, 1968), vol. 2, p. 733.

† See Appendix IV, pp. 360–71.

‡ G. Barbero, *Land Reform in Italy* (FAO, Rome, 1961) and G. E. Marciani, *L'Esperienza di Reforma Agraria in Italia* (SVIMEZ, Rome, 1966), have evaluated the effects of the Italian land reform. The changes in the land reform areas and their side-effects on Italian agriculture are considerable and have, no doubt, increased production and farm income in the areas concerned.

According to periodic estimates by the Italian Ministry of Agriculture, the value of the gross marketable production per hectare at constant prices in the land reform areas rose by 114 per cent during 1953–63, the greatest rise being in those of Sardinia, Campania, Apulia and Calabria, while the real growth was 8.5 per cent per annum compared to the national average of 2.6 per cent.

See also E. B. Shearer, 'Italian Land Reform Re-appraisal', *Land Economics*, vol. 44, no. 1 (1968), pp. 101 ff.

In the truly underdeveloped countries it has as yet had only a limited effect and it remains to be seen to what extent it is at all feasible within a socio-economic framework where powerful vested interests dominate the administration and control the very machinery designed for implementation. In the countries of South Asia, to quote Myrdal;

> agricultural policy has courted the worst of two worlds: equality has not in fact been promoted, with the result that people have become discouraged and cynical, while efficiency has not been adequately recognized and rewarded... [Under such conditions] it might be preferable to make a deliberate policy choice in favour of capitalist farming by allowing and encouraging the progressive cultivator to reap the full rewards of his enterprise and labour, while approaching the fundamental issues of equality and institutional reform from a different angle and by different policy means.*

He is clearly of the opinion that a modified capitalist path of development cannot tolerate passive and parasitic landownership on the part of those who reap the surplus of the agricultural sector but contribute nothing to its productive performance, and that much could be accomplished, therefore, by a tax system that places severe penalties on the income of non-participating landowners. He also mentions the feasibility of modest redistributive schemes, far less radical than those discussed, which would offer a minimal form of social security to the landless agricultural workers by allowing them to produce a modest income in kind which would enhance their status and dignity.

In our view, however, there is nothing to support the contention that a restricted 'land reform', based on heavy taxation and the redistribution of small subsistence plots, would be easier to implement. Given the power structure in underdeveloped countries, any unwelcome taxation is sure to be contested by the vested interests, as was the case in the Philippines and in several Latin American countries. As to the 'modest redistributive scheme', its ultimate effect will be very small indeed, since the mere ownership of a tiny, unviable plot, given the risks of tropical agriculture, lack of credit, etc., will very soon lead to renewed insecurity, dependence and stagnation, and in the end, therefore, to disappointment and misery rather than to enhanced status and dignity.

* G. Myrdal, *Asian Drama*, pt. 2, chap. 26, pp. 1379 ff.

It seems safe to state that a redistribution of land* can be carried out within the existing constitutional framework only on the following two assumptions: first, that peasant organizations are given the chance to develop freely and establish a political and social movement that will attempt to level out the social and economic differences on the village level and represent the peasants' interests on the highest political level. And secondly, that Technical Assistance efforts are concentrated on changes in the socio-economic structure of underdeveloped countries and that a willingness to accept such changes is a precondition for technical and financial support in other fields. If the West would only stop the economic, political or military support of the vested interests in the feudalistic systems, their control over land and labour would soon cease to be profitable and induce them to compromise with the advancing peasant movements—or even to sell out.

But current assistance from the United Nations' Technical Assistance and Western bilateral aid is an effective support for the continued oppression of any movement for or by the peasants in underdeveloped countries. It may be argued, of course, that it would be difficult to prevent private foreign investments; but this is a weak argument for, as matters stand today, private investors are apprehensive of the underdeveloped world's political instability and very seldom act unless they are backed by government or international guarantees. What is needed in order to secure a peaceful change in the power structure is that multilateral and bilateral Technical Assistance be based on a realistic understanding of the true conditions prevailing in underdeveloped countries. But such an understanding seems farther away than ever and is hardly more than a chimerical hope.

Land Redistribution Initiated by Revolutionary Action

In any country marked by rural misery, revolutionary movements, whatever their origin and apparent objectives, will necessarily lead the struggle for land. Yet they no longer aim, unlike the French

* See part II, chapter 7, p. 262.

Revolution 180 years ago, exclusively at a more egalitarian distribution of individual land ownership since in the twentieth century the need is for large-scale production in agriculture as well as industry. Accordingly, the outstanding characteristic of land redistribution under revolutionary conditions, and indeed its most distinguishing feature, is its aspirations towards increased and more effective production rather than compliance with the peasants' claim for ownership to land.

The revolutions in Eastern Europe, in Asia and in Latin America during the past fifty years all shared the conviction that the land belongs to the nation as a whole and that collective or state farming are the most expedient means of ensuring agricultural development. With the exception of Cuba and Algeria where the large and efficient plantations producing export crops were kept intact for national economic reasons, the socialization of agriculture proceeded in two consecutive stages: a preliminary distribution of estate land to small peasants and landless workers followed relatively quickly by a second stage of collectivization.

The description and analysis of land redistribution initiated by revolutionary action is bound to deal with the problems, strategy and results of the second stage rather than with the actual redistribution procedure which is part of the revolutionary process itself and in all cases consists of a rapid, wholesale expropriation of large landholdings without compensation. This stage is, and will always be, marked by the specific character of the revolution and, particularly, of the environment in which the revolution takes place. Once this stage has been accomplished, planners even in the centrally directed economics have to tackle the fundamental problems of land policy, farm structure, incentives, and productivity of land and labour. From the viewpoint of the man-land relationship, an analysis and assessment of socialist agricultural policy and its ultimate effects upon rural society and upon the role of agriculture in overall economic development may contribute to a better understanding of the potential importance of collective and state farming in agrarian reconstruction in underdeveloped countries.

The most urgent problem is to decide upon the new type of land tenure. The variety of socialist tenure types is very considerable, ranging from different forms of collective or state

TABLE 9
Global Agricultural Output

Country	1955–1959 to 1960–1964	1960–1964 to 1965–1969	1964	1965	1966	1967	1968	1969	1970 Plan
	Average compound rates		Percentage increase over preceding year						
Albania									
Total	..	..	1.6	− 4.0	12.5	12	2.5	ca.10	17
Crop output	..	..	7.8	− 6.8	..	..	..	..	..
Animal output	..	..	6.3	− 5.4	..	..	..	..	..
Bulgaria									
Total	5.3	4.7	11.4	1.8	14.3	3.5	− 8.7	2.4	12
Crop output	5.4	4.6	10.3	− 1.5	19.0	1.8	−15.4	ca. 6.4	..
Animal output	5.1	5.0	13.7	8.3	5.8	6.9	− 3.1	− 4.7	..
Czechoslovakia									
Total	0.9	2.5	3.0	− 5.4	11.1	5.5	5.6	0.9	0.6
Crop output	0.2	1.7	1.2	−14.4	21.4	5.3	6.3	1.1	..
Animal output	1.5	3.2	7.3	3.2	3.0	5.8	5.0	0.8	..
Hungary									
Total	1.4	2.7	6	− 5	8	4	1	5–6	1
Crop output	0.8	2.7	3	− 6	12	4	− 1	ca.10	..
Animal output	2.7	2.7	10	− 4	4	5	5	− (1–2)	2–3

TABLE 9
continued

Country	1955–1959 to 1960–1964	1960–1964 to 1965–1969	1964	1965	1966	1967	1968	1969	1970 Plan
	Average compound rates		Percentage increase over preceding year						
Poland									
Total	2.8	3.2	1.3	7.7	5.4	2.5	4.5	− 4.7	3
Crop output	2.9	3.7	0.5	8.4	5.5	3.9	5.4	− 8	4
Animal output	2.7	2.4	2.3	6.6	5.4	0.3	2.9	0.5	1
Rumania									
Total	2.5	2.5	6.3	6.7	14.0	1.8	− 3.7	4.8	16
Crop output	..	..	3.3	6.4	16.5	− 1.9	− 3.9	..	..
Animal output	..	..	14.7	4.5	12.3	7.7	− 3.0	..	..
Soviet Union									
Total	3.0	3.5	14.6	1.8	8.9	1.6	3.2	− 3.2	8.5
Crop output	2.8	..	29.0	− 8.3	12.7	0.1	4.8	..	..
Animal output	3.2	..	− 1.6	17.0	3.4	3.3	1.6	..	..

SOURCE: United Nations Economic Commission for Europe, *Economic Survey of Europe in 1969* (New York, 1970), Part 2, Chap. 1, Table 6 (based on statistical year books, plans and plan-fulfilment reports).

farms to peoples' Communes, as in China, to regional economic planning units on the Cuban model. But on examination, it appears that any one of these tenure types already has been or certainly could be realized in non-socialist countries as well. It must be understood, of course, that neither system is universally acceptable and that their applicability in different environments must be appraised in terms of incentives, efficiency of farm management and available administrative resources. All these systems, however, offer the opportunity of large-scale agriculture, the application of advanced technology, a more efficient labour utilization, and, last but not least, of economy of available administrative and extension staff resources.

It can no longer be denied that during the sixties socialist farming has led to technical progress and considerable growth in agricultural output. According to the *Economic Survey of Europe in 1968,* most Eastern European countries had been able to 'improve their levels of global agricultural output though the fillip of the weather was lacking and the general progress in 1966 has lifted the standards for comparison'.* In that year, most socialist countries in Europe had actually reached the stage when the principal problem is to create economic conditions appropriate for the transition to capital-intensive agriculture.

The *Economic Survey* also points out that the general economic reforms in Eastern European agriculture have created the need for new measures which will prevent the weak structure of the agro-business complex from becoming a bottleneck in the development of the economy. As a matter of fact, several socialist countries have introduced changes in the established institutions and organizations in order to align agriculture with the other sectors of the economy.

The general trend towards a liberalization of socialist agriculture is obvious almost everywhere in Eastern Europe. To an increasing extent farms are authorized to establish auxiliary enterprises for processing their own produce, for services and even for individual or cooperative trading. During the past few years, the share of the farm sector has increased considerably and the income of full-

* United Nations, Economic Commission for Europe, *Economic Survey of Europe in 1968.* Prepared by the Secretariat of the Economic Commission for Europe (New York, 1969), pp. 134 ff.

time collective farmers and state farm workers is gradually approaching urban wage levels.*

1. THE SOVIET UNION

The history of Soviet agriculture may be divided into three distinct phases—the inter-war period, the immediate post-war period, and the Khrushchev and Kosygin period. It is a story of peasant usurpation of land, power and class conflicts in the villages, state interference and compulsion, serious peasant dissatisfaction and, finally, the growing success of collective and state farms. The ruthless liquidation of the *kulaks* which dissolved the old village communities, subdued the rural population's resistance to subsequent government policies such as compulsory deliveries of agricultural produce, and the forced establishment of collective farms (*kolkhozes*) and state farms (*sovkhozes*).

And yet the vital problems of socialist agriculture do not differ essentially from those of individual farming in developed countries where agriculture is an essential part of overall development;

---

* *Economic Survey of Europe in 1968*, p. 136. The theoretical foundation for the liberalization of socialist agriculture is the recognition, contrary to Marxist doctrine, that land has a specific value, that there are differences in the productivity of national resources and that, consequently, the rent differential should be absorbed by the state. This was already confirmed in the decree on Land Nationalization, signed by Lenin in February 1918, and later by the fact that the original motor and tractor stations in the Soviet Union charged collective farms for the work performed roughly in accordance with the productivity of the land. See J. Wilczynski, 'Towards Rationality in Land Economics under Central Planning', *The Economic Journal*, vol. 79, no. 315 (September 1969), p. 542, fn. 4. (*Kolkhozes* in the Krasuodar Region paid 150 kg. of grain for ploughing 1 hectare of land for grain cultivation, but those in Byelorussia only 35 kg.)

This deviation from Marxist doctrine has been firmly established in recent years by new schools of socialist economists who, despite disagreement on the method of determination, acknowledge the need for a land valuation in monetary terms for planning purposes which would lead to a better allocation of agricultural resources and increased labour productivity. See ibid., p. 545 and fns.

The practical implication of the inclusion of rent in the cost of agricultural production will make land-intensive primary products less economical as compared with labour-intensive production and thus strengthen the position of agricultural labour.

namely, how to provide incentives for increased production of food and other agricultural commodities; how to make the cultivators accept technical innovations; and how to extract from agriculture the savings and manpower needed for industrial development. Efforts to tackle these problems are based on such agricultural policy measures as price formation and marketing, farm organization, mechanization and, finally, the distribution of income from agriculture. In the course of its fifty years of existence the Soviet Union has experimented with a variety of agricultural programmes which to start with were a process of trial and error. For more than three decades their principal objective was to promote agriculture for the furtherance of industrial development, and only during the past two decades have they been designed with a view to increasing the incentives for the farming population. Compulsory deliveries have been replaced by a controlled market economy; agricultural prices have been increased considerably; motor and tractor stations have been incorporated into the collective farms; and the rigid administration of agriculture has been loosened in order to permit the farm units to buy their own machinery and market their own surplus production.

The emotional reaction against the violence and human suffering which accompanied the enforced collectivization in Soviet Russia has led many observers to misjudge socialist farming in general and the performance of Soviet agriculture, in particular. They hold the system of collective farming itself responsible for the slow development of agriculture, although it cannot be proved to what extent, if at all, individual farming would have done better under the pressure of an exacting price policy and an onerous system of compulsory deliveries. Just as certain experts on underdeveloped countries tend to underestimate the impact of outdated tenure conditions on labour productivity and land use, some critics of Soviet agriculture are inclined to rest their case on the fictitious assumption that collective tenure is primarily responsible for the relatively poor performance of Soviet agriculture between 1917 and 1938* and that any other type of tenure would have been able to protect effectively the economic and social interests of the peasants against a hostile price and market policy. They seem to forget completely that during this period collective farm-

* See D. Mitrany, *Marx against the Peasant* (London and New York, 1961).

ing was hardly more than an expedient tool for levying direct taxes in kind which the state needed for expanding the industrial sector and for mobilizing unutilized and underutilized labour for capital formation. Unless these facts are recognized it is impossible to make an objective appraisal of collective agriculture.

When describing the particular effects of land redistribution in Soviet Russia it would be futile to resume the old discussion on collective versus individual farming since this would neither add to our general knowledge of Soviet agriculture nor contribute to an interpretation of the role of collective and state farms in economic development—Marxists and anti-Marxists are anyway equally boring when they discuss the merits and demerits of collective farming. Instead we shall attempt to assess the development and performance of Soviet agriculture in relation to general economic development. Recent literature on the subject clearly indicates that a reappraisal of socialist agriculture is under way in Western economic thinking although it has not yet become common knowledge.

The final decision on a nationwide collectivization of agriculture was made in the mid-twenties on the basis of the successful performance of the few existing state and collective farms which had been established in the 1917–24 period.* Although their yields per acre were only slightly better than the average obtaining on the peasant farms, the output levels were achieved with substantial savings in manpower. Collective and state farming provided the organizational framework for the mobilization of seasonal unemployed labour for capital formation and was soon able to lengthen the work-year per person in agriculture from around 120 days to approximately 185–190 days.† It has also been reported that the collective farms contributed labour equal to an annual average of about one million yearly workers.‡

Contrary to the belief held by many Western experts on Soviet

* C. K. Wilber, 'The Role of Agriculture in Soviet Economy', *Land Economics*, vol. 45, no. 1 (February 1969), pp. 87 ff.

† US Congress, Joint Economic Committee, *Comparisons of the United States and Soviet Economies*, 86th Congress, 1st Session, 1960, p. 213.

‡ A. Kahan, 'The Collective Farm System in Russia: Some Aspects of its Contribution to Soviet Economic Development' in *Agriculture in Economic Development*, C. Eicher and L. Witt (eds.), (New York and London, 1964), pp. 252–5.

conditions, Soviet agriculture was an aid, not a handicap to development. Their judgment is usually based on an unfair comparison of present-day Soviet yields with those obtaining in the United States without making allowance for 'geographic and cultural differences, relative capital endowments, the element of time and differential development strategies'.* The situation appears in quite a different light when comparing Soviet agricultural growth with other countries. In that case both total and per capita average annual growth rates of agricultural production since 1928 have been higher in the Soviet Union. Given that the average annual growth in output per man also compares quite favourably (1928–59: USSR 3.1 per cent and USA 3.4 per cent)† there is little justification for the argument that the collective farm system has been a disincentive to Soviet agriculture.

When it was decided some fifteen years ago to finally improve the economic position of agricultural labour by changes in the distribution of investment funds and of the terms of trade for agriculture, collective and state farms proved not only a suitable instrument for raising the level of living of the rural population, but they continued, though at a more moderate rate, to provide savings for industrial investments.‡ The improved financial situation was due also to a new arrangement whereby the collective farms gradually obtained access to direct bank credits instead of having to rely on advance payments on state purchases. By 1967, about 23,000 collective farms worked with bank credits.

Achievements have also been impressive with regard to increased labour productivity.§ Between 1950 and 1964 the number of man-hours declined by 9 per cent despite an increase of 41 per cent in the agricultural area. During the same period, inputs in agriculture increased roughly by one-third while output rose by 70 per cent. Despite the exceptionally poor growing conditions in 1963, the straight annual growth average of net agricultural

* C. K. Wilber, art. cit., p. 91.
† Ibid., p. 91, table 1 and p. 92, table 2.
‡ R. Dumont (*Sovkhoz, kiolkhoz, ou le problématique communisme*, Paris, 1964) recognizes this fact although he is otherwise still strongly impressed by those aspects of early soviet agricultural policy which denied agriculture a fair chance of development.
§ US Congress, Joint Economic Committee, 'New Directions in the Soviet Economy', in *Economic Performance, Part II-B*, 89th Congress, 2nd Session, 1966, pp. 346 ff.

output for 1961–65 was still 2.7 per cent compared to an average of 3.8 per cent for the entire period. It is significant that livestock production participated in this favourable development despite a heavy setback in 1963–64; in 1965, the livestock index was 212 (1950=100) as against 184 in 1960 and 137 in 1955. Within the one year of 1965–66, global agricultural output increased by 10 per cent and the gross income of collective farms by about 15 per cent.* Although conditions in 1967 were less favourable than during the previous year, the growth rate of agricultural output was maintained and even slightly increased, and the average rate of expansion of some 5 per cent over the last four-year period bodes well for the future.†

During the period 1964–68, in fact, the global agricultural output increased at an average rate of nearly 6 per cent. Compared to this performance and in view of the unfortunate weather situation that year, the decline of 3.2 per cent in 1969 cannot be considered a serious setback. Under equally bad weather conditions in 1963, the decline had been as great as 7.5 per cent. The final figures for the agricultural sector in 1969 confirm the progress in agro-techniques and farm management achieved in recent years.‡

The agricultural situation in 1969 was marked by an extraordinary cereal harvest in the Ukraine which had increased by 31 per cent and reached an all-time high of 36.5 million tons, but at the same time by a continued weakness in livestock production. To remedy the latter, a new policy is under way which will gradually transfer livestock production to large-scale, fully mechanized enterprises.

On the other hand, outside investments in agriculture showed a favourable development and among other things the target for deliveries of chemical fertilizers was exceeded by 7 per cent.

It is self-evident that this considerable progress was due largely to the education and training of a qualified labour force. Despite the increasing number of specialized agricultural schools and colleges, the mechanization of agriculture proceeds at such a pace that a shortage of qualified people will be a serious problem for Soviet agriculture for some time to come.

* *Economic Survey of Europe in 1966*, chap. 2, pp. 14, 18.
† *Economic Survey of Europe in 1967*, chap. 2, pp. 19, 23.
‡ *Economic Survey of Europe in 1969*, pt. 2, chap.1, pp. 56 ff.

Many observers attribute the Soviet agricultural development in the past decade to the high productivity of the private plots on the collective farms (one-fourth to one hectare and recently reduced to 2000 m² for irrigated and 5000 m² for other land) and are inclined to believe that individual farming and marketing provided the incentive for the record performance. It cannot be denied that, in proportion to its relative size, this 'private' sector has played a considerable role, particularly in livestock and meat production* and that the private plot, to some extent at least, realized the Agrarian Creed of the Soviet farmer. But this over-simplified interfarm comparison of productivity proves little more than the continued existence of a prejudice against Soviet agriculture which ignores the fact that the private plots are complementary to, rather than competitive with, collective agriculture since they are operated with machinery, agricultural requisites, stock animals and feeding stuffs belonging to the collectives and that, accordingly, the operators have access to a larger number

TABLE 10

USSR: Indexes of net Agricultural Production, 1950–65
(1950 = 100)

	Total	Crops	Livestock		Total	Crops	Livestock
1950	100	100	100	1958	155	143	172
1951	97	91	105	1959	149	122	185
1952	104	102	110	1960	150	124	184
1953	106	97	119	1961	163	135	200
1954	109	99	123	1962	161	129	204
1955	126	118	137	1963	153	118	199
1956	141	138	145	1964	170	157	186
1957	141	126	160	1965	171	141	212

SOURCE: US Congress, Joint Economic Committee, 'New Directions in the Soviet Economy,' in *Economic Performance, Part II-B*, 89th Congress, 2nd Session, 1966, p.346.

* See *Progress in Land Reform, Fourth Report*, p. 82, and fn. 182; and A. N. Sakoff, 'The Private Sector in Soviet Agriculture', *FAO Monthly Bulletin of Agricultural Economics and Statistics*, vol. 11, no. 9 (September 1962).

TABLE 11

USSR: Average Annual Rates of Growth of net Agricultural Output: Selected Periods, 1951–65[a]

	Straight annual average	Moving average for 3 years[b]
1951–64	3.8	3.7
1951–53	2.0	2.4
1954–55	9.2	8.7
1956–59	4.2	4.8
1960–64	2.6	1.7
1961–65	2.7	—

SOURCE: 'New Directions in the Soviet Economy'.
[a] The base year for the calculations shown in each line is the year before the stated initial year of period, i.e., the average annual rate of increase for 1951–53 is computed by relating production in 1953 to base year 1950.
[b] Average annual rates of growth were computed by relating the 3-year average for the terminal year (for example, output in 1953 as the average for 1952, 1953, and 1954) to a similar 3-year average for the base year (1950).

TABLE 12

USSR: A Comparison of the Value of net Farm Output, 1950–64
(In billions of rubles)[a]

	Net output for 5-year period	Average annual output
1950–54	133.08	26.62
1955–59	184.02	36.80
1960–64	205.32	41.06

SOURCE: 'New Directions in the Soviet Economy'.
[a] Billions of rubles in 1959 prices. Computed by moving the total value of output for sale and home consumption in 1959 (38.48 billion rubles).

H

TABLE 13

USSR: Indexes of Inputs Used by Agriculture, 1950–64
(1950 = 100)

	1950	1951	1952	1953	1954	1955	1956	1957	1958	1959	1960	1961	1962	1963	1964
Labour:															
Man-days[a]	100	N.A.	91	93	95	100	101	98	98	98	94	94	94	91	91
Employment[b]	100	96	93	93	92	93	94	96	101	99	95	94	96	94	95
Fixed capital[c]	100	111	122	134	146	164	187	209	234	260	286	310	342	384	432
Current purchases	100	110	112	138	145	152	158	169	184	193	203	221	239	262	279
Productive livestock[d]	100	105	110	113	121	131	141	151	162	170	172	176	184	187	187

SOURCE: 'New Directions in the Soviet Economy'.

[a] All man-days expended in farm activity.

[b] Limited to persons principally or exclusively engaged in farm activity.

[c] Average of stocks at end of given and previous year. Includes value of draft animals.

[d] Average of stock values at end of given year and previous year.

N.A. = Not available.

of production factors than the actual area allocated to them.* From an economic and technical point of view, the private plot must be considered part of the collective rather than an isolated individual farm household. It may be assumed, however, that the steady development and consolidation of the collective and state farm economy may gradually increase the returns from agriculture to such an extent that the private plots will lose their significance as a source for satisfying the personal requirements of the collective farmers.† The modernization of Soviet agriculture is a task of tremendous dimensions; the need for a more rapid transfer of research results to the farm sector was officially recognized in a decree of October 1968, but the level of capital assets per agricultural worker is still comparatively low, though electro-energy supplies to the farm sector rose by as much as 21 per cent in 1968.‡

In its analysis of the general achievements of agriculture in the Soviet Union and the Eastern European countries the *Economic Survey of Europe in 1966*§ states that although it is difficult to define the respective parts played by the various elements—weather, techniques, and incentives—'one thing is nevertheless certain; even if the weather has assisted the improvement, government measures are assuming an increasingly important role. There is no doubt that the present approach to the problems in the agricultural sector is undergoing profound changes under the pressure of general economic development and that the harmonious and comprehensive integration of agriculture into the rest of the economy is initiated.' And the survey for 1967‖ even concludes that 'the preference of agriculture tends to confirm the tendency observed in recent years which points to a diminished dependency of agricultural performance on changes in weather conditions'.

This seems to be due in the first place to the continued decentralization and liberalization which has finally broken the isolation of agricultural enterprises and gradually links them to one

* 'Land Reform and Organization of the Peasants into Cooperatives in the USSR' (RU : WLR /66/49), p. 5. Paper submitted to the World Land Reform Conference, FAO, Rome, 1966.
† *Soviet Financial System* (Moscow, 1966), p. 163.
‡ *Economic Survey of Europe in 1968*, pp. 138–9.
§ Chapter 2, p. 15.
‖ *Economic Survey of Europe in 1967*, chap. 2, p. 1.

another as well as to state industries with regard to planning. Secondly, it stems from the gradual revision of prices, by a policy which has established a price level for agricultural produce that not only covers production costs but leaves a reasonable profit margin which also secures the accumulation necessary for expanded food production. Finally, old prejudices have been overcome and, gradually though not openly as yet, the ground rent of agriculture is being reinstated into tax and price regulations.

One should, however, beware of drawing the hasty conclusion that the rationalization of socialist agriculture, reluctantly started in the late fifties and accelerated during the early sixties, signals the introduction of a capitalist agriculture. In fact, all that this illustrates is that dominant economic thought in the Soviet Union has recognized that the law of values leads to the formation of profits even in socialist economics.* The organizational framework of Soviet agriculture has likewise been subject to gradual changes. Whereas, after years of debate, collective farms were given preference over state farms as the more appropriate tenure system, the introduction of similar methods of planning, and directives for accounting and labour remuneration has gradually reduced the differences between the two types of tenure. And today, state farms play an important role in agriculture and are even considered by some observers to be the leading socialist enterprise in the countryside, since by definition they are free from any trace of private ownership. It seems safe to assume, however, that this was a deliberate development based on very realistic considerations. The rate at which both unusually prosperous and very poor collective farms are being converted into state farms is probably due to the fact that the state needs the high profits of the former for fulfilling its economic responsibility to the latter. In addition, state farms prove to be the more efficient since collective farms could not be expected to carry the risk of the inevitable crop fluctuations which follow the reclamation of virgin land. In the past ten years or so, the state farm sector consisting of relatively few but very prosperous state enterprises has developed into a kind of agricultural clearing house which supports the poor and more risky undertakings that need state guarantees or very considerable investment. The increasing number of backward collec-

* J. Liberman, 'The Soviet Economic Reform', *Foreign Affairs*, vol. 46, no. 1 (New York, October 1967), pp. 53 ff.

tive farms converted into state farms, however, has weakened the general financial position of the state farm sector and, according to the *Economic Survey of Europe in 1966*, it was not considered strong enough to take over full economic responsibility for enterprise activity.

The first practical step towards increasing the efficiency of state farms was taken in the spring of 1967 when 406 state farms were selected to operate on the basis of autonomous economic accounting under the assumption that income has to cover both operating expenses and new investments. They are free to decide the level of employment and the utilization of available funds, but have to pay considerably increased wages. In order to strengthen the economic basis of these well-selected farms their delivery prices have been raised to the level of those paid to local collective farms. It will be interesting to see whether this reorganization affords a solution to the financial problem of the state farm sector.

When analysing the position of the human factor in the course of agricultural development in the Soviet Union two major factors must be considered. The first is that Soviet Russia has had to develop its economy without any outside aid or credit and in the face of a world-wide opposition, and accordingly it fell to the collective farms to provide the capital and food needed for industrial expansion. The other is the impact of the Second World War which, with its toll of 20 million of the active population, the drain on the economy, the devastation of the countryside, and the subsequent Cold War led to a setback in development which took years to overcome. As has happened in the Western world during periods of rapid development, the heaviest burden fell on one particular group: in England it was the first two generations of factory workers and in the United States the most recent wave of immigrants; in the Soviet Union the peasants had to suffer, on their neglected soil—albeit for the development of a socialist economy and not for the profits of private enterprise.

Until the mid-fifties one of the weakest parts of Soviet agriculture was the system of labour remuneration and it cannot be denied that throughout this period the private plots helped to keep Soviet agriculture and the Soviet farmer afloat. The state paid exceedingly low prices for the compulsory deliveries of food and agricultural raw materials needed for the expanding industrial sector, and the volume exacted was arbitrarily fixed and therefore tended to in-

crease with the growth of the industrial population rather than
with that of agriculture.

The combined effect of the volume and price of the deliveries
to the state was that any incentive on the part of the peasants
on collective farms to increase production was removed. And
even when the pressure on the agricultural sector had somewhat
abated, the prices for the scarce manufactured goods were fixed
at a level so much higher than that for agricultural produce, that
little room was left for any material incentive. Due to this unparalleled concentration on industry, agriculture in the Soviet
Union was a neglected sector of the economy and the people
working and living under such unfavourable conditions were dissatisfied and frustrated.

Despite some improvements in the system of remuneration on
collective farms the gap between income from industry and agriculture continued to widen. Even in the late fifties when fixed
monthly cash payments, based on labour input, results and the
collective farms' potential were introduced and supplemented by
an annual bonus, which was calculated according to net profits,
the overall level of agricultural wages lagged far behind those of
industry.

It was not until the mid-sixties that the government decided
to tackle seriously the problem of agricultural income, and the
resolution of 16 May 1966 'On Raising the Material Incentives of
Collective Farmers'* represents a turning point for the peasants in
the Soviet Union and amounts to a kind of agrarian reform of
Soviet agriculture. It recommends among other things, that, in
distributing their gross income, the collective farms shall give
labour remunerations, in cash and kind, to their members on a
guaranteed monthly basis which thus recognizes agricultural labour
as a cost factor just like other costs. This is a decisive step forward
which will enhance the economic function of the human factor in
collective agriculture. Moreover, the guaranteed monthly payments
will become a test of each collective farm's efficiency, as the labour
remuneration fund must now be established at the planning stage
and cannot be used any longer to cover up the costs of errors
and mismanagement. According to recent information† the implementation of this resolution caused some difficulties in the

* *Economic Survey of Europe in 1966*, chap. 2, p. 19.
† *Economic Survey of Europe in 1968*, p. 140.

economically weak collective farms, but by the end of 1968, it was reported that the income of the members of a number of collective farms had almost reached the guaranteed level. An earlier experiment with guaranteed cash remunerations seems to have already convinced the farmers that any additional effort to strengthen the economy of their collective will increase their own material well-being.*

Currently, experiments are under way to improve incentive on state farms by establishing work brigades which are to be remunerated according to performance.

2. OTHER EASTERN EUROPEAN COUNTRIES

Apart from Poland and Yugoslavia, the other socialist countries of Eastern Europe more or less followed the Soviet pattern of agrarian reconstruction, although their course of action was generally less violent and tense. In all of them the redistribution of expropriated land to individual peasant families was soon followed by the collectivization of agriculture, which was to be most widespread in *Rumania* and *Bulgaria* where collective farm enterprises dominate the countryside.

In both these countries, peasant farming was adapted to socialist agriculture by the gradual integration of the holdings into some kind of common-land-use like joint farming, cooperative land improvement and irrigation schemes, which introduced the peasants to the advantages of collective action.

The principal economic motives underlying the collectivization of agriculture in Eastern Europe may be summed up as follows: first, to reduce and possibly eliminate the discrepancy between the large-scale industrialization which was planned and an agricultural production carried out on millions of extremely fragmented holdings; and secondly, to make possible the changeover from extensive to intensive cultivation by the use of modern agricultural equipment and machinery, which could only be used on large surface areas.

The initial stages were extremely difficult throughout Eastern Europe for, as in the Soviet Union, a backward and devastated

* K. Oschapkin, 'Erfahrungen mit der Geldvergütung der Arbeit in den Kollektivschaften', *Internationale Zeitschrift der Landwirtschaft, DDR* (Berlin, 1967), pp. 23 ff.

agriculture which was badly in need of reorganization, had to carry the burden of industrialization. After a long period of centralized supervision and administration, the last decade has seen a general trend towards liberalization which has given greater incentives to the collective farms. New principles were applied with the object of strengthening their independence with regard to planning, management and finance, and substituting indirect measures for the exaction of centrally planned targets. In Rumania,* the introduction of stable prices for agricultural products and of surplus prices for surplus production acted as important incentives to additional effort.

Since the reorganization of agriculture in Poland and Yugoslavia which followed the revolutionary redistribution of land to peasants and workers differs substantially from the general pattern outlined above, we will deal with the particular types of socialist tenure which have emerged in these two countries in somewhat greater detail.

In *Poland*, the collectivization of agriculture was a transitional stage only. The tenants and landless workers who had become owner-cultivators through the redistribution of the large estates were at first obliged, for a limited period of five years, to join *land distribution cooperatives* for the common cultivation of the newly acquired land. This, however, proved to be an unsatisfactory approach since the set limit of five years made it impossible for the cooperatives to set long-term targets or accumulate sufficient funds for the investments and improvements needed to raise the new owners' standard of living. It became increasingly difficult to maintain a spirit of solidarity and one after another the members used their right to withdraw at the end of the stipulated period. The frequent reorganization of the cooperatives caused by the withdrawals inevitably adversely affected land utilization and production. It has been said that this type of collective farming never comprised more than 7 per cent of the peasant families. A few cooperatives still exist and some have even been reestablished, mostly by new peasant-owners who lack the experience to manage on their own.

* 'Agrarian Reform and Recent Measures for Agricultural Development in Rumania' (RU:WLR/66/51), p. 5. Paper submitted to the World Land Reform Conference, FAO, Rome, 1966.

In view of the individualistic Polish peasantry's general opposition to the cooperatives, and the given economic conditions which did not permit the capital investment needed for mechanized large-scale farming, the government decided, in 1956, to abandon the plan for the collectivization of agriculture and concentrate instead on establishing viable family farm units. Since then peasant farming has dominated Polish agriculture. Ninety-four per cent of the rural population operate individual holdings that together comprise 85 per cent of the agricultural area and account for 88 per cent of agricultural production and 82 per cent of market deliveries.* Collective farms comprise only 1 per cent and state farms barely 13 per cent of the agricultural area.

The general effect of a centrally directed economy is undoubtedly to reduce gradually the family farm pattern. But this is a long-term development, and in the meantime the most important problem is to raise the general level of peasant farming and improve cultivation methods. In order to hasten this development it was decided to revive and strengthen the *agricultural circles,* on old form of mutual assistance among the Polish peasantry which had been founded by enlightened estate owners and Church dignitaries in the latter half of the nineteenth century for the purpose of raising the educational level of the peasants. These circles, which had been an important instrument for developing the rural areas after the First World War when Poland had once more become a sovereign state, had lost much of their influence during the first decade of reorganization and collectivization after the Second World War.

But after 1956, they reassumed their role as an important rural institution. They are financed by the Agricultural Development Fund which was established in order to lighten the burden of compulsory deliveries. The state pays the difference between compulsory and open market prices into this fund, on the understanding that 80 per cent shall be redistributed to the farmers for investment commensurate with their deliveries, while 20 per cent shall be used for the administration and activities of the agricultural circles.

By 1968, the agricultural circles had a membership of about

* 'Structural Changes and Development of Peasant Farms in Poland' (RU:WLR/66/16), p. 13. Paper submitted to the World Land Reform Conference, FAO, Rome, 1966.

1.5 million, or almost one-third of all peasant farmers, and handled more than 26 per cent of the total investment in the peasant farm sector. Their main activity is to provide agricultural extension, mechanized farm equipment, fertilizers and improved seeds to the peasants. It is interesting to note that mechanization is not yet considered an urgent need, as sufficient manpower is still available in most parts of the country for the cultivation of the average family farm and labour-saving machinery as such is not economically attractive due to the prevailing shortage of alternative employment. In other words, the favourable man-land ratio (between 1931 and 1950 the per capita availability of land had increased from 0.96 to 1.44 hectares) not only made large-scale collective farming less pressing but ensured that the speed of mechanization would remain commensurate with overall economic and industrial development. Poland is probably the only country in Europe where the number of draught-horses has increased since 1966.

The greatest merit of the agricultural circles is that they are making the peasant farmer increasingly aware of the necessity for innovations and of the opportunities available for improving their professional and social standing. According to a field study carried out in 1967, the members of the agricultural circles are very active and make good use of the extension services. Their farms are better equipped and more productive than those of other farmers and their standard of living is considerably higher.*

The relative increase in efficiency of the Polish system of small farms is largely the result of their gradual integration into a kind of cooperative 'agro-business' through government contracts for crops and animal products. Although this institutional framework is not yet fully developed and only comprises about 50 per cent of all farms, it is the nucleus of a socialist system of vertical integration which supports the continued existence of the family farm system within a centrally directed economy. The changeover to larger units in agriculture may eventually become necessary, but as long as this depends on the increase of employment oppor-

* B. Galeski, 'The *Agricultural Circle* as a Main Form of Mutual Assistance Among Poland's Farmers'. Paper submitted to the Third Session of the Working Party on Agrarian Structure in Europe, Bucharest, June 1968 (ECA: AS/68/13, FAO, Rome, 1968).

tunities in the industrial centres, private farm ownership in Poland will persist longer than was originally intended.

Unlike collective farming, state farms have become an important factor in Polish agriculture.* The first state farms were established in order to take over the cultivation of expropriated large estates during the period of redistribution. Today, they comprise 2,500,000 hectares, or 13 per cent of the agricultural area. Their principal functions are: to conduct agricultural research and practical training; to produce improved seeds and high-quality livestock for distribution to peasant farmers; to set an example by using rational farming methods and thereby supporting the state in its efforts to carry out its agricultural policy and, particularly, to have some control over the domestic market with regard to the most important food items.†

To begin with, the state farms under the direct supervision and administration of the Ministry of Agriculture were linked directly to the state budget with regard both to expenses and revenue. This complete dependence, however, produced a feeling of indifference and had a negative effect upon their performance. With the change in agricultural policy in 1956, they were given authority to plan their own activities and handle their own economy. The state should no longer impose the production lines but simply provide the necessary economic incentives through cheap credits and even through grants if unfavourable conditions should arise. This clear division between production and investment has undoubtedly boosted the activity of the state farms, and their actual role in Polish agriculture by far exceeds their rather modest share in the agricultural area. They have become an important part of the 'agro-business' and their educational and practical activities strongly support the family farm sector.

Polish agricultural production has shown an upward trend for several years. In 1968 global output growth was 4.4 per cent compared to 2.3 per cent in 1967 and an average of 6.5 per

* 'Structural Changes and Development of Peasant Farms in Poland' (C/66/26). Paper submitted to the World Land Reform Conference, FAO, Rome, 1966.

† In 1964, the state farms supplied 34.6 per cent of the bread grain, 22.2 per cent of the milk, and 13 per cent of the cattle for slaughter sold on the market; in 1965 their gross output accounted for 10.9 per cent of the total agricultural production.

cent in the two preceding years; while in 1968, capital investment in agriculture had increased by about 5 per cent.

In 1969, the agricultural output growth declined 4.7 per cent partly because of adverse weather conditions. Although this decline is not very serious, it is unfortunate that Polish farmers are so slow to adapt to technical progress; they continue to use outdated feeding methods and pay too little attention to silage and other modern means of feed preservation. The *Economic Survey of Europe in 1969** emphasizes that great efforts seem to be needed to teach the small private farmers to use chemical fertilizers properly and that more than 10 per cent of them do not use any at all. There is no doubt that this reluctance of the small peasant farmers is the price which Poland has to pay for the maintenance of peasant farming.

Other factors limiting agricultural expansion in Poland are a progressive fragmentation of farm holdings and a decreasing efficiency of the agricultural labour force. The *Economic Survey of Europe in 1967* reports that more than 51 per cent of private farm holdings are under 5 hectares, that almost 5 per cent of arable land is owned by farmers aged above 60, and that an estimated one million holdings are run by women.†

In an effort to remedy these shortcomings, the government passed new legislation early in 1968 for a large-scale land consolidation programme. In addition to the structural changes envisaged, this law also deals with problems of farm management and provides, among other things, that inadequately cultivated land shall be put to better use or, under certain circumstances, be put up for auction where the state has the right to pre-emption; farmers considered too old to operate their holdings effectively are to be retired and given a monthly pension as well as the right to the lifelong use of a plot of land of up to one hectare. This programme is expected to bring about fundamental structural changes which will improve agricultural production.

The particular structure of Polish agriculture is of more than theoretical interest to underdeveloped countries. The peasant has become owner of the land that he tills and carries out most of his farming activities with no great measure of interference; yet, he

---

* p. 62.

† *Economic Survey of Europe in 1967*, chap. 2, pp. 26–7; and *Economic Survey of Europe in 1968*, chap. 2, p. 142.

has been freed from his traditional isolation through the agricultural circles and is gradually being integrated into national agricultural production by government contracts that encourage him to take on responsibility. Thus while the long-term prospects for increased production and income from farming are favourable, the rate and speed at which the individual farmer can advance economically is determined by the interests of the society as a whole. This, moreover, gives him added security because the very factor which determines the limits of personal success protects him at the same time against the disastrous consequences of personal failure.

Despite private ownership of the land, this socialist variant of individual farming is quite distinct from the Western pattern of family holdings. Neither the farmer nor his cooperative association has the possibility of making final decisions since the price and marketing policy as well as investment trends are part of the central plan for overall development.

Yugoslavia represents another example of a revolutionary land redistribution that did not follow the usual pattern. During the Second World War when the country was under German occupation, the partisans had spontaneously redistributed the land in many of the villages, and immediately after the liberation in 1945, the large estates and all land belonging to the German minority was expropriated by law. More than 1,600,000 hectares of agricultural land were thus made available for redistribution through a general land fund established for this purpose. For the actual expropriation procedure public hearings were organized by peoples' committees on the spot, whose decisions could be appealed against in the local district courts.*

A considerable part of the expropriated land, particularly in the vast fertile plains of Vojvodina and Slovenia, was used for the resettlement of peasants, preferably partisans, from agriculturally depressed areas. The remarkable speed with which the redistribution of land was carried out did not leave time, however, for careful advance planning. Only 300,000 hectares were set aside for large state and collective farms, while a total of

---

* 'Agrarian Reform and Economic Development in Yugoslavia' (RU:WLR/66/18), pp. 6–7. Paper submitted to the World Land Reform Conference, FAO, Rome, 1966.

about 790,000 hectares were distributed in private ownership to landless peasants, to the owners of unviable holdings of less than 20 hectares, and to small peasant-producer cooperatives.*

The effect of this first radical redistribution, however, fell far below expectations. The lack of proper planning has led to an undue fragmentation of the farm land and the shortage of adequate extension services for the new settlers from the hill regions who lacked both experience and implements for the rational cultivation of the fertile plain land led to a considerable decline in both production and market supplies.† Despite their limited number and functional weaknesses it was the large state and collective farms that kept Yugoslavian agriculture afloat during the critical years of the late forties and early fifties, and proved their potential capacity for integrating individual peasant holdings.

The slow rate of growth in agricultural production soon proved a serious obstacle to industrial expansion, and between 1949 and 1951 the gap between aggregate demand for agricultural products and actual supply had widened to such an extent that government interference was called for. Under the circumstances, large-scale collective production seemed the only solution and a countrywide collectivization drive brought about one-fifth of the total arable area into the 'peasant-producer cooperatives'. But this also failed to bring about the desired increase in productivity, as the establishment of cooperatives was not accompanied by improved methods of cultivation and adequate extension services. One after the other they broke up and agricultural unemployment increased far beyond the absorption capacity of the industrial sector. In 1953, a new land redistribution policy was introduced by law‡ which reduced the ceiling for private holdings from 20 to 10 hectares. Contrary to former expropriation practices, the government now purchased the surplus land with bonds payable over a period of twenty years and transferred it almost exclusively to the state farms and those peasant-producer cooperatives still in existence, in order to increase agricultural employment and, at the same time, strengthen the socialist sector in agriculture.

The Law on Socially Owned Land Fund marks the beginning of a new agricultural policy in Yugoslavia. Compulsory deliveries

* Ibid., p. 8.
† Ibid., p. 9.
‡ 'Law on Socially Owned Land Fund, 1953', ibid., p. 11.

were abolished and rigid central planning gradually gave way to a more liberal price policy that provided badly needed incentives for increased production and the introduction of modern machinery. In 1957, the Federal Peoples' Assembly passed a resolution demanding the expansion and consolidation of the large-scale collective enterprises.*

The enlarged socialist sector of agriculture received considerable government support and soon reached a relatively high technological standard and level of production. Although in 1961 it comprised only about 10 per cent† of the agricultural area, it accounted for 16 per cent of the gross agricultural output and its rate of growth was well above that of the private farms. Taking into account the shortage of capital and staff resources in Yugoslavia during the late fifties and early sixties, the priority given to investment in the socialist sector of agriculture should not be regarded as a socialist bias. It was a sound economic policy which gradually came to benefit the individual peasant farmers, who through cooperation with the socialist enterprises in their neighbourhood were able to improve their cultivation methods and farm organization.

In more recent times, the private sector, which still dominates agriculture, has also been given additional incentives through price increases, bonuses for quality, and local price supplements. The coexistence of individual and collective ownership has given rise to unique forms of cooperation between individual holdings and collective farm enterprises, one of which entitles the private farmer entering into cooperative cultivation agreements with either state or collective farms to participate for a period of three years in delivery contracts which guarantee fixed minimum prices. By 1968 about 45 per cent (25 per cent in 1960) of the over 2.6 million individual holdings had entered cooperative cultivation agreements with socialist farm enterprises; and nearly 20 per cent of the 6 million hectares of crop land belonging to individual holdings, was being ploughed by machines belonging to socialist farms.‡

* 'Resolution on Methods of Promoting Agriculture and the Cooperative System', ibid., p. 13.

† By 1966, about 14 per cent of total agricultural area. (Ibid., p. 14).

‡ 'Cooperation and Mutual Aid Among Farm Producers in the Federal Socialist Republic of Yugoslavia'. Paper submitted to the Third Session of the Working Party on Agrarian Structure in Europe, Bucharest, 1968 (ECA:AS/68/4E FAO, Rome).

Another interesting form of cooperation, encouraged and largely financed by the government, is a kind of combined undertaking between private farms and other branches of the economy, particularly in the sphere of food processing, which may well be considered a specific form of vertical integration which aims at saving labour and creating specialized production units in definite branches of the economy.*

The pace of industrialization and urbanization is gradually reducing the number of individual smallholders and many of the farmers who do not work jointly with the large socialist farm enterprises earn more than half their livelihood through non-agricultural activities. The socialist sector is taking advantage of this development and, with the help of government credit, it purchases or leases an increasing number of these unviable holdings, particularly in the fertile plains of Vojvodina. Yet, it has been emphasized that this does not mean that the intention is to liquidate private holdings, but is rather an effort to rationalize and improve peasant farming and, above all, to improve its growth rate, which, in comparison with the socialist sector, is very low. It must be emphasized, however, that the greater part of total farm production and, with a few exceptions, of market deliveries, is still supplied by the individual farms which employ about 50 per cent of the labour force, cultivate about 85 per cent of the arable land and produce nearly 90 per cent of the livestock. Increasing industrialization and absorption of rural labour will eventually disintegrate the private sector but, as in Poland, this is unlikely to happen in the near future.

Since 1965, when a new agricultural policy improved the terms of domestic trade, stimulated investment and the use of fertilizers, there has been considerable agricultural progress in Yugoslavia. Land values increased and the area of agricultural land for sale declined from 140,000 hectares in 1964 to 3,000 hectares in 1966 and to 2,500 in 1967, while the price for land rose from about 1,000 new dinars per hectare in 1964 to 7,500 in 1967, less people left agriculture, and many part-time smallholders even went back to full-time farming which provided better income prospects.† At that time the new policy had changed Yugoslavia's main agricultural problem from that of insufficiency of supplies

* Ibid, p. 7.
† *Economic Survey of Europe in 1967*, chap. 1, p. 95.

and increasing dependence on food imports to a difficulty in finding markets.

Whereas in 1968 there was a decline in agricultural production which was closely connected with the trade policy of the European Common Market,* agricultural output in 1969 increased by 7–8 per cent.† The crop and livestock production is also recovering from earlier setbacks as new cooperative regulations ensure the sale of livestock and some cereal and food crops at favourable prices for three to five years ahead.

Agricultural development in Yugoslavia is yet more proof of the often contested flexibility of tenure systems within centrally planned economies. As in Poland, land redistribution was carried out in a way which left room for the continued existence of private peasant farming. But in Yugoslavia the socialist sector's greater production capacity in agriculture has counterbalanced the lower growth rate of individual farms and thus made possible the sustained rate of industrialization.

3. SOCIALIST COUNTRIES OUTSIDE EUROPE

The revolution that ended thirty years of civil war and 200 years of foreign intervention in *China* is fundamentally an agrarian revolution of gigantic dimensions. In contrast to Tzarist Russia where the revolutionary movement spread from the urban centres into the countryside, the Chinese movement began by winning the support of the peasants and established its principal bases in rural areas.

The Chinese land reform represents probably the most far-reaching and flexible reorganization of agriculture ever carried out within the short span of one generation. It started with a primitive but practical redistribution of land, draught animals, implements and houses confiscated from large landlords and rich peasants who did not work the land themselves. In this way, 40 to 50 per cent of the arable land was handed over to the poor peasants and landless labourers who together accounted for 60 to 70 per cent of the rural population. This giant reform was implemented relatively smoothly, with a minimum of bloodshed, for seldom has a country been as ready as China was for radical

* *Economic Survey of Europe in 1968*, p. 74.
† *Economic Survey of Europe in 1969.*

changes in the agrarian structure. The authority and esteem of the ruling landowners and warlords had been hopelessly compromised by their cooperation with the Japanese invaders and foreign capitalist interests, while the misery of the peasants after half a century of increasing oppression and civil and international warfare had reached the point of no return. In many districts taxes were levied for forty years in advance; tenancy was increasing rapidly and so were rents.*

But, in addition, the literate among the peasants and, in particular, the intellectuals had been ideologically prepared for revolutionary changes by the teachings of Sun Yat Sen who, at the turn of the century, had already recognized that the land problem is one of the principal issues in the struggle for independence and national development and that the equalization of land ownership is the basis for the realization of the Principle of Livelihood.† True, in earlier writings he asserted that the feudal system in China had been abolished 2,000 years ago, and simply advocated the rights of the state to acquire the unearned increments of the rising land values caused by industrial and commercial development. 'The nationalization of the increase of land values,' he said then, 'is the true policy to effect the equal distribution of land; it is the basis of the Principle of the People's Livelihood.'‡ But he soon realized that this alone would not do away with the unfair distribution of land, and that only a 'land to the tiller' policy could alleviate rural misery'.§ Yet, the Kuomintang made no effort to realize Sun Yat Sen's policy. It only carried out some feeble land reform measures such as rent reduction, and otherwise openly sided with landlords in oppressing the peasant population.

The first attempt at land redistribution was far from being a success. In practice, it merely increased the number and the relative social and economic standing of the medium-sized holdings, while many of the new, small, peasant farms did not receive a fair share of draught animals and farming implements. In addition,

---

* Audrey Donnithorne, *China's Economic System* (London and New York, 1967), p. 36.

† Sun Yat Sen, *San Min Chu I, Three Principles of the People* (Shanghai, 1927), pp. 409 ff., 430 ff., 434.

‡ Quoted from T'ang Liang-Li, *The Foundations of Modern China* (London, 1928), pp. 136–7.

§ 'Third Lecture on Min Sheng' in Tsung-li and Ch'uan-chi (eds.), *San Min Chu-I Discourses* (Shanghai, 1930), I, p. 152.

they soon got into economic difficulties because the landlords and merchants who used to be their most important source of credit had left the countryside and no institutions had as yet been established to provide the necessary cash loans. It was almost inevitable that within a few years new and distinct class differences were to emerge in the rural areas. Some peasants did improve their lot but many more were unable to manage and had to sell their land, house and animals to those who were in a position to take advantage of the situation. In the area of the present Yangyi Commune, 200 peasant families sold their land and 100 their houses in the course of 1951.* Gradually it became obvious that individual farming would not solve the huge problems of the hundreds of millions of Chinese peasants who were disillusioned after the horrors of the civil war and the high expectations of the past decades. At this stage the revolutionary government decided to choose the road of collectivization. It encouraged the peasants to form cooperatives and, in particular, *mutual work teams* composed of a number of households which during farming seasons pooled their land, animals and equipment, while retaining private ownership of these. This first step, which was in line with the Chinese peasant tradition of mutual assistance, soon took on a more permanent character, and any additional animals and implements which the teams were able to acquire were considered common property.

From this more developed form of mutual work teams the logical transition was made to the final collectivization of Chinese agriculture. At first the teams were changed into *lower agricultural producer cooperatives* where the members pooled everything— land, labour, animals and implements—and received a share of the produce, usually 30 to 50 per cent, as a dividend for their particular piece of land; while the remainder, after the deduction of expenses, was allocated according to work performed. With increased production and income from agriculture, these co-operatives were changed into *higher agricultural producer cooperatives*, which no longer paid dividends to the original owners but regarded the land as collective property operated on a cooperative basis. Finally these were reorganized to form the present-day Communes.

* Isabel and David Crook, *The First Years of Yangyi Commune* (London and New York, 1966), p. 6.

By 1956, more than 95 per cent of the peasant households had been collectively organized into one form or another, mostly, however, into 'higher' cooperatives. This stage was reached sooner than expected, mainly because the poor peasants, disappointed by the first land redistribution, were easily convinced by the well-organized collectivization campaign that they could only gain by their voluntary participation in collective units. It seems that real opposition was limited to the few medium-sized and rich peasants in the villages, who, however, could hardly go against the general trend because of their dependence upon irrigation, marketing, credit and other matters of mutual concern.

A favourable price policy for agricultural products gave great support to the collectivization drive and although the Chinese peasants had to live through periods of uncertainty with regard to grain prices, the government's share in the profit from grain transactions was at no time as high as it used to be in the Soviet Union.*

In the summer of 1958 it was decided to amalgamate the agricultural cooperatives into the large units of People's Communes for the purpose of establishing multi-purpose units which should be able to manage their own agricultural, industrial, commercial, cultural and military affairs. Although the Communes have encountered considerable difficulties and even periodic set-backs, largely because of unrealistic calculations and natural catastrophies it seems safe to state that, at the present stage of development, they represent a workable solution to the complex economic and social problems of the immense Chinese population.

The principal objective of the Communes is to firmly establish a collective socialist agriculture *prior* to mechanization†—an aim that has drawn heavy criticism from Soviet observers who insist that agricultural development through mechanization should pre-cede collectivization. But, as we have already said, the Communes are meant to be far more than large-scale mechanized agricultural units on the Russian model. They are envisaged as the backbone for the social organization of the future communist society and

* A. Donnithorne, op. cit., p. 361.
† Han Suyin, *China in the Year 2001* (London and New York, 1967), pp. 42 ff.

as the main instrument for a gradual *urbanization* of the country-side and *ruralization* of the cities. Although their establishment was in keeping with the decentralization policy in 1957-58 and the optimism that accompanied the First Great Leap Forward, the principles underlying their organization were not commensurate with the factors that actually determine the rhythm and volume of production. It has been emphasized quite rightly that the administrative machinery of any single Commune must be organized according to its particular functions. The later transfer of certain administrative responsibilities from the Commune at large to the working teams on the village level seems to be a realistic step towards aligning the administrative framework of agriculture with the existing state of the production forces.* The fact that this transfer, which simplifies planning and administration and helps to rationalize distribution, is made mainly in those Communes where hoe and sickle are still the principal farm implements is a tribute to the flexibility of the Chinese concept of socialist agriculture.

The three-level structure of the Communes (work teams, production brigades and communes) is particularly suited to adapting the peasants to changes in agricultural techniques and in the tasks of production forces. As long as manual labour is still the principal production factor, management and accounting will continue to rest largely with the working teams; at the early stage of mechanization the level of command goes to the production brigades; and only when the stage of tractors, combine harvesters and other heavy farm equipment has been reached is it transferred to the Commune at large which also handles the coordination of industrial and overall communal activities.

The composition of the Commune is undoubtedly a most suitable institutional framework for the gradual introduction of technical innovations and creates an administrative 'infrastructure' for the transfer of responsibilities which encourages the substitution of labour for capital wherever needed and provides an essential incentive for additional efforts. It has been observed quite rightly that remuneration on the work team level may easily be associated with individual performances and thus puts pressure to

* A. Donnithorne, op. cit., pp. 55 ff., and I. and D. Crook, op. cit., p. 218.

bear on those members of the team who work slowly or do not show any initial interest.*

It has been repeatedly argued that the transfer of responsibilities within the Communes together with their reduction in size were the direct result of the failure of the Great Leap and represent the capitulation of Commune administration to village individualism. It is true, that between 1958 and 1962, the reduction in the average size of the Communes from about 5,000 to 1,800 households, almost tripled their number from 26,000 to 74,000. But, although this represents a withdrawal from an advanced position that could not be defended due to the massive size of the labour forces in the various Communes it cannot possibly be seen as the 'liquidation' of the Communes and a return to the former system of small producer cooperatives. The very number of 74,000 Communes is low in both absolute and relative terms compared to the 740,000 producer cooperatives in 1958.† The ever-increasing literature on conditions in China,‡ which either praises or refutes the achievements of the Chinese Communes and the way in which the Chinese government is using them to promote agricultural development seems to agree on one point at least: that the Communes represent a considerable concentration of manpower and material and carry out irrigation, drainage and soil conservation through an effective utilization of labour. The emphasis which the Chinese government now places on the need for increased mechanization of agriculture indicates that considerable progress must have been achieved by the full utilization of labour.§ The cultural Revolution has reinforced the original socialist principles

* A. Donnithorne, op. cit., p. 53.
† I. and D. Crook, op. cit., pp. 280 ff.
‡ Among others: Chao Kuo-chun, *Agrarian Policy of the Chinese Communist Party* (Bombay, 1960); G. Dutt, *Rural Communes of China* (London, 1967); W. Hinton, *Fanshen. A Documentary of Revolution in a Chinese Village* (New York and London, 1966); I. and D. Crook, *The First Years of Yangyi Commune*; A. Donnithorne, *China's Economic System*; A. Eckstein, *Communist China's Economic Growth and Foreign Trade* (New York and London, 1966); W. F. Wertheim, 'Recent Trends in China's Population Policy'. Paper submitted to the UN World Population Conference, Belgrade, August-September, 1965; Han Suyin, *China in the Year 2001*, particularly pp. 60 ff. (see also chap. 2, pp. 32 ff. of this book on problems of labour utilization).
§ *Le Monde* (9.12.1969).

and further strengthened the ideological incentives for a continued rural integration.

In *Cuba* the changes in the land distribution pattern after the revolution are quite different, mainly because the economy of this small country was based on relatively modern and effective plantations rather than on peasant farming with deep-rooted traditions. Before the revolution, 57 per cent of the agricultural area, about 5,000,000 hectares, were in the hands of large local and foreign landowners of which 13 United States sugar-cane plantations alone controlled almost 1,200,000 hectares.

The actual redistribution of land was relatively simple. The revolutionary government expropriated the large plantation units and limited landownership in the remaining part of the agricultural area to 30 *caballarías* (402 hectares) but soon lowered the ceiling to 5 *caballerías* (67 hectares) giving the tenants full ownership rights.*

The greatest problem was whether or not to redistribute the plantation land to the landless workers. The government chose to maintain the efficient agricultural production units—a few years later, Algeria followed their example and preserved the estates of the French *colons*—and established the National Institute for Agrarian Reform (INRA), the aim of which was to centralize the management of the estates particularly with regard to the allocation of raw materials and technicians. After a few years of experimentation in development planning the government decided to concentrate on agriculture and more specifically on the development of sugar production. From then on the countryside has benefited from ever-increasing investment (like the Carlos Manuel Cespedes dam in the Province of Oriente which today irrigates 125,000 acres for the cultivation of sugar-cane and rice) and has been favoured with regard to the distribution of both food supplies and educational resources. In the last analysis, those who have most benefited from the Cuban Revolution are the agricultural workers† who for the first time in the history of the island are experiencing security and rising real wages.

* C. R. Rodriquez, 'Cuatro años de reforma agraria', *Cuba Socialista*, año III (May 1963).
† E. H. Jacoby, 'Cuba: The Real Winner is the Agricultural Worker', *CERES, FAO Review*, vol. 2, no. 4 (July-August 1969), pp. 29 ff.

No doubt the realistic approach of the Cuban government to land redistribution has contributed substantially to the successful implementation of the land reform. By refraining from an emotional redistribution of land, it prevented not only a repetition of the agricultural and social crises which have marked the first years of socialist agriculture in Eastern Europe, but also the emergence of a peasant middle class in the plantation areas which would have become an obstacle to further revolutionary developments.

An initial move to reorganize the sugar plantations on a cooperative basis was of brief duration only. The INRA, and particularly Fidel Castro himself, very quickly realized that, under Cuban conditions, cooperative sugar farming would prove a failure from the agricultural as well as political point of view. The relatively high measure of autonomy at the individual cooperative units entailed a risk of uncoordinated action and even of black market operations which, in the end, may have jeopardized an agricultural policy that aims at adequate wages and social security for all agricultural workers. The 620 sugar-cane cooperatives that had been established by 1961 were converted into state farms and by this move a strong agricultural worker element has come to exist side by side with the peasant farmers.

The agrarian reform in Cuba, however, is only ten years old and is still in the process of adapting the organization of agriculture, particularly that of sugar production, to the formidable socio-economic changes caused by the revolution. After a period of centralization during the years 1961–63, there followed a policy of decentralization in which groups of 10–15 state sugar farms directed sugar production with a considerable measure of autonomy more or less in accordance with regional administrative expediency. Since 1966, however, the heavy pressure to reach the target of 10 million tons of sugar by 1970,* and the con-

* In the middle of 1970 it became clear that Cuba would not reach the ten-million-ton sugar target but that the final result would be close to eight and a half million tons. Although this remains a record crop both for Cuba and for other sugar-producing countries, there is no doubt that the production costs in terms of labour were very high and that the unyielding attitude of the government had led to some serious disturbances in the economic field. This has also been recognized in a statement by Fidel Castro.

sequent shortage of agricultural labour, has given rise to a renewed trend towards centralization.

There are indications that Cuba is about to establish a completely new type of socialist agriculture based on large units of regional economic planning which seem to represent a kind of land consolidation that offers increased possibilities for the utilization of land and labour. There is little doubt that such a large-scale plan for centralization, which excludes the competition of the state farms on the labour market will be able to cope more efficiently with the labour shortage. It is too early, of course, to judge whether the regional economic planning units will become the final form for Cuban socialist agriculture; but the fact that the Cuban government is facing the present critical shortage of labour by introducing an agricultural organization which allows for rapid adjustments in the distribution of labour and at the same time economizes on staff resources, is certainly yet more proof of its flexibility.

The socialist sector of Cuban agriculture, however, comprises only about 60 per cent of the agricultural area. The remaining 40 per cent is composed of about 230,000 farm units, partly owned by former tenants. It is of considerable interest to note that these individual peasant holdings, whose average size does not exceed 2.3 *caballerías* (26.8 hectares), account for 85 per cent of the total Cuban tobacco production.

Due to the particular structure of agriculture at the time of the revolution, the Cuban peasantry was already firmly wired into the circuits of market production, and the land reform did not have to concern itself with the reorientation of subsistence agriculture as a major problem.* But in the interests of harmony between the socialist and private sectors of agriculture, it became necessary to control the production activities of the peasant farmers and, above all, to prevent the free play of market forces from frustrating the efforts of agrarian reform as was the case in Mexico after the agrarian revolution. For this purpose a state agency, the National Association of Small Farmers (ANAP) was established to guide the activities of the peasant farmers and provide the necessary credit and technical knowledge.

Through this and some other agencies the government not only

* A. Pearse, 'Subsistence Farming Is Not Dead', in *CERES, FAO Review*, vol. 2, no. 4 (July-August 1969), p. 41.

controls agricultural prices, but is also for all practical purposes, the only buyer of private farm produce and agricultural land. Although this at present secures the position of the individual farmers, it is difficult to believe in the continued existence of a private sector within the otherwise socialized agriculture of Cuba. If they become firmly established, the new regional economic planning units will not only replace the state farms in the rice and sugar areas but may even bring about a reorganization of the tobacco and possibly also of the coffee industries, which will finally lead to the full economic integration of individual farmers. It is not unlikely, however, that the reduced demand for agricultural labour following upon an increased mechanization of agriculture may call into question the merits of an agricultural system that not only multiplies the hazards of central planning and investment and requires a strong central bureaucracy but also prevents the agricultural worker from identifying himself with a distinct socialist enterprise. But irrespective of any organizational changes, the very policy of the government which, in addition to its monopoly on land acquisition, aims at increasing the wages of the agricultural workers in order to narrow and eventually close the existing gap in agricultural incomes, will gradually squeeze out the private sector in agriculture. This, however, is a long-term prognosis and for the next decade or two peasant farming will probably persist, particularly in tobacco production where fixed prices based on a detailed system of standardization still guarantee the private farmer an income well above that of the agricultural worker. Yet, the fact that the number of private tobacco farms— at present amounting to about 24,000 units—declined by 500 in 1966–67 and by 1,000 in 1968 seems to indicate a gradual diminishing of the private sector.

Present political considerations may still justify the continued existence of the private agricultural sector despite its relatively high costs of production and higher income level. But there is little doubt that government control of land, labour and credit as well as of price and market developments will ultimately establish a land distribution pattern that will equalize the income from agricultural work and allow the necessary adjustment between rural and urban living conditions. The dedicated enthusiasm of the youth brigades working in the remote rural areas is one of the most effective means by which the government can reach these objectives.

CONCLUSIONS

We have dealt at length with land redistribution and the reorganization of agriculture in socialist countries in order to disprove the unfortunately widespread notion that socialist agriculture follows only one given pattern that is inseparable from communist policy. The variety of socialist tenure types and the different ways in which they are being adjusted to changes in economic and social conditions clearly show that an ideal model for socialist agriculture is as fictitious as is an ideal, generally applicable, model for individual farming and that, even in socialist countries different tenure systems do exist side by side. Accordingly, in planning agricultural development for underdeveloped countries an attempt could well be made to approach the man-land problem by allocating land for collective farming or other 'socialist' tenure types in order to increase production and income from agriculture. This would be particularly expedient in the wide field of rural settlement considering that joint action and mutual assistance are time-honoured traditions in many parts of the underdeveloped world. It has been emphasized that compulsory collective farming is nothing but a means to control the farmers politically and to tax them either directly or through adverse terms of trade, but that its effect on agricultural output is to reduce it.* But this is a generalization that has been amply disproved by the increase in productivity and level of living obtained by collective farming in the Soviet Union, Eastern Europe and China during the last decade. Yet some economists commit the error of over-emphasizing the term 'compulsory', and do not recognize that there are different degrees and shades of compulsion which can hardly be distinguished from the so-called 'voluntary' obligations of individual settlers in non-socialist countries. It is true that in certain cases extreme compulsion accompanied the initial stages of a revolutionary reorganization of the economy and society but it is equally true that they were often combined with a whole range of administrative persuasion and direction which finally led to increased agricultural production.

In the last analysis, therefore, it is the unique dimension of collective farming which determines its importance for overall

* W. A. Lewis, *Development Planning: The Essentials of Economic Policy* (London and New York, 1966), p. 47.

agricultural development even if at first its quantitative performance may fall short of that obtained by successful individual
farming. But it seems highly unlikely that collective farming will
be given a fair trial outside the socialist countries as long as
multilateral and bilateral Technical Assistance remain so strongly
biased in favour of individual farming and continue to design
piecemeal development programmes that only benefit small sections of the population.

CHAPTER SEVEN

Tenancy Reform—A Dilemma

Reforms of landlord-tenant relationships are less dramatic than changes in the land redistribution pattern, but far more difficult to accomplish. Although a rational step towards improvement on the micro-economic level, they affect the very substance of human relations between the farming family and the outside world, usually represented by the landlord and his social environment. In large parts of the underdeveloped world *tenancy at will* (of the landlord) is the traditional type of tenure which leaves the cultivator without any security whatever. True, in many cases this type of landlord-tenant relationship may continue for generations and it has been maintained that the often paternalistic attitude of the landlord provides a high measure of security and almost customary rights for the tenant family. But such a viewpoint does not take into account the fact that the landlord is more interested in exploiting the man than the land and, consequently, has an economic interest in keeping the heavily indebted tenant on the land.

Land redistribution is a surgical operation, whereas tenancy reform is an internal cure. The objective of any purposeful tenancy law is to guarantee security of occupancy, fair compensation for improvements at termination of lease, controlled rents, and the cancellation of all onerous conditions in the lease; in short, to align the working conditions of the tenant as closely as possible to those of the owner-operator so that the main difference lies in the payment of rent. The economic justification of tenancy reforms is the certainty that equitable tenancy conditions stimulate continued farming, increased production and improved cultivation practices and that only tenants who are assured of a decent standard of living and security of tenure will be inclined to make improvements which contribute to the development of agricultural resources. But even if all this is accepted and enacted by law, two fundamental problems remain to be solved: first, how to encourage the tenant cultivator to insist on his legal rights and secondly how to prevent the landlord from either bringing into contempt the new regulations or contriving arrangements that in reality evade the spirit of the reform.

The generally favourable tenancy regulations in advanced countries are of little value as an example to the underdeveloped part of the world. For here pressure on land, lack of alternative employment possibilities for the rural population, and scarcity of external food supplies push rent levels to ever-increasing heights. Moreover, political power and social prestige come from landownership while hard labour, misery and inequality before the law is the lot of the tenants whose only privileges are to show gratitude for the paternal kindness occasionally extended by the landlords in times of emergency, and pay for it with perpetual indebtedness and servitude.

To alter this state of inequality by reform legislation poses innumerable problems among which probably the most crucial ones are the cost and efficiency of the administrative machinery needed for implementation. It has been pointed out quite rightly that 'a country where landlord-tenant problems are acute is almost by definition a country which simply cannot afford the administrative costs of fielding an inspectorate large enough to perform the task'; and that this task calls for 'indefinitely recurring costs, and indefinitely expandable costs, since infinite possibilities of evasion are offered by such a multifaceted contract as that between landlord and tenant'.* We may add that a country with acute landlord-tenant problems is also, almost invariably, a country whose organs of administration lack the skill, honesty and independence required to perform this task. The number of tenancy laws consigned to oblivion in Asia, the Near East, and Latin America amply testify to the fact that it is the administrative machinery itself which by indifference, collusion and bribery has stultified the original purpose of the tenancy regulations.

In vast areas of underdeveloped Asia and Latin America sharecropping in its various forms is still the prevailing type of tenancy.

* *Progress in Land Reform, Fourth Report*, p. 29.

In India, for example, a recent survey* ascertains that roughly half of the tenanted land seems to be under *de facto* sharecropping and only one-fifth is completely free from it; and that the incidence of both tenancy and actual sharecropping is significantly higher in wet or irrigated areas with inflated land values than in areas without assured rainfall. This confirms that the economic importance of tenancy is far greater than national statistics lead one to believe.

The defects of tenancy are well-known; the tenant is not very interested in improving the land since he cannot be sure of ever enjoying the fruits of his effort and investment; if a sharecropper, he will be reluctant to invest money in technological innovations or increase his labour input unless he is convinced that his share in the marginal increase in output will actually augment his income. If he works on a 50–50 basis, an expense of, say, 100 rupees for fertilizer, will be worth his while only if the total increase in output exceeds 200 rupees. Otherwise his own returns will at best cover his outlay and neither increase his income nor reward his additional work. These defects are characteristic of all types of tenancy which do not ensure the economic security of the tenant farmer by a fixed rent. Yet, they are often neglected in the so-called 'packages of improved agricultural practices' which are designed to encourage increased production, but which only calculate the rates of return expected from owner-cultivators and tenants with fixed rent, without taking into consideration the much lower returns from the sharecroppers' investment.

It has been argued that the negative effect of sharecropping tenancy upon agricultural development could be greatly reduced were input costs to be shared in the same proportion as returns, and that this would ensure the sharecroppers a marginal rate of return comparable to that of an owner-cultivator.† Theoretically, this is a logical proposal but, in practice, it is bound to encounter considerable resistance. Firstly, it is usually contrary to local institutions and custom and, particularly, to the landowner's interest in maximizing his own returns which under certain market conditions may even increase despite declining output. In parts of India and almost everywhere in Latin America, the landowner

* A. K. Sen and T. C. Varghese, 'Tenancy and Resource Allocation', *Seminar*, no. 8 (New Delhi, May 1966).
† Ibid.

is on his guard against even the most modest institutional change lest it shake the foundation of what is for him a most profitable landlord-tenant relationship. Secondly, a considerable part of the costs, namely the cultivator's labour, cannot really be shared by the landowner without breaking up the entire structure of the established tenure system. Cost-sharing, of course, should be encouraged wherever possible, but it is naïve to believe that it can ever take the place of tenancy reform.

It has also been argued that overall returns from additional inputs even if scaled down by sharecropping tenancy, are often so high that net returns may still provide an incentive for the tenant-cultivator. But even this argument is logical in theory only; it does not take into account the psychological fact that in the underdeveloped world the peasant is generally not a businessman calculating in terms of future returns but a poverty-stricken cultivator who lives so near the subsistence level that he considers any extra expenditure, such as for fertilizers, a risky venture.

Many attempts have been made through decrees and laws to correct the most conspicuous wrongs of the landlord-tenant relationship and provide some legal protection for the tenant-cultivator: lease in writing; minimum period for occupancy and automatic extension of the lease; limited number of reasons for eviction; rent ceilings; limitations on subletting; compensation for improvements and discomfort at termination of lease; and right of preemption to the leased property. None of these provisions, however important, will have any effect under conditions that are intrinsically hostile to the tenant-cultivator. Written leases are of little use in areas with a high rate of illiteracy and even the strictest provisions against unjustified termination of leases can, and will, be evaded wherever the local judges side with the landowners in defending the *status quo*. It cannot be repeated often enough that it is the established power structure, not legislative measures, which determine the landlord-tenant relationship and that, therefore, protective tenancy laws will have the desired effect only when the tenant has achieved a certain amount of bargaining power and an economic and social position that enables him to insist on his rights. In the State of Bombay a former tenant-cultivator once told me that he not only pays rent instalments to the government but, in order to play safe, continued to pay rent to his former landlord. The lack of confidence and security, fostered by the disappointments of countless peasant generations, often adds to the difficulties of implementing tenancy reform programmes, and only in rare cases have tenancy laws actually strengthened the social and economic position of the tenants and increased their bargaining power for dealing with the landlord.

Of all underdeveloped areas, Latin America probably boasts the largest record of unimplemented tenancy laws. Ever since the early twenties, Chile and Argentina have had a series of laws regulating tenancy contracts, the present ones dating from the mid-forties. Peru has had legislation controlling the disastrous *yanaconaje* system and certain aspects of conventional tenancy contracts since the late forties, but it remains to be seen whether the recent land reform laws will actually improve tenant conditions; and laws stipulating conditions for farm workers and tenants have been on record in Brazil, Ecuador, Colombia, and Guatemala for more than a generation. A CIDA report states that if the already existing laws had been implemented effectively, the Latin American cultivators would have had greater security and a considerably higher share in the income from farming than he has today.* But present conditions clearly prove that the laws not only failed to protect the tillers but in many cases even worsened their situation.

Field studies reveal that, in Chile, the average income from farming of the *inquilino* (tenant) families is between 1/80 and 1/230 of the landlord's returns, and that in Colombia, Peru and Argentina the legal regulation of tenancy contracts was, in practice one of the major reasons for the eviction of thousands of small tenants. In Argentina alone, the total number of tenants declined by as much as 25 per cent during the decade following the enactment of legislation introducing protective tenancy in 1947, and there is ample evidence that most of them had been ejected from their farms by landlords who refused to comply with the provisions of the tenancy legislation. Similar reactions have been reported from Colombia where mass expulsion of tenants was the landlords' answer to a law providing ownership rights to tenants

---

* See *Land Tenure Conditions and Socio-economic Development of the Agricultural Sector in Seven Latin American Countries,* pp. 34 ff. See also *Progress in Land Reform, Fifth Report;* Chapter 1 reflects more the legal than the factual situation.

who had worked the land for more than ten years; while, in Brazil, the attempts by tenants to enforce their legal rights were met with violence and assassinations.

In India the open opposition against post-independence tenancy laws was less outspoken, but the existing structural system gave the landowners countless opportunities to prevent their effective implementation. Laws prohibiting the ejection of tenants were effectively enforced in only 9 per cent of the total cultivated area in Gujarat; and it has been confirmed that the largest number of ejections in recent times occurred between 1951 and 1956, the years following the enactment of the Tenancy and Agricultural Land Act.*

Equally unsuccessful was an attempt to check the widespread practice of rack-renting. Another investigation on the effects of the Bombay Tenancy Act,† reveals that the control measures proved completely ineffective and that there was an 'almost total absence of any sign of lowering the share of cash rents or any changes in the tenancy praxes'. The investigation points out that the ineffectiveness of the Act is entirely due to the failure to implement it; landlords have not even been prevented from continuing the common practice of raising the rent rather than lowering it when changing tenants. The authors admit that they were extremely surprised to find that the landlord even feels in a strong enough position to declare the actual amount of rent he receives, and sees no reason whatever for concealing it. Tenancy reform in India has not altered the landlord-tenant relationship and despite some recent improvements here and there the menace of ejection and rack-renting is as widespread as ever, and further increases the insecurity of the tenant-cultivators and the stagnation in the tenanted areas.

In the United Arab Republic a relatively successful piece of tenancy legislation was implemented in connection with the

* M. B. Desai, *Report on Enquiry into the Working of the Bombay Tenancy and Agricultural Land Act 1948, as Amended up to 1953 in Gujarat* (*excluding Baroda District*) (The Indian Society of Agricultural Economics, Bombay, 1958), p. 75.

† V. M. Dandekar and G. J. Khudanpur, *Working of Bombay Tenancy Act 1948, Report of Investigation* (Gokhale Institute of Politics and Economics, Publication no. 35, Poona, 1957), pp. 110 ff.

Agrarian Reform Law of September 1952 and affected at least 50 per cent of the cultivated area and approximately 40 per cent of all farms. The rents which had reached astronomical heights owing to population pressure and the lack of legal protection were fixed at a maximum of seven times the land tax which lowered the average rent level by approximately 33 per cent. In the case of sharecropping, the requirements of the Law were relatively modest and only reduced the share due to the landlord to a maximum of 50 per cent of the crop produced, although all expenses were to be shared equally. But, as in India, the redistribution of land had given rise to a relatively large group of medium-sized landowners who having gained considerable political and social influence not only impeded for years any further improvements in the tenant situation, but frequently abused the existing tenancy legislation.* Yet, the much-publicized threats of exposure and penal sanctions were reasonably effective and by the end of the fifties most big or medium-sized landowners (50–200 *feddans*) observed the legally stipulated rents. On the other hand, the vast majority of tenants and sharecroppers who rent their land from the very numerous small absentee landlords, often their own relatives, were made to pay rents far higher than the legal rates,† and in 1960, the instance of rent control violations was estimated at 80 per cent.

New laws‡ in 1962 and 1963 enforced a stricter observance of existing tenancy legislation. And in 1966 an Amendment, according to which one copy of the tenancy agreement has to be deposited with the cooperative, finally provided the tenant with a greater measure of security. In 1969 the number of sharecroppers declined to 24 per cent of the tenants and the increase in tenants' income was estimated at about 60 million Egyptian pounds annually.§

The present tenancy legislation in the Philippines‖ provides a

---

* G. S. Saab, *Egyptian Agrarian Reform 1952–1962* (London and New York, 1967), p. 145.
† Ibid., pp. 145–6.
‡ Laws no. 139 of 1962 and no. 17 of 1963.
§ S. A. Marei, 'Overturning the Pyramid', *CERES, FAO Review,* vol. 2, no. 6 (November-December 1969), pp. 48 ff.
‖ Contained in the Agricultural Land Reform Code (Act no. 3844), Approved 8 August 1963.

wealth of detailed regulations that should help the tenants, when
eventually promoted to the status of 'leaseholders', to acquire
the skill and self-confidence needed to manage their own holdings.
But since the Land Reform Code as such carefully avoids infringing upon the prerogatives of the landowners and provides
gradual institutional adjustments and minor modifications only, it
is doubtful whether it will actually diminish the state of
dependency of the Filipino peasant on a countrywide scale.

In *Ceylon*, on the other hand, the Paddy Lands Act 1 of 1958
as amended up to 1964, presents a new approach to problems of
tenancy in the rice areas where for generations insecurity of tenure
has been the limiting factor for increased production. This Act
provides for maximum rents of either 25 per cent of the gross
yield or 12 bushels of paddy per acre; for permanent and inheritable cultivation rights; and for the setting up of Cultivation
Committees composed of twelve members all of whom are to
be elected from amongst cultivators for a term of 3 years only.
These Committees have very considerable mandatory duties to
protect the interests of tenant-cultivators and agricultural workers
of which the most important are: to maintain the Paddy Land
Register that shows the extent of land and the name and tenure
of its cultivator; to work for the development of paddy cultivation; to exercise communal functions such as control and regulation of water for irrigation and collection of an acreage levy from
all the cultivated paddy lands, at the maximum rate of 6 rupees
per acre per season; to protect agricultural labourers through
fixing the wages payable to them; and to prepare the implementation of schemes ensuring the efficient cultivation of paddy lands,
the consolidation of holdings and the establishment of collective
farms. But most important of all, the Cultivation Committee is
responsible for the *collection of rent and loan repayments from
cultivators on behalf of the persons entitled thereto.*

The content and wording of the Ceylon Paddy Lands Act
suggest that legislation of this kind, if properly implemented,
could be a suitable instrument for freeing the tenant-cultivator
from his bondage and traditional submission. He no longer has
to face the landlord in person since the Cultivation Committee
acts as his intermediary, and for all practical purposes secures
him the status of an independent cultivator who has entered into

Hello Amanda,

We hope you are not
working too hard?

Peace did
I ask you
which you were
away. He's been
really. It's just
a pentill. Phillis

P.S. Can't brother
it, [illegible]

an agreement to pay a fixed amount of 25 per cent of his crop returns.

Yet, a recent evaluation study* comes to the conclusion that by and large the implementation of the Paddy Lands Act has been ineffective. People are in general still bound by tradition rather than by the Law which at times is even regarded as somewhat 'immoral', and tenant-cultivators still frequently pay the customary rent of half their produce—usually without getting receipts, although these are stipulated by the Act. Although 15,000 out of about 35,500 cases of eviction were decided in favour of tenant-cultivators, less than 2,700 restorations have been made. It is only natural that such an ineffective performance should make the tenants lose confidence in the protection promised them under the Act, and so they continue to pay the customary rent in order to try and keep the landlord happy and thus avoid eviction.

The Cultivation Committees perform some of their functions rather well but are unequal to the task of affording true protection to either tenant-cultivators or agricultural workers. The report concludes that protection of tenants is only possible when the personal relationship between landlord and tenant has been broken and that the enforcement of fixed agricultural labour wages will depend upon the emergence of a strong organization of agricultural workers. We may add that a strong organization of tenant-cultivators would also facilitate the enforcement of the protective tenancy legislation. Despite its faulty implementation there can be no doubt that the disruption of the personal landlord-tenant relationship as envisaged by the Ceylon Paddy Lands Act is a prerequisite for any practical approach to a reform of tenancy conditions.†

The oppressive tenancy arrangements in underdeveloped countries are also largely responsible for the defective market

---

* United Nations, FAO, *Report to the Government of Ceylon on the Working of the Land Paddy Act*. Prepared by Ameer Raza (Rome, 1970).

† In May 1970, Mrs Sirimavo Bandaranaike and her party, the United Front, an organization of three radical parties, won the Parliamentary election and once again Mrs Bandaranaike has become Prime Minister. It can be expected that the Paddy Lands Act will now be implemented and that the fundamental problem of the tea and rubber plantations will also be taken up.

mechanism that further weakens the position of the tenants both as producers and consumers. Until he is allowed to handle the sale of his own share of the produce the tenant remains but an appendage to the land and the landlord, whose dominant position rests upon his ability to keep his tenants in a state of indebtedness, is thus inclined to limit their opportunities for earning a cash income.* Tenancy systems that entitle the landlord to demand compulsory services from his tenants and control the production and sale of their crop are the main reason for the extremely small participation of peasants in cash market transactions. On large sheep farms in certain parts of Latin America, the tenant families are even obliged to wash, spin and weave the landlords' share of the wool into blankets and rugs, while in some provinces of the Philippines, the owner of the land claims the right to handle the marketing of his tenants' share of the produce.

It is a mistake to even attempt to reorganize the marketing system in tenancy infested areas without first reforming the inequitable tenancy arrangements which keep the tenants in a state of total dependence upon the landlord. Up to now a neglected aspect of the landlord-tenant relationship is the psychological readiness of the tenants to submit to the landlord's will. Tenancy reforms should aim at preventing the landlord from using coercion and, therefore, at reducing as much as possible any personal contact between landlord and tenant. Arrangements such as the Cultivation Committees of the Ceylon Paddy Lands Act, which not only prevent the landlord or his agents from personally collecting rent and loan repayments but also act as mediators in case of dispute, would give the tenants a fair chance to protest against any abuse of their new rights. But even this kind of reform encounters numerous difficulties and can only be successfully implemented if strong, independent peasant organizations encourage the tenants to demand collectively that which they are too weak to claim individually. The extent to which governments encourage active tenant organizations, therefore, is a major proof of their sincerity with regard to the implementation of tenancy reforms.

The publicity given to the content and ultimate objective of the tenancy reform is equally important proof of this since only

* R. J. Clark, *Land Reform and Peasant Market Participation in the Northern Highlands of Bolivia*, Land Tenure Center Reprint, no. 42 (University of Wisconsin, 1968).

widespread information can prevent misinterpretation and circumvention. At public meetings and through the mass media and adult education government officials should enlighten the tenants on their new rights and obligations. Mobile arbitration units should be sent out periodically to the villages to settle current disputes and control local officials, in order to prevent decisions in contempt of the law being made under the influence of local pressure groups.

Provided that an adequate relationship exists between rent for the land and returns from agricultural production, tenancy as such—and this is clearly evident in developed countries like the United Kingdom, Belgium and Sweden—has the great advantage of leaving the tiller's capital free to work within the agricultural enterprise rather than tying it to the land. The peasants, who lack administrative experience and opportunities for alternative employment, have a long way to go before they will be in a position to both rent land and make a decent living from cultivating it. It may even be argued that as a tenure type, tenancy can function effectively only within the framework of a developed economy, and that a successfully implemented tenancy reform indicates a relatively advanced stage of economic and social development.

CHAPTER EIGHT

Land Consolidation–
The 'Small' Land Reform

Land consolidation is also a structural reform on the micro-economic level. Its main purpose is to remedy excessive sub-division and fragmentation and prepare the ground for improved cultivation practices and a higher standard of living for the farming population. Land consolidation, however, is not only of importance in underdeveloped countries; it has become a permanent feature of the agricultural policy of almost all developed countries. It is the prerequisite for reorganizing fragmented holdings, where the efforts of the farming families are disproportionate to the limited economic results, and has the effect of raising their standard of living to a level comparable to that of industrial workers. In countries where socialist agriculture has introduced large-scale farm operations, the problems of excessive fragmentation have been solved and land consolidation operations are of no further relevance.

In large parts of the underdeveloped world the continued process of subdivision and excessive fragmentation has produced a farm structure that prevents adequate application of labour and rational crop patterns and, consequently, keeps the farming family's income at subsistence level—even below it. The reasons are manifold, but all of them can be traced back to defective institutions. In the Moslem countries of the Near East and Southeast Asia rigid inheritance laws, particularly in areas with a great population pressure, have led to progressive subdivision and fragmentation of agricultural holdings. The minute holdings reduce the capacity for economic survival, increase the incidence of indebtedness and soil-mining and, worst of all, demoralize the rural communities whose members increase in inverse ratio to the declining income possibilities. In the fragmented farm areas the peasants become the easy prey of land grabbers and money-lenders to whom they will pledge or sell their land, bit by bit, in order to survive. Concentration of land ownership combined with increased tenancy is the inescapable result. But even additional income from non-agricultural activities does not always counteract the trend to fragmentation. On the contrary, the peasant who finds himself in the possession of cash is inclined to invest in land. The peasants from Calabria and Sicily, for example, who have gone to work in northern Italy or abroad use whatever money they can spare to purchase a piece of land even if it is economically meaningless. Consolidation is a most valuable instrument for helping to raise the tiller from an appendage to the land to its master. The man who has to subsist on the returns from a minute holding or has to walk for hours to reach his scattered plots cannot be expected to sense the dignity of labour and execute his work effectively and with foresight. He will remain the slave of the land even if he is its owner.

Land consolidation, however, is much more than the reallocation of parcels. It is a reorganization of farm land which is adjusted to the ever-changing demographic and technological development and, if combined with adequate education and extension, it is often an indispensable supplementary measure to land redistribution. The failure of the Indian land reform to substantially increase agricultural production is due largely to the fact that it did not improve the farm structure and only carried out consolidation operations in a few areas.

Throughout the world, subdivision and excessive fragmentation are inherent defects of old peasant communities. A distinction has to be made, however, between fragmentation that provides the farmer with a number of separate plots serving different production purposes, and which is, therefore, justified under certain physical and economic conditions and the excessive fragmentation of farm land into unviable holdings. We shall not deal with the merits and demerits of the former since they present problems of management rather than of structure, but shall concentrate instead on land consolidation as a means of remedying the meaningless division of farm units by a defective agrarian system.

Since the Second World War, in many areas of Western Europe

experience has shown that it is possible to adjust agriculture to changes in the demographic and technological situation while aligning the still backward areas with overall development through a reorganization of holdings combined with as much construction and improvement as possible. In the Netherlands, for example, land consolidation was closely associated with land reclamation, in Sweden with the rationalization of the forestry industry, and in Western Germany with the resettlement of refugees.

The developed countries, in fact, treat land consolidation as a permanent process of adjustment which is as necessary as the continued rationalization of industry and relatively easy to carry out from a technical point of view. In many underdeveloped countries, however, the very symptoms of underdevelopment, such as inadequate or spurious land records; lack of proper soil classification; and inefficient administrative bodies may render the implementation of land consolidation programmes extremely difficult. For while land improvements and effective infrastructures will facilitate cultivation and marketing for the new farm units, the mere reallocation of plots will only remedy the excessive fragmentation of a farm area in the short term without substantially helping to increase production or income.

In areas, for example, where drainage and irrigation works are under consideration, land consolidation operations should be planned and possibly implemented beforehand. Otherwise later costly adjustments of the canal systems may become necessary as was the case in the vast Ganges-Kobadek irrigation scheme in East Pakistan where land consolidation had not been planned prior to the completion of the irrigation works, or in Greece, where the final effect of a large-scale land consolidation scheme involving about 180,000 hectares was greatly reduced because it was not coordinated with the irrigation works in the same area.

Yet, even well-designed and well-timed land consolidation programmes encounter immense difficulties in excessively fragmented areas, particularly when the holdings are composed of plots belonging to different owners. This is the case in Malta and Gozo, for example, where over 112,000 plots belonging to 12,000 different holdings are still waiting to be consolidated.* Somewhat more

* United Nations, FAO, *Report to the Government of Malta on the Development of Agricultural Resources* (ETAP 409, Rome, 1955), p. 52.

successful was the East Ghor Canal Project in Jordan, a combined land consolidation and redistribution scheme involving the irrigation of about 120,000 *dunums* (c. 56,000 acres) of land. This area had been divided amongst 3,666 farmers of whom 36 per cent owned less than ten *dunums*, a few per cent more than 500 while only 10 owners had more than 1,000 *dunums* each. With the implementation of the combined scheme, 2,491 farmers became owners of new holdings of between 30 and 200 *dunums*, but since the allocations were made on the basis of previous ownership, only the ten owners who originally had more than 1,000 *dunums* received the maximum allocation of 200. Though it did not fully eliminate inequalities, the scheme has undoubtedly improved the land distribution pattern in this area.*

Despite the contention that in countries with a great pressure of population priority should be given to increasing agricultural output, the consolidation of fragmented holdings primarily serves to increase labour productivity. The idle manpower abundant in all excessively fragmented agricultural areas could be usefully employed in the improvement and construction works needed for the implementation of any large-scale consolidation scheme. Road construction and the digging of drainage and irrigation canals could become part of community development schemes, as happened in certain parts of the Punjab in India, where consolidation operations were greatly accelerated by the organization of labour teams.

In the course of time two clearly distinct land consolidation procedures have emerged: (1) improvement of the farm size and resettlement patterns by purposeful changes in the property rights in land; and (2) improvement of the land use pattern without changing the existing rights in land.

The first of these procedures is particularly suited to the congested areas of Asia, the Near East and Southern Europe, as well as to those regions of Latin America where the predominance of large estates has pushed the indigenous peasants into inhospitable hill areas where they practise subsistence farming on minute patches of land with an excess input of labour. In order to 'loosen up' a congested area or village by regrouping the scattered plots

* *Progress in Land Reform, Fourth Report*, p. 91.

and creating space for new farm buildings and a more adequate road system, some of the owners will have to be transferred to the outer limits of the area under consolidation. Such a 'resettlement', however, calls for an appraisal of the soil and the location of the different plots and frequently it might be necessary to offer the farmers more land than they give up in order to make them accept the change. The emotional resistance of the peasant owner who firmly believes in the superior quality of his particular plot, small as it may be, should be overcome to whatever extent possible by persuasion, compensation and, if necessary, by some compulsion. The implementation of land consolidation schemes, in fact, is a crusade against prejudice, inertia and suspicion, and only when the large majority has been convinced of the advantages of the scheme can the active participation and support of the peasants be counted upon. Experience has shown that a psychological readiness to accept the changes involved in land consolidation is greatest among the women, who suffer most under the excessive fragmentation of the minute holdings and are, therefore, more amenable to any proposal that may improve their situation.

In tribal areas, marked by subdivision and excessive fragmentation rather than by congestion, land consolidation presents problems of a somewhat different nature. In many parts of East Africa —Uganda for example—where the peasants do not live in compact villages but have settled on one of their scattered plots, a regrouping should be carried out in order to improve their methods of production. In other tribal areas, however, where no unutilized land is available, consolidation operations should be started as early as possible and, certainly, prior to any registration of individual titles. This latter point is extremely important since registration of titles to fragmented holdings will freeze the defective settlement pattern and make any attempts to introduce a more rational outlay of individual holdings far more difficult for a long time to come; this is particularly evident in some African territories where registration of titles had been favoured by the colonial authorities as a measure to increase security of tenure. As important as this may be, it is the rational organization of the substance of land and not the mere act of registration which is the decisive factor in development.

Like all other agrarian reform measures, land consolidation operations should be planned in strict accordance with the particular conditions in the region and the specific social and cultural characteristics of the farming people. This is particularly valid where the psychological effect of new settlement patterns upon the farming families is concerned. In the developed countries, the belief of but a generation ago that living quarters and holding should be as close as possible no longer holds true due to the rapid development of modern communications and, particularly, of mechanized transport which makes it possible to cover distances of 5 to 10 kilometres within a few minutes. Today, the advantages of well-organized villages far outweigh the benefits derived from home and field being in close proximity. In less developed or underdeveloped countries, experience has likewise proved that isolated homesteads not only present psychological difficulties but considerably increase the costs of extension, rural aid and social amenities. Unless there is some specific technical reason for the close combination of home and holding, such as intensive market gardening, dairy farming, etc., group settlements at some distance from the fields are preferable.

Consolidation operations which affect land use, on the other hand, are much easier to carry out since, by definition, they do not affect the property rights in land and, consequently, do not mobilize the defence mechanism of the peasants. The Gezira Scheme in the Sudan, for example, can be looked upon as a kind of large-scale consolidation scheme at the land use level, which helps the farmers to apply more rational and economic methods of cultivation. Their scattered plots which led to endless hours of walking, were regrouped into solid blocks of land for the large-scale cultivation of cotton, sorghum and fodder crops. In addition to saving time and energy, these blocks guarantee a far more economic use of water by making possible the rectangular layout of the irrigation canals which minimizes the loss of water in the fields.

The introduction of block-farming combined with a three-year crop rotation scheme in certain land reform areas of the UAR was equally successful. Land in selected, excessively subdivided and fragmented areas was pooled and then divided into three large blocks each given over to the cultivation of one crop only. The members of the scheme cultivate jointly three parcels of land, one in each of the blocks; this gives them the possibility of large-scale farming with machinery and cultivation methods that have increased production considerably above that obtained on the dispersed plots. Following the successful experiment in the land reform areas, similar projects were started on a voluntary basis in other communities and by 1965 block-farming was practised in large parts of the country. There is no doubt that this has increased production and made pest control, irrigation and drainage as well as the timing of agricultural operations more effective.

Despite the many advantages, however, one should not over-estimate the effect of land consolidation upon the actual economic position of the farmer. In reality, he is only exchanging the total output from his small fragmented holding with a correspondingly small share in the crop from the rationally cultivated block. Even if this share may earn him a somewhat larger income with less effort, the smallness of his property will remain the limiting factor; unlike land redistribution, land consolidation at the land use level does not enlarge the individual holdings and, consequently, it does not change the pattern of income distribution, which is the only thing that could initiate an economic and social breakthrough for the peasants.

Although the urgent need for land consolidation is recognized in all quarters, opinion is divided regarding the administrative procedures for its implementation. Here we are also faced with the problem of taking into account the particular stages of economic, social and cultural development for which no model can be devised that is valid for all environments. This holds true particularly for the degree of 'compulsion' to be applied and experience in various parts of the world proves that the final choice between the various degrees of 'voluntary' or 'compulsory' methods must be made on the basis of the prevailing cultural, economic and social climate of the country concerned. Consequently, the implementation of land consolidation in developed Western or Westernized countries is bound to be different from that in the still tradition-bound areas of the underdeveloped world. In large parts of Africa, for example, where the spirit of neighbourhood and village cooperation is still alive, some means of direct compulsion against obstinate outsiders rather than being considered offensive may be regarded as a way of carrying out another of the time-honoured reallocations of land. In the individualistic developed countries, on the other hand, more sophisticated methods of compulsion have to be applied, as in the Netherlands and Switzerland, for example, where the absence of any owner from a decisive meeting on a consolidation scheme is registered as his consent to the suggested procedure.

In reality, however, the degree of compulsion is not the decisive point. Far more essential to the success of land consolidation is the cooperation of the peasants concerned, and once this has been ensured by education, persuasion and the demonstration of successful attempts in the past, compulsory praxes hardly need to be applied. Yet, their continued active participation is necessary and at all stages of implementation they should be made responsible, entirely or partly, for some aspects of the scheme. This can be done either by organizing community programmes as in the Punjab and in Kenya, or by appealing to their sense of self-help and cooperation as was done in many European countries and also in Japan, particularly for the execution of construction works. The peasants' active participation in improving the land will undoubtedly strengthen their emotional attachment to the new holdings.

Equally important, however, is the close coordination of the administrative bodies concerned with the various aspects of agricultural improvement. Unless the entire agrarian structure is taken into consideration the danger exists that an inconsistent and piecemeal approach will disrupt the implementation of land consolidation and thus jeopardize the project as a whole. As in all instances of meaningless and prestigious competition between the various branches of administration, the man on the land will be the one who suffers the most.

Another harassing problem is the financing of the extremely costly land consolidation operations. Although most governments are legally authorized to expropriate against compensation any land needed for public use, their position is more difficult when it comes to acquiring land for enlarging uneconomic private holdings. In some European countries, like Sweden and Denmark, special land funds have been established which purchase the additional land needed for consolidation purposes. On the other hand, acquisition or expropriation of land for roads, school and hospital buildings, shopping centres, etc. in an area under consolidation should not encounter undue difficulties. If properly prepared the peasants will understand that their respective losses will be inconsiderable compared to the benefits and the increase in land values due to the consolidation.

Public funds, of course, will always be needed but the final success of a consolidation programme does not only depend on the capital available, but even more on an adequate combination of capital and self-help. Even in the developed countries where financing is no major problem, the farmers have to participate in the cost of works of common interest and the establishment of a land consolidation fund. In the underdeveloped countries, however, where government funds as a rule are rather limited, the purposeful use of idle and underemployed manpower may largely compensate for the shortage of capital, provided that the administration simplifies and speeds up the consolidation programme in order to make full use of the limited staff resources available.

Since land consolidation is almost always combined with other agricultural development programmes, it is difficult to appraise its specific effects. In most cases, however, where land consolidation is an integral part of an agricultural development programme, a considerable increase in the productivity of land and labour and frequently also in the area under cultivation has been observed. The importance of land consolidation in excessively fragmented agricultural areas is clearly evident from the following evaluation of a consolidation project in the Lucknow district in India,* which is based upon detailed land records relating to the periods 1953–55 and 1960–62, i.e., the years preceding and following its implementation.

The consolidation operations, which covered 3 villages with 2,758 acres, increased the average size of the plots from 0.37 to 0.61 acres, i.e., by 65 per cent. The number of plots of less than 0.1 acres, however, was lowered by more than 70 per cent while that of plots comprising one acre or more increased by 17.1 per cent. Still more important is the fact that while the net area put under seed in the consolidation scheme increased by more than 30 per cent through the extension of cultivation to previously

* S. K. Agarwal, 'Consolidation of Holdings: A Case Study of the Lucknow District', *The Economic Review*, vol. 18, no. 10 (New Delhi, December 1966).

unused land, it actually declined in the control villages, where holdings had not been consolidated.

The total irrigated area increased by 3 per cent and the area under double cropping by 6.8 per cent, but it is of interest to note that the area under canal irrigation (the cheapest form of water supply) increased by 6 per cent while that irrigated from wells and tanks actually declined. The extension of both cultivated and irrigated areas led to an increase of 20 per cent of the gross cropped area over a period of 5 or 6 years—the greatest extension taking place in those areas under the labour-intensive wheat and paddy crops. Despite its smallness, the scheme clearly demonstrates that in underdeveloped countries where land is the limiting factor, land consolidation is a suitable instrument for bringing about an extension of the crop area.

The final problem remains of how to keep the consolidated farms intact and prevent renewed subdivision and fragmentation. A concerted effort through legislation, administration and education is needed in order to prevent the landholder from voluntarily subdividing his holding once again, or being forced to do so by circumstances.

In an area in Malaysia, where the titles for new holdings contained a specific clause prohibiting subdivision, I saw an interesting example of evasion. On a holding, whose owner had been dead for five years, the sons had settled in permanent houses each on 'his' part of the property according to the laws of Moslem inheritance. True, they had obeyed the letter of the law and left the title intact in the name of the dead father, but for all practical purposes they had subdivided the property and established non-viable units that would not appear in the land records.

The legislation against subdivision and fragmentation, therefore, must be combined with other measures such as alternative employment possibilities, adequate credit arrangements that will allow one son to take over the holding and compensate his co-heirs, a fair amount of education and, above all, information about the disadvantages of a rigid interpretation of the inheritance rules. Many underdeveloped countries, among them India, Pakistan, Kenya, Uganda and the Sudan, make considerable efforts in this respect which may substantially reduce the incidence of renewed subdivision and fragmentation.

Wherever land consolidation has been successfully implemented, it provides the basis for improved cultivation methods, better communication and market outlets, and thus increases the psychological readiness of the farmers to accept innovations that prepare the ground for a more dynamic agricultural development. Yet, significant though it may be for the reorganization of the farm structure, this 'small' land reform does not bring about a redistribution of income and is, therefore, no substitute for land redistribution in areas with a highly defective income distribution pattern.

Land consolidation is not a limited programme to be accomplished within a given period of time, but is a continuing action which is needed for adjusting agriculture to the continuing processes of demographic change and technological development.

CHAPTER NINE

Settlement Policy in the Context of Development

The sedentarization of man is a time-honoured process that has been going on for millenniums; and vast regions of the world are still faced with the challenge of expanding agriculture by the settlement of nomadic peoples. But even established agriculture is not a permanent feature and time and again the exigency of development calls for a reorganization of man or land, or of both. In advanced and underdeveloped countries alike such changes always touch upon the Agrarian Creed and constitute, therefore, a psychological as well as a physical and economic problem.

In the context of national development, land settlement* is an agrarian reform programme particularly designed to relieve the pressure in overpopulated rural areas and promote a more homogeneous distribution of land and labour. Settlement schemes, therefore, should not be considered as local projects, but must be planned according to future need in *all* regions of the country and appraised in terms of overall national development.

Land settlement schemes are frequently the follow-up of land redistribution or land consolidation in order to provide a new setting for the man on the land which will make him stronger, more effective, healthier and better prepared to shoulder the new economic and political responsibilities of citizenship. The move to new land is generally associated with the notion of liberation from the bondage of serfdom and repression. But it may also mean eviction, deprivation and the emergence of misery-ridden

---

* Although it would be more logical to restrict the use of the word *settlement* to mean the sedentarization of nomads and apply the term resettlement for all activities implying the move of sedentary people from one area to another, we will adhere to the established broad usage of *settlement* in both cases.

communities as in some parts of Latin America where, in the name of land reform, the redistribution of almost inaccessible public domain land, unsuitable for normal market operations, forces the peasants away from their organized social and traditional relationships, bad as they may be, and lures them into an economic and social vacuum. Such a resettlement, however, has nothing in common with structural reforms but is merely a stratagem in the fight for the maintenance of the *status quo* which frequently takes the form of civil war.

The ultimate objective of land settlement is to increase agricultural production either by reclaiming and cultivating hitherto unused land or reorganizing and intensifying the exploitation of already cropped land. Any such programme, however, will be meaningless unless it is commensurate with the general socio-economic and technological trends and, above all, if it does not speed up agricultural development. Costly settlement schemes have been designed and implemented as show-pieces that remain suspended in mid-air and have no value whatsoever for global agricultural development. They are but an irresponsible waste of scarce resources, as in the case of some schemes in Western Nigeria* where a few thousand settlers recruited from among primary school graduates enjoy the most favourable conditions while millions of their fellow countrymen remain underprivileged. Schemes of this kind are likely to introduce elements of hostility, suspicion and insecurity in the entire region and even in the life of the settlers themselves who fear the day when the lavish government support will be withdrawn.

It would be equally wasteful and undesirable, however, to reproduce in new settlements the non-viable holdings, outdated cultivation practices and poor returns which characterized the agriculture of the old villages; yet, it is not always easy to decide where to draw the line between waste of capital and investment in future progress. Generally speaking, it is safe to say that the standard of a new settlement scheme is satisfactory when there is good reason to assume that it can be reproduced on a countrywide scale within a period of, say, ten to fifteen years.

The concept of purely agricultural settlement as a means of

* United Nations, FAO, 'Agricultural Development in Nigeria 1965–1980' (Rome, 1966, as yet unpublished), chap. 21, pp. 339 ff.

promoting rural development is no longer valid. Present-day farming does not stand alone but is closely interrelated with a whole series of non-agricultural factors. Any agrarian reform policy must take this into account and must ensure that agricultural and industrial activities are linked together in rural settlement planning.*

Considering the physical limitations of land settlement and, consequently of possibilities for alternative employment, industrial enterprises in the neighbourhood will provide an outlet for the growing population and an insurance against the subdivision and fragmentation of land. The combination of agricultural and industrial employment opportunities is the most effective means of reducing the exodus from the land, and has the effect of changing the village from a refuge for old people to a modern centre for rural development. In areas where scarcity of land and water is the limiting factor for increasing income from agriculture, near-by rural industries will provide the supplementary income needed to make part-time farming an acceptable way of life.

It would be inadvisable, of course, to combine highly specialized industries with new rural settlements where the lack of transportation facilities and skilled labour may cause serious problems. The industries should be engaged primarily in the processing of agricultural products, such as sugar refining, cotton ginning and canning and preferably should be located as near to the source of raw material as possible.

Such a coordination of agricultural and industrial activities in rural settlements will also expand the village market for agricultural products; this will increase contact between the village and the outside world and break down the invisible wall that today isolates the peasants from the currents of change and progress. It will make the life of the settlers more meaningful since a stratified community provides a variety of interests and more efficient and cheaper services. But, most important of all, it will prevent the inevitable industrial development from turning the

---

* R. Weitz, *Agriculture and Rural Development in Israel—Projection and Planning* (The National and University Institute of Agriculture, Hebrew University of Jerusalem, 1963), pp. 120 ff. See also R. Weitz and A. Rokach, *Agricultural Development, Planning and Implementation* (Dordrecht, 1968).

village into an industrial slum, as happened in Western Europe
and the east coast of the United States, when industry invaded
the rural areas and caused a malignant growth of industrial villages
which combined the worst of both worlds.

Manufacturing industries using agricultural products as raw
material may likewise be of importance whereas auxiliary industries without specific connection with local conditions are less
desirable. True, the latter may provide additional employment*
but if they are not integrated into the rural pattern they tend to
hinder rather than support agricultural development. The type of
rural industry and its location, therefore, are of considerable importance and should reconcile to the largest extent possible the
needs of industrial production with the real interests of the settlement. Thus, other factors besides cost calculations and rentability
must be taken into account, but the fact that this may to some
extent discourage private industrial enterprise is not altogether a
disadvantage since cooperative rural industries are anyway a
better way of accelerating social development in the new communities.

The history of settlement reflects an endless waste of human
and material resources. Thus, the settlement of the North American
continent, carried out by spontaneous and selfish action on the
part of individuals, was one of the most costly and wasteful
ventures of modern times. It was certainly successful, but it
involved the loss of invaluable agricultural resources and hundreds of thousands of human lives, because it was based on the
expendability of land and human labour. Although modern ethics
and economic thinking deprecate this kind of settlement and
recognize the need for careful advance planning, there is a serious
difference of opinion regarding the concern for the human
factor.

While it is generally agreed that the most advanced methods
and techniques should be applied when planning the physical
layout and economic potentialities of settlement, the human problems are frequently neglected. Certainly, cost-benefit calculations
are an essential part of adequate planning; but experience has
proved time and again the urgent need for an advance appraisal

* R. Weitz, op. cit. Under the specific conditions in Israel auxiliary
industries might be recommendable, due to the geographic, demographic and social town-land relationship.

of the social benefits.* The multifarious features and side-effects of settlement cannot be expressed in purely quantitative terms, but the fact that they do not lend themselves to measurement does not make them nonexistent.

Land settlements have been organized for a variety of reasons, such as to mitigate population pressure and unemployment, facilitate diversification of agriculture, compensate war veterans, pacify unruly population groups or strengthen national defence. Occasionally, they are being used for experiments in new human relationships. All these motivations are justifiable under certain conditions; but the fundamental criterion for rural settlement as part of land reform is that it provides a flexible and progressive framework for human activities which will assure a 'new deal' for the man on the land. This may seem a difficult task but in practice the procedure is logical and straightforward: controlled acquisition of land, carefully determined outlay and type of farms, adequate institutions and a fair distribution of agricultural and non-agricultural activities.

It may happen, of course, that political pressure or emergency situations call for solutions that distort this concept of settlement and compromise its fundamental principles. Prompt settlement action, for instance, may be needed to appease landless minority groups or provide homesteads for large numbers of refugees. Governments, of course, should deal with such situations as generously as possible; but they must not pretend that this is, or can ever be, settlement in the true sense of the word.† To confuse development programmes and emergency solutions may lead to costly deviations and even jeopardize an originally sound settlement policy.

* See D. R. Gadgil, 'Integration of Land Settlement Policies into the Economic and Social Development Planning of Countries', *FAO Monthly Bulletin of Agricultural Economics and Statistics,* vol. 8, no. 10 (1959), pp. 1–7; and D. Christodoulou, 'Land Settlement: Some Oft Neglected Basic Issues', *FAO Monthly Bulletin of Agricultural Economics and Statistics,* vol. 14, no. 10 (October 1965), pp. 1–6.

† The 'New Villages' established by the British authorities in Malaya to control Chinese squatters and peasants who supported the guerrillas during the Emergency of 1952–55, were unable to survive with the exception of a very few in privileged locations.

The settlements of limited professional groups like war veterans is likewise a false conception of settlement and the fact that it has been tried repeatedly throughout history does not increase its chances for success. The men returning to civilian life after years of enforced obedience and subordination are not psychologically fit, hardworking as they may be, for the cooperative action and community work needed in rural development. It may be questioned, therefore, whether the food aid and other assistance granted for the establishment of such projects in Taiwan could not have been put to better use elsewhere in the country. There is no doubt, however, that small groups of veterans would be an asset and it may be worth while to encourage their incorporation into different settlements rather than concentrating them in schemes of their own.

We have stressed repeatedly that rural settlement must be planned with a view to overall national development. But even careful planning cannot always anticipate all future trends, which may call for immediate adjustments. In Libya, for example, the sudden rapid growth of the oil industry jeopardized a scheme for the settlement of nomads, because the planned income targets, originally far above the income level of the tribes, suddenly appeared unrealistically low compared to the wages offered by the oil industry. Long-term settlement projects, therefore, require the careful observation of income trends in other sectors and should be adjusted as early as possible.

Careful attention should likewise be given to existing tenure conditions since in many areas, otherwise suited to settlement, land records are often spurious or nonexistent. This is particularly important in Africa where customary communal ownership is still alive and where land acquisition may, therefore, constitute an offence against established rights in land which may ultimately lead to friction and even warfare. In order to avoid conflicts between customary and statutory laws regarding ownership rights, sociological and legal investigations should precede actual settlement planning. In areas where periodic grazing and shifting cultivation obscure existing rights in land, imprudent land acquisition has frequently led to injustice and discord which eventually jeopardized the very existence of the new settlement. It is paradoxical to deprive some people of part of their land in order to resettle others, unless the former gain some advantages from the change, such as soil improvement, irrigation, or infrastructures.

It is equally important that advance planning of the size and layout of the farm units should be made on the basis of their expected productive capacity, of the number of families to be settled and, above all, of the agricultural and capital resources available. These factors will suggest whether preferences should be given to large-scale collective or state farms or to individual peasant holdings.

The ultimate decision on the type of tenure to be used in a settlement scheme, however, should depend on the intended land use and on the social and economic level of the settlers. From the point of view of the settler's pride as landholder it makes little difference whether he is given full ownership rights or a secure and inheritable leasehold, except in areas like Kenya where the European type of freehold rights in the White Highlands had become a status symbol for the new Kikuyu settlers. It has been stated quite rightly, however, that 'the surest way to deprive a peasant of his land is to give him a secure title and make it freely negotiable...'* And there is no doubt that leasehold rights for individual farmers in a settlement would facilitate the control of subdivision and fragmentation, of overgrazing and other wasteful land use. While the new settler is still inexperienced in farm management and unaccustomed to commercial transactions it would certainly be inadvisable to start a settlement scheme with a tenure system that gives him the right to mortgage or even sell his new holding. The cultural background of the settlers, therefore, is of decisive importance in selecting the most suitable tenure type.

An often neglected aspect of settlement planning is how to treat the indigenous population in a new settlement area. The settlement of Javanese peasants in Sumatra bears witness to the serious difficulties which arise when the local people have not been considered as part of the settlement plan. Advance sociological research could have provided invaluable information that would have mitigated the unavoidable hardship of adjustment and facilitated the gradual integration of old-timers and newcomers. Even in the relatively well-planned settlement scheme of Gal Oya

* *Report of the Working Party on African Land Tenure, 1957–1958* (Nairobi, 1958), para. 10.

in Ceylon, clusters of poverty-stricken, old peasant farms can be found around the prosperous settlement area.

The complete integration of everybody within a settlement area is in the interests not only of the indigenous peasants, but also of the new settlers for money-lenders and shopkeepers may use the distressed groups within a settlement area to gain a foothold from where they can penetrate the new community and gradually undermine its institutional pattern. A Filipino official concerned with land reform has explained that his government abandoned its former settlement policy in favour of tenancy reform and land redistribution mainly because of the high cost of duplicating in new areas, social facilities which had already been established in the areas from which the settlers came, and because of the tendency for tenancy to develop in the new settlements.* This reasoning is particularly interesting because it shows that rural settlement alone is no substitute for land reform. Yet, it is not altogether convincing since almost by definition land settlement implies, or should imply, the improvement and expansion of economic and social facilities. The 'tendency to renewed tenancy', therefore, could not have developed had adequate institutions and tenure arrangements been introduced from the outset of the settlement schemes.

Migratory movements and the dissolution of tribal systems in Africa have facilitated settlement schemes of considerable magnitude which we will deal with more extensively below.† Here, we will only refer briefly to their purpose and specific role in overall development.

When the European monopoly in the White Highlands of Kenya was eventually broken after independence, the government purchased these lands for the settlement of African peasants in order to maintain agricultural production and, at the same time, relieve population pressure in the Kikuyu areas. The new settlements are based on full ownership and seem to have had a stabilizing effect on the economy of the country which, due to a sharp drop in prices for land and grade cattle in the Highlands after the liquidation of the European farms, was on the verge of collapse. At the same time, however, they brought land values in the Kikuyu areas down to a more realistic level by decreasing the

* *Progress in Land Reform, Fourth Report*, p. 59, para. 278.
† See chapter 12.

demand for land. Furthermore, they occasioned a much larger input of labour relative to other factors of production; this not only replaced capital to a considerable extent but also reduced the foreign exchange component within the farming sector. This is highly important for countries like Kenya where there is shortage of capital but abundance of readily available labour. At present, the value of imported capital goods per 1,000 acres of settlement land is about one-half or one-third of that in large-scale farm units, the difference being due mainly to reduced imports of machinery.*

In Uganda, land settlement has frequently been designed to create barriers of settlement as a defence against the reinvasion of the tsetse fly from areas already cleared.† Different criteria are, of course, applied to the planning and implementation of such schemes and any cost-benefit appraisal of their value, therefore, should include not only the benefits to the settlers themselves, but also the benefits to those farmers behind the barrier who are given protection against the reinvasion of the tsetse fly.

Inevitably, such a multi-purpose project involves the specific difficulty of phasing the settlement schemes to coincide with the anti-tsetse operation, and of coordinating the planning and budgeting negotiations with yet another government department.

But whatever the objectives, or combination of objectives, of a specific settlement project, the fundamental problem is to establish from the very outset a social structure that will exclude the emergence of a farming hierarchy which is privileged by the size and quality of their holdings. Large differences in farm size within a settlement scheme and its institutions will necessarily jeopardize the position of the smallholders because leadership, and with it the authority to allocate credit and other resources, will be concentrated in the hands of the large and economically stronger farmers. It even entails the risk that the small owners or their families may accept additional work on the larger farms and thus reestablish a social dependence contrary to the objectives

* J. W. Maina, 'Land Settlement in Kenya' (RU: WLR 66/20). Paper submitted to the World Land Reform Conference, FAO, Rome, 1966.
† *Progress in Land Reform, Fourth Report*, p. 67, para. 323.

of settlement. This happened in the Gal Oya settlement scheme and was the main reason for the decision to change the farm size pattern.

Another problem of far-reaching importance is that of settler selection and opposing criteria have been proposed none of which is universally valid. Some planners want to settle only young married couples without children; others prefer large families. Some stress previous farming experience, while others want to give first priority to inexperienced landless people in order to reduce the pressure in congested rural areas. Any one of these may be justifiable under specific demographic, social and agricultural conditions, but what really matters is the subsequent decisions on education, training, extension, housing and farm outlay. It is safe to say that the degree to which these decisions correspond to the needs of the group selected will in the end determine the success or failure of the settlement project. In Israel, for example, adequate institutions changed inexperienced immigrants into successful farmers, although probably no planner would ever have considered pedlars from the ghettos of North Africa and intellectuals and businessmen from Central and Eastern Europe as eligible groups for agricultural settlement. The one criterion which cannot be justified under any circumstances is political favouritism. Any selection reflecting a political bias will carry with it elements of factional strife, injustice and inequality which will be detrimental to the pattern of human relations in the new community.

Land settlement implies a new start free from time-honoured dividing lines and prejudices. Education and extension services will help to reduce the power of traditionalism and gradually integrate the settlers into the new institutional pattern. The young settlers will probably not become as attached to the soil as did their elders in the old villages; but they may achieve instead a stronger community and cooperative spirit that will increase the possibility of social and economic progress.

The often only modest success and the many failures of settlement schemes have been largely due to the lack of proper training in the particular conditions of the new environment. Traditions and patterns of life from the old areas should be respected in order to secure the feeling of continuity; but they must not be allowed to shape the way of life in the new settlements. The Indonesian transmigration scheme's mistake in transplanting entire

Javanese villages with their established traditions and cultivation methods into the entirely different world of Sumatra is largely responsible for the misfortune of some of the settlement programmes; the Javanese peasants, accustomed to wet agriculture, received little guidance in how to tackle the problems of dry farming in the new surroundings. It is most important, therefore, to coordinate training with the actual tasks to be performed in the settlement. Pre-training for settlement under the generally optimum conditions of farm institutes is not altogether advisable as it may entail a disdain for manual labour and even arouse expectations that can seldom be immediately fulfilled in the new settlement.

Finally, there is the problem of appraising the staff resources available for the organization of administrative machinery to implement the scheme, and particularly, for the establishment of civic and cooperative institutions through which the settlers can actively participate in the attainment of local government. Even the most effective administration, however, cannot guide the gradual transfer of responsibilities if the social organization of the community does not exclude caste and class divisions.

Although small settlement projects may be carried out directly by government departments, planning and implementation of large projects, particularly in ex-colonial countries, should not be left to an administration that by tradition is used to commanding the peasants and not to inviting their participation.

It is difficult to put forward a general formula for the progressive administration of settlement schemes, but it seems that only an independent agency, set up for the particular purpose of dealing with all aspects of large land settlement projects, is able to handle the programme with the flexibility needed to avoid unnecessary friction and with a certain degree of continuity even in periods of adverse political developments.*

Settlement of Nomads

The aura of romanticism that surrounds the life of nomads is in sad contrast to their difficult existence. Nomadism is a people's

* See part 2, chapter 14.

specific response to the harsh bio-climatic conditions of arid areas,* and the impermanence of settlement affects their social structure and particularly their land tenure situation. The nomads' life centres on water supplies that are either owned in common by various tribes or used by agreement with settled farmers in exchange for dung, milk or small cash payments. The often vague rights to those water sources which are not commonly held are frequently the reason for continued conflicts and even warfare between nomadic groups and sedentary cultivators. While in the past nomads were often the stronger and in exchange for 'protection' could claim much more than water by way of tribute from the oasis cultivators,† their position today is getting increasingly more vulnerable due to the population increase in the settled areas and the emergence of strong civic and political state organizations. The sedentarization of the nomads has become a structural necessity for the governments of underdeveloped countries where herdsmen still graze their flocks over nearly 10 million square miles.‡ The most serious charge against nomadism is that it wastes, or inefficiently utilizes, the available natural resources. Like all generalizations, this charge is not quite fair. It is evident that some nomadic groups are more efficient resource-users than others and succeed in gaining for themselves what is, by local standards, a relatively high income as, for instance, the Basseri of Iran, or, Sudanese nomads, who even use natural resources which would be unexploitable by any other mode of life.§ Nevertheless, it remains true that the very institution of nomadism implies a wasteful utilization of certain resources which can only be rectified by institutional reforms. The most serious is the tendency to overstock grazing land which is exacerbated as the population grows, and not only depletes the natural pastures but leads to an impoverishment of the nomads themselves which, in turn, increases the social costs of the government in terms of a low level of education and standard of living. It is extremely important

---

* R. G. Fontaine, 'FAO Ecological Studies as a Basis for Agricultural Development' in *IUCN (International Union for Conservation of Nature and Natural Resources)*, p. 340.

† *Progress in Land Reform, Fourth Report*, p. 53, para. 246.

‡ W. Allan, *The African Husbandman* (Edinburgh and New York, 1965), p. 288.

§ *Progress in Land Reform, Fourth Report*, p. 54.

that the difficult and costly undertaking of integrating nomads into the civil life of the nation and bringing them within the orbit of education and welfare services has proved technologically feasible and psychologically acceptable in countries such as the USSR, UAR, Sudan and Saudi Arabia. Despite the widespread notion that all nomads prefer a life of freedom without restraint and have an inborn contempt for settled life, experience in the Western Desert of the UAR seems to indicate that it is, in fact, a matter of social distinction. I have personally met a Bedouin sheik who years ago had had a permanent house built for his immediate family on an olive plantation near a water source. He retained a magnificent tent simply to receive his guests in, while the poorer members of his clan continued their nomadic life as herdsmen. To my mind, there is no doubt that they would also be prepared to settle as agriculturists if only the necessary water supplies could be provided to raise permanent crops. The gradual disintegration of the nomadic tribes in areas relatively close to the air bases and oil fields of Libya also seems to indicate an inclination to give up their itinerant existence if attractive occasions arise.

The settlement of nomads and their economic integration into the civil life of the nation requires, however, continued attention in order to prevent the exploitation of a population group that has no bargaining power and hardly any knowledge of economic transactions. The planned sedentarization of nomads, therefore, is much more complex than other land settlement schemes for whereas these need but a few years of adjustment, it involves a social and psychological transformation that may take decades to accomplish. The magnitude of the settlement scheme is determined not only by the number of nomads to be settled but even more by the often considerable amount of agricultural resources in terms of pasture, water and livestock which they control.

In the Near East and North Africa efforts have been made to transform the traditional pastoral economy of the nomads by considerable public investment in large-scale settlement schemes.* Due to the enormous costs and the long-term aspect of the project, only one section of the nomads in an area, and in all probability

* M. Riad El Ghonemy, 'Land Reform and Economic Development in the Near East' (RU: WLR/66/E), p. 7. Background Paper for the World Land Reform Conference, FAO, Rome, 1966.

the smaller one, can be settled in the initial stages. It is of great importance, therefore, that alongside settlement action, efforts should be made to improve the nomads' pastures and provide as much education and welfare as possible within the framework of their nomadic existence. If this is neglected, the whole settlement scheme may flounder as the gains of the one group will be counterbalanced by the losses of the others whose grazing areas are gradually deteriorating. This will cause tension and friction between the settled and unsettled nomads, whereas improved pastures may encourage the herdsmen to raise more livestock and even to become suppliers to the settled groups.

Furthermore, particular attention must be given to the power relations within the tribes and effective counter-measures should be worked out at the planning stage in order to avoid the often feudal tribal structure being reproduced in the settlement. More land and high offices to the sheik and his family entail the great danger that they will take on themselves the leadership of the settlement and its institutions, and on the strength of their education, political relations and economic experience will dominate even the cooperative organizations to the disadvantage of the majority of the settled families.

The social aspects of nomad settlement planning are highly complicated since they call for a complete change in the mode of existence and values. A well-conceived system of education and extension, based on thorough sociological research, must be provided in every sphere of community life and continued for many years. As it is the women who carry the main burden of the transition from tent to house, home economics should be given a more prominent position in the extension work than they are given in other settlement schemes.

The invasion of the Italian settlements in Libya at the end of the Second World War by nomadic tribes, and their continued struggle with the Libyan government to be recognized as the legitimate owners of this land is proof of their vital interest in settled agriculture under favourable conditions. The much-publicized fact that a few may still pitch their tents next to their house does not prove the contrary and implies hardly more than an understandable attachment to a traditional pattern of living.

Forest Settlements

The problems of forestry and impermanence of settlement are closely interrelated. Rational forest development frequently infringes upon the customary rights of nomads to shifting cultivation or grazing in forest areas, and adequate measures, therefore, are needed to arrive at an acceptable compromise between the interests of traditional societies and the requirements of economic development of timber land free from customary usufructuary rights. Such a compromise should be easier to achieve once the concept of state control of all forest lands has been recognized, and in most forest regions of the world, forestry departments deal with the legal and institutional matters associated with the allocation of forest land for settlement and production. In Africa communal rights to forest land have been legalized and the transition from subsistence to market economy has accelerated the clearing of these for agricultural use. In Asia most forest land is state-owned and private ownership is recognized in a few countries only. In the countries of Latin America the situation is somewhat different since here forest development is a problem of distribution rather than of the area available; and this has provoked pressure for a change in the landholding pattern which, so far, is being partly resolved through forest settlements.* In fact, most of the land offered to settlers is located in state-owned forest areas which are not only sparsely populated but also fertile. But settlement on forest land is still largely uncontrolled and causes a considerable deterioration of forest resources. Although in many parts of Latin America forest development is linked with land settlement to an increasing extent, this is not yet sufficiently reflected in appropriate administrative and institutional arrangements or in action programmes which are designed to control the settlers.

In the context of agrarian reform, forest settlements may become tremendously important in countries with a scarcity of arable and pasture land; and 'farm forestry', as it is called in Scandinavia is a type of settlement which could be applied to the

---

* *Progress in Land Reform, Fifth Report*, p. 173.

K

forest areas of underdeveloped countries,* particularly if it is organized on a cooperative basis. Such schemes could be carried out by allocating forest plots of adequate economic size which include a small area of arable land. There is little doubt that our development strategy in the past has neglected one of the under-developed countries' most important resources, the forests,† and that land settlement could be a suitable means of integrating the forest into development projects. In this, the progressive nature of forest institutions will be of great help.‡

There is no doubt that land settlement is a most effective means of relieving population pressure in congested areas and increasing agricultural production. But settlement planning is still fraught with difficulties and there is still no completely valid answer to this problem—all we can state with confidence is that conscientious planning alone does not guarantee lasting success. The settlement has to be kept viable under changing demo-graphic, economic and technological conditions and must be organized, therefore, with a degree of flexibility that will permit the necessary adjustments to be made.

* 'Forestry and Agrarian Reform' (RU: WLR/66/B). Background paper prepared by J. Prats-Llaurado in collaboration with C. Petrin for the World Land Reform Conference, FAO, Rome, 1966.
† The Pearson Report (*Partners in Development. Report of the Commission on International Development*, New York, 1969), com-prising about 400 pages, does not even mention forestry.
‡ In connection with some land reform programmes, experiments in cooperative forest settlements have been carried out as, for in-stance, the forest *ejidos* in Mexico and the forest *asentamientos* in Chile.

CHAPTER TEN

Collective and Cooperative Farming Activities - Not a Socialist Monopoly

In many socialist countries the terms 'collective' and 'cooperative' farming are used synonymously and this has created a good deal of confusion in current literature on the subject. In practice, however, any form of group farming is based on a cooperative scheme the organization of which varies from country to country and under different social, political and physical conditions. In the first place there is the loose cooperation between individual farmers at times of sowing and harvesting such as in mutual aid societies and joint ownership of more costly farm equipment. Secondly, there is the more closely knit cooperation between agricultural producers who pool their land to form a single unit which they cultivate in common, each member, however, retaining the ownership rights to his land and receiving for it a commensurate share of the returns. And thirdly, there is total cooperation where all the land and means of production are owned collectively by a group of producers who divide the returns from farming either on the basis of individual labour input or on the principle of fair sharing according to need.

The first form of cooperation is less interesting in this context because of its limited impact on the agrarian structure. The second form may or may not directly lead to structural changes in agriculture, whereas the third is representative of a socialist organization of agriculture although not necessarily of a country-wide socialist political system. Although the last two forms are both based on common-land-use, centralized management and economies of scale, they differ essentially with regard to the distribution of returns. In this chapter, therefore, only the third form will be denoted as *collective* farming, while the term *collective* farming will be used only for those types of common-land-use

292 Programme of Agrarian Reform

practices that explicitly emphasize individual ownership in land and a corresponding share in the returns.

In the post-war discussion on agricultural development in backward areas, most Western economic literature associated collective farming with revolution, violence and peasant exploitation. During the cold war, particularly, it was conveniently identified with communism and depicted as the arch-enemy of the peasants in the underdeveloped world. Gandhi, however, was a stout defender of the merits of all forms of cooperative farming as long as they were based on non-violence.*

The success of individual farming in the relatively small agricultural sector of the Atlantic countries was held up as an ideal and books like *Marx Against the Peasant*† provided scientific arguments for resisting changes in the concept of free ownership in those parts of the world where the peasant who tills the land is seldom its owner. The patent success of collective farming in Israel was 'excused' on the grounds of unusual circumstances and, quite wrongly, of the religious zeal of the Israeli settlers. During the first post-war decade not one honest study on the comparative merits and demerits of collective farming was published, and even for the United Nations agencies the topic was almost taboo. It was not until 1956, that it became possible to organize a study group on problems of individual and group settlement for the European region,‡ and for a long time this remained FAO's only effort to deal with any kind of group farming. But as so often during the past twenty years, development out-paced economic research, and when socio-economic studies finally began to appear on the issue of common-land-use, the advantages of this type of farming in many parts of the world had already struck the unbiased observer. And all the critics could do was to attack it as a tremendous exploitation of human effort and a sacrifice of freedom—as if exploitation and waste had not

* M. K. Gandhi, *Co-operative Farming* (Ahmedabad, 1959), pp. 10 ff.
† D. Mitrany, *Marx Against the Peasant.*
‡ United Nations, FAO, *Report of the Study Group on the Problems of Individual and Group Settlement for the European Region, Tel Aviv, Israel, April-May 1956* (1956/19, Rome, 1956).

always marked the decisive stages of economic and industrial evolution in the West—while, ironically, they hardly ever mentioned the lack of 'freedom' in the feudal and semi-feudal areas of the underdeveloped world.

If we seek to determine the role of collective farming in agrarian reform, we must answer two fundamental questions. Firstly, whether the principle of cooperation can be applied at all in agricultural production and if so, in what form and to what extent. And secondly, whether cooperation is likely to influence the power structures in the villages and thus affect the agrarian structure too.

There is no doubt that collective farming as a tenure system should not be treated as a monopoly of the socialist countries; it is a rational means for increasing agricultural production and creating a less depressed society in underdeveloped countries. Provided that there is no discrimination against collective farming, it can happily coexist with individual tenure types, as is the case in Israel and Tanzania. The coexistence of capitalist and socialist tenure types in agriculture should, indeed, be as feasible as the mixed economy in industry, banking, services and communications in Western Europe.

The time when individual tenure types could monopolize agriculture is at an end. The continued subdivision and fragmentation of holdings and the growing rate of landlessness is making millions of peasants increasingly aware of their state of isolation and frustration. Working their minute plots with outdated implements for returns hardly exceeding mere subsistence, they are becoming increasingly less susceptible to the argument that collective farming will reduce them to a state of still greater frustration and exploitation. The increasing evidence of the success of collective farming in the socialist world, and China in particular, is making them aware of the obvious advantages that can be gained from working the land in larger units.

At this stage, therefore, when development is sliding back in large parts of the underdeveloped world and the time-tested devices can no longer cope with the task in hand, we must try to analyse the reasons for the widespread negative attitude of the Western world to collective farming. Some observers, of course, are carried away by their emotional reaction to political systems in which collectivization plays the predominant role. But many others rest their case on some unfortunate experiments in group agriculture in non-socialist countries, although they have not carried out a thorough investigation of the reasons for the meagre results and frequent failure. This is true, for example, of the argument against cooperative farming in India, so well set out by Myrdal,* that the Indian village, as it at present exists does not provide the social harmony needed for the transformation in economic incentives which needs to take place. This may be true, but it is also true that many of the ventures in cooperative farming as practised in India were treated by landlords, absentees in particular, as a convenient device for receiving the benefits of the preferential treatment and subsidies given to cooperatives by government agencies without actually assigning their lands to a common pool. They could continue to exploit the peasants and claim their conventional share of the crop with the result that the traditional status distinctions were maintained and with them disharmony in the villages. It must not be thought, therefore, that the failure of the Indian experiment is due to shortcomings in the actual system of cooperative farming. It failed because of weaknesses in the land and tenancy laws and, above all, in their implementation, which made it impossible to remove the obstacles standing in the path of other agrarian reform measures designed to promote agricultural development in India.

It has also been argued that collective farming does not offer the tiller land ownership as an incentive and for this reason is doomed to failure unless introduced by compulsion.† A growing understanding of the real causes underlying the social and economic misery and the stagnation of smallholders despite legal ownership to the land is, however, gradually undermining this argument. Many observers advocating owner-cultivation as a cure to all the underdeveloped countries' ills are, at the same time, impressed by the Gezira scheme in the Sudan where the tenants have lost any affection they had for their own plots when they first entered the scheme decades ago. It is quite obvious that the emotional, and even economic, incentive value of landownership will decline commensurately with the increased income from a growing productivity of land and labour. Other assertions such

---

* G. Myrdal, *Asian Drama*, vol. 2, pp. 1346 ff.
† W. A. Lewis, *The Theory of Economic Growth* (London and Homewood, Ill., 1957), pp. 64 ff., 120 ff.

as collective farming kills the initiative of the peasants and their capacity for a positive reaction to incentives, or that it is inevitably labour-displacing and, therefore, leads to growing underemployment in congested areas, are becoming almost nonsensical the more we get to know about agricultural progress in China and the USSR.*

Yet, some observers state that the collectivization of agriculture in the immense rural areas in China was a gradual process starting with the establishment of mutual aid teams, and that the transition to the various stages of cooperation was relatively easy once the peasant had understood how little he could gain from his own plot and had been impressed by the better credit terms, implements, housing and marketing obtainable through collective farming. It is, in fact, most likely that the majority of the millions of peasants in Vietnam, North Korea and China were not compelled by force to join such schemes but learned through careful information to recognize that working the land in larger units means better supplies, better facilities and, quite simply, a better way of life.

As for the labour-displacing effect of collective farming, the Chinese experience proves the contrary. The collectivization of Chinese agriculture mobilized the huge army of idle labour for the construction of irrigation and drainage works, for terracing and other forms of capital formation.† It has been assumed, quite rightly, that the impressive progress in Chinese agriculture in a relatively short period of time would have been impossible without the capacity of collective farming for mobilizing labour and substituting labour for capital.‡

Despite dominant Western thought, it is becoming increasingly difficult to deny that group agriculture is a realistic possibility for rendering agriculture more meaningful in many under-

* See T. J. Hughes and D. E. T. Luard, *The Economic Development of Communist China* (London and New York, 1961), p. 167; and chapter 7, subsections on the USSR and China and the sources quoted there.

† T. J. Hughes and D. E. T. Luard, op. cit., p. 166.

‡ W. F. Wertheim, 'Recent Trends in China's Population Policy', para. 17.

developed countries. Wherever agricultural development is impeded by a limiting factor—be it land, water, labour or extension staff—it entails full use of the existing resources without immediately infringing upon the personal rights in land. Given the present land distribution pattern in the majority of underdeveloped countries with their millions of minute holdings, it is almost ridiculous to speak about preserving the right to decide farm management since, from the point of view of development, it has no economic meaning whatsoever.

Just as whole-hearted government support is necessary for the successful implementation of agrarian reform, it is indispensable for the organization of any cooperative venture. The Agro-Economic Research Centre for Gujarat and Rajastan in India has made an interesting case study on the fate of a collective farming society in the Jaipur District (State of Rajastan)* which clearly shows how little assistance and guidance on the part of government agencies would have been needed in order to rescue this voluntary initiative.

The village under investigation, Ganeshpura, accessible both by road and rail, was established on a tract of uncultivated land, by 10 families, numbering 75 members who left a nearby village because of a quarrel with the local *Jagirdar*. They received land for settlement from the district authority, the amount depending on size of family, and from the very outset tried to overcome the difficulties of reclaiming the new land and constructing a well for drinking water and irrigation by voluntary common effort. A government subsidy covered only one-third of the costs for the well and the remaining two-thirds were shared by the villagers and so was the complicated procedure of drawing water.

In contrast to other small villages, the inhabitants of Ganeshpura led a harmonious community life; caste relations were altogether cordial and even the lowest caste had access to the well. The villagers were not destitute. They had some cash, as their contribution to the well proves, and their holdings were large compared to those in many other villages. Their main problems were usurious rates for credit and a shortage of labour and bullocks for farm

* K. M. Choudhary, *The Organization and Disintegration of a Collective Farming Society. A Case Study in a Gramdan Village* (Sardar Patel University, Vallabh Vidyanagar, Ad hoc Study no. 2, June 1963).

operations. Every year, in fact, a considerable part of the land was left uncultivated. Informal cooperation at the time of ploughing, weeding, harvesting, etc. had become common practice and they were thus ready to follow the advice of a Gramdan* leader that they form a collective farming society in order to obtain cheaper loans, technical help and other facilities from the government.

They formed the society in June 1959 and applied for a loan from the Cooperative Bank in Jaipur and for subsidies to buy a water-lifting pump and perhaps a tractor so that they could irrigate and cultivate a larger area of the dry land. But their high hopes were disappointed.

None of the government agencies responsible nor the Gramdan movement gave them any concrete assistance despite promises made from time to time. They had to start collective cultivation on their own and even get the seeds from money-lenders at the customary usurious rates of interest. As all the members were illiterate with the exception of one who could sign his name, they could not understand how to keep accounts, or the necessary records of attendance. They applied for a subsidy for qualified secretarial help which was refused. As a result great problems arose with regard to sharing and disposing of the crop. In the end they decided to use the crude method of members contributing plough-units (i.e., one male and one female labourer, one plough and one pair of bullocks) as the basis for sharing; but thereafter the members sold their part of the crop individually.

Neither of the agencies set up to encourage and facilitate co-operation among farmers fulfilled its task. The Gramdan leader who had persuaded the villagers to form the society soon lost interest and only seldom visited them to discuss their problems and difficulties. And the government officials never bothered to investigate the real needs and give appropriate advice. Even the credits eventually extended by the Cooperative Bank for the buying of seeds only arrived after the sowing season was over with the result that the villagers distributed the money amongst themselves and largely used it for consumption purposes. This re-established individual interests and weakened the spirit of

---

* A movement initiated by Vinoba Bhave in which the landholders of a village surrender their proprietory rights in favour of the village community.

solidarity. After the second ill-timed loan the members failed to repay it within the stipulated time and thus forfeited their chances of any further loans from the bank.

The collective farming society that had been started with such high expectations only lasted a year; by the second year it had already begun to disintegrate and in the third year, though still existing on paper, it completely fizzled out.

It is obvious from the thorough analysis that the pathetic failure of the Ganeshpura collective farming society was due neither to the concept of collective farming nor to apathy or ill-will on the part of the peasants but to the lack of adequate support and guidance on the part of the responsible authorities.

And this, in turn, leads to the inescapable conclusion that any kind of common-land-use farming in backward areas needs careful preparation and skilled guidance in farm management and operation. This may seem a formidable task, but compared to the efforts that would be needed in order to raise the level of the millions of undersized individual farms it seems less so.

Any form of agricultural cooperation will, in fact, reduce the hitherto insurmountable problem of limited staff resources to manageable proportions by more effectively utilizing the skilled staff available. It provides the possibility, for example, of placing the more efficient farmers in key positions and relieving the less advanced ones from the burden of farm management decisions and, still more important, it increases the production performance of the extension worker.*

It is against this background that we must consider yet another precondition for all cooperative farm types, namely, the size and internal structure of the agricultural production unit. It is often forgotten that cooperation involves complex sociological problems and that the optimum size of a unit, therefore, is not determined by economic considerations alone but must be considered in conjunction with the organizational and sociological problems which arise from too large a community, particularly with regard to the active participation of the members in farm management

* See appendix III.

decisions.* The entire internal structure must provide a maximum of encouragement for individual initiative and give the members the possibility of gradually controlling the management itself.

Some observers consider cooperative farming to be the optimum choice in densely populated backward rural areas. This type of farming remains of an individual kind for all functions that can be executed within the limited boundaries of a single unit, while all other tasks such as planning, financing of investments and large equipment as well as supply and marketing is handled by the cooperative society. This system, which more or less corresponds to the *moshavim* in Israel, has, of course, certain merits from the standpoint of the individual farmer, but, unlike the collective farm, it does not provide a strong link with the national economy and necessarily retains an individual orientation.†

In Israel, a series of studies on the comparative profitability of the *moshav* (individual) and *kibbutz* (collective) come to the conclusion that in the Israeli setting neither system presents definite advantages or disadvantages. Good, average and poor performances are found in both cases and differences in degree are greater than any fundamental difference between the two systems.‡ In other words, the average profitability is more or less the same. While this does not exclude the possibility that an efficient individual farmer may have a higher productivity rate than an efficient *kibbutz*, the badly-managed individual farm will be infinitely worse off, since no *kibbutz* will delegate the responsibility for management to an inefficient manager even if he is a good worker.

Individual and collective farms exist side by side in Israel and neither system is given economic preference. They work under

* T. Bergman, 'Factors Influencing Optimum Size and Decision-Making in Cooperative Farms', *Papers and Proceedings, International Centre on Rural Cooperative Communities* (Tel Aviv, March 1969), pp. 18 ff.

† F. Van Dam, *Collective Farming in Densely Populated Underdeveloped Areas* (Academisch Proefschrift, University of Amsterdam, June 1961).

‡ See *Graphic Illustration of the Profitability of Agricultural Branches in 1964–65 and 1965–66* (Institute of Farm Income Research in Cooperation with the Central Bureau of Statistics, Tel Aviv, December 1967); and Jehuda Lowe, *Kibbutz and Moshav in Israel: An Economic Study in International Explorations of Agricultural Economics* (Iowa State University, 1964), pp. 126 ff.

equal conditions with regard to price relations, taxes and subsidies, and are both 'going' concerns. It must be added, however, that without the support of highly effective service cooperatives the individual farmers would be unable to compete successfully with the *kibbutz*.

In Mexico, on the other hand, where government policy and organized public opinion has turned against collective farming since the end of the Cardeñas administration in 1940, only a few of the rather successful *ejidos* established by the Revolution have been able to resist the artificial pressures to weaken them and provoke their failure.* Despite some recent attempts to stimulate collective exploitation, particularly in the newly established livestock *ejidos*, this type of farm organization is clearly on the decline. And, once again, not because it proved a failure but because of the increasing incompatibility between a collective farming system and the Mexican variety of capitalism.†

Despite its many obvious advantages as a tenure type that will strengthen agriculture and promote its integration into overall national development, collective farming, if rashly introduced into tribal areas, may impede the further development and progress of the rural masses. We must be aware of the danger that traditional communities all too frequently conceal their exploitation of the lower strata and the existence of a rigid structure based on inequality in the application of resources and the distribution of income.‡ Collective farms, therefore, should not be organized in backward or tribal areas before the possible impact of traditional institutions has been established by sociological research.

But on the other hand, a prominent group of Indian specialists§ actually warn against individual allotments of land being assigned in any form to groups of tribal or low caste people as this entails the risk that the resourceless members of the community will soon be demoted to labourers while the benefits will accrue to those who supply the capital and assume the authority to make deci-

* M. A. Durán, *El agrarismo Mexicano* (Mexico, 1967), p. 19.
† R. Stavenhagen (ed.), *Agrarian Problems and Peasant Movements in Latin America* (New York, 1970).
‡ T. Balogh, *The Economics of Poverty* (London, 1960; New York, 1967), p. 246.
§ Government of India, Ministry of Home Affairs, *Report of the Special Working Group on Cooperation for Backward Classes* (New Delhi, September 1962), vols. 1 and 2, pp. 116 ff.

sions. Moreover, those traditional ways of life which preserve social cohesion and prevent any disintegration which may lead to the isolation of the individual should be carefully preserved.

It is equally important, however, that the organization and ideology of group agriculture, particularly in densely populated underdeveloped areas, do not become self-centred but recognize the responsibility towards the economy and society as a whole. If this important aspect is neglected or ignored there is a risk that the new large units will develop into islands of economic success and high standards of living in an ocean of social and economic distress not altogether unlike the prosperous foreign plantations in the colonial territories. It is an outstanding characteristic of collective farming that, as an institution, it can link agriculture to overall social and economic development, as is happening to an ever-increasing degree in the socialist countries. Collective farming, therefore, should not be judged on its own merits but in relation to the economy as a whole. Its permanent success can only be ensured by a flexible policy that adjusts the social and cultural individuality of the people to the objectives of national development.

CHAPTER ELEVEN

Programmes Complementary to Land Reform

The frequent failure, or at best limited success, of social reform programmes are due neither to faulty planning nor defective implementation but to the misconception that they alone can change the quality of society and bring about a redistribution of income and wealth. But once the outdated structures preventing the rational utilization of available resources have been removed such programmes are important and even prerequisite measures for defending the new land distribution pattern by establishing an institutional framework that will give the peasants protection and incentives and help them to overcome traditional psychological inhibitions, social prejudices and formidable taboos.

In this respect the much praised community development programmes are extremely useful, but if launched in isolation they will only have a superficial effect as it is the man-land relationship with its attendant social and political order which determines the distribution of income and status and, therefore, the range of any social reform programme. Many economists and sociologists, however, do not realize this causality and still believe in the expediency of 'soft' reforms. The United Nations shares this belief and during the past decade numerous community development programmes have been planned and carried out in underdeveloped countries in an effort to bring about the urgently needed changes in the village societies. In the prevailing setting of outdated institutions, however, they fail to achieve the desired end and often have the effect of widening the gap between rich and poor besides releasing cheap labour for undertakings which are not always in the interests of the people. The rigid class system is bound to act in its own interests and, in the absence of basic changes, this can only distort even the most well-meaning reform programme.

An account of a project to bring sanitary drinking water and improved roads to the Valle de la Esperanza in El Salvador shows the persistent psychological influence of a semi-feudal structure upon the organization of community activities. Despite their need for both drinking water and roads, the villagers did not participate whole-heartedly in its implementation because painful experiences in the past had convinced them that any improvements would benefit the large landowners alone. Although this particular project was exceptional, the fact that the class-divided village society usually ignored the interests of the people had fostered distrust, resentment and frustration even against a government project which had honest intentions.*

There are a number of measures which are complementary to land reform; each one is important under certain conditions and at different stages of agricultural development and they have all been referred to in earlier chapters. At this point, however, we will limit ourselves to discussing reform programmes in the fields of credit, taxation and education because of their particular importance in carrying out agrarian reconstruction in under-developed countries.

Agricultural Credit

Most observers agree that the credit situation in underdeveloped countries is largely responsible for the vicious circle of poverty and indebtedness; that credit transactions with destitute peasants do not attract commercial banks and are, therefore, usually handled by landlords and traders at exhorbitant rates of interest; and that this pernicious credit system can only be abolished if the peasants gain access to institutional credit at fair rates channelled through cooperative organizations. But here opinion divides, as to whether the new agricultural credit institutions should use the bulk of the credit available to expand and strengthen the larger farm units, or whether it should be used to improve the lot of the small peasant holdings. Obviously, the final decision between

* G. Huizer, 'Community Development, Land Reform and Political Participation', *American Journal of Economics and Sociology*, vol. 28, no. 2 (April 1969).

these two options will strongly influence social stratification in the rural community and decide the trend of agricultural development.

In an earlier chapter* we have pointed out that the future of agriculture in underdeveloped countries is determined by the social and economic development of the peasant community as a whole. It could, of course, be argued that credit investments in the more efficient and larger farm units may to some extent improve conditions in the surrounding countryside. But recent experiences in Mexico and India, have shown the limited cumulative effects of a credit policy that gives rise to a new type of capitalist farm, which tends to develop into the kind of commercial enterprise which is likely to shift investment to other sectors of the economy in case of unfavourable agricultural prices. Moreover, these large farm units may even contribute to the exploitation of the small farmers by their dominant position in the market, as is the case in Mexico. Instead of improving conditions in the peasant communities, they will increase the underutilization of labour as they will inevitably use a considerable part of the loans extended to buy labour-saving equipment. It is difficult to conceive how this can be prevented under the prevailing economic and political conditions.

On the other hand, it is also true that the benefit of institutional credit to small farmers who in large parts of the underdeveloped world are at best subsistence cultivators is limited. Their most pressing problem is the smallness of their holdings and even generous credit arrangements cannot remedy the structural non-viability of these.† Even if they were to make farming profitable in terms of cost and return, the surplus would still be too meagre to both maintain the farming family and repay the loan. According to official Indian statistics, the national average of overdue repayments of outstanding loans is as large as 22–25 per cent, while it is as high as 71 per cent in Assam, 48 per cent in Bihar and 45 per cent in Rajasthan.‡ In other words, although institu-

---

* Chapter 3.

† 'Credit for Small Farmers', *Economic and Political Weekly*, vol. 4, no. 82 (9.8.1969) pp. 1293 ff., emphasizes the difficulties of this type of credit in the absence of land reform.

‡ M. L. Dantwala, 'Institutional Credit in Subsistence Agriculture,' *International Journal of Agrarian Affairs*, vol. 5, no. 1 (December 1966).

tional credit extended to subsistence cultivators may relieve a momentary crisis, it cannot stabilize their economy and thus neither improves agricultural development nor social stratification unless preceded by agrarian reforms, including the consolidation of holdings.

In fact, it is well-nigh impossible to conceive a cooperative system on the village level which can avoid reflecting the existing power structure particularly in the sensitive field of agricultural credit. Time and again we have seen how through their influence and business experience the larger farmers automatically take over the management and operation of the credit institutions and direct the lending to their own advantage leaving but little benefit, if any, to small cultivators.

The Indian *Rural Credit Follow-up Survey, 1959–60** analyses the effect of dominant vested interests in the cooperative credit and marketing societies. It points out that at the management level in the central office they can arbitrarily decide the credit limits to be set by the local society and the policy regarding respite for payments due, while at the local level money-lenders, traders, and large farmers use their economic and social powers to press for large loans at concessionary rates of interest.

In many Latin American countries credit cooperatives like other service associations are generally ineffective and often a complete failure which is detrimental to cooperative principles and expectations. The main reason for their failure is that the rural élite prevents their attempts to improve the institutional setup because it regards successful peasant cooperation as a potential menace. Nevertheless new cooperatives are constantly being formed because cooperation has become a slogan in government policy programmes. Moreover, it forms an important part of what has been called 'intellectual colonialism', i.e., the abuse of a Western social concept in order to distract the people's attention in times of political and social crises.†

In the final analysis, therefore, institutional credit alone cannot solve the financial and technical problems of the small peasant. It is, however, a complementary and indispensable measure with-

---

* Reserve Bank of India (Bombay, 1962), p. 210.
† O. Fals Borda, 'Formation and Deformation of Cooperative Policy in Latin America' (not yet published).

out which land redistribution and/or consolidation programmes will have no lasting effect, but will remain halfhearted measures that can only prolong the economic agony of the small cultivator.

Taxation

Underdeveloped countries have been reluctant to introduce fair land taxes, and generally still prefer the more simple systems of indirect taxation, price fixing or marketing boards, to a taxation policy that would require realistic land assessments. Concentration of landownership, favoured by the social prestige and political power which derives from landed properties and the control of agricultural labour, prevents the introduction of a taxation system that is just to the small farmer and burdens the powerful land-owner; hence the continued inflation of land values and the per-petuation of a feudalistic land distribution pattern. To put it more simply, the maldistribution of land in underdeveloped countries is largely a consequence of the correlation between low assess-ments and high market prices for agricultural land. When Magsaysay, the late President of the Philippines, failed to get his tax reform bill through the Senate in the early fifties, he had lost the battle for land reform, for this bill would have been the only legal means of forcing down land values to a reasonable level, diminishing land speculation, encouraging the cultivation or resale of idle land and making the settlement of landless people at rational costs possible.*

The weight and incidence of indirect taxes particularly on con-sumption goods are a heavy burden on the peasants. But they yield a high and constant revenue as the demand for basic con-sumption items like food, textiles and fuel is relatively inelastic and will not decrease substantially if liable to taxation. But as a side-effect it will automatically increase the economic power of the landlord-cum-trader, to whom the poor peasant will turn for credit at usurious terms when the tax burden further reduces his low income and increases his need for loans in cash or kind.

Despite the obvious interdependence between power structure,

* E. H. Jacoby, *Agrarian Unrest in Southeast Asia* (Bombay, 1961), p. 200.

taxation policy and peasant misery it is still an open question whether a rational taxation policy is at all feasible under the prevailing political conditions in underdeveloped countries.* It may be possible, of course, to achieve some minor socio-economic improvements and mitigate the most outrageous injustices by gradually increasing land assessments. This, however, will not solve the agrarian problem although it may lend some support to the underprivileged. On the other hand, a tax reform which is strong enough to change the balance of power and considerably reduce the market values of land will have to be carried out in the teeth of powerful vested interests and it is most unlikely that such a bill would ever pass a Parliament controlled by the very interests it sets out to weaken.

Thus once more we have a reform measure which will have marginal importance only if introduced in isolation but which, if closely coordinated with land redistribution, may serve as a useful instrument for strengthening the effect of the structural change. The introduction of progressive taxes on land based on potential yields will have a two-fold effect. First, it will induce the owners to either cultivate or sell idle land and secondly, it will provide an incentive for the cultivator to exceed the level of productivity on which the assessment of his land is based. Such a development orientated taxation (in more advanced areas combined with taxes on agricultural income) will also discourage the continued speculation in land which, by raising land values, increases social inequality and retards development.† An effective tax administration, on the other hand, will improve land surveys and the registration of titles, since taxation officials cannot be expected to collect revenues unless they are in a position to determine land ownership and fix liabilities.‡ In many cases, in fact, the intervention of fiscal agencies has actually increased the security of ownership and reduced the incidence of litigation. Indirect systems of

* In view of experiences in the Philippines and Latin America, it is difficult to share Gunnar Myrdal's views on the prospect of a progressive taxation policy (*Asian Drama*, p. 1380).

† T. Balogh, *The Economics of Poverty*, p. 340.

‡ Philip M. Raup, 'Agricultural Taxation and Land Tenure Reform in Underdeveloped Countries' in *Agricultural Taxation and Economic Development. Papers and Proceedings of the Conference on Agricultural Taxation and Economic Development, January 28 to February 3, 1954* (Cambridge, Mass., 1954), p. 257.

taxation, however, will unfavourably affect the tenure situation as was the case in colonial India, where the *Zamindars* using their semi-fiscal authority turned themselves into powerful landlords.

The interdependence between agricultural and economic development in underdeveloped countries makes it desirable that some of the savings of the 70 and 80 per cent of the population engaged in agriculture should be transferred to industry. This is always a most painful process but particularly in areas where agriculture is in a state of stagnation. Yet, even under improved conditions due to the new institutions and incentives established by agrarian reform, peasants should not be taxed before increased production has actually led to a substantial increase in returns. Agricultural taxes must never lower the peasants' standard of living but should simply postpone the full enjoyment of a part of their higher income. It might be useful, therefore, if taxes were withheld by the marketing cooperative that handles the sales of their produce, an arrangement that would also reduce the cost of fiscal administration. The new capitalist farmers' agricultural income on the other hand, should be realistically taxed, as are incomes from commerce and industry.*

In the centrally planned economies of Eastern Europe the administrative machinery of the state and collective farms is responsible for transferring savings from agriculture to industry. At first this was done by rather rough and often doubtful methods which during the last decade, however, have developed into a sophisticated and flexible taxation system that has become part of their organizational structure.

The collection of taxes in peasant communities has almost always been combined with force, humiliation and contempt. In order to prevent taxation from acting as a disincentive and make the peasants understand that in connection with land reform it is a kind of 'forced saving' carried out in their interest, they must be shown that part of the taxes are being plowed back into agriculture, into better roads, better markets, better community institutions and even into rural industries which will expand the domestic market and increase employment possibilities.

---

* Wolf Ladejinsky ('Green Revolution in Bihar, the Kosi Area: A Field Trip', *Economic and Political Weekly*, vol. 4, no. 39, Bombay, 27.9.1969), states that farmers prospering by the green revolution have no taxation burden 'to speak of'.

Taxes must lose the taint of dues and tributes extorted by superiors and come to be recognized by the peasants as their natural contribution to building new communities in which they themselves participate. It is of great importance, therefore, that the taxation system should be straightforward and not too difficult to understand; but it is even more important that the peasant should not be called upon to pay more than the marginal costs of agricultural improvements, such as water rates, if he is already adequately taxed.

The Role of Education

Improved education is the natural consequence of structural changes and no genuine agrarian reform can avoid raising the educational level of the people. But education within the framework of a stagnant and class-ridden society will always reflect and perpetuate the prevailing power relations. In almost all the former colonies, the system of education has remained a legacy from the past and still represents the philosophy of the old masters*, and more specifically of the colonial administrators who were not interested in socio-economic changes but, at best, in creating a national élite in their own image. The crux of the matter is the close interdependence between education and institutional reforms. Higher education in Liberal Arts and Law may enhance the gracious living of the upper class, but is not an instrument for raising agricultural productivity; for the bulk of the people education will acquire a meaning only if and when institutional changes have taken place.

A recent investigation on the economic efficiency of small-holders in Central Gujarat† states that the main indicator for the lack of investment in the human factor is the level of literacy on small farms. In the area under investigation the average rate of literacy was 59.4 per cent; but while it was 84 per cent for the

* J. S. Coleman (ed.), *Education and Political Development* (Princeton, N.J., 1965), pp. 36 ff.
† V. S. Vyas, *Economic Efficiency on Small Farms of Central Gujarat. Report of the Seminar on Problems of Small Farmers,* Seminar Series, no. 7 (Indian Society of Agricultural Economics, Bombay, 1968).

large farmers, only 40 per cent of the smallholders were able to read and write and most of them had only attended school for a year or two. Likewise, the correlation is obvious between literacy and the adoption of improved praxes so that generally speaking misery and lack of education go hand in hand.*

A successful agrarian reform, however, will increase the peasants' self-confidence and stimulate their interest in agricultural development. It will thus provide an adequate background for a progress-oriented education that will bring to the surface the latent qualities of intellect, common sense, energy, resourcefulness and prudence.†

The social revolutions which have taken place this century in underdeveloped countries have all been followed by educational revolutions. This is true of the Mexican revolution which set up primary schools in every *ejido*, of the Russian and Chinese revolutions with their massive literacy campaigns and of the Cuban revolution that organized a young peoples' crusade against illiteracy in the backward areas of the country.‡

It cannot be denied that revolutionary movements bring to the fore unused resources of energy to cure the ills of society; but the real reasons for progress in the educational field are the changes in the social structure and the emergence of new community institutions. It is almost painful to have to stress this point over and over again: but it is apparently necessary in view of the voluminous literature on the extraneous forces which are, in

* K. M. Choudhary, *Factors Affecting Acceptance of Improved Agricultural Practices. A Study in a IADP District in Rajasthan.* Research Study no. 9 (Agro-Economic Research Centre, Vallabh Vidyanagar, 1965).

† E. H. Jacoby, 'Agrarian Structure and Land Settlement', in *Report of the UN Conference on the Application of Science and Technology for the Benefit of Less-Developed Countries* (Geneva, October 1962).

‡ This remarkable campaign against illiteracy was carried out by the *Conrado Benitez* brigades, comprising more than 100,000 students and schoolchildren trained in the techniques of 'alphabetization' and equipped with an ABC called 'Venceremos' (we shall overcome). The members of the brigades were sent out to the most isolated parts of the country where they lived and worked with the peasants teaching them to read and write in the evenings and on holidays. This close contact created a feeling of solidarity between workers and peasants, between the generations and between city and village. Two years after the revolution illiteracy had practically been eliminated in Cuba.

one way or another, identified with technical progress or increased knowledge, and are judged to produce a measurable 'residual factor' with lasting impact, capable of preventing the decline in return on investment otherwise to be expected. If such a quantitative relationship is accepted, however, this means nothing less than the complete neglect of social, economic and institutional problems and justifies the continuance and expansion of an educational structure that disregards the need for a balanced programme of long-term development.

In an attempt to justify the 'residual factor' Jan Tinbergen* designed a model for the investment needed in education in order to ensure a given rate of economic growth. This mathematical exercise, that simply assumes the existence of a stable relationship between education and economic progress without considering the manifold variables of economic and social realities is highly abstract and reveals a surprising indifference to the actual forces ruling society.†

Were it really possible to achieve or retard economic progress by merely increasing or reducing the quantity of production factors, which are assumed to be homogeneous and interchangeable —then development strategy should be the easiest thing in the world!

But there is the 'residual factor'; and it is certainly a fallacy to assume that an educational system, such as that in the United States, for example, which has been accompanied by a certain growth rate, would be equally successful under different conditions. Indeed, numerous facts indicate that such a system cannot succeed in underdeveloped countries for the simple reason that their institutional structure, far from supporting progress as in the Western world, actually impedes development. And this also explains why, in the absence of institutional reforms, extension services and agricultural colleges, training camps and exhibitions, have so little effect upon the general level of agricultural cultivation.

* J. Tinbergen and H. Correa, 'Quantitative Adaptation of Education to Accelerated Growth', *Kyklos, Internationale Zeitschrift für Sozialwissenschaften*, vol. 15 (1962), pp. 776 ff. See also E. A. G. Robinson and J. E. Vaizey (eds.), *The Economics of Education* (London and New York, 1966).

† T. Balogh, *The Economics of Poverty*, pp. 87 ff., 89, 103, brilliantly attacks Tinbergen's theory.

The widespread lack of understanding of the interdependence between education and institutional reforms is reflected in the often unrealistic suggestion that agricultural education should be adjusted to the fundamental requirements of social and economic progress which the underdeveloped countries face. In his controversial book, *Transforming Traditional Agriculture*,* Theodore Schultz describes at length the difficult process of learning and emphasizes the role of schooling and on-the-spot training, but fails to recognize that the problems of education in underdeveloped countries are directly connected with the existence of a social structure that by its very nature dulls the peasant's interest in the process of 'learning'. Neither does he seem to realize that the Danish Folk High Schools which he holds up as an ideal method of education for underdeveloped countries were closely associated with the liberation of the peasants and the start of the cooperative movement, i.e., with fundamental, institutional changes. Moreover his assumption that under competitive conditions an increasing number of the farms owned by absentee landlords will be taken over by owner-operators because of their greater efficiency is most unrealistic.† Indeed it is difficult to understand *how* he visualizes competition between small owner-cultivators and absentee landlords in a society where the institutional framework is based on an intricate system of repressions that excludes the very spirit of competition.

In large areas of Asia and Latin America, education in Law and Liberal Arts is still considered the *non plus ultra* target of academic learning, although neither is suitable for combating backwardness and may even retard or reverse the process of development.‡ As long as such a 'colonial' system of higher education continues to set the values for society, the basic requirements for progress will be sadly neglected. What is really needed is a down-to-earth educational system that is an integral part of long overdue institutional changes, and thus has to be dedicated to agricultural progress and socio-economic advance.

* T. W. Schultz, *Transforming Traditional Agriculture* (New Haven and London, 1964).
† Ibid., pp. 172, 119. See also G. Myrdal, *Asian Drama*, p. 1547, fn. 5.
‡ T. Balogh, 'Education Must Come Down to Earth', *CERES, FAO Review*, vol. 1, no. 2 (March-April, 1968), p. 60.

Apart from outstanding results on a few model farms in certain communities, the overall picture of backward rural areas has changed but little during the past decade despite numerous, often well-meant, educational programmes. Even those enthusiastic graduates from agricultural colleges who actually return to their villages, are only able to apply their acquired knowledge to a limited extent and soon revert to the customary methods of cultivation. Their failure to 'reform' cultivation is usually blamed on the stubbornness, lack of adaptability and passive resistance of the villagers, but hardly ever on the terrible problem of education within an outdated socio-economic framework. It is not 'backward mentality', but the undervaluation and low returns of agricultural labour, and consequently its apparent futility, that are the main cause of the peasants' fatalistic attitude.

The close interdependence between education and institutional development also explains why the outdated educational systems die so slowly. Balogh's striking remark that 'British sluggishness might have something to do with the perpetuation of a classical arts education and the disdain for technical training',* points to the truth, that in developed and underdeveloped countries alike the system of education is determined by the spirit of the ruling group. In the underdeveloped world where education has been geared to the image of the successful landlord, the smart lawyer-politician and the sophisticated administrator, rather than helping in the tough job of developing a backward society, it has helped to perpetuate the peasants' bondage.

Inherited educational establishments constitute strong inhibitions and blocks to development,† and it is a fallacy to expect that the mere achievement of political independence can produce the needed changes. The requirements of a modern state demand an agonizing reappraisal of existing educational institutions that will shift the emphasis from misunderstood humanistic ideals to economic and social realities. The need to converge educational and institutional changes was well understood by Maulana Abul Kalam Azad, the great Indian scholar, who felt that the basic problem is how to form new minds that will respond creatively to the emergent forces in national life and that education, there-

---

* *The Economics of Poverty*, p. 90, fn. 7.
† G. Myrdal, *Asian Drama*, p. 1649.

fore, should be directed towards raising the nation's economic
well-being as well as its intellectual and spiritual potential.*

Japan, the USSR and Israel have been rightly quoted as examples
of a high rate of literacy, of institutional progress and economic
advance.† Their exceptional economic growth can only be explained in terms of the unique interaction between economic,
socio-cultural and powerful political factors. Despite the differences
and variations in their socio-economic development (an interesting
field by the way for specialized institutional research), the educational process in all three countries has been coordinated with
institutional changes that encouraged the people to accept innovations and to develop initiative and foresight.

It is imperative that education in the underdeveloped world
should be primarily focused on improving the quality of rural
society. This alone would be a revolutionary change as the aristo-
cratic, century-old educational institutions were used mainly as a
means of escaping the rural environment. Primary education for
children as well as adults should concentrate principally on arith-
metic. Reading and writing is essential, of course, but the peasant
who cannot reckon properly will be cheated in the market as he
was in the past, or become an easy prey to the manipulations of
fraudulent officials.

The content of secondary and university education, on the other
hand, needs an entirely new approach that corresponds to the
requirements of rural progress. The textbooks, almost always imported from the West, need to be rewritten to fit the specific
socio-economic and, in particular, agricultural problems of the
countries concerned. Agricultural economics, for instance, ought to
be taught with a view to tropical agriculture and the problems
of rural underdevelopment; courses in cooperative organization are
more important than in commercial banking, and problems of land
policy and market factors should be given a central place in the
curriculum.

In many underdeveloped areas, however, elementary rural education is still the most pressing need. Apart from the rudiments
of general knowledge, the children should be taught the needs

* K. G. Saiydain, *The Humanist Tradition in Indian Education
and Thought* (Bombay, 1966), pp. 138–9.
† K. W. Kapp, 'In Defence of Institutional Economics', *Swedish
Journal of Economics*, vol. 70, no. 1 (March 1968), p. 11.

of the community to which they belong, and the school ought to be the centre of village life providing education and information for both young and old.

For almost a century, progress in the Scandinavian countries has been strongly supported by a broad enlightenment movement supported by peasant and labour organizations and to some extent by the Church. From its inception it was based on lectures, study groups and easily read publications in all fields relevant to the technical and cultural progress of society but, in addition, it aimed at creating a countrywide awareness of the great political and economic issues of the day and provided the necessary background for people to decide where they stood on these. The movement is still active but a considerable part of its programme has been taken over by radio and television which up until now have resisted the pressure of commercialization. This broad concept of adult education has made an invaluable contribution to the overall economic and social progress and democratic development of the Scandinavian people and is largely responsible for their mature judgment in controversial political situations.

If adjusted to local traditions, objectives and socio-economic realities, such an approach to education could well be attempted in underdeveloped countries in order to make the people conscious of the necessity for land reform, cooperation and other institutional improvements. This, of course, does not suggest a *transfer* of the Scandinavian method, but the application of an educational system that does not scorn the interdependence between socio-economic problems and everyday life within the community.

It has almost become commonplace to stress the need for educating the women in underdeveloped countries where they have been, and often still are, repressed by religion and tradition. There is little doubt that one of the greatest obstacles to development in the Near East and large parts of Southeast Asia is the Moslem woman's low level of education. Educational programmes, therefore, should not only provide equal opportunities for boys and girls but should even give preference to the education of women. This would accelerate the entire process of education since women are not only the wives of men but also the mothers of the next generation.

In most underdeveloped countries, however, there is a scarcity of both financial and staff resources for education. The change-over to a more realistic and much less status-oriented educational system should, therefore, be focused on improving the quality of education in accordance with the needs of the rural community* and reducing the ever-increasing number of university graduates for whom not enough jobs are available and most of whom have not acquired any useful kind of knowledge or skill.

Efforts, therefore, should be concentrated on vocational training in the administration of the rural community as well as in technical skills. It is true that well-equipped agricultural schools and farm institutes exist almost everywhere in the underdeveloped world but on the whole they fail in their purpose and swallow up a disproportionate amount of the countries' financial and staff resources. Isolated from what is happening in the villages they provide sophisticated agricultural training in artificial surroundings, and the students graduate armed with a fund of knowledge that has little practical importance but makes them feel too superior to go back to farmwork and entitled to a desk job in administration.† Training in actual fieldwork and learning-by-doing are undoubtedly superior and cheaper methods for transferring the knowledge and skills needed for the application of modern technology.‡ When, therefore, the Regional Seminar on Agriculture of the Asian Development Bank complains that it is the lack of financial support which has caused the existing stagnancy in the training and guidance of farmers in nearly all Asian countries, it overlooks the important fact that even increased expenditure cannot change the misdirection of education within an obsolete institutional framework.§

* L. Cerych, *Problems of Aid to Education in Developing Countries* (New York, 1965: London, 1966), p. 201.

† United Nations, FAO, *Report to the Government of Nigeria on the Farm-Settlement Scheme in the Western Region* (FAO/EPTA 1720, Rome, 1963).

‡ Ingvar Svennilson, 'The Strategy of Transfer', in Daniel L. Spencer and Alexander Woroniak (eds.), *The Transfer of Technology to Developing Countries* (New York, 1967).

§ Asian Development Bank, *Papers and Proceedings. Regional Seminar on Agriculture Held in Conjunction with the Second Annual Meeting of the Board of Governors of the Asian Development Bank* (Sidney, April 1969), p. 44.

Two additional aspects of agricultural training ought to be mentioned in this context. The first is the considerable time-lag between research results and their application in most underdeveloped countries and the subsequent slow progress in agriculture. Although it may be true that administrative shortcomings, lack of staff and friction between different services are partly responsible, it is primarily a symptom of an institutional framework that by its very nature prohibits the rational dissemination of technological knowledge to the millions of peasant households. The poor extension services and lack of understanding of the real needs of the rural population are not due to ill-will on the part of the individual officers but merely an expression of the lack of social cohesion within a defective institutional system.

The second point is that foreign advice on the farm level is frequently useless. Foreign experts, unfamiliar with the people's mentality, and living according to their own accustomed standards, are hardly ever in a position to effectively guide the peasants in underdeveloped countries. The actual extension work, therefore, should preferably be conducted by the countries themselves. But if foreign advisors were willing to adjust their superior knowledge to the actual needs of rural development, they could make a valuable contribution by providing the organized training of teachers, extension officers and administrators for cooperative organizations and rural centres.* Teachers' training is the most effective foreign aid to education. But once again, institutions which are too large and too well-equipped are of little use if they are out of touch with reality. Smaller training centres in the rural areas with a curriculum geared to the needs of the rural community should multiply the number of teachers in a relatively short time. Considering the serious shortage of teachers in underdeveloped countries, it would be wise, for a time at least, to place less emphasis on examinations and degrees and concentrate on developing a proper attitude in the young teachers. The educational campaign in countries like Cuba was most successful even though the 'teachers' were hardly more than schoolchildren. Unfortunately, however, the governments of many underdeveloped countries and their highly trained advisers still insist on academic

* R. Dumont, 'A World Strategy for Fertilizers', in *CERES, FAO Review*, vol. 1, no. 1 (January-February 1968), p. 46.

standards of education which are of little practical use and, in addition, are both costly and time-consuming.

Rural education, in fact, must be rooted in the environment where it is going to be applied and this raises some doubt as to the advantage of training people from underdeveloped countries in the colleges and institutions of the Western world. It may be useful for some post-graduates who want to specialize but will be meaningless and even dangerous for young students whose intellectual understanding of the problems at home is still so imperfect that they will be utterly unable to integrate themselves into the community—if they return at all.

CHAPTER TWELVE

Adjustment of Traditional Tenure Systems and Land Policy in Africa

In many parts of the vast continent of Africa, the man-land relationship is still determined by the time-honoured institutions of static tribal societies that for centuries have had but limited contact, if any, with the world around them. These traditional tenure systems guarantee a high measure of security to the man on the land, but function at the same time as a bulwark against any changes in the customary standards of life and work. Colonial conquest, which brought with it commercial penetration, the introduction of cash crops and Western administration and concepts, gradually broke down the wall of isolation and exposed the traditional communities to the superior technology and particular values of a fundamentally different economic system. Today, the pace and substance of change is well on the way to disintegrating the traditional society. Land, once an object of undisputed and eternal value, has become an ordinary commodity for which foreigners, local speculators and a growing population are competing, while the prestige and wealth derived from the possession of cattle is being undermined by the cash earnings of the younger people who have gone to work outside the community. There is no doubt that one of the greatest problems of development in Africa is how to adjust these tradition-ridden societies to the requirements of agricultural progress and socio-economic advance and how to finally decide whether to channel this dynamic process to the advantage of all Africans or leave it to favour the few.

The process of disintegration of the traditional society is commonly referred to as the *individualization of land tenure*, a typical

Western concept implying that the dissolution of communal tenure automatically leads to individual ownership of land. This over-simplification of a complicated developmental process has proved highly dangerous in the African setting and has encouraged land manipulations not only by foreign commercial interests but also by tribal chiefs, tempted by the prospect of becoming feudal lords or capitalist farmers. In Malawi, for instance, influential tribal people returned to their community after years of absence in order to claim their share in the communal land and establish capitalist farms without paying any compensation to the tribe; in other places speculative land transactions were made possible by changing tribal land into Crown land and thus making it available for sale.

Unlike the economic and social stagnation in rural South Asia, Latin America and the Middle East, Africa south of the Sahara is in the midst of a dynamic transformation of traditional values and customs which has caught the imagination of the bulk of the people and not only of the upper strata of society. The continual tribal conflicts have made the peasants doubt the meaning of customary values that no longer correspond to reality, and many of them are eager to make a new start. Under these circumstances, a constructive land policy would be a most re-warding task since the peasants' psychological readiness to accept innovations and consequently the transition to a market economy, would inspire their participation in the development of a new society that would relatively quickly raise the low level of labour productivity and increase returns from agricul-ture.

Prevailing tenure conditions in large parts of Africa are one of the greatest obstacles in the way of agricultural development. As long as their population balance was more or less stable the African peasants enjoyed a relatively high degree of economic and social security. But under the pressure of outside forces the customary institutional framework began to disintegrate and this gradually increased the need for alternative tenure systems. The impact of Western legal and economic concepts isolated time-honoured values and even brought their removal from reality into clear relief without, however, making a positive contribution to the cultural and social life of the people. The role of land as a regulating device for the routine of tribal life was gradually re-

duced and with it the traditional values, taboos and attitudes.*
This released impulses and propensities that hitherto had been
safely channelled and controlled by the tribal society. Thus the
Mau Mau movement in Kenya was the passionate reaction of
tribal people who had lost their identity and secure place in the
community. Or we may take the recurring waves of social irregu-
larities and crimes in the mining areas of southern Africa as further
evidence of the close interdependence between communal stability,
values and social behaviour.

The eventual breakdown of the customary tribal tenure under
the pressure of new economic, technological and demographic
developments is a natural process. No institutional arrangements
exist that do not have to be changed, adjusted, or replaced in
the course of time. The passionate desire of some anthropologists
to safeguard outdated forms of social life doomed to disappear
may be understandable but is not very helpful in the given circumstances. Changes are a welcome necessity if, as an integral part
of socio-economic development, they strengthen the foundation
of society by increasing the opportunities for the development of
resources and human energy. But if they are restricted to land
distribution without improving all the interlinked social rights
and obligations they will impede the emergence of new values
and the establishment of a more suitable social structure.

The East Africa Royal Commission was the first official body
to air these problems and clearly point out the risks involved in
the transition from tribal subsistence to a modern money economy.
It recognized that 'the economic security of the society no longer
depends on the subsistence which each individual attempts in
isolation to wring from the environment with the unaided efforts
of the family or kinship group, but on the combination of the
highly specialised efforts of the community as a whole'.† This

---

* In certain areas, however, the chief rather than the land is the
focal point in tribal life. In Buganda, for instance, the peasants
had both the right of occupation of the land and the freedom to
choose the chief whom they wished to serve; they were not serfs
bound to the soil but enjoyed a political and social relation to their
chief. H. W. West, 'The Mailo System in Buganda. A Preliminary
Case Study in African Land Tenure' (unpublished ms., 1964), p. 7.
† *Report of the East Africa Royal Commission, 1953–55* (Cmd.
9475, HMSO, London, 1956), pp. 48 ff.

statement holds true not only for traditional tenure but for full individual ownership too. The Report of this Commission recommends that the test of land *needs* should be replaced by a test of land *use* and that 'policy concerning the tenure and disposition of land should aim at the individualization of landownership, and at a degree of mobility in the transfer and disposition of land which, without ignoring existing property rights, enable access to land for its economic use.' Yet, it does not identify individualization of land tenure with private ownership and states explicitly that modern African society should be based on property 'owned individually as well as by agencies for communal action such as cooperatives.'*

The discussion of land problems was taken up at the Conference on African Land Tenure in East and Central Africa at Arusha, Tanganyika, February 1956.† The Report of this Conference further analyses the existing tenure conditions in East and Central Africa but, contrary to the Royal Commission, it arrives at the unwise conclusion that future land policy must take into account that 'Africa is in a transitional stage between communal rights and exclusive individual land ownership.'‡

The Working Party on African Land Tenure (1957–58), established for the Colony and Protectorate of Kenya, continued the discussion on the merits and demerits of full individual land ownership and its Report cautions against a too hasty individualization of land tenure:

> We felt [it says] that, individual ownership being such a new concept to the majority of Africans, it was desirable in the early stages to give Divisional Boards a very wide discretion which will enable them to forbid, for instance, if they so wish, the alienation of land outside the tribe, clan or family group, and also to exercise some restraint over the newly emancipated landowner who wishes to sell his land to the detriment of his family. It has been proved in many countries that the surest way to deprive a peasant of his

---

* Ibid., p. 346, para. 1 and p. 52, para. 12. By emphasizing the test of land use, however, the Report supports the interests of the European settlers and the capitalist African farmers.
† *Report of the Conference on African Land Tenure in East and Central Africa Held at Arusha, Tanganyika, February 1956* (Special Supplement to the *Journal of African Administration,* October 1956).
‡ Ibid., p. 24.

land is to give him a secure title and make it freely negotiable, and we do not think that anybody will seriously challenge the need for control in the early stages.*

In the African countries formerly under French control,† the traditional systems are no less defective. France had tried to 'modernize' her colonies by a registration of land which encouraged individual ownership as well as European settlement and capital investment. It was not until the fifties that the French colonial administration began showing somewhat greater concern for the protection of customary rights by prohibiting 'vacant' land from being automatically reverted to the state and thus no longer legally available for alienation. Although this to some extent reduced the flow of European settlers, another law of about the same time (1955) considerably strengthened the chiefs' jurisdiction and provided a means of circumventing the protection of tribal land. From now on the chiefs were legally more or less free to 'cede' their tribal rights to uninhabited forest land for the establishment of large plantations to be worked by migrant wage labour. In the Ivory Coast and the Cameroons, this loophole in the legislation which enabled tribal chiefs to infringe arbitrarily upon the communal ownership to non-utilized land and draw large incomes without working slowed down development considerably.‡ Thus, far from improving rural conditions as was its intention, the legislation had the completely opposite effect of creating an agrarian situation in which the bulk of returns from agriculture automatically accrued to those who merely controlled the land.

The individualization of traditional tenure systems in Africa has not got off to a very promising start and, if not checked in time, will continue to benefit only those who have the power and capital to use the land for commercial exploitation. In Sierra Leone, the tribes in the Protectorate justly fear that they may be dispossessed once speculators and traders from Freetown are entitled to buy up agricultural land in all parts of the country. Even prior to independence, a high government official openly

* *Report of the Working Party on African Land Tenure, 1957–1958* (Nairobi, 1958), p. 45, para. 101.

† See R. Dumont, *False Start in Africa* (London and New York, 1967), pp. 127 ff.

‡ Ibid.

complained to me about it being unfair that tribal people from the Protectorate were free to buy land anywhere, while residents in the Freetown area were barred by law from acquiring land in the Protectorate. In the tribal environment, however, it would be extremely dangerous to create a free land market or, more specifically, to establish negotiable ownership rights in land when land transactions can lead to the dispossession of whole tribes, villages or clans. It is an unforgivable mistake to continue associating the fundamentally different agrarian situation in Africa with the Western concept of landownership.

The individualization of tribal tenure should be considered as one of the many processes of adjustment and differentiation connected with economic and social progress and not as a trend towards unrestricted ownership rights. The association of a person or a group of individuals with a particular unit area of land is not an end in itself; it is only a side-effect of the particular stage of economic development where land has changed from expanse to asset and its advantages and defects must be determined on the basis of criteria such as productivity of land and labour, distribution of income, social cohesion, etc. The fundamental problems are how to prevent the process of individualization from leading to a final separation between land ownership and actual cultivation and how to ensure that the man on the land will reach a level of social integration that makes him a partner in and not the victim of agricultural development.

Unfortunately, their close contacts with the West have shaped the minds of the political élites, who almost everywhere uphold the concept of free ownership based on the registration of individual rights in land as the only possible alternative to communal tenure. But many traditional societies have only just begun to come to terms with economic reality and in such cases there is a pressing need to give priority to a constructive land policy in order to avoid their cultural and economic collapse. For once the institutional planner will face the challenging task of *preventing* rather than *remedying* and will thus be able to avert the emergence of an agrarian structure that for centuries has caused misery and stagnation for the man on the land in rural Asia and Latin America. There is still time to forestall such a development on the African continent by planning and introducing tenure systems and rural institutions that will put an end to the increasing loss of land to speculators and traders* and by remodelling the outdated forms of social life.

It was a great temptation, of course, to hasten the individualization of land tenure in order to boast local agricultural progress, and colonial administrations were inclined to satisfy the claims for ownership rights of those indigenous farmers who succeeded in getting ahead in the community. Unfortunately, this typical colonial trend did not end with independence and the present administrations, trained in the spirit of the colonial powers, continue to single out pioneer farmers for ownership at the expense of the bulk of the people or favour the emergence of small and often non-viable farm units.

It has been emphasized quite rightly that the thousands of individual holdings created at great expense in the old settled Kikuyu areas of Kenya are most likely a misdirection of scarce resources which will set up a land tenure pattern and farming system with inbuilt structural weaknesses from the start.† Given the urgent need for the rapid modernization of agriculture it is reprehensible that a typically European smallholder economy should be reproduced on African soil when structural changes will undoubtedly be necessary in a few decades to facilitate the use of modern machinery and technology. It is even more reprehensible when there is still time to reorganize African agriculture on the basis of traditional communal obligations and allocation of duties and the communal execution of public works.

The World Land Reform Conference recognized the crucial importance for Africa of avoiding the concentration of land ownership, landlessness and the wasteful use of land that have marked agricultural history on other continents. And it emphasized the urgency of developing new types of tenure and cooperation which promise to increase both labour productivity and the use of capital and advanced technology so that the African communities

* M. H. Hussain, *Customary Land Tenure in the Context of a Developing Agricultural Economy* (EPTA 1853, FAO, Rome, 1964).
† D. Christodoulou, 'Basic Agrarian Structural Issues in the Adjustment of African Customary Tenures to the Needs of Agricultural Development' (RU: WLR/66/C), p. 8. Paper submitted to the World Land Reform Conference, FAO, Rome, 1966.

may enter the modern world in harmony with their sense of values and potentialities.*

Specific Aspects of Present Land Policy in Africa

The countries of Africa are critically aware of the urgent need to expand and modernize their agriculture particularly through the settlement and resettlement of tribal people. In the absence of clearly defined land policies, they are experimenting with a variety of solutions which are frequently, however, so strongly influenced by Western concepts and achievements that they have the opposite result to what was intended despite some isolated progress here and there.

Models of tenure structures such as the partnership arrangement of the Gezira scheme in the Sudan, the nucleus plantation in Nigeria, the *paysannat* in the Congo and the various types of group and collective farming which have been introduced in Dahomey and Tanzania have both advantages and defects and their failure or success in other African environments depend on the actual conditions and the people's cultural background. The same is true of the individual settlements of the Israeli *moshav* type which have been established in Western Nigeria; they are not conventional villages of individual agriculturists but self-governing communities which control not only economic matters but all aspects of life in the village.† Partnership arrangements, such as the Gezira scheme, depend not only upon efficient management but also to a great extent upon the ready cooperation between foreign capital and the local government and labour force. Nucleus plantation schemes have been rather successful in Nigeria where the central plantation with its processing factory is surrounded by smallholdings mainly growing the same crop as the plantation and using its processing services. The whole enterprise is usually started and run by a foreign firm with the understanding

* *Report of the World Land Reform Conference 1966* (UN, New York, 1968), pp. 112, 113.
† M. Frank, *Cooperative Land Settlement in Israel and their Relevance to African Countries* (Basle, 1968), p. 50.

that once developed, it is to be purchased by the association of farmers and managed either as a cooperative organization or company in partnership with the government. But it is difficult to establish a proper balance between the need to manage the plantation in such a way that the foreign capital can be repaid within a relatively short period with profit to the investors and the long-term interests of the enterprise.

The *paysannat* type of production unit calls for a highly organized peasantry strengthened by supervising cadres and comprising tenure, production, supporting services (including extension), mechanization, processing facilities and administrative structure. Although this system clearly promotes the commercialization of agriculture without disturbing the tenure arrangements, it does so at the expense of the voluntary participation of the people and can easily be misused by commercial enterprises for exploiting the peasantry. For all practical purposes, it needs an almost military regimentation and a centralized administration that may not be conducive to the development of local initiative.

Group farming has also been tried with varying degrees of success in several African countries. Although the cooperative or collective type of production unit has the advantage of a certain familiarity with the time-honoured communal tenure, it is to a very considerable extent an educational challenge and its accomplishments will depend on the extent to which it provides 'social' rather than 'individual' incentives to a group of producers.* There is no doubt that such an institutional approach would help the African countries to remedy the excessive fragmentation of the farm units held under customary law and use more effectively the capital and know-how available for modernizing their agriculture and overcoming the standstill caused by the piecemeal approach of adjudication procedures.

African settlement policy also presents a variety of more or less applicable models. In Kenya, for instance, post-independence land policy was inspired by the prosperous European settlements in the White Highlands where initiative and individual success had determined the farmers' incomes. An increasing number of

---

* *Provisional Indicative World Plan for Agricultural Development*, pp. 400 ff.

European estates have been purchased by the government for redistribution to African settlers, particularly from the over-populated Kikuyu areas. There are two types of settlement schemes: the low-density schemes located on poor soil or steep slopes where the average size of the farms is 30 acres, and the high-density schemes in fertile and populated areas with farms averaging 10 acres. It is too early to judge the final socio-economic effect of this large-scale settlement policy, although in the low-density schemes well-organized extension services and con-siderable capital investments for the carefully selected settlers have led to an increase in output.* Yet, the very fact that the size and even quality of the farms is determined by the capital re-sources of the individual settlers has introduced from the very beginning an element of inequality which may render the develop-ment of adequate community institutions in the settlements more difficult.

In Uganda the new settlements are likewise based on the in-dividual ownership of viable plots of land.† The government invests a considerable amount of capital in the mechanical clearing of unused land for the establishment of 'group settlements' of in-dividual farmers who receive government subsidies for tractors and technical services. Although the farmers are encouraged to market their products cooperatively, the settlements are strictly individualistic as well as uni-tribal and cannot be expected to contribute appreciably to social and national integration.

In Tanzania, on the other hand, post-settlement policy is being focused to an increasing extent on changing social relationships as well as the land tenure and land use patterns by reorganizing and mobilizing the peasant population. While to begin with priority was given to improving and developing agricultural pro-duction, the Arusha Declaration of 1967 opened the way for a new settlement strategy that aims at the social and economic

* See Edith Whetham, 'Land Reform and Resettlement in Kenya', *East African Journal of Rural Development*, vol. 1, no. 1 (January 1968); J. D. MacArthur, 'The Evaluation of Land Reform in Kenya' (RU: WLR/66/L). Paper submitted to the World Land Re-form Conference, FAO, Rome, 1966; and P. A. Reid, 'Report on the Mission to Kenya to Review Land Settlement Policies' (IBRD Liaison Representative, FAO, Rome, 1965, unpublished).

† D. G. R. Belschaw, *An Outline of Research in Uganda, 1945–1963* (East African Institute of Social Research, Kampala, 1963).

transformation of rural life by organizing *Ujamaa Vijijini*, i.e., multi-tribal 'collective socialist villages'. In these, efforts are to be pooled according to capacity, returns are to be shared equally and the land tenure structure is to follow as closely as possible the communal traditions prevailing in the area. This approach should not be too difficult to realize as long as land is plentiful and those peasants unwilling to join the villages can receive their customary allocations elsewhere. But it remains to be seen whether it will be successful in areas where land is scarce as in the Kilimanjaro, in the coastal plains, and in certain areas round Lake Victoria. The government is aware of this problem and plans to precede the introduction of the socialist village concept in these areas by a more intensive education of the peasants in socialist thinking.

The village scheme has not yet taken definite form and some observers consider it less successful, at least in the short run. It is clearly evident, however, that agricultural policy in Tanzania is trying to avoid the dominant influence of successful individual farmers or of one particular tribe as in Kenya, and is aiming instead at a national land policy that will greatly reduce and probably eliminate altogether the scourge of landlessness.*

* On land policy in Tanzania see: *First Five-Year Plan for Economic and Social Development 1964–1969*, vol. 1: 'General Analysis', vol. 2: 'The Programmes' (Government Printer, Dar es Salaam); 'The Modernized Village Approach' in *Rural Development Planning Seminar* (University College, Dar es Salaam, 1966, mimeographed); A. O. Ellman, 'Kitete Land Settlement Scheme in Northern Tanzania', *Land Reform, Land Settlement and Co-operatives*, no. 1 (FAO, Rome, 1967); O. A. Sabry, 'Alternative Systems of Land Tenure and Farm Structures for New Holdings in Tanzania' (RU: LT/69/4), Paper submitted to the Second Panel of Experts on Land Tenure and Settlement, FAO, Rome, May 1969; A. Segal, 'Cooperative Farms in Tanzania', *Atlas* (October 1965), pp. 204 ff.; and R. Dumont and M. Mazoyer, *Développement et Socialisme* (Paris, 1969), pp. 133–60.

The *Second Five-Year Plan for Economic and Social Development, 1969–1974*, vol. I: 'General Analysis' (Government Printer, Dar es Salaam, 1969), pp. 26 ff, mentions besides the Ujamaa villages (1) the establishment of state farms extending over 250,000 acres as these are most suitable for certain agricultural outputs which benefit from mechanization and large-scale irrigation and need centralized management of a large-scale operation and (2) the

A number of African governments attempt to raise agricultural production and income through the cooperative cultivation and marketing of certain plantation crops. In Cameroon 'plantation cooperatives', supported by the government, the Cameroon Development Corporation and some international fruit companies, had already been started by the fifties and have successfully operated not only in the important field of banana production but also in the cultivation of coffee, cocoa and tobacco.

The International Labour Organization,* however, expressed some anxiety that the Cameroon plantation cooperatives may eventually encounter serious difficulties partly because their number is increasing so rapidly that the training of qualified officers is lagging behind, and partly because their members show a marked trend towards instability. It has been estimated that within one working season alone, 15–20 per cent of the cooperative workers have changed domicile and even their names.

In the Ivory Coast, the banana plantation cooperative 'Coba Fruit' seems to have succeeded in improving the planters' income due to a whole series of common services such as technical research, transportation and marketing as well as quality inspection.

In Dahomey, the government even attempts to tackle the problems of ownership rights and landless labour by establishing so-called 'compulsory' cooperatives in zones which appear, on the basis of soil and other surveys, to have development possibilities. All farmers within a zone thus demarcated by the government are called upon to form a cooperative farming unit by contributing land and/or labour against corresponding shares in the aggregate enterprise. One share is equivalent either to about 1.5 hectares of land or to 200 days of work per year and in this way the landless worker is placed on an equal footing with land-owning peasants. The cooperatives receive long-term government loans

---

transformation of cooperative societies, mostly concerned with marketing, into production orientated cooperatives through the development of cooperative farming units from amongst their members at the primary level.

* United Nations, ILO, *Plantation Workers: Conditions of Work and Standards of Living* (Geneva, 1966), p. 24.

for carrying out the necessary development works in the zone
and for the initial expenses of technical equipment and management. By 1964, two such cooperatives had been formed comprising
600 and 4,000 hectares respectively, for the cultivation of oil
palms. The farmers themselves are in charge of management but
the government has two representatives on the Board. These cooperatives promise to increase social integration in rural areas by
giving landless labour an equal share in the management and
achievements of the cooperative unit.* Despite a number of technical and organizational problems as yet unsolved, the Dahomey
type of cooperative farming could prevent the further deterioration of social stratification in areas where the individualization of
land tenure has already given rise to a landless peasantry.

Yet, cooperative enterprises, however efficient, cannot remedy
the shortage of capital and technical know-how in agriculture
which is inherent to underdeveloped countries. The governments,
therefore, are faced with the serious problem of how to attract
the kind of outside capital and expertise which does not ultimately lay hands upon the surplus earnings so badly needed for
overall development. It is difficult to see how this problem can be
solved while African countries unwisely continue to compete for
foreign investment in plantations, as this enables capital interests
to play off one country against the other and settle matters on
their own terms.†

It is easy to see that the adjustment of traditional tenure systems
to the requirements of agricultural development comprises a
variety of measures which must be applied simultaneously if they
are to prevent the still abundant land resources from being sold
out to disloyal tribal chiefs, traders and foreign capital interests.

Almost throughout Africa, therefore, the first objective of current land policy should be the settlement of landless peasants and
of tribal people from overcrowded areas into new communities
based on the traditional inclination towards mutual-help. A new
land policy is more easily applied to areas where the unity of

---

* D. Christodoulou, *Report of the Development Center on Land
Policy for West African Countries, Freetown, Sierra Leone, Dec. 63-
Jan. 64* (EPTA 1860, FAO, Rome, 1964), pp. 20–1.
† See chapter 5, part II.

the tribal society is as yet undisturbed by open or disguised ownership rights in land and where settlement would thus be a means
of preventing the disintegration of tribal tenure and social cohesion. Even where tribal unity is already broken a satisfactory
solution such as the Dahomey cooperative experiment may still be
found, but a negligent land policy in such areas may have
disastrous consequences. In Swaziland, for instance, no efforts
whatsoever were made to counteract the continuation of unjustified
adjudication of rights with the result that a large squatter population has emerged which today constitutes a serious economic and
social problem in large parts of the country.* This thoughtless
land policy has created an agricultural slum and a gap between
constitutional and customary law which will be extremely difficult
to bridge.

Countries like Cameroon, Malagasy and Tunisia, on the other
hand, have adopted land policies that hold brighter prospects for
the future as a result of synchronized institutional arrangements.
In Cameroon, an imaginative legal reform of the land tenure
system has preceded the resettlement of the mountain people in
the eastern part of the country.† After thorough legal and socio-
economic investigations, a law was passed in 1959 which recognized that all land belonged to the various tribal communities
except for the public domain, in its strict sense, and the private
property of the state. This repudiated the French colonial concept
that 'vacant land' belongs to the state. Although the Law of 1959
thus protected the legitimate interests of the tribal communities,
it prevented the government from utilizing excess tribal land and
water resources in order to relieve the pressure in densely populated areas. Through decrees and amendments‡ the main law now
enables the government to reduce the areas under customary law
to the level of the tribal communities' actual needs and to use
the surplus to establish a national collective patrimony available

---

* See J. C. D. Lawrance, *Report on Squatters on Farms in Swaziland* (HCP BC 225).
† A. Bessis, *Rapport au gouvernement du Cameroun sur les
problèmes de la réforme foncière au Cameroun oriental. Loi No.
59–47, 17.6.1959, portant organisation dominale et foncière* (EPTA
1872, FAO, Rome, 1964).
‡ Décret-loi No. 63–2, 9.1.1963, fixant le régime foncier et dominale
au Cameroun oriental; Décret No. 64–9, 30.1.1964; Décret No.
64–10, 30.1.1964.

for redistribution. If efficiently implemented, such a land policy will promote nationwide social and economic development. It should be added that land grants from this national patrimony are only provisional and may be revoked if the land is not used within the period specified by the agricultural development plan.

Current land policies in Malagasy and Tunisia also seem conducive to a better utilization of natural resources and improved institutional arrangements. Legislation provides the establishment of so-called 'aires de mise en valeur rurale' (AMVR), which are clearly defined areas to be developed for organized rural settlement. In these areas, modern farm techniques, extension and institutional arrangements are to be enjoyed by the original inhabitants as well as the new settlers; subdivision of holdings is prohibited, and any change in ownership must first be authorized by the administration; the size of individual holdings has a fixed ceiling and excess land is to be expropriated by the government against compensation; consolidation operations are to be enforced in case of excessive fragmentation; and in the zones earmarked for irrigation landowners are obliged to join so-called agricultural water groups.*

The achievements of settlement in Africa will largely depend upon the way in which the land has been obtained. The first step towards a national land policy which will promote the integration of the tribal communities is undoubtedly that the government should acquire the land to be settled and, due to the deep-rooted traditions and customs, determine the future tenure arrangements on the basis of sociological and legal research. Haphazard legislative action will only create problems not solve them.† The highly acclaimed enclosure policy is thus a narrow-minded and even dangerous procedure that ignores the very essence of the man-land relationship because it singles out the privileged few and

* P. J. van Dooren, in 'State-controlled Changes in Tunisia's Agrarian Structure', *Tropical Man* (Royal Tropical Institute of Amsterdam, Leiden, 1968), pp. 59 ff., gives a detailed description of land policy in Tunisia.

† On legal aspects of settlement, see F. M. Mifsud, *Customary Land Law in Africa* (FAO Legislative Series, no. 7, Rome, 1967).

isolates the majority of the people often leaving them without
land.

The adjustment of traditional tenure systems by synchronized
institutional changes is a prerequisite for a long-term national
land policy wherever customary agrarian and social structures
impede the development of whole areas and population groups.
The great variety of regional characteristics on the African continent prevents the formulation of a general policy for adjusting
traditional societies. Differences in population patterns and farm
types, in social structures and property consciousness suggest
different priorities for certain types of tenurial and institutional
arrangements. This may seem a cumbersome approach to development, but it is the only possible way of paying due attention to
the social, economic and legal aspects of the man-land relationship and of correcting maladjustments wherever they occur.

CHAPTER THIRTEEN

Administration – The Crux of Land Reform Programmes

It is an outstanding characteristic of underdevelopment that agricultural land is an extremely sensitive factor in the economic life of the people. In many countries all literates have a piece of land and even in large parts of Italy, Portugal and Spain, many professional people and small businessmen own landholdings worked by sharecroppers or tenants. This social phenomenon extends far into the ranks of the political parties that associate themselves with changes in the agrarian structure and it dominates even more the entire rural scene from the village councils to the regional legislative and administrative bodies. The latter are of overriding importance as in countries where religion and tradition still govern the distribution and inheritance of land, matters concerning agriculture, such as land tenure, land use, production etc., are still considered a regional rather than a national prerogative. In Malaysia, for example, all land policy matters, with the exception of some recent settlement schemes of the federal administration, are handled with a large measure of independence by the various states. The same is true of India where the Planning Commission of the Government in New Delhi designs the agrarian reform programmes but where the actual legislation and execution is left to the state governments. In Nigeria, land policy is totally a local prerogative although this country's immense tribal problems urgently call for a national land policy.*

Against this background it can be easily understood that it is the implementation not the formulation of land reform which poses the greater difficulty and that, ironically, the fact that the *small*

* United Nations, FAO, 'Agricultural Development in Nigeria 1965–1980' (Rome, 1966, as yet unpublished), p. 338.

landlords dominate the regional and rural institutions which are charged with the administrative aspects of implementation is often the reason why land reform has failed to change the balance of power in rural areas.

It is of fundamental importance, therefore, that the administration of land reform should be raised to the national level and the complex process of implementation given due consideration at the planning stage. The very scope of the programme should be determined according to the administrative potential of the country concerned and formulated in a clear and easily understood way. Sophisticated legal formulations will automatically only favour those strata in society which have the financial means to acquire an education or employ a lawyer and these are nearly always composed of the very interests that are opposed to changes in the man-land relationship.

Experience has proved time and again that an inefficient administration is the greatest obstacle in the way of carrying out the intended structural changes, since the large vested interests, even if defeated on the political level, fight back with renewed strength when it comes to the actual implementation of land reform. They find ready allies in the multitude of small landholders in the rural areas who have their own stake in maintaining the *status quo*. Through evasion and corrupt practices this alliance has in many cases caused a spurious implementation of even reasonably well-formulated agrarian reform programmes, and this has later been used as a most effective argument against further attempts at land reform, as happened in India.

It is obvious, therefore, that the entire fabric of prevailing administrative praxes ought to be changed in order to break up the traditional allegiance of the old ministries of agriculture to the powerful landowning and commercial groups and establish a new bureaucracy that will gradually develop a vested interest in the implementation of land reform. It is very tempting to suggest that land reform planning should automatically comprise the establishment of a *separate administrative agency* in which status and career are dependent upon the speed and efficiency with which implementation is carried out. In this way, at least somebody would be anxious to provide the services needed by the peasants in order to strengthen their position against the superior social and economic forces in the rural community.

In order to foster such an attitude, however, it is imperative that overstaffing on the lower level should be carefully avoided, as in underdeveloped countries this usually means that the field officers are being underpaid which reduces their resistance to tempting offers of collusion and bribery. Adequate salaries and training in public services are, therefore, most important prerequisites if attempts to increase the employees' loyalty and their competence to handle the task in hand are to succeed. This may even be the beginning of an attack against what Myrdal calls the 'soft' state* that is characterized by a general lack of social discipline, by deficiencies in legislation and particularly by a readiness to disregard or circumvent the law.

It is true, of course, that the very existence of two types of bureaucracy different in outlook, structure and quality may introduce a kind of schizophrenic feature into public administration. But we consider this a minor evil made acceptable by the possibility of a more successful implementation of agrarian reform which will give rise to new institutions that may gradually supplant the old bureaucracy, absorb its administrative functions and, above all, do away with the inherited colonial legacy of commanding the peasants instead of inviting their cooperation.

But just as it is necessary to shift the responsibility for implementation from the old bureaucracy in the ministries of agriculture, it is essential to check the influence of the landed interests on the regional, provincial and village levels. In the first place, all important policy-decisions, such as the principles governing redistribution of land, compensation payments and ceiling levels as well as the use of agricultural resources, should be made by the central administrative agency since only an overall land policy will contribute to the integration of agriculture and of the man on the land into the national economy.† Secondly, and most important, the local officials' position in the field must be strengthened; at present he is badly paid, regarded with contempt, and is often a tool of the landowning interests rather than a trustworthy link with the administration. In the planning of land re-

---

* *Asian Drama*, chap. 18, sects. 13–14.

† E. H. Jacoby, 'Can Land Reform Help to Establish the Rural Base for National Development', in R. Robinson and P. Johnston (eds.), *The Rural Base for National Development* (Cambridge University Overseas Studies Committee, 1968), pp. 15 ff.

form programmes due attention should, therefore, be given to the
status, training and remuneration of the officers in the field in
order to strengthen their integrity when dealing with the powerful
persons or groups whose land and activities they are employed to
administrate. In addition, they should be committed to report
their appraisal of the progress of implementation in their districts
directly to the central agency. This fundamental change on the
field level would undoubtedly prevent at least some of the more
dangerous shortcomings in the implementation of reform programmes, which so frequently cause the repudiation of the very
concept of land reform.

Another practical function of a new administrative agency which
is genuinely interested in improving the procedure of implementation should be to encourage a feeling of solidarity between interests within the rural community and the growth of communal
rights and obligations.* In other words it should support the
formation of peasant and worker organizations and secure their
active participation in bringing about the desired changes.
Promoting such a 'development from below' would not only ensure a more rapid transition to a new society but also strengthen
the land reform legislation. If the peasant is given a feeling of
responsibility and constructive partnership he will become aware
of his rights and even dare to insist upon them if the need should
arise. In an earlier chapter† we explained how village committees
backed by peasant organizations reduce contact between landlord
and tenant by handling rent payments and important management
matters and how multi-purpose cooperatives take over the credit
and marketing functions of the trader-cum-moneylender. With the
help of peasant organizations a similar approach could be applied
on the judicial level in order to prevent disputes in land matters
being handled exclusively by the local landed groups. The position
of the peasants would also be considerably strengthened if the
administrative agency were to send out mobile courts at regular
intervals to pass judgment on ownership or tenancy disputes in
the villages.

* See L. Oppenheimer, 'Regional Economy as an Historical Stage
of Development and the Permanent Element of Social Structure
from Below', *Internationales Symposium, Deutsche Wirtschaftspolitische Gesellschaft* (Berlin, 1967).
† See chapter 7.

A settlement project in La Julio-Jobe Dulce, State of Aragua in Venezuela offers an excellent example of the integration of peasant organizations in the implementation of land reform. The success of this pilot project was due largely to the existence of a strong peasant union which dated from 1948, and took an active part in implementing the land reform in this and the surrounding communities through a well-planned and non-violent invasion of those estates which were affected by the law. An evaluation of this project, carried out in 1963, notes that a common nucleus of living together with the union had been successfully established in the community.*

It is well-known that in tribal areas, particularly in Africa south of the Sahara, the transition to a money economy frequently tempts the tribal chief to assume the prerogatives of a feudal lord. In such areas, therefore, cooperatives and other institutions should be organized which are closely related to the communal pattern of social behaviour, in order to reduce the authoritarian pressure of the chiefs and lay the foundation for a community spirit.

The transition to new socio-economic institutions presents numerous problems particularly where rural settlement schemes are part of the agrarian programme. It may be necessary, for instance, to postpone the decision on the final tenure type until an analysis of the relevant economic, social and psychological factors have established the effect of education and extension upon the maturity of the individual settlers and, consequently, the need for possible changes in the original production targets. The Chilean concept of *'asentamiento campesino'* is one administrative method of establishing a transitional type of tenure during the interval between the redistribution of estate land and the final decision on the desirability of collective or individual ownership under the

---

* United Nations, ECLA, *Report of a Community Development Evaluation Mission to Venezuela*, prepared by Caroline F. Ware, Rubén Dario Utria and Antoni Wojcicke (TAO/VEN/15, New York, 1963), para. 36.

See also Carola Ravell, 'Community Development in Venezuela', in Inter-American Development Bank, *Community Development. Theory and Practice* (Mexico City, April 1966), pp. 158–66; and G. Huizer, 'Peasant Unrest in Latin America' (CIDA, 1967, unpublished), p. 220.

given circumstances.* Another is the one applied by the British administration in Kenya which was reluctant to give African settlers, unfamiliar with the concept of individual ownership, the right to alienate land and so committed the divisional boards to restrain the new landowners from unwise land transactions.†

In other words, the efficient administration of agrarian reform programmes does not necessarily mean the quick implementation of a succession of decisions based on a rigid application of static principles, but rather doing whatever is necessary to underline the inherent logic of the programme and promote its objectives. Implementation is more than an administrative technique; it is a dynamic process focused upon changes in a defective man-land relationship and should use, therefore, complementary measures such as improved credit, marketing and education in order to avoid bottlenecks and quicken the process towards greater productivity of land and labour.

An efficient implementation should also disseminate information on land reform legislation and establish services that, as we have already said, will strengthen the participation of peasant and worker organizations. The proper timing of all these measures would be a challenging but not too difficult task for the new agency were it not for the crucial problem of providing and training in a short time a competent extension staff. As a shortage of field workers has time and again jeopardized noteworthy development programmes, it is essential, as we have repeatedly emphasized, that in planning tenure reforms preference should be given to a form of collective farming which allows a minimum of extension workers to achieve maximum results.

There remain two crucial administrative problems of implementation which deserve particular attention. The first is whether the reforms should be carried out simultaneously on a country-wide scale or by piecemeal action in a few districts at a time. Many countries, particularly in Latin America, have chosen the latter approach partly because they consider it easier, more accept-

* See 'The Chilean Agrarian Reform' (RU: WLR/66/40). Paper submitted to the World Land Reform Conference, (FAO, Rome, June 1966); and the 'Inter-American Development Bank Report, 1967', p. 98.
† *Report of the Working Party on African Land Tenure 1957–58,* para. 101.

able and less of a strain on their scarce staff resources for administration and extension. In our view, this is a realistic attitude as their backward socio-economic structure goes hand in hand with administrative incapacity and immaturity and thus a countrywide approach is automatically excluded. But if peasant organizations were allowed to participate in the implementation, or collective production units were established, it would be possible to economize with the available professional staff and carry out countrywide land reform programmes almost everywhere. Considering the ever-increasing impact of outside forces upon rural conditions, the countrywide approach has become a precondition for the successful implementation of agrarian reform programmes.

As to piecemeal action or the phasing of land reform, it is true that this allows the concentration of scarce staff resources on certain measures in given districts. But from the psychological, political and social point of view, such a phasing is extremely risky since it may discourage landowners in adjoining districts from making the necessary investment in production and even induce them to anticipate developments by eviction of tenants and the proforma sale of land above the ceiling level to relatives.

The other crucial problem is how to verify and evaluate the achievements and failures of land reform so that the government can make the necessary legal adjustments and improve the performance of the administrative agency if needed.* No fundamental reform can avoid errors at one stage or another; and the more controversial the issues, the greater the risk of mistakes, evasions and deviations. Even the most ingenious planning authority cannot foresee all relevant developments and undesirable side-effects and a proper evaluation of the entire gamut of reform measures is therefore necessary. This, of course, will make it a rather costly procedure but considering its importance for the success of the entire programme and its educational value for the staff of the administrative agency, it must be regarded as a

---

* See E. H. Jacoby, *Evaluation of Agrarian Structure and Agrarian Reform Programs* (FAO Agricultural Studies no. 69, Rome, 1966); and Government of India, Ministry of Food and Agriculture, *Report of the Working Group of the Government of India and the Food and Agriculture Organization of the United Nations on Methods for Evaluation and Effects of Agrarian Reform* (New Delhi, August 1958)

worthwhile investment rather than an unnecessary expenditure.

Such an evaluation, however, should also include the administrative machinery itself in order to determine whether it actually complies with the reform legislation and provides the stipulated services to the peasants or whether a possible failure is due to an incorrect interpretation of the legislation, lack of staff resources or bias against the objectives of the reform. It is of decisive importance, therefore, that the evaluation of land reform is carried out by an independent organization which has no connection with the implementing agency.* This is not the place to give an exhaustive description of evaluation procedures, but it should be pointed out that a *transitional evaluation* must be carried out concurrently with the implementation and answer the following questions:

1. Does implementation serve the immediate objectives of the legislation? What difficulties are encountered in realizing them? Is the programme still in step with the trend of general economic development, or does it need to be adjusted?
2. Does implementation produce the desired effect in the rural community? What is the reaction of the losers, the beneficiaries and the administrative staff at the village level, and to what extent have favourable or unfavourable conditions for implementation been established or promoted?

This evaluation should also analyse any unexpected side-effects of implementation, determine the reason for their appearance and recommend remedial action if they are undesirable. Land redistribution in India during the fifties, for example, indirectly led to mass evictions in many areas and thus actually increased the insecurity of tenancy. No doubt, an independent evaluation service at that time could have prevented a great deal of injustice and human misery.

A *subsequent evaluation* should be conducted when the implementation is thought to be completed in order to appraise the effect of land reform in the context of agricultural and economic development, taking into account actual as well as intended changes. In this case the following questions should be posed:

* *Report of the Working Group of the Government of India and the Food and Agriculture Organization of the United Nations, op.cit.*

1. What were the effects of land reform upon the underprivileged sections of the rural population?
2. Has land reform actually promoted the village economy and has it—directly or indirectly—also contributed to improved conditions in the non-rural sectors?

It has been argued that evaluation should be restricted to appraising the actual effectiveness of implementation and, undoubtedly, this would make the procedure easier and, in addition, concentrate the limited administrative resources on the most important issues. In my view, however, such a limited approach would fail to evaluate the general trend of the programme and the expected or unforeseen long-term effects of changes in the agrarian structure which will be of decisive importance for future land policy programmes.

An inefficient land policy administration is detrimental to agricultural and socio-economic development in all political environments. It is true that land reform initiated by revolution will have eliminated the vested interests that support the *status quo;* but this alone does not solve all administrative problems. Historically, all revolutions come to an end (though China and Cuba make great efforts to the contrary) and in Mexico as well as Eastern Europe, highly centralized, bureaucratic systems have succeeded the *ad hoc* revolutionary governments. Centralization and decentralization on various levels and in different spheres of government and individual activities, therefore, must be re-examined from time to time in the light of new experiences, new developments and new challenges. And this inevitably calls for an evaluation of the ultimate effects of structural changes on the man-land relationship as well as of implementation.

CHAPTER FOURTEEN

Defence of Land Reform

In the preceding chapters we have repeatedly stressed the importance of keeping a watch on the implementation of land reform programmes by periodic evaluations of their immediate as well as long-term effects on rural conditions and overall development and of adjusting original guidelines if necessary. But evaluation alone is not enough. Given the formidable impact of internal and external forces intent on restoring the *status quo*, the entire development policy must be geared to the ultimate objectives of land reform: an equitable income distribution and an improved quality of society. Otherwise the social and economic progress achieved through land reform will deteriorate even faster than the time it took to be produced. Development is, in fact, identical with land reform and therefore *land reform is a continued uphill battle in which every step forward must be guarded against the opponents of change*. And it is in this battle that measures in the fields of education, credit and marketing assume more than complementary importance and may even become the spearhead—or the Achilles' heel—of the defence of land reform.

Take only the redistribution of Friar land in the *Philippines* in 1902 which ended in a complete fiasco. More than 165,000 hectares were purchased for $7,240,000 by the administration for subdivision and sale to approximately 60,000 tenants. But illiteracy and lack of adequate credit and marketing facilities soon forced the new owners into fatal indebtedness and within less than one generation they had lost their land again to large landowners, traders and even to the Church.

It is practically impossible, for obvious reasons, to prevent the deterioration of land reform programmes that are carelessly designed and half-heartedly implemented. In *South Korea*, for example, the widespread evasions during the implementation of the agrarian reform legislation continued with added strength when the programme was thought to be completed. The restrictions on transfer of farm land, which should have been enforced by county and sub-county land adjustment committees, had never been effective. Moreover the Farm Household Survey of 1963 reveals that the category of 'borrowed land' amounts to 20 per cent of all paddy land; and this despite a law prohibiting tenancy and an official statement to the effect that tenancy had been reduced to one per cent on cultivated land. Other investigations report on considerable land accumulations,* and the Farm Land Survey,† conducted at the end of 1965, concludes that the land reform has neither protected nor promoted the growth of the small farmers and that some powerful former landlords are still influential community leaders. It is difficult to imagine how it could be otherwise. The complementary measures designed to strengthen the owner-cultivator's financial position and provide education and guidance were never effectively introduced. The Land Reform Law did not allow the farmers to mortgage their land; but since they did not have access to other sources of reasonable credit, they often had to return to the old system of usurious loans. The result is that land accumulation is increasing and tenancy is returning although tenant farming has been prohibited by both Constitution and land reform legislation.

But this is not all. The South Korean land reform never included forest land, although more than 70 per cent of the surface area was under forest by the end of 1950. Consequently, the large-scale land reclamation projects in these areas carried out by the government under the Land Reclamation Act of 1962, are not subject to restrictions regarding size of holdings and tenancy. In this way two different kinds of land policy are currently in force, one for the old cultivated areas and the other for newly reclaimed lands. This, of course, has a most unfortunate influence on morale, particularly in the administration, and

* *A Study of the Land Tenure System in Korea* (Korean Land Economics Research Center, Seoul, 1966), pp. 197 ff., particularly p. 227.
† Quoted by Ki Hyuk Pak, 'Economic Effects of Land Reform in the Republic of Korea', *Land Reform, Land Settlement and Co-operatives*, no. 1 (FAO, Rome, 1968), pp. 13 ff.

weakens the achievements of land reform by strengthening the forces opposed to it.

Nowhere, however, has failure to defend the achievements of land reform impeded promising rural development and progress as much as in *Mexico*, where the memory of the successful agrarian revolution is still cherished by the nation although its very spirit has been submerged in the economic and political realities of today. It is true that the Mexican agrarian revolution of 1910–17 accomplished a large-scale redistribution of land that eliminated the *latifundia* system: in 1910, one per cent of the population controlled 97 per cent of the total land area while today about 900,000 individual holdings of up to 5 hectares and 1.5 million *ejido* units control 48.7 per cent of the cultivable and 46.5 per cent of the irrigated land. But complementary measures to defend these achievements were either not thought of or neglected by the land policy of subsequent governments and gradually large holdings monopolizing land, water and other resources at the cost of the small cultivators (private or *ejidal*) have become the rule rather than the exception in many parts of the country.

The reluctance to control the dynamic forces of capitalist development in the fields of marketing, credit and trade gave rise to a *neo-latifundism* particularly in the rich, irrigated areas of the North-west where owners evaded the size restrictions on land for private ownership by registering part of the large landholdings under different names of family members or friends. Still more important, this reluctance has encouraged the emergence of a new social class, a rural-urban bourgeoisie which is concentrated in the regional towns. It is composed of merchants, store-owners, public officials and professionals who largely control the capital accumulation generated by agricultural activity, credit and markets and thus, up to a certain point, the social processes in the rural areas. The land reform which succeeded in destroying a dominant oligarchy has degenerated into a tutelary policy that 'protects' the lower strata of peasantry by a rigid wall of regulations; manipulated by a powerful bureaucracy, they have proved detrimental to agricultural improvement. At the risk of oversimplification it could be said that this bureaucracy, appointed to defend the achievements of agrarian reform, largely perpetuates the subsistence agriculture of the small cultivators.

Its agricultural policy and political and administrative bias have deprived the *ejido* sector of its competitive capacity; hence, the fallacy of the inefficient *ejidos*. Serious studies of Mexican agricultural development show that, given the same conditions, *ejidos* and individual farm units can work the soil with equal efficiency.* Others state that defamation of the *ejido* has all the characteristics of a self-fulfilling prophecy, for they are now denied those very technical and financial requirements which are necessary to improve their efficiency. In fertile regions, the value of agricultural production from *ejidos* and from private farms of over 5 hectares corresponds roughly to their respective amounts of arable land, while in poor regions private farms are as unproductive as *ejido* plots. It is neither the *ejido* institution nor the collective *ejido* which has failed but the slow and cumbersome *ejido* policy—or even the lack of one—which for more than three decades has fomented practices that are so often denounced.† The greater concentration of capital in large private farms does not contribute substantially to increased production; yet, it contributes to the displacement of manpower and growing landlessness. The *ejido* system is without doubt a positive achievement of Mexican agrarian reform, but its ultimate success has been prevented by the complex of political and economic relationships that has come to rule the economic life of the country.

Developments in Mexico are an example of an unfinished agrarian reform whose limited achievements are cherished by the people but offer no hope for future development. The *laissez-faire* policy that failed to control the free play of market forces and the circumvention of the reform laws is mainly responsible for the reappearance of corruption and *caciquism* in the Mexican countryside. The agrarian reform has become a static system of old-established relationships which is inadequate to serve the country's need for economic and agricultural development. Mexican economists are increasingly aware of the need for 'reforming land reform'‡ in order to free the peasants from the paralysing effect

---

* S. Eckstein, *El ejido colectivo en México* (Mexico City and Buenos Aires, 1966), pp. 205 ff.
† R. Stavenhagen, 'Social Aspects of Agrarian Structure in Mexico', op. cit.
‡ M. A. Durán, *El agrarismo Mexicano* (Mexico City, 1967), p. 19.

of uncontrolled market forces and for providing an existence for the ever-increasing numbers of landless agricultural workers. But not even a continuing land redistribution could possibly solve these formidable problems. There is an urgent need for a new agricultural policy and, above all, for legislation that will protect the over 3,300,000 landless peasants who today live as pariahs in the rural areas and urban shanty towns and who, in the final analysis, are victims of a sterile complacency with the first successful achievements of the agrarian reform.

Contrary to Mexico, *Japan* has successfully defended and further increased the achievements of its land reform programme from the fifties. Strict observance of the Agricultural Land Law of 1952, which controlled the transfer of rights in farm land, limited the possession of tenanted land to a few special cases and protected the rights of tenants, has prevented both the acquisition of additional lands and the emergence of a new type of absentee landlord. A rigid implementation of the Law over a period of fifteen years, effectively defended the new agrarian structure created by the land reform, while at the same time agriculture and industry developed rapidly and the whole economic picture dramatically changed.

By the beginning of the sixties the growing exodus from rural to industrial areas had caused a manpower shortage in agriculture which could only partly be relieved by mechanization. Once again the Japanese government proved its flexibility. It recognized that the land tenure system created by the reform of the fifties was about to become an obstacle to the further development of agriculture and that the time was ripe for a reappraisal of land policy. In 1962, it passed an amendment to the Agricultural Co-operative Association Law and authorized cooperatives, limited companies, joint stock companies, unlimited partnerships and agricultural cooperative associations to acquire titles to farm land. This broke with the original principle of only allowing individual ownership to farm land and has caused an increase in the average size of agricultural enterprises the extent of which will depend on future agricultural policy.* Japan seems convinced of the need to

* Takekazu Ogura, (ed.), *Agricultural Development in Modern Japan* (Japan-FAO Association, Tokyo, 1963), pp. 147, 148.

enter a new stage of land reform in order to promote large-scale production and farm management unrestricted by land-lease regulations and ceilings on the amount of land acquired. A public agency in charge of the transfer of agricultural land is shortly to be established.*

Everywhere the story of land reform underscores the importance of a flexible defence of institutional achievements and, once it has been implemented, confirms the need for a continuing review of agrarian conditions. Permanent institutional regeneration is a prerequisite for ensuring an equitable pattern of land distribution which will protect the farming population against the risks of the free play of market forces and ensure a high level of agricultural productivity. There is no end to land reform—just as there is no end to demographic changes, technological progress and economic development. Land reform is a permanent feature of any dynamic economic system.

Demographic and technological developments pose the same questions to every new generation: is your land distribution pattern still adequate even if it was established by land reform? If not, how will you redistribute the land? And how will you make the farmers efficient or protect their accomplishments in the light of new developments? The developed countries ask themselves these questions, and for many decades they have given priority to costly programmes for land consolidation, agricultural credit, education and settlement. Since the Second World War the socialist countries have permanently reappraised their agriculture with a view to improving its performance by institutional adjustments. Yet, strangely enough, the interests vested in the outdated agrarian systems of underdeveloped countries succeed time and again in convincing Western politicians, governments and experts that socio-economic progress is compatible with the continuance of a repressive land policy.

The problem of man and land will remain the key issue in development wherever agricultural production is the mainstay of the population. Underdevelopment, owing to the entrenched

* Paper submitted by the Japanese Government to the Joint FAO/ECAFE/ILO Seminar on Implementation of Land Reform in Asia and the Far East, Manila, 1969 (FAO, Room, 1969, mimeographed).

monopolies of landownership, education and the control of credit and labour markets by the privileged few, still prevails in one-third of the world and is the prime reason for the economic and cultural crises of our age. Present Western assistance to under-developed countries which comforts and supports these monopolies, contributes in fact to the perpetuation of misery and stagnation and future generations will consider it to be as great an offence against international morality as was colonial exploitation.

Appendix I

Technical Assistance for the Financing of Land Reform Programmes*

It goes without saying that any social policy involves considerable expense; this holds true particularly for land reform programmes in underdeveloped countries where large, long-term investment is needed in addition to capital expenditure in acquiring land for redistribution. The latter, however, is relatively modest (in Latin America an estimated 18 per cent of the total), compared to the costs of the complementary measures necessary to increase the productive capacity of the new peasant owners. Accordingly, it is essential that land redistribution is not financed independently but considered part of the national budget for agricultural development. The new owner-cultivators can hardly be expected to pay the costs of the comprehensive development programmes which, given the usual conditions in underdeveloped areas, will include land improvements like irrigation and drainage, provision of working capital and current investment which taken together will amount to many times the actual land value. In addition, rapid agricultural development calls for effective extension, improved education and local research stations with sufficient land for experiment and demonstration.

Naturally, governments may want to reduce the high costs per family either by increasing the number of units to benefit from the programme or by establishing state or collective farms. They may even postpone less urgent investments until a certain economic stability has been reached or even incorporate small-scale, preferably cooperative, industries in order to increase the number

---

* This section draws largely on information provided by: T. T. Carroll in 'Issues of Financing Agrarian Reforms; the Latin American Experience' (RU: WLR/66/5). Paper submitted to the World Land Reform Conference, FAO, Rome, 1966; 'Report of the Peru Mission composed of T. Balogh, K. Owada, and J. Patton', (FAO, Rome, 1964, unpublished); the *Report of the World Land Reform Conference, FAO, Roome, 1966* (UN, New York, 1968); and the 'Report of Meeting on Financing Integral Agrarian Reforms, Santiago, Chile, August-September 1965' (FAO, Rome, 1966, mimeographed).

of beneficiaries. Although any of these steps may facilitate financing and extend the programme to a larger number of families, they may also delay the anticipated increase in agricultural production.

The almost complete lack of even the most important infrastructure in many underdeveloped countries, particularly in Latin America, will further increase the investment necessary. From the point of view of financing land reform it should be possible, of course, to distinguish between the direct and indirect financial requirements, that is to say, between the initial capital costs of land acquisition and improvements, and the additional expenses involved in the necessary institutional arrangements. Despite its modest share of total costs, investment in the acquisition of land for redistribution is of specific psychological and political importance since it represents the first step towards a change in the power structure of the rural society.

The World Land Reform Conference came to the conclusion that the entire financial requirements of agrarian reform programmes should be considered as part of the overall cost of economic and social development and that it might, therefore, be unwise to make too much distinction between the initial expenses for land acquisition and the subsequent costs of rural development connected with the tenure changes. Whatever the truth, the thing that needs to be stressed is that the investments in all land reform and agricultural development programmes should be made in such a way that they increase employment and, as far as possible, substitute labour for capital.

At various stages of development, tenure conditions determine the relationship between capital investment and income distribution, and accordingly investments in land improvement have different effects before and after land reform. In the former case, such investments are mainly in the interests of large and medium landowners and middlemen while in the latter, it will benefit the peasants to whom land has been redistributed.

Given the limited financial resources in most underdeveloped countries, comprehensive land reform programmes require outside financial assistance. And yet, urgent as they may be, grants and credits from international sources will serve their purpose only if the responsible organizations would stop hiding behind their statutes, and generously support not only the building up of resources, but also institutional developments. The Report of the World Land Reform Conference observes correctly the contradictory attitudes of international agencies with regard to the implementation of institutional reforms; on the one hand, they demand that the administrative and technical services of the projects which they support be strictly controlled while, on the other, they refuse to contribute to the costs of the administrative personnel needed. This lack of understanding and generosity, as it were, compels the new peasant owners or collective farms to shoulder financial obligations disproportionate to the productive capacity of the land and, consequently, at variance with the desired redistribution of income and subsequent increase in the standard of living of the rural population. If the amortization rates to be paid by the new owners are as high as their former rents this will be a disincentive for additional effort. This was the case in large parts of India, where the limited success of land reform was probably also due to the high instalments.

Accordingly, the peasants in an area of land reform should not be obliged to repay investment in infrastructures, land reclamation and land improvement. Their financial contribution to the costs of land reform should be restricted to that part of public expenditure from which they benefit directly and personally: the acquisition of land, the construction of a new house, and the interest rates on agricultural credit. But even these payments should be made in long-term instalments at the most favourable terms possible.

The governments of some Latin American countries have requested that international organizations guarantee the whole or a part of the agrarian bonds which they issue to the landlords as compensation for land expropriated, hoping in this way to free themselves from the financial burdens of large-scale land reform programmes. Tempting as it may be, this suggestion has most serious implications; first, the very prospect of such an international guarantee would boost land values and, consequently, compensation which, in turn, would increase the amortization payments by the new peasant owners far beyond the productive capacity of their land. Meanwhile the agrarian bonds or cash to an equivalent value would probably soon leave the country for the more favourable climate of Switzerland. And secondly, given the instability of Latin American currencies, there is little doubt that such an arrangement would indemnify the landlords against losses through devaluation and inflation, and perhaps even encourage the landlord-dominated governments to devaluate the national currency at the expense of the international agencies. Since it may be assumed that compensation payments to landlords do not create any assets and that their volume is determined by political rather than by economic considerations, an international guarantee of the agrarian bonds would merely finance the export of national capital, and in the final analysis defeat the very objectives of land reform. Direct international aid, on the other hand, would be a valuable contribution to solving the crucial problem of financing, if it were to provide generously the capital funds needed for the additional investment in agriculture which alone can ensure the success of land reform.

Appendix II

Land Redistribution and Organization of Agriculture in Israel

With regard to land redistribution and organization of agriculture, *Israel* presents a unique case. Despite certain quasi-revolutionary elements, the prevailing land distribution pattern results neither from true evolutionary nor from true revolutionary developments but from a large-scale purchase of land and recently also from land aquisition by war.

The first *kibbutzim*, collective immigrant settlements, which were established on more or less barren land purchased from feudal Arab estates, are noteworthy in the context of this study. They prove that it is possible to develop an effective agriculture under most adverse conditions without sacrificing the dignity of human labour. Although the *kibbutzim* today represent only a minor part of agricultural producers in Israel, they have not lost their capacity for development and adjustment which originally provided security and incentives for the Jewish immigrants.

It may be true that the spiritual and social values of the *kibbutzim* are on the decline and that they no longer dominate Israeli agriculture, but the fact remains that they were once the catalyst for agricultural development and the school for citizenship and civic responsibility.

Despite the capitalist economy of Israel, and the increasing importance of the *moshavim*, a more recent type of cooperative individual farm settlement, the *kibbutz* as a collective tenure type has been able to hold its own. Even today the *kibbutzim* account for one-third of total agricultural output and in addition for more than 5 per cent of the national industrial production. They were in fact the pioneers of rural industrialization and still contribute substantially to regional development. In the mid-sixties, 225 *kibbutzim* comprised 82,000 out of a total Jewish agricultural population of about 300,000 and 50 per cent of the agricultural area in the original State of Israel.

The very fact that the land purchased for settlement was not distributed to the individual immigrants created a genuine community spirit and established at a very early stage a group identity which automatically prevented the pursuit of personal interests.

The political, historical and social background of the *kibbutzim* differs essentially from that of the collective farms in socialist countries. Yet, their initial contribution and continued capacity for economic progress cannot but confirm the purposiveness of collective tenure systems for speeding up agricultural and economic development in areas with limited natural and staff resources and a population inexperienced in farming.

Appendix III

Comparative Requirements of Extension and Farm Services of Collective or State Farms and Individual Peasant Holdings

The growing recognition of the importance of educational and extension activities for agricultural development has underlined the necessity for increasing the generally limited numbers of skilled staff in underdeveloped countries and providing the resources needed for the expensive training particularly at the senior and intermediary levels.

During the past few years various agencies have done some studies on the requirements for professionally trained manpower. Of these the FAO studies in connection with the Indicative World Plan* are of particular interest as they are concerned not only with the quantitative and qualitative assessment of trained manpower requirements and their financial implications but also with the development of a proper manpower strategy. Though dealing with the specific conditions in various underdeveloped regions, these studies have the unfortunate shortcoming of assuming that individual peasant farming will remain the predominant tenure type, and neglect the possible emergence during the coming decades of collective or state farms in various regions of the underdeveloped world. The methodology of assessing manpower requirements is thus based on the agricultural family.†

The FAO studies deal in detail with various requirements and policies according to population concentration, farming experience, level of labour and farm management efficiency but fail to take the fundamentally different requirements of disparate tenure types

* *Provisional Indicative World Plan for Agricultural Development* C 69/4, FAO, Rome, 1969). See, in particular, 'Africa South of the Sahara'. Regional Study Prepared for the Indicative World Plan (FAO, Rome, 1968); and 'South America'. Regional Study Prepared for the Indicative World Plan (FAO, Rome, 1968). The chapters on 'Requirements and Policies for Trained Manpower at the Professional and Technical Levels' are of special interest.

† *Provisional Indicative World Plan for Agricultural Development,* p. 431.

into consideration. They have worked out, for instance, that in the land reform areas of Latin America and Africa the minimum target for the intensification of extension work needed should be one field worker to 500 farm families and one supervisor to 5 intermediary-level officers; special ratios have been worked out on staff requirements for farm services like land use, soil conservation, animal health, etc., and the organization of cooperatives.

Obviously, in areas where collective or state farms are the prevailing tenure types, the professional and technical requirements with regard to numbers, composition and supervision of the agricultural extension service staff will be entirely different. While only a limited number of the peasant-owners in backward areas have some farming experience and the majority need the extension staff's direct help in the fields of operation and management, collective or state farms can select the more capable peasants for key positions in the management. These can then, through direct and permanent contact with extension workers in the various fields, disseminate the imparted knowledge to the labour force of the farm. This more intensive utilization of the extension service will, however, affect both the number and qualifications of the staff, particularly during the early stages of agricultural development when there is a greater need for extension in the techniques of management.

The studies rightly emphasize the importance of extension services for the women who in many countries in addition to rearing the children, play an important part in agricultural production, trading, processing and marketing, and thus in the development of the rural society. But just as it is obvious that extension should take account of the problems of rural women, it should also be evident that this particular form of extension service can be more easily and economically extended to collective and state farms than to individual peasant holdings.

Generally speaking, the concentration of farming activities into large production units together with a certain streamlining of credit and marketing will make it easier to economize with staff resources and, in particular, will reduce the problems of supervision. It may even be possible to further rationalize extension as has been done in Israel, for example, where the establishment of joint advisory and educational services by groups of *kibbutzim* have lowered costs and facilitated a large-scale standardization of production. Such favourable results, however, can only be expected if the administrative policy is guided by objective considerations rather than by a political bias that may induce the management to place people who are not necessarily the most capable in key positions.

Just as it can be said that, from the point of view of development, the system of individual peasant farming has failed in the past, it can be claimed that collective or state farms have also been unsuccessful in some countries and even responsible for a decrease in the efficiency of production. For the planning of future extension services, however, the potential capacity of either system for utilizing the staff resources available should be given priority. A thorough investigation, therefore, should also be made of the quantitative and qualitative requirements and policies for trained manpower both at the professional and technical levels of the various types of collective and state farming in order to determine:

Firstly, the extent to which they can be expected to economize with staff resources as compared to individual peasant holdings; and the additional number of specialists needed according to the type of farming.

Secondly, the extent to which they can reduce the gap between research and extension through direct contact with the experiment stations.

Thirdly, the extent to which they will need more qualified staff for extension in business management and auditing than the peasant farms.

And *finally*, the extent to which they need specialized extension and supervision in order to handle variables like climate and soil, market demands, and standardization of production in comparison with individual peasant holdings.

Appendix IV

Deterioration of the Social Stratification in Rural Areas of Central Luzon*

Because of the heavy pressure of population the majority of agricultural holdings in the Philippines are extremely small. According to the 1960 Agricultural Census, only 0.1 per cent of all farm units are over 100 hectares while over 60 per cent are below 3 hectares and more than 12 per cent are less than 1 hectare. Together all these small units comprise only 25 per cent of the total agricultural area while the few farms of 100 hectares and over account for more than 10 per cent. Table 1 shows that general tenure conditions are highly unfavourable inasmuch as 54.2 per cent of all farms are operated by tenants and part-owners.

TABLE 1 †

Tenure conditions	Number of farms	Percentage	Farm area	Percentage
Total Philippines	2,167,500	100.0	7,772,000	100.0
Owners	968,000	44.7	4,133,000	53.2
Part owners	311,000	14.3	1,140,000	14.7
Tenants	865,000	39.9	2,000,000	25.7
Farm managers	2,500	0.1	365,000	4.7
Other tenure systems	21,000	1.0	134,000	1.7

* This appendix on the social stratification in the rural areas of Central Luzon has been written with the valuable assistance of Amanuens Leif Ståhl, Stockholm.

† The tables in this appendix are all based on the following statistics: *Census Atlas of the Philippines, Vol. V* (Commission of the Census, Commonwealth of the Philippines, Manila, 1940). *Yearbook of Philippine Statistics 1946; 1948 Census of the Philippines; Summary Report on the 1948 Census of Agriculture; 1960 Census of the Philippines*, Vol. II: 'Agriculture, Summary'; *1960 Census of the Philippines*, Vol. II: 'Population and Housing, Summary'; and *Labor Force, May 1966 (Series no. 20) and Special Release no. 80 Series of 1968* (all published by Bureau of the Census and Statistics, Republic of the Philippines, Manila). *World Bank Atlas. Population per Capita Production and Growth Rates* (IBRD, Washington DC, 1969).

Overall economic development is likewise most unsatisfactory. In 1967, the per capita GNP amounted to only $180 and the economic growth rate to 0.8 per cent while the population increase was as high as 3.4 per cent.* Equally unfavourable is the employment situation. According to official statistics, total unemployment in rural areas rose from 435,000 to 529,000 between May 1966 and May 1968.† It is evident that these figures cover unemployment in both agricultural and non-agricultural industries. But from the point of view of the present analysis a distinction between the two is of minor importance as non-agricultural unemployment in rural areas is practically identical with agricultural unemployment. The increasing unemployment is particularly unfortunate when we consider that the country enjoys a maximum of financial and technical support from the United States and this proves only too clearly the limitations of an aid policy that does not take the social structure and the interests of the majority of the population into consideration.

The precarious economic situation, and particularly the unfortunate changes in the land distribution pattern, take on almost dramatic proportions in the central provinces of Luzon, the principal island of the Philippine Archipelago. The following tables analyse certain developments in the rural areas of Bulacan, Cavite, Laguna, Nueva Ecija, Pampanga, Rizal and Tarlac. We have chosen to deal with these seven provinces of Central Luzon for several reasons: first because they comprise a major part of the rural population of this island and have had, and still have, a considerable influence upon the general social and economic pattern of the country; secondly, because they are marked by such a high concentration of landownership that actual agricultural production is largely in the hands of tenant-cultivators; thirdly, because they are still the traditional centre of agrarian unrest with recurrent dramatic conflicts between peasants and landlords; and finally because the steady stream of landless peasants migrating to the metropolitan area of Manila principally comes from these areas.

* IBRD, *World Bank Atlas, Population Per Capita Product and Growth Rates* (Washington DC, 1969).
† Republic of the Philippines, Bureau of the Census and Statistics, *Labor Force, May 1966 (Series no. 20), Special Release no. 80 Series of 1968.*

TABLE 2

Tenure conditions	Number of farms	Percentage	Farm area	Percentage
Total (7 provinces)	211,000	100.0	660,000	100.0
Owners	42,000	19.9	125,000	18.9
Part owners	22,000	10.6	84,000	12.7
Tenants	143,000	67.8	391,000	59.2
Farm managers	328	0.2	50,000	7.6
Other tenure systems	3,000	1.5	11,000	1.6

Table 2 reveals that the number of farms operated by tenants and part-owners in these provinces is almost four times as large as that operated by owners and that as much as 50,000 hectares, i.e., 7.6 per cent of the total area in farms, is controlled by only 328 farm managers.

According to the 1960 Census, the agricultural area in these seven provinces has been increased by 127,000 hectares since 1948, mainly in Nueva Ecija, Pampanga and Tarlac. Yet, this has in no way improved the employment opportunities for the rapidly growing agricultural population, and the formidable growth of Metropolitan Manila and the adjoining province of Rizal during the post-war period is largely a result of the massive exodus from the countryside.

TABLE 3

	Population increase between the years:	
	1939–1948 (per cent increase)	1948–1960 (per cent increase)
Total Luzon	21.5	41.5
Bulacan	23.6	35.1
Cavite	10.1	44.0
Laguna	14.9	46.9
Nueva Ecija	12.2	30.1
Pampanga	11.0	48.2
Rizal	51.3	116.4
Tarlac	23.7	30.5

TABLE 4

| | Population increase between the years: | |
	1939–1948 (per cent increase)	1948–1960 (per cent increase)
Total Luzon	21.5	41.5
Total Luzon without Metropolitan Manila	16.3	39.1
Metropolitan Manila	60.4	54.6
Total Philippines	20.2	40.8

In addition between 1948 and 1960 changes have taken place in the land distribution pattern which disclose certain trends that most likely still continue. Tables 5–8 have been compiled partly on the basis of the 1948 and 1960 Agricultural Censuses and partly on available local data in order to provide the statistical basis for a comparative analysis of the changes in the number and area of farms within the different size groups.

It must be assumed, of course, that the general increase in the number of farms during this period, particularly in the groups comprising 5–20 hectares, was largely due to the lull in the quasi-civil war situation in Central Luzon in the early fifties when some of the better-off farmers, who had left the rural areas because of the political tension, returned to the land. But even so, the changes observed during this period clearly point to a serious deterioration in the social stratification in the rural areas of these important provinces which shows itself in an ever-increasing gap between small and exceedingly large farm units.

Analysing these tables, we find that the number of farms in the smallest size group (less than 1 hectare) has increased by 9 per cent while the area within this size group has declined by 22 per cent. In the 1–2 hectares group farm numbers rose by 22.7 per cent whereas the total farm area increased by only 17.5 per cent. Even in the 10–20 hectares group the increase of 26.1 per cent in the number of farms was accompanied by an extension of the farm area of only 18.2 per cent.

The full significance of these changes emerges with unmistakable clarity if we compare them with those in the group of 20 hectares and over. Here the number of farms has declined by 7.7 per cent

TABLE 5
Number of Farms by Size Groups (in ha.)

Province	Number of farms less than 1.0	Number of farms 1.0 and under 2.0	Number of farms 2.0 and under 3.0	Number of farms 3.0 and under 5.0	Number of farms 5.0 and under 10.0	Number of farms 10.0 and under 20.0	Number of farms 20.0 and over
1948							
Bulacan	2,544	9,125	8,516	5,314	1,561	224	51
Cavite	2,528	7,285	6,966	5,096	1,802	286	103
Laguna	3,439	4,783	4,128	3,952	2,597	686	272
Nueva Ecija	1,636	9,225	16,502	17,284	4,139	606	193
Pampanga	1,161	3,376	4,666	6,688	3,394	265	71
Rizal	2,084	3,198	1,958	1,222	546	180	89
Tarlac	1,537	7,330	8,934	10,067	3,548	430	104
Total	14,929	44,322	51,670	49,623	17,587	2,677	883
1960							
Bulacan	2,717	12,753	9,349	5,102	1,556	325	52
Cavite	2,400	7,835	6,429	5,180	1,704	303	54
Laguna	2,765	6,528	5,220	5,309	3,491	920	193
Nueva Ecija	2,128	9,568	18,038	21,844	6,172	572	244
Pampanga	1,889	5,089	6,696	8,064	4,058	336	71
Rizal	2,670	3,746	2,052	1,195	482	325	52
Tarlac	1,706	8,876	9,877	10,255	4,149	594	149
Total	16,275	54,395	57,661	56,949	21,612	3,375	815

TABLE 5 continued

Province	Number of farms less than 1.0	Number of farms 1.0 and under 2.0	Number of farms 2.0 and under 3.0	Number of farms 3.0 and under 5.0	Number of farms 5.0 and under 10.0	Number of farms 10.0 and under 20.0	Number of farms 20.0 and over
Difference between 1948–1960							
Bulacan	173	3,628	833	− 212	− 5	101	1
Cavite	128	550	− 537	84	− 98	17	− 49
Laguna	− 674	1,745	1,092	1,357	894	234	− 79
Nueva Ecija	492	343	1,536	4,560	2,033	− 34	51
Pampanga	728	1,713	2,030	1,376	664	71	0
Rizal	586	548	94	− 27	− 64	145	− 37
Tarlac	169	1,546	943	188	601	164	45
Total	1,346	10,073	5,991	7,326	4,025	698	− 68
Percentage of total	9.0	22.7	11.6	14.8	22.9	26.1	− 7.7

TABLE 6
Area of Farms (in ha.) by Size Groups

Province	Area of farms less than 1.0	Area of farms 1.0 and under 2.0	Area of farms 2.0 and under 3.0	Area of farms 3.0 and under 5.0	Area of farms 5.0 and under 10.0	Area of farms 10.0 and under 20.0	Area of farms 20.0 and over
1948							
Bulacan	1,394	12,451	19,475	18,586	9,501	2,711	3,254
Cavite	1,245	8,952	15,204	17,678	10,503	3,252	3,508
Laguna	1,346	6,358	9,192	15,035	16,224	8,980	10,406
Nueva Ecija	786	12,484	37,546	59,746	25,631	7,628	9,407
Pampanga	497	4,381	10,576	23,990	20,555	3,394	4,013
Rizal	1,118	4,012	4,309	4,234	3,431	2,360	4,216
Tarlac	913	9,989	18,263	34,687	18,164	5,536	5,471
Total	7,299	58,627	114,565	173,956	104,009	33,861	40,275
1960							
Bulacan	1,128	16,765	21,049	17,820	9,465	3,936	4,524
Cavite	936	9,489	13,825	17,961	10,266	3,464	1,780
Laguna	801	8,096	11,493	18,752	22,294	10,974	14,105
Nueva Ecija	768	12,431	40,625	75,444	37,058	6,910	44,495
Pampanga	650	6,556	14,756	28,407	24,656	3,916	5,938
Rizal	605	4,618	4,486	4,145	3,062	3,705	2,369
Tarlac	763	10,957	21,949	36,259	25,468	7,119	12,857
Total	5,651	68,912	128,183	198,788	132,269	40,024	86,068

TABLE 6 *continued*

Province	Area of farms less than 1.0	Area of farms 1.0 and under 2.0	Area of farms 2-0 and under 3.0	Area of farms 3.0 and under 5.0	Area of farms 5.0 and under 10.0	Area of farms 10.0 and under 20.0	Area of farms 30.0 and over
Difference between 1948–1960							
Bulacan	− 266	4,314	1,574	− 766	− 36	1,225	1,270
Cavite	− 309	537	−1,379	283	− 237	212	−1,728
Laguna	− 545	1,738	2,301	3,717	6,070	1,994	3,699
Nueva Ecija	− 18	− 53	3,079	15,698	11,427	− 718	35,088
Pampanga	153	2,175	4,180	4,417	4,101	522	1,925
Rizal	− 513	606	177	− 89	− 369	1,345	−1,847
Tarlac	− 150	968	3,686	1,572	7,304	1,583	7,386
Total	−1,648	10,285	13,618	24,832	28,260	6,163	45,793
Percentage of total	− 22.6	17.5	11.9	14.3	27.2	18.2	113.7

TABLE 7

Number of Farms by Size Groups (in ha.)

Province	Number of farms 20.0 and under 50.0	Number of farms 50.0 and under 100.0	Number of farms 100.0 and under 200.0	Number of farms 200.0 and over
1948				
Bulacan	47	2	1	1
Cavite	88	13	2	0
Laguna	225	32	11	4
Nueva Ecija	152	27	6	8
Pampanga	53	9	5	4
Rizal	77	4	1	7
Tarlac	83	8	6	7
Total	725	95	32	31
1960				
Bulacan	35	8	4	5
Cavite	47	5	2	0
Laguna	143	30	11	9
Nueva Ecija	125	34	18	67
Pampanga	44	12	10	5
Rizal	43	4	4	1
Tarlac	96	26	17	10
Total	533	119	66	97
Difference between 1948–1960				
Bulacan	− 12	6	3	4
Cavite	− 41	− 8	0	0
Laguna	− 82	− 2	0	5
Nueva Ecija	− 27	7	12	59
Pampanga	− 9	3	5	1
Rizal	− 34	0	3	− 6
Tarlac	13	18	11	3
Total	−192	24	34	66
Percent of total	− 26.5	25.3	106.3	212.9

TABLE 8

Area of Farms (in ha.) by Size Groups

Province	Area of farms 20.0 and under 50.0	Area of farms 50.0 and under 100.0	Area of farms 100.0 and under 200.0	Area of farms 200.0 and over
1948				
Bulacan	1,129	108	118	1,899
Cavite	2,382	913	213	—
Laguna	5,900	2,036	1,557	913
Nueva Ecija	3,839	1,625	824	3,119
Pampanga	1,511	615	647	1,240
Rizal	1,880	260	105	1,971
Tarlac	2,180	431	756	2,104
Total	18,821	5,988	4,220	11,246
1960				
Bulacan	922	522	565	2,515
Cavite	1,239	300	241	—
Laguna	3,965	2,117	1,529	6,494
Nueva Ecija	3,568	2,268	2,131	36,528
Pampanga	1,307	784	1,449	2,399
Rizal	1,134	257	559	418
Tarlac	2,588	1,772	2,111	6,386
Total	14,723	8,020	8,585	54,740
Difference between 1948–1960				
Bulacan	− 207	414	447	616
Cavite	− 1,143	− 613	28	—
Laguna	− 1,935	81	− 28	5,581
Nueva Ecija	− 271	643	1,307	33,409
Pampanga	− 204	169	802	1,159
Rizal	− 746	− 3	454	− 1,553
Tarlac	408	1,341	1,355	4,282
Total	− 4,098	2,032	4,365	43,494
Percent of total	− 21.7	33.9	103.4	386.6

N

while the farm area has increased by as much as 113.7 per cent; the only possible interpretation of this development is that a considerable concentration of ownership rights has taken place.

In Table 7, which lists the number of farms in a series of groups according to size ranging from 20 to 200 hectares and over, we find that the greatest increases, of 106.3 and 212.9 per cent, in the two largest size groups have occurred partly at the expense of the 20–50 hectares group. In absolute figures, the number of farms in these two groups has increased by 100 units during the same period in which the number of farms in the groups of less than 1–10 hectares increased by as much as 28,760 units! If, in addition, we compare these increases with the corresponding figures for the farm area, (Table 8) we find that the area of farms of 200 hectares and over has expanded by 43,494 hectares, or 386.6 per cent, while the increase in area of the farm units of less than 10 hectares adds up to a mere 75,347 hectares, or to less than 17 per cent. Even if the post-war trend towards large-scale agriculture is taken into consideration, the progressive concentration of ownership in the largest size groups accompanied by an ever-increasing number of small farm units clearly indicate the detrimental changes which have taken place in the rural social stratification.

It may be of interest in this connection to point out that of the total increase of 43,494 hectares in the area of the largest size group, the province of Nueva Ecija alone accounts for 33,409 hectares and that, incidentally, this figure corresponds almost exactly to the area of 33,780 hectares put under irrigation in that province since 1948. Although this, of course, may be mere coincidence, it could be that politically powerful large landowners have been able to acquire beforehand what was to become the most valuable rice land in Nueva Ecija.

The above changes in the number and size of farms clearly reflect an unhappy social polarization in rural areas which expresses itself in increasing rural and urban unemployment, economic stagnation and political unrest. The pronounced expansion of the large estates is certainly of far greater importance than are the modest agrarian reform measures hailed by political propaganda and is the true reason for the continued political and economic crises. Developments in the Philippines in fact may be considered a 'reverse land redistribution' and clearly prove that agrarian reform programmes are without any practical effect in an environment where technical and financial assistance support an economic policy which primarily serves the interests of the privileged few.

Bibliography

Public Documents

AFRICA, BRITISH REPORTS

Report of the East African Royal Commission, 1953–55. Cmd. 9475. HMSO, London, 1956.

Report of the Conference on African Land Tenure in East and Central Africa Held at Arusha, Tanganyika, February 1956. A Special Supplement to the *Journal of African Administration* (London, October 1956).

Report of the Working Party on African Land Tenure, 1957–1958 (Government Printer, Nairobi, 1958).

ASIAN DEVELOPMENT BANK

Asian Agricultural Survey, Vol. II (Manila, 1968).

Papers and Proceedings. Regional Seminar on Agriculture Held in Conjunction with the Second Annual Meeting of the Board of Governors of the Asian Development Bank (Sidney, Australia, April 1969).

COMITE INTERAMERICANO DE DESARROLLO AGRICOLA (CIDA)

Brazil: Land Tenure Conditions and Socio-economic Development of the Agricultural Sector (Pan American Union, Washington, DC, 1966).

Peru: Land Tenure Conditions and Socio-economic Development of the Agricultural Sector (Pan American Union, Washington, DC, 1966).

Land Tenure Conditions and Socio-economic Development of the Agricultural Sector in Seven Latin American Countries. Edition prepared for the World Land Reform Conference, Rome, 1966 (Pan American Union, Washington, DC, 1966).

INDIA

Report of the Team for the Study of Community Projects and National Extension Service, Vols. I-III (Committee on Plan Projects, Government of India, New Delhi, 1957).

Review of the First Five-Year Plan (Government of India, New Delhi, 1957).

The National Sample Survey, Eighth Round: July 1954-April 1955 (The Cabinet Secretariat, Government of India, Calcutta, 1958).

The National Sample Survey, Sixteenth Round: July 1960-June 1961, Tables with Notes on Agricultural Holdings in Rural India (No. 113) (The Cabinet Secretariat, Government of India, Calcutta, 1967).

The National Sample Survey, Seventeenth Round: Tables with Notes on Agricultural Holdings in Rural India (The Cabinet Secretariat, Government of India, Calcutta, 1968).

Report of the Working Group of the Government of India and the Food and Agriculture Organization of the United Nations on Methods for Evaluation and Effects of Agrarian Reform (Ministry of Food and Agriculture, Government of India, New Delhi, August 1958).

India: A Reference Annual 1958 (Ministry of Information and Broadcasting, Government of India).

Seventh Evaluation Report on Community Development and Some Allied Fields (Progress Evaluation Organization, Planning Commission, Government of India, New Delhi, 1960).

Third Five-Year Plan, 1961–1966 (Planning Commission, Government of India, New Delhi, 1961).

Rural Credit Follow-up Survey, 1959–60. General Review Report (Economic Department, Reserve Bank of India, Bombay, 1962).

Report of the Special Working Group on Cooperation for Backward Classes, Vols I and II (Ministry of Home Affairs, Government of India, September 1962).

Report of the Committee of Direction on Cooperative Farming (Department of Cooperation, Ministry of Community Development and Cooperation, Government of India, New Delhi, 1965).

Report on the Evaluation of the Rural Electrification Programme (Programme Evaluation Organization, Planning Commission, Government of India, New Delhi, 1965).

Cooperative Sugar Factories in India (Ministry of Food and Agriculture, Community Development and Cooperation, Government of India, New Delhi, 1966).

Studies in Economics of Farm Management for Six Typical Regions in the Country (Ministry of Food and Agriculture, Community Development and Cooperation, Government of India, New Delhi).

INTER-AMERICAN DEVELOPMENT BANK

Social Progress Trust Fund. Sixth Annual Report, 1966 (Washington, DC, 1966).

INTERNATIONAL BANK FOR RECONSTRUCTION AND DEVELOPMENT (IBRD)

World Bank and International Development Association, Annual Report, 1966–67. (Washington, DC, n.d.).

*World Bank and International Development Association, Annual Report,
1968* (Washington, DC, n.d.).
*World Bank and International Development Association, Annual Report,
1969* (Washington, DC, n.d.).
World Bank Atlas. Population per Capita Product and Growth Rates
(Washington, DC, September 1969).
'Annual Address by Robert S. McNamara, President of the Bank and
its Affiliates', in *1969: Annual Meetings of the Boards of Governors,
Summary Proceedings* (Washington, DC, 1969).

ISRAEL

*Graphic Illustration of the Profitability of Agricultural Branches in 1964–
65 and 1965–66* (Institute of Farm Income Research in Cooperation
with the Central Bureau of Statistics, Government of Israel, Tel Aviv,
December 1967).

KOREA (SOUTH)

A Study of the Land Tenure System in Korea (Korea Land Economics
Research Center, Seoul, 1966).

MEXICO

Censos Agrícola-Ganadero y Ejidal IV, 1960 (Mexico City, 1965).

THE PHILIPPINES

Census Atlas of the Philippines, Vol. V (Commission of the Census,
Commonwealth of the Philippines, Manila, 1940).
Yearbook of Philippine Statistics 1946 (Bureau of the Census and
Statistics, Republic of the Philippines, Manila).
1948 Census of the Philippines (Bureau of the Census and Statistics,
Republic of the Philippines, Manila).
Summary Report on the 1948 Census of Agriculture (Bureau of the
Census and Statistics, Republic of the Philippines, Manila).
1960 Census of the Philippines, Vol. II: 'Agriculture, Summary' (Bureau
of the Census and Statistics, Republic of the Philippines, Manila).
1960 Census of the Philippines, Vol. II: 'Population and Housing' (Bureau
of the Census and Statistics, Republic of the Philippines, Manila).
*Labor Force, May 1966, (Series no. 20) and Special Release no. 80 Series
of 1968* (Bureau of the Census and Statistics, Republic of the Philippines, Manila).

TANZANIA

'The Modernized Village Approach', in *Rural Development Planning Seminar* (University College, Dar es Salaam, 1966, mimeographed).

Second Five-Year Plan for Economic and Social Development, 1969–1974, Vol I: 'General Analysis'; Vol. II: 'The Programmes' (Government Printer, Dar es Salaam, 1969).

UNITED NATIONS

United Nations Conference on Trade and Development (UNCTAD)

Towards a New Trade Policy for Development. Report by the Secretary-General of UNCTAD (New York, 1964).

Trade Expansion and Economic Cooperation Among Developing Countries, Report of the Committee of Experts (Geneva, 1966).

The Terms of Financial Flows and Problems of Debt-Servicing. Paper Prepared by the UNCTAD Secretariat for the Second UNCTAD Conference in New Delhi, 1968 (TD/7/Supp. 3, Geneva, 18 October 1967).

The Outlook for Debt-Service. Paper Prepared by the UNCTAD Secretariat for the Second UNCTAD Conference in New Delhi, 1968 (TD/7/Supp. 5, Geneva, 31 October 1967).

Problems and Policies of Financing. UNCTAD, Second Session, vol. 4 (TD/7, Geneva, 1968).

Towards a Global Strategy of Development. Report by the Secretary-General of UNCTAD to the Second Session of the Conference (UN, New York, 1968).

The Significance of the Second Session of UNCTAD. Report by the Secretary-General of UNCTAD to the Secretary-General of the United Nations (TD/96, Geneva, 7 May 1968).

Towards a Global Strategy of Development. Report by the Secretary-General of UNCTAD to the Second Session of the Conference (UN, New York, 1968).

Department of Economic and Social Affairs

Progress in Land Reform, Third Report (New York, 1962).

Progress in Land Reform, Fourth Report (New York, 1966).

Progress in Land Reform, Fifth Report (New York, 1970).

World Economic Survey 1965.

Report on the World Social Situation 1967 (New York, 1969).

A Study of the Capacity of the United Nations Development System (The Jackson Report), vols. 1 and 2 (Geneva, 1969).

Economic Commission for Africa

'The Demographic Situation in West Africa', *Economic Bulletin for Africa*, vol. 6, no. 2 (UN, New York, 1966).

Economic Commission for Asia and the Far East

Economic Survey of Asia and the Far East 1965. Prepared by the Secretariat of the Economic Commission for Asia and the Far East (UN, Bangkok, 1966).

Economic Survey of Asia and the Far East 1967. Prepared by the Secretariat of the Economic Commission for Asia and the Far East (UN, Bangkok, 1968).

Economic Survey of Asia and the Far East 1968. Prepared by the Secretariat of the Economic Commission for Asia and the Far East (UN, Bangkok, 1969).

Economic Commission for Europe

Economic Survey of Europe in 1966. Prepared by the Secretariat of the Economic Commission for Europe, Geneva (UN, New York 1967).

Economic Survey of Europe in 1967. Prepared by the Secretariat of the Economic Commission for Europe, Geneva (UN, New York, 1968).

Economic Survey of Europe in 1968. Prepared by the Secretariat of the Economic Commission for Europe, Geneva (UN, New York, 1969).

Economic Survey of Europe in 1969. Prepared by the Secretariat of the Economic Commission for Europe, Geneva (UN, New York, 1970).

Economic Commission for Latin America

Geographical Distribution of the Population of Latin America and Regional Development Priorities (E/CN. 12/643, Mar del Plata, Argentina, May 1963).

Report of a Community Development Evaluation Mission to Venezuela. Prepared by Caroline P. Ware, Rubén Dario Utria and Antoni Wojcicke (TAO/VEN/15, UN, New York, 1963).

Economic Bulletin for Latin America, vol. 13, no. 2 (UN, New York, November 1968).

Feder, Ernest, 'Report on Land Tenure Problems in Latin America' (not yet published).

United Nations Conferences (Papers to)

Jacoby, Erich H., 'Agrarian Structure and Land Settlement', in *Report of the UN Conference on the Application of Science and Technology for the Benefit of Less-developed Countries* (UN, Geneva, October 1962).

Wertheim, W. F., 'Recent Trends in China's Population Policy'. Paper submitted to the United Nations World Population Conference, Belgrade, August-September, 1965.

Davis, Kingsley, 'Conceptual Aspects of Urban Projections in Developing Countries', in *Report of United Nations World Population Conference, 1965*, vol. 3 (UN, New York, 1967).

UNITED NATIONS SPECIALIZED AGENCIES

Food and Agriculture Organization (FAO) Rome

Report to the Government of Malta on the Development of Agricultural Resources (Report no. ETAP 409, Rome, 1955).

Report of the Study Group on the Problems of Individual and Group Settlement for the European Region, Tel Aviv, Israel, April-May 1956 (Meeting Report no. 1956/19, Rome, 1956).

'Interim Report of the FAO Mediterranean Project'. Prepared by a team headed by Thomas Balogh (Rome, 1957, as yet unpublished).

Report to the Government of Nigeria on the Farm-Settlement Scheme in the Western Region (Report no. FAO/EPTA 1720, Rome, 1963).

'Report on the Seventh Regional FAO Conference for Asia and the Far East, Manila 1964' (Rome, 1965, as yet unpublished).

'Report of the Meeting on Financing Integral Agrarian Reforms, Santiago, Chile, August-September, 1965' (Rome, 1966, mimeographed).

'Agricultural Development in Nigeria 1965–1980' (Rome, 1966, as yet unpublished).

'FAO Mission to the Philippines, March-May 1967' (Rome, 1967, mimeographed).

'Cooperation and Mutual Aid Among Farm Producers in the Federal Socialist Republic of Yugoslavia'. Paper submitted to the Third Session of the Working Party on Agrarian Structure in Europe, Bucharest, June 1968 (Report no. ECA: AS/68/4E, Rome, 1968).

Memorandum on FAO/Industry Cooperative Program (Report no. WS/57103, Rome, 15 March 1967).

Summary Record of the Fifth Session of the General Committee, FAO/Industry Cooperative Program (Report no. IP: G/69/13, Rome, May 1969).

Paper submitted by the Japanese Government to the Joint FAO/ECAFE/ILO Seminar on Implementation of Land Reform in Asia and the Far East, Manila 1969 (Rome, 1969, mimeographed).

Provisional Indicative World Plan for Agricultural Development (Report no. C 69/4, Rome, August 1969).

'Africa South of the Sahara: Requirements and Policies for Trained Manpower at the Professional and Technical Levels'. Regional Study prepared by R. Rowat for the Indicative World Plan (Rome, June 1968).

'South America'. Regional Study prepared by R. Rowat for the Indicative World Plan (Rome, May 1968).

Report to the Government of Ceylon on the Working of the Land Paddy Act. Prepared by Ameer Raza (Rome, 1970).

Abensour, Emanuel S., *Principles of Land Tenancy Legislation* (FAO Legislative Series, no. 6, Rome, 1966).

Bessis, A., *Rapport au gouvernement du Cameroun sur les problèmes de la réforme foncière au Cameroun oriental. Loi No. 59–47, 17.6.1959, portant organisation dominale et foncière* (Report no. EPTA 1872, Rome, 1964).

Christodoulou, D., *Report of the Development Center on Land Policy for West African Countries, Freetown, Sierra Leone, December 1963-January 1964* (Report no. EPTA 1860, Rome, 1964).

Dandekar, V. M., 'Motivating Farmers to Increase Agricultural Production'. Paper submitted to the Seventh Regional FAO Conference for Asia and the Far East, Manila, 1964 (Rome, 1964).

Galeski, Boguslau, 'The *Agricultural Circle* as a Main Form of Mutual Assistance Among Poland's Farmers'. Paper submitted to the Third Session of the Working Party on Agrarian Structure in Europe, Bucharest, June, 1968 (Report no. ECA: AS/68/13, Rome, 1968).

Hussain, M. H., *Customary Land Tenure in the Context of a Developing Agricultural Economy* (Report no. EPTA 1853, Rome, 1964).

Jacoby, Erich H., *Inter-Relationship Between Agrarian Reform and Agricultural Development* (FAO Agricultural Studies, no. 26, Rome, 1953).

Jacoby, Erich H., *Evaluation of Agrarian Structure and Agrarian Reform Programs* (FAO Agricultural Studies, no. 69, Rome, 1966).

Jacoby, Erich H., *Agrarian Reconstruction* (Basic Studies, no. 18, Rome, 1968).

Kawharu, I. H., 'Supplementary Report on Maori Land Tenure and Social Organisation' (Research Project, André Mayer Fellowship Paper, Rome, 1963, mimeographed).

Madiman, S. G., *Land Reform and Institutional Planning in India* (FAO Document no. RU: MISC/68/15, Rome, April 1968).

Mifsud, Frank M., *Customary Land Law in Africa* (FAO Legislative Series, no. 7, Rome, 1967).

Moral-López, Pedro, *Principles of Land Consolidation Legislation* (FAO Legislative Series, no. 3, Rome, 1962).

Myrdal, Gunnar, 'The United Nations, Agriculture, and the World Economic Revolution'. Address to the Latin American Conference on Food and Agriculture, held in Viña del Mar, Chile, 18 March 1965.

Nyerere, Julius, *McDougal Memorial Lecture* (Rome, November 1963).

Sabry, O. A., 'Alternative Systems of Land Tenure and Farm Structures for New Holdings in Tanzania'. Paper submitted to the Second Panel of Experts on Land Tenure and Settlement, Rome, May 1969 (Report no. RU: LT/69/4).

Papers to the World Land Reform Conference, Rome, 1966 (Convened jointly by the UN, New York, and FAO in association with the ILO, Geneva):

'Issues of Financing Agrarian Reforms; the Latin American Experience', by Thomas T. Carrol (Report no. RU: WLR/66/5, Rome, 1966).

'Basic Agrarian Structural Issues in the Adjustment of African Customary Tenures to the Needs of Agricultural Development', by D. Christodoulou (Report no. RU: WLR/66/C, Rome, 1966).

'Land Reform and Economic Development in the Near East', by M. Riad El Ghonemy (Report no. RU: WLR/66/E, Rome, 1966).

'The Evaluation of Land Reform in Kenya', by J. D. MacArthur (Report no. RU: WLR/66/L, Rome, 1966).

'Land Settlement in Kenya', by J. W. Maina (Report no. RU: WLR/66/20, Rome, 1966).

'Forestry and Agrarian Reform', by J. Prats-Llaurado in collaboration with C. Petrin (Report no. RU: WLR/66/B, Rome, 1966).

'The Chilean Agrarian Reform' (Report no. RU: WLR/66/40, Rome, 1966).

'The Experience of State Farms in Poland, (Organization, Production, Assistance to Peasant Farms)' (Report no. RU: WLR/66/26, Rome, 1966).

'Structural Changes and Development of Peasant Farms in Poland' (Report no. RU: WLR/66/16, Rome, 1966).

'Agrarian Reform and Recent Measures for Agricultural Development in Rumania' (Report no. RU: WLR/66/51, Rome, 1966).

'Agrarian Reform and Economic Development in Yugoslavia' (Report no. RU: WLR/66/18, Rome, 1966).

'Land Reform and Organization of the Peasants into Cooperatives in the USSR' (Report no. RU: WLR/66/49, Rome, 1966).

Report of the World Land Reform Conference, Rome 1966 (UN, New York, 1968).

International Labour Organization, (ILO), Geneva

Plantation Workers: Conditions of Work and Standards of Living (Geneva, 1966).

Social Development in the Americas. Report of the Director-General on the Eighth Conference of American States Members of the International Labour Organization in Ottawa, 1966 (Report no. 1, Geneva, 1967).

'Report on the Study of the Role of Peasant Organizations in the Process of Agrarian Reform in Latin America' (Geneva, 1969, mimeographed).

UNITED STATES OF AMERICA

Congress, Joint Economic Committee

Comparisons of the United States and Soviet Economies (86th Congress, 1st Session, Washington, 1960).

'New Directions in the Soviet Economy', in *Economic Performance, Part II-B* (89th Congress, 2nd Session, Washington, 1966).

Congress, Senate, Committee on Foreign Relations

Survey of the Alliance for Progress, Problems of Agriculture (90th Congress, 1st Session, Washington, 1967).

USSR

Soviet Financial System (Progress Publishers, Moscow, 1966).

Books

Abaya, Hernando J., *The Untold Story of the Philippines* (Malaya Books, Quezon City, The Philippines, 1967).

Allan, William, *The African Husbandman* (Oliver & Boyd, Edinburgh: Barnes & Noble, New York, 1965).

Alsberg, Karl L., *Land Utilization Investigations and their Bearing in International Relations* (Institute of Pacific Relations, New York, 1933).

Aziz, Ungku A., *Subdivision of Estates in Malaya, 1951–1960* (University of Malaya, Kuala Lumpur, 1962).

Balogh, Thomas, *The Economics of Poverty* (Weidenfeld & Nicolson, London, 1960: The Macmillan Company, New York, 1967).

Barbero, Guiseppe, *Land Reform in Italy* (Food and Agriculture Organization, Rome, 1961).

Behrendt, Richard F., *Soziale Strategie für Entwicklungsländer* (S. Fischer Verlag, Frankfurt am Main, 1965).

Belschaw, D. G. R., *An Outline of Research in Uganda, 1945–1963* (East African Institute of Social Research, Kampala, Uganda, 1963).

Brown, Murray, *On the Theory and Measurement of Technological Change* (Cambridge University Press, Cambridge, 1966).

Cerych, Ladislav, *Problems of Aid to Education in Developing Countries* (Published for the Atlantic Institute by Praeger, New York 1965: Pall Mall Press, London, 1966).

Chao Kuo-chun, *Agrarian Policy of the Chinese Communist Party* (Asia Publishing House, Bombay, 1960).

Clairmonte, Frederick, *Economic Liberalism and Underdevelopment. Studies in the Disintegration of an Idea* (Asia Publishing House, Bombay, 1960).

Coleman, James S. (ed.), *Education and Political Development* (Oxford University Press, London: Princeton University Press, Princeton, N.J., 1965).

Crook, Isabel and David, *The First Years of Yangyi Commune* (Routledge & Kegan Paul, London: Humanities Press, New York, 1966).

Currie, Lauchlin, *Accelerating Development: The Development and the Means* (McGraw Hill, New York and London, 1966).

Dam, F. van, *Collective Farming in Densely Populated Underdeveloped Areas* (Academisch Proefschrift, University of Amsterdam, June 1961).

Dandekar, V. M. and Khudanpur, G. J., *Working of Bombay Tenancy Act 1948. Report of Investigation* (Gokhale Institute of Politics and Economics, Publication no. 35, Poona, India, 1957).

Donnithorne, Audrey, *China's Economic System* (George Allen & Unwin, London: Praeger, New York, 1967).

Dore, Ronald P., *Land Reform in Japan* (Oxford University Press, London and New York, 1959).

Dumont, René, *Sovkhoz, kolkhoz, ou le problématique communisme* (Editions du Seuil, Paris, 1964).

Dumont, René, *False Start in Africa* (André Deutsch, London: Praeger, New York, 1967).

Dumont, René, and Mazoyer, Marcel, *Dévelopment et Socialism* (Collection Esprit, 'Frontière Ouverte', Editions du Seuil, Paris, 1969).

Dutt, Gargi, *Rural Communes of China* (Asia Publishing House, London, 1957).

Durán, Marco Antonio, *El agrarismo Mexicano* (Siglo XXI Editore, Mexico City, 1967).

Eckstein, Alexander O., *Communist China's Economic Growth and Foreign Trade* (McGraw Hill, New York and London, 1966).

Eckstein, Salomón, *El ejido colectivo en México* (Fondo de Cultura Económica, Mexico City and Buenos Aires, 1966).

Edel M., and Ballesteros, J., *The Colonization of Papaloapan* (To be published by the Centro de Investigaciónes Agrarias, Mexico).

Eicher, Carl, and Witt, Laurence (eds.), *Agriculture in Economic Development* (McGraw Hill, New York and London, 1964).

Fanon, Frantz, *The Wretched of the Earth* (MacGibbon & Kee, London: Grove Press, New York, 1965).

Firth, Raymond, *Essays on Social Organization and Values* (Athlone Press, London: Humanities Press, New York, 1964).

Flores, Edmundo, *Tratado de Economia Agrícola* (Fondo de Cultura Económica, Mexico City, 1968).

Frank, André Gunder, *Capitalism and Underdevelopment in Latin America. Historical Studies of Chile and Brazil* (Monthly Review Press, New York and London, 1967).

Frank, Michael, *Cooperative Land Settlement in Israel and their Relevance to African Countries* (Kyklos Verlag, Basle, 1968).

Franz, Günther, *Der deutsche Bauernkrieg* (Gentner Verlag, Darmstadt, 1956).

Galbraith, J. K., *American Capitalism. The Concept of Countervailing Power* (rev. ed., Hamish Hamilton, London, 1957: 2nd rev. ed. Houghton Mifflin Co., Boston, 1965).

Gandhi, Mohandas Karamchand (Mahatma), *Co-operative Farming* (Navajivan Publishing House, Ahmedabad, India, 1959).

Golay, F. H., *The Philippines: Public Policy and National Economic Development* (Cornell University Press, Ithaca, N.Y., 1968).

Han Suyin, *China in the Year 2001* (C. A. Watts & Co., London: Basic Books, New York, 1967).

Hinton, William, *Fanshen. A Documentary of Revolution in a Chinese Village* (Monthly Review Press, New York and London, 1966).

Hopcraft, Arthur, *Born to Hunger* (Heinemann, London: Houghton Mifflin Co., Boston, 1968).

Hughes, T. J., and Luard, D. E. T., *The Economic Development of Communist China* (Oxford University Press, London and New York, 1961).

Jacoby, Erich H., *Agrarian Unrest in Southeast Asia* (Asia Publishing House, Bombay, 1961).

Kapp, K. William, *Hindu Culture and Economic Planning in India* (Asia Publishing House, London, 1963).

Kotovsky, Grigory, *Agrarian Reforms in India* (People's Publishing House, New Delhi, 1964).

Krassowski, Andrzej, *The Aid Relationship* (Overseas Development Institute, London, 1968).

Laxminarayan, H. and Kanungo, Kissen, *Glimpses of Cooperative Farming in India* (Asia Publishing House, London, 1967).

Lewis, William Arthur, *The Theory of Economic Growth* (George Allen & Unwin London: Richard D. Irwin, Homewood, Ill., 1957).

Lewis, William Arthur, *Development Planning: The Essentials of Economic Policy* (George Allen & Unwin, London: Harper & Row, New York, 1966).

Lindqvist, Sven, *Slagskuggan—Latinamerika inför 70 talet* (Bonniers, Stockholm, 1969).

Lowe, Jehuda, *Kibbutz and Moshav in Israel: An Economic Study in International Explorations of Agricultural Economics* (Iowa State University Press, Ames, Iowa, 1964).

Marciani, G. E., *L'Esperienza di Reforma Agraria in Italia* (SVIMEZ, Rome, 1966).

Meek, C. K., *Land Law and Customs in the Colonies* (Oxford University Press, London, 1949).

Mehring, Franz, *Zur deutschen Geschichte* (Soziologische Verlagsanstalt, Berlin, 1951).

Mitrany, David, *Marx Against the Peasant* (Collier-Macmillan, London, and New York, 1961).

Moore, Barrington Jr., *Social Origins of Dictatorship and Democracy* (Beacon Press, Boston, 1966: Allen Lane, The Penguin Press, London, 1967).

Myrdal, Gunnar, *Value in Social Theory. A Selection of Essays on Methodology*, ed. by Paul Streeten (Routledge & Kegan Paul, London, 1958).

Myrdal, Gunnar, *Asian Drama. An Inquiry into the Poverty of Nations* (Allen Lane, The Penguin Press, London: Pantheon, New York, 1968).

Myrdal, Gunnar, *The Challenge of World Poverty: A World Anti-Poverty Program in Outline* (Pantheon, New York, 1970).

Ogura, Takekazu (ed.), *Agricultural Development in Modern Japan* (Japan-FAO Association, Tokyo, 1963).

Pande, V. P., *Village Community Projects in India* (Asia Publishing House, Bombay, 1967).

Pearson, Lester B. (Chairman), *Partners in Development. Report of the Commission on International Development* (Praeger, New York, 1969).

Proudhon, P.-J., *Qu'est-ce que la propriété? Ou recherches sur le principe du droit et du gouvernement. Premier mémoire* (Prévot, Paris, 1841).

Robequain, Charles, *Malaya, Indonesia, Borneo and the Philippines* (Longmans, Green, London, 1954: Humanities Press, New York, 1958).

Robinson, E. A. G. and Vaizey, J. E. (eds.), *The Economics of Education* (Macmillan, London: International Economic Association, New York, 1966).

Robinson, Ronald, and Johnston, Peter (eds.), *The Rural Base for National Development. Papers and Impressions of the Sixth Cambridge Conference on Development Problems* (Cambridge University Overseas Studies Committee, 1968).

Rosen, George, *Democracy and Economic Change in India* (Cambridge University Press, London: University of California Press, Berkeley, 1967).

Saab, Gabriel S., *Egyptian Agrarian Reform 1952–1962* (Oxford University Press, London and New York, 1967).

Saiydain, K. G., *The Humanist Tradition in Indian Education and Thought* (Asia Publishing House, Bombay, 1966).

Schultz, Theodore W., *Transforming Traditional Agriculture* (Yale University Press, New Haven, Conn., 1964).

Sovani, N. V., *Urbanization and Urban India* (Asia Publishing House, Bombay, 1966).

Stavenhagen, R., (ed.), *Agrarian Problems and Peasant Movements in Latin America* (Anchor Books, Doubleday, New York, 1970).

Streeten, Paul, *Economic Integration. Aspects and Problems* (A. W. Sythoff, Leyden, 1961).

Sun Yat Sen, *San Min Chu I, Three Principles of the People* (Shanghai, 1927).

T'ang Liang-Li, *The Foundations of Modern China* (Noel Douglas, London, 1928).

Tarlok Singh, *Poverty and Social Change. With a Reappraisal*. 2nd. ed. (Orient Longmans, New Delhi, 1969).

Tobata, Seiichi (ed.), *The Modernization of Japan I* (Institute of Asian Economic Affairs, Tokyo, 1966).

Warriner, Doreen, *Land Reform in Principle and Practice* (Clarendon Press, Oxford: Oxford University Press, New York, 1969).

Weber, Max, *General Economic History*, trans. by Frank H. Knight (Collier-Macmillan, London and New York, 1961).

Weber, Max, *The Religion of India*, trans. and ed. by H. H. Gerth and D. Martindale (The Free Press, Glencoe, Ill., 1958: Collier-Macmillan, London, 1967).

Weitz, Raanan, *Agriculture and Rural Development in Israel—Projection and Planning* (The National and University Institute of Agriculture, Hebrew University of Jerusalem, 1963).

Weitz, Raanan, and Rokach, Avshalom, *Agricultural Development, Planning and Implementation* (D. Reidel, Dordrecht, 1968).

Wolf, Erich R., *Peasants* (Prentice-Hall, Englewood Cliffs, N.J. and London, 1966).

Articles and Monographs

Abo-Lughod, Janet L., 'Urbanization in Egypt: Present State and Future Prospects', *Economic Development and Cultural Change*, vol. 13, no. 3 (Chicago, April 1965).

Agarwal, Santosh Kumar, 'Consolidation of Holdings: A Case Study of the Lucknow District', *The Economic Review*, vol. 18, no. 10 (New Delhi, December 1966).

Aziz, Ungku A., 'Poverty and Rural Development in Malaysia', *Kajian Ekonomi Malaysia*, vol. 1, no. 1 (Kuala Lumpur, June 1964).

Aziz, Ungku A., 'Fundamental Obstacles to Rural Development with Special Reference to Institutional Reforms'. Paper submitted to the South Asia Symposium at the Institute of International Economic Studies (Stockholm, September 1969, mimeographed).

Baba, Keinosake, 'Structure of Agricultural Income Distribution', *Quarterly Journal of Agricultural Economy*, vol. 9, no. 3 (Tokyo).

Balogh, Thomas, 'Agricultural and Economic Development, Linked Public Works', *Oxford Economic Papers*, new series, vol. 13, no. 1 (February 1961).

Balogh, Thomas, 'The Mechanism of Neo-Imperialism', *Bulletin of the Oxford Institute of Statistics*, vol. 24, no. 3 (1962).

Balogh, Thomas, 'Education Must Come Down to Earth', *CERES, FAO Review*, vol. 1, no. 2 (Rome, March-April, 1968).

Bardhan, Kalpana, 'Size of Holdings and Productivity, Further Comment', *Economic Weekly*, vol. 16, no. 34 (Bombay, 1964).

Barraclough, Solon L., 'Employment Problems Affecting Latin American Agricultural Development', *FAO Monthly Bulletin of Agricultural Economics and Statistics*, vol. 18, nos. 7–8 (Rome, July-August 1969).

Barraclough, Solon L., *Agricultural Policy and Strategies of Land Reform*, (Social Science Institute, Washington University, St. Louis, Mo., Sage Publications, 1969).

Bergman, Theodor, 'Factors Influencing Optimum Size and Decision-Making in Cooperative Farms' in *Papers and Proceedings, International Centre on Rural Cooperative Communities* (Tel Aviv, March 1969).

Boerma, A., 'Trade and Aid', *Mediterranea, Révue des Problèmes Agronomiques Mediterraneens*, no. 23–24 (Paris, July-August 1968).

Brown, Lester R., 'A New Era in World Agriculture'. Paper submitted to the First Annual Senator Frank Carlson Symposium on World Population and Food Supply, Kansas State University, December 1968 (USDA 3773–68, United States Department of Agriculture).

Byrnes, Francis C., *Some Missing Variables in Diffusion, Research and Innovation Strategy* (The Agricultural Development Council, New York, March 1968).

Chaudhuri, Sachin, 'Going Back on Land Reform', in *Economic Planning and Social Organisation* (Published by the *Economic and Political Weekly*, Bombay, 1969).

Chonchol, Jacques, 'From Isolation to Unity', *CERES, FAO Review*, vol. 1, no. 3 (Rome, May-June 1968).

Chossudovsky, Evgeny M., 'UNCTAD and Co-existence: Part One— From Geneva to New Delhi', *Co-Existence*, vol. 6, no. 2 (Oxford, July 1969).

Choudhary, K. M., *The Organization and Disintegration of a Collective Farming Society. A Case Study in a Gramdan Village*, Ad hoc study no. 2 (Agro-Economic Research Centre, Sardar Patel University, Vallabh Vidyanagar, June 1963).

Choudhary, K. M., *Factors Affecting Acceptance of Improved Agricultural Practices. A Study in an IADP District in Rajasthan*, Research Study no. 9 (Agro-Economic Research Centre, Sardar Patel University, Vallabh Vidyanagar, 1965).

Christodoulou, D., 'Land Settlement: Some Oft Neglected Basic Issues', *FAO Monthly Bulletin of Agricultural Economics and Statistics*, vol. 14, no. 10 (Rome, October 1965).

Clark, Ronald James, *Land Reform and Peasant Market Participation in the Northern Highlands of Bolivia*, Land Tenure Center Reprint, no. 42 (University of Wisconsin, 1968).

Clark, Ronald James, *Problems and Conflicts over Land Ownership in Bolivia*, Land Tenure Center Reprint, no. 54 (University of Wisconsin, 1969).

Dandekar, V. M., 'Utilization of Rural Manpower', *The Economic Weekly* (Bombay, February 1962).

Dandekar, V. M., *The Demand for Food and Conditions Governing Food Aid During Development*, Study no. 1 (Gokhale Institute of Political and Economic Research, Poona, 1965).

Dantwala, M. L., 'Institutional Credit in Subsistence Agriculture', *International Journal of Agrarian Affairs*, vol. 5, no. 1 (London, December 1966).

Davis, Kingsley, *Population Policy: Will Current Programs Succeed?* Population Reprint Series, no. 258 (Institute of International Studies, University of California, Berkeley, n.d.).

Desai, M. B., *Report on Enquiry into the Working of the Bombay Tenancy and Agricultural Land Act 1948, as Amended up to 1953 in Gujarat (Excluding Baroda District)* (The Indian Society of Agricultural Economics, Bombay, 1958).

Dooren, P. J. van, 'State-controlled Changes in Tunisia's Agrarian Structure', in *Tropical Man*, Yearbook of the Anthropology Department, Royal Tropical Institute, Amsterdam (Leiden, 1968), vol. 1.

Dore, Ronald P., 'Land Reform and Japanese Economic Development', in Seiichi Tobata (ed.), *The Modernization of Japan I* (Institute of Asian Economic Affairs, Tokyo, 1966).

Dumont, René, 'A World Strategy for Fertilizers', *CERES, FAO Review*, vol. 1, no. 1 (Rome, January-February 1968).

Edgeworth, F. Y., 'The Theory of International Values', *Economic Journal*, vol. 4, no. 1 (London, March 1894).

Eisenstadt, S. N., 'Some New Looks at the Problem of Relations Between Traditional Societies and Modernization', *Economic Development and Cultural Change*, vol. 16, no. 3 (Chicago, August 1968).

Ellman, A. O., 'Kitete Land Settlement Scheme in Northern Tanzania', *Land Reform, Land Settlement and Cooperatives*, no. 1 (FAO, Rome, 1967).

Feder, Ernest, 'The Rational Implementation of Land Reform in

Colombia and its Significance for the Alliance for Progress', *America Latina,* vol. 6, no. 1 (Rio de Janeiro, January-March, 1963).

Finch, Bob and Oppenheimer, Mary, 'Ghana: End of an Illusion', *Monthly Review* (New York, July-August 1966).

Flores, Edmundo, *Land Reform and the Alliance for Progress,* Policy Memorandum no. 27 (Center of International Studies, Princeton University, N.J., 1963).

Gadgil, D. R., 'Integration of Land Settlement Policies into the Economic and Social Development Planning of Countries', *FAO Monthly Bulletin of Agricultural Economics and Statistics,* vol. 8, no. 10 (Rome, October 1959).

Gadgil, D. R., 'The Fourth Plan: Evolution of New Policy and Planning Strategy—II', *Indian and Foreign Review,* vol. 6, no. 5 (Delhi, 15.12.1968).

Giri, V. V., 'Jobs for Our Millions', (excerpts from forthcoming book of same title), *Indian and Foreign Review,* vol. 7, no. 12 (New Delhi, 1.4.1970).

Goodman, Seymour S., 'Problems of the External Sector of Developing Countries', *The Developing Economies,* vol. 7, no. 3 (Tokyo, September 1969).

Goodwin, R. M., 'The Optimal Growth Path for an Underdeveloped Economy', *Economic Journal,* vol. 71, no. 284 (London, December 1961).

Haberler, Gottfried von, 'An Assessment of the Current Relevance of the Theory of Comparative Advantage to Agricultural Production and Trade, *International Journal of Agrarian Affairs,* vol. 4, no. 3 (London, May 1964).

Hobsbawm, E. J., 'Peasants and Rural Migrants in Politics', in (Claudio Veliz(ed.), *The Politics of Conformity in Latin America* (Oxford University Press, London, 1967).

Huizer, Gerrit, 'Community Development, Land Reform and Political Participation', *American Journal of Economics and Sociology,* vol. 28, no. 2 (April 1969).

Hurrenius, Hannes and Olof Åhs, *The Sweden-Ceylon Family Planning Pilot Project* (Demographic Institute, University of Gothenburg, 1968).

Idenburg, P. J., 'Political Structural Development in Tropical Africa', *Orbis,* vol 11, no. 1 (Foreign Policy Research Institute, University of Pennsylvania, Spring 1967).

Jacoby, Erich H., 'Can Land Reform Help to Establish the Rural Base for National Development' in Ronald Robinson and Peter Johnston (eds.), *The Rural Base for National Development* (Cambridge University Overseas Studies Committee, 1968).

Jacoby, Erich H., 'Cuba: The Real Winner is the Agricultural Worker', *CERES, FAO Review,* vol. 2, no. 4 (Rome, July-August 1969).

Jakhade, V. M., *Presidential Address to the Twenty-Ninth All-India Agricultural Economics Conference 1969,* Andrah University, Waltair (Published by the Indian Society of Agricultural Economics, Bombay, 1969).

Javits, Jacob K., 'Urgencies in Latin America. Last Chance for a Common Market', *Foreign Affairs*, vol. 45, no. 3 (New York, April 1967).

Johnson, B. L. C., 'Recent Developments in Rice Breeding and Some Implications for Tropical Asia'. Paper submitted to the Conference on South East Asian Society and Environment, School of Oriental and African Studies, London, 9–11 September 1969.

Jolly, Arthur Leonard, 'The Economic Evaluation of the Asentamientos of the Agrarian Reform 1966 and 1967' (Instituto de Capitación e Investigación en Reforma Agraria (ICIRA), Santiago, Chile, April 1968, mimeographed).

Kahan, Arcadius, 'The Collective Farm System in Russia: Some Aspects of its Contribution to Soviet Economic Development', in Carl Eicher and Laurence Witt (eds.), *Agriculture in Economic Development* (McGraw Hill, New York and London, 1964).

Kaneda, Hiromitsu, 'Economic Implications of the "Green Revolution" and the Strategy of Agricultural Development in West Pakistan', *The Pakistan Development Review*, vol. 9, no. 2 (Karachi, Summer 1969).

Kapp, K. William, 'In Defence of Institutional Economics', *Swedish Journal of Economics*, vol. 70, no. 1 (Stockholm, March 1968).

Karst, Kenneth L., *Latin American Land Reform: The Uses of Confiscation*, Land Tenure Center Reprint no. 20 (University of Wisconsin, 1963).

Kenadjian, B., 'Disguised Unemployment in Underdeveloped Countries' (Ph. D. Dissertation, Harvard University, 1957, mimeographed).

Kuznets, Simon, 'Economic Growth of Small Nations', in *Economic Consequences of the Size of Nations. Proceedings of a Conference held by the International Economic Association*, edited by E. A. G. Robinson (Macmillan, London, 1966).

Kuznets, Simon, 'Quantitative Aspects of the Economic Growth of Nations. Level and Structure of Foreign Trade: Long-Term Trends', *Economic Development and Cultural Change*, vol. 15, no. 2, pt. 2 (Chicago, January 1967).

Ladejinsky, Wolf, 'The Green Revolution in Punjab: A Field Trip', *Economic and Political Weekly*, vol. 4, no. 26 (Bombay, 28.6.1969).

Ladejinsky, Wolf, 'Green Revolution in Bihar, the Kosi Area: A Field Trip', *Economic and Political Weekly*, vol. 4, no. 39 (Bombay, 27.9.1969).

Landsberger, Henry A., *The Role of Peasant Movements and Revolt in Development: An Analytical Framework*, International Institute for Labour Studies, Geneva (Bulletin no. 4, February 1968).

Laxminarayan, H. and Kanungo, Kissen, 'Glimpses of Cooperative Farming in India', *Agricultural Economics Research Centre*, University of Delhi (1967).

Le Monde, 'La modernisation de l'agriculture Chinois explique les bonnes récoltes de ces dernière années' (Paris, 9.12.1969).

Liberman, Jevsei, 'The Soviet Economic Reform', *Foreign Affairs*, vol. 46, no. 1 (New York, October 1967).

Lindbeck, Assar, 'Handelspolitik gentemot U-länder', in *U-hjälp utveckling?* (Wahlström & Widstrand, Stockholm, 1969).

Lin Pao, 'Long Live the Victory of the People's War', *The People's Daily* (Peking, 3.9.1965).

Lodge, George C., 'U.S. Aid to Latin America: Funding Radical Change', *Foreign Affairs*, vol. 47, no. 4 (New York, July 1969).

Long, Erwin J., 'The Economic Basis of Land Reform in Underdeveloped Economies', *Land Economics* (Wisconsin, May 1961).

Metcalf, Thomas R., *Landlords without Land: The U.P. Zamindars Today*, South Asia Reprint Series, no. 274 (Institute of International Studies, University of California, Berkeley, 1967).

Myint, H., 'An Interpretation of Economic Backwardness', in A. N. Agarwala and S. P. Singh (eds.), *The Economics of Underdevelopment* (Oxford University Press, London, 1958).

Myrdal, Gunnar, 'Economic Effects of Population Development' in *Economic Development Issues and Policies*, P. S. Lokanathan 72nd Birth Commemoration Volume (Bombay, 1966).

Ominde, S. H., *The Population Factor in Kenya's Economic Development*, International Institute for Labour Studies, Bulletin no. 3 (Geneva, November 1967).

Oppenheimer, Ludwig, 'Regional Economy as an Historical Stage of Development and the Permanent Element of Social Structure from Below', *Internationales Symposium, Deutsche Wirtschaftspolitische Gesellschaft* (Berlin, 1967).

Oschapkin, K., 'Erfahrungen mit der Geldvergütung der Arbeit in den Kollektivschaften', *Internationale Zeitschrift der Landwirtschaft, DDR* (Berlin, 1967).

Pak, Ki Hyuk, 'Economic Effects of Land Reform in the Republic of Korea', *Land Reform, Land Settlement and Cooperatives*, no. 1 (FAO, Rome, 1968).

Parsons, Kenneth M., 'Poverty as an Issue in Development Policy: A Comparison of the United States and Underdeveloped Countries', *Land Economics*, vol. 45, no. 1 (Wisconsin, February 1969).

Pearse, Andrew, 'Trends of Agrarian Changes in Latin America', *Latin American Research Review*, vol. 1, no. 3 (University of Texas, 1966).

Pearse, Andrew, 'Subsistence Farming Is Not Dead', *CERES, FAO Review*, vol. 2, no. 4 (Rome, July-August 1969).

Powell, John Duncan, *The Role of the Federazion Campesina in the Venezuelan Agrarian Reform Process*, Land Tenure Center Reprint, no. 26 (University of Wisconsin, December 1967).

Raup, Philip M., 'Agricultural Taxation and Land Tenure Reform in Underdeveloped Countries', in *Agricultural Taxation and Economic Development. Papers and Proceedings of the Conference on Agricultural Taxation and Economic Development, January 28 to February 3, 1954* (Cambridge, Mass., 1954).

Reynolds, Lloyd G., *Economic Development with Surplus Labour: Some Complications*, Economic Growth Center Paper no. 133 (Yale University, New Haven, 1969).

Rodriguez, Carlos Rafael, 'Cuatro años de reforma agraria', *Cuba Socialista*, Año III (Havana, May 1963).

Rosenstein-Rodan, P. N., 'Problems of Industrialization of Eastern and Southeastern Europe', *Economic Journal*, vol. 53, no. 210 (London, September 1943).

Sakoff, A. N., 'The Private Sector in Soviet Agriculture', *FAO Monthly Bulletin of Agricultural Economics and Statistics*, vol. 11, no. 9 (Rome, September 1962).

Sandberg, Laars G., 'Worldwide Farming Just Around the Corner', *Economic Development and Cultural Change*, vol. 15, no. 1 (Chicago, October 1966).

Sen, Amartyra Kumar, 'An Aspect of Indian Agriculture', *Economic Weekly* (annual no., Bombay, February 1962).

Sen, Amartyra Kumar, 'Size of Holdings and Productivity', *Economic Weekly* (annual nos., Bombay, February and May 1964).

Sen, Amartyra Kumar and Varghese, T. C., 'Tenancy and Resource Allocation', *Seminar*, no. 8, *Farms and Food: A Symposium on Our Land Relations and Agricultural Growth* (New Delhi, May 1966).

Sen, S. R., 'Growth and Instability in Indian Agriculture', Address to the Twentieth Annual Conference of the Indian Society of Agricultural Statistics, 10–12 January 1967, Waltair, India.

Sethi, J. D., 'Technological Development and Economic Growth', *Indian and Foreign Review*, vol. 6, no. 3 (New Delhi, November 1968).

Shearer, Eric B., 'Italian Land Reform Re-appraisal', *Land Economics*, vol. 44, no. 1 (Madison, Wisconsin, 1968).

Stavenhagen, Rudolfo, 'Classes, Colonialism and Acculturation', *Studies in Comparative International Development*, vol. 1, no. 6 (Social Science Institute, Washington University, St. Louis, Mo., 1965).

Stavenhagen, Rudolfo, 'Social Aspects of Agrarian Structure in Mexico', in R. Stavenhagen (ed.), *Agrarian Problems and Peasant Movements in Latin America* (Anchor Books, Doubleday, New York, 1970).

Sternberg, Marvin J., 'Chilean Land Tenure and Land Reform' (Ph.D. Dissertation, University of California, Berkeley, September 1962, mimeographed).

Sukhatme, P. V., 'The World Hunger and Future Need in Food Supply', *Journal of the Royal Statistical Society*, ser. A, vol. 124 (London, 1963).

Svennilson, Ingvar, 'The Strategy of Transfer', in Daniel L. Spencer and Alexander Woroniak (eds.), *The Transfer of Technology to Developing Countries* (Praeger Special Studies in International Economics and Development, New York, 1967).

Taylor, Jim, 'Some Findings and Implications of Land Tenure Center Research in Nicaragua', *Land Tenure Center Newsletter*, no. 26 (University of Wisconsin, April 1967-February 1968).

Tello, Carlos, 'Agricultural Development and Land Tenure in Mexico', *Weltwirtschaftliches Archiv*, vol. 101, no. 1 (Kiel, 1968).

Tha, L. K., 'Price Policy in a Developing Economy' (Shri Ram Memorial Lecture), *Indian and Foreign Review*, vol. 5, nos. 15 and 16 (New Delhi, 1968).

Thiesenhusen, W. and Brown, Marion, 'Paper Prepared for an Overall

Survey Conducted by the Subcommittee on American Republic Affairs',
Land Tenure Center Newsletter, no. 26 (University of Wisconsin,
April 1967–February 1968).

Thome, Joseph R., 'The Bolivian Reform: The Need for a Faster Title
Distribution Process', *Land Tenure Center Newsletter*, no. 24 (University
of Wisconsin, 1.8.1966).

Thome, Joseph R., 'A Brief Survey of the Chilean Agrarian Reform
Program', *Land Tenure Center Newsletter*, no. 28 (University of Wisconsin, September 1968–February 1969).

Thorner, Daniel, 'Indian New Farms: New Class Rises in Rural India',
The Statesman (New Delhi and Calcutta, 1.11.1967).

Tinbergen, Jan and Correa, H., 'Quantitative Adaptation of Education to
Accelerated Growth', *Kyklos, Internationale Zeitschrift für Sozialwissenschaften*, vol. 15 (Berne, 1962).

Tomosugi, Takashi, 'The Land System in Central Thailand', *The Developing Economies*, vol. 7, no. 3 (Institute of Developing Economies, Tokyo,
September 1969).

Tuma, Elias H., 'The Agrarian Based Development Policy in Land Reform',
Land Economics, vol. 39, no. 3 (Wisconsin, August 1963).

Viner, Jacob, 'Gains from Foreign Trade', in *International Trade and
Economic Development* (Clarendon Press, Oxford, 1957).

Viner, Jacob, 'Stability and Progress in the World Economy', in *The First
Congress of the International Economic Association* (London, 1958).

Vyas, V. S., 'Land Reform Legislation', *Seminar*, no. 8 (New Delhi, May
1966).

Vyas, V. S., Tyagi, D. S., and Misra, V. N., *Significance of the New
Strategy of Agricultural Development for Small Farmers—A Cross-
Section Study of Two Areas* (Agro-Economic Research Centre for
Gujarat and Rajasthan, Sardar Patel University, Vallabh Vidyanagar,
1968).

Vyas, V. S., *Economic Efficiency on Small Farms of Central Gujarat.
Report of the Seminar on Problems of Small Farmers*, Seminar Series,
no. 7 (Indian Society of Agricultural Economics, Bombay, 1968).

Weiner, Myron, 'India: Two Political Cultures', in Lucien W. Pye and
Sydney Verba (eds.), *Political Culture and Political Development*
(Princeton University Press, Princeton, N.J., 1965).

Wertheim, W. F., *Evolution and Revolution: Sociology of a World on the
Move*, Nieuwe reeks, voorpublikaties no. 1 (Zuid-en Zuidoost-Azie
Antropologisch-Sociologisch Centrum, University of Amsterdam, 1967).

Wharton, Clifton R. Jr., 'The Green Revolution: Cornucopia or Pandora's
Box?', *Foreign Affairs*, vol. 47, no. 3 (New York, April 1969).

Whetham, Edith, 'Land Reform and Resettlement in Kenya', *East African
Journal of Rural Development*, vol. 1, no. 1 (Nairobi, January 1968).

Wilber, Charles K., 'The Role of Agriculture in Soviet Economy', *Land
Economics*, vol. 45, no. 1 (Madison, Wisconsin, February 1969).

Wilczynski, J., 'Towards Rationality in Land Economics under Central
Planning', *The Economic Journal*, vol. 79, no. 315 (London, September
1969).

Wolf, Erich R., 'On Peasant Rebellions', *International Social Science Journal*, vol. 21, no. 2 (UNESCO, Paris, 1969).

Yudelman, M., 'Planning the Rural Sector in the National Economy—From the Donor's Point of View' in Ronald Robinson and Peter Johnston (eds.), *The Rural Base for National Development: Papers and Impressions of the Sixth Cambridge Conference on Development Problems* (Cambridge University Overseas Studies Committee, 1968).

Index